NEW MEXICO PERSONAL INCOME TAX GUIDE

2017 EDITION

(FOR 2016 TAX RETURNS)

MICHAEL RASHKIN, JD, LLM

TAX TREND PUBLICATIONS, LLC

Editorial Staff

Editor in Chief........**Pamela Revak-Cartier, JD, LLM**
Production and Graphics......................**Vaclay Vlasak**

LIMIT OF LIABILITY - DISCLAIMER OF WARRANTY

This book is meant as a resource book and is sold with the understanding that the publisher and the author are not providing any legal, accounting, or other professional services and that the information in this book should not be relied upon as such and may not be used to disclaim any tax penalties. If legal, accounting, or other expert assistance is required, the services of competent professionals should be sought. Although the author and publisher have made every effort to ensure that the information in this book was correct at press time, the author and publisher do not assume and hereby disclaim any liability to any party for any loss, damage, or disruption caused by errors or omissions, whether such errors or omissions result from negligence, accident, or any other cause. The publisher and the author make no representations or warranties with respect to the accuracy or completeness of the contents of the work and specifically disclaim all warranties of fitness for a particular purpose.

First Printing, December 2016

ISBN 978-0-9983127-0-5

© 2016, Tax Trend Publications, LLC
21780 Via Regina
Saratoga, CA 95070
http://www.taxtrendpublications.com

No claim is made to original government works; however, within this product or publication, the following are subject to the copyright of Tax Trend Publications, LLC: 1) the gathering, compilation, and arrangement of such government materials; 2) the magnetic translation and digital conversion of data, if applicable; 3) the historical, statutory and other notes and references; and 4) the commentary and other materials.

All rights reserved
Printed in the United States of America

PREFACE

It is difficult not to fall in love with New Mexico. It is a beautiful and varied state with friendly people and an ease of life that draws you in. My wife and I have often dreamed of moving there and we once placed an offer on a beautiful house in Santa Fe. Unfortunately, once we got the report on the weak foundation, we had to let it go. At that time, I became interested in the New Mexico tax system and looked for a guide to give me an overview of the tax laws. I was surprised to find that there was no such book. It was at that moment that the idea for this book was born.

I have been working in tax law over 40 years and during that time I have used many federal and state tax guides and generally found them to be unsatisfactory. The prime intention of the authors of these guides seems to be to summarize complex tax matters in as few words as possible. As a result, these guides are often incomprehensible and provide little context and background of the laws they are describing.

This book takes a different approach. The book's entire focus is on the reader, and as the author I have endeavored to make the book readable, interesting (to the extent possible in book such as this), comprehensible, navigable, comprehensive, and practical. When a tax professional or a taxpayer looks up a question in this book, I hope he or she will find the issue, understand the explanation, and know how to plan for it and treat it on the tax return.

This book is perhaps more than just a guide, but I did not intend to make it a treatise. Yet, the coverage of the subject is much more than typical guides. One state guide I reviewed covers individual taxes in 40 pages, while this guide is over 400 pages. As a result, I have been able to provide lengthy descriptions of issues that need that kind of coverage. For example, film production incentives have their own chapter. It is an important incentive for the growth of the film industry in New Mexico and there is no good way to describe such a complex incentive in a short summary piece.

I hope, as a result, you enjoy this book and find it useful. Please place any comments or suggestions for improvement, on the publisher's web site.

Michael D. Rashkin
Saratoga, California

ABOUT THE AUTHOR

Michael D. Rashkin is author of *Taxation of Research and Development Tax Incentives: Federal, State, and Foreign*, which evolved into the *Practical Guide to Research and Development Tax Incentives*, both of which were published by CCH. Mr. Rashkin is a recognized expert in the area of research incentives and has been invited twice to speak before the Senate Finance Committee on this subject. While as the head of the Apple Computer tax department, he pioneered the use of stock option income as compensation for calculating the R&D credit and won the landmark case in Tax Court establishing this principle, which is still in effect today. He has also introduced the use of commissionaires in international planning in the early 1980's, a business arrangement which is wide use today among multinational corporations.

Mr. Rashkin received his JD. from St. John's School of Law and his LLM from the New York University Graduate School of Law. Beginning his career in 1972 he concentrated on working for high technology corporations, such as Digital Equipment Corporation (6 years), Apple Computer (13 years), and Marvell Technology (16 years), where he also served as CFO. He has also served as a tax consultant to many Silicon Valley companies, specializing in establishing international tax structures.

He has spoken on business and tax matters before many groups, including: The Commonwealth Club, the Internal Revenue Service, the California Bar Association, the World Trade Institute, Panel Publishers, Santa Clara Valley Chamber of Commerce, MIT/Stanford Venture Lab, and the Tax Executive Institute. His articles have appeared in the Santa Clara Computer and High-Technology Law Journal, The Tax Executive, The International Tax Journal, Tax Notes and Tax Notes International, among others.

Throughout his career as a tax department director, he has been in charge of tax matters for multinational corporations where his focus has been on a practical understanding of the tax law so as to ensure compliance and minimize tax burdens. As an author he puts that experience good use for the benefit of his readers of this guide.

This book is dedicated to my understanding wife Zdena
and to the open and friendly people of New Mexico

CONTENTS

Chapter	Page
KEY DATES	25
KEY RATES	27
1. INTRODUCTION TO THE NEW MEXICO PERSONAL INCOME TAX	29
2. THE NEW MEXICO PIT IN TEN EASY STEPS	37
3. OUTLINE OF THE NEW MEXICO PIT RETURN (FORM PIT-1) –	55
4. FILING REQUIREMENTS, EXEMPT STATUS, AND ESTIMATED TAXES	61
5. RESIDENCY	93
6. MILITARY PERSONNEL – INCOME, FILING, RESIDENCY, AND DOMICILE	101
7. TAXABLE INCOME AND NET INCOME	111
8. ADJUSTMENTS TO ADJUSTED GROSS INCOME	135
9. COMPUTING THE TAX ON TAXABLE INCOME	155
10. CREDITS AGAINST THE INCOME TAX	183
11. BUSINESS-RELATED CREDITS	189
12. FILM PRODUCTION TAX INCENTIVES	275
13. REFUNDABLE CREDITS AND REBATES	313
14. VOLUNTARY CONTRIBUTION OF REFUNDS	335
15. INTEREST AND PENALTIES	341
16. AUDITS AND DISPUTES	357
17. TAX ADMINISTRATION	383
18. RECORD RETENTION REQUIREMENTS	399
19. COLLECTION AND ENFORCEMENT	407
APPENDIX	427
INDEX	435

TABLE OF CONTENTS

Key Dates   25
Key Rates   27

CHAPTER ONE - INTRODUCTION TO THE NEW MEXICO PERSONAL INCOME TAX   29

¶1.1 OVERVIEW   29
¶1.2 HISTORY OF THE PERSONAL INCOME TAX   31
¶1.2.1 Tax rate changes   32
¶1.2.2 Benefits for low-income taxpayers   32
¶1.2.3 Adoption of federal adjusted gross income   33
¶1.2.4 Economic, Environmental, and Social Objectives   33
¶1.2.5 Withholding and Estimated Tax   34
¶1.2.6 The Personal Income Tax Today   34
¶1.3 STRUCTURE OF THIS BOOK   34
¶1.4 REFERENCES TO FEDERAL AND NEW MEXICO INCOME TAX FORMS AND TO WEBSITES   36

CHAPTER TWO
THE NEW MEXICO PIT IN TEN EASY STEPS   37

¶2.1 STEP 1: ENTER AGI AND OTHER FEDERAL INFORMATION   37
¶2.2 STEP 2: MAKE ADJUSTMENTS TO FEDERAL AGI ON PIT-ADJ   38
¶2.3 STEP 3: ADDITIONAL EXEMPTION FOR LOW- AND MIDDLE-INCOME TAXPAYERS, AND DEDUCTION FOR UNREIMBURSED MEDICAL EXPENSES   41
¶2.4 STEP 4: CALCULATE TAXABLE INCOME   42
¶2.5 STEP FIVE: DETERMINE RESIDENCY   42
¶2.6 STEP SIX: ALLOCATE AND APPORTION INCOME   43
¶2.7 STEP SEVEN: CALCULATE TAX ON TAXABLE INCOME AND LUMP SUM AMOUNTS   44
¶2.8 STEP 8: CLAIM NON-REFUNDABLE CREDITS FOR TAXES PAID TO ANOTHER STATE AND BUSINESS-RELATED TAX CREDITS   45
¶2.9 STEP 9: SUBTRACT REFUNDABLE LOW-INCOME REBATES AND CREDITS AND REFUNDABLE CREDITS DUE ALL TAXPAYERS   51
¶2.10 STEP 10: SUBTRACT WITHHOLDING AND ESTIMATED TAX AND ADD ANY INTEREST AND PENALTIES TO DETERMINE TAX DUE

| OR AMOUNT OF REFUND | 54 |

CHAPTER THREE
OUTLINE OF THE NEW MEXICO PIT RETURN (FORM PIT-1) 55

¶3.1 Overview of Form 2016 PIT-1	55
¶3.2 Outline of Form 2016 PIT-1	54
¶3.3 Filling out the form	60

CHAPTER FOUR - FILING REQUIREMENTS, EXEMPT STATUS, AND ESTIMATED TAXES 61

¶4.1 Imposition of Tax on Individuals	61
¶4.2 Taxpayer requirements for filing returns and payment of tax	62
¶4.2.1 Individuals required to file	62
¶4.2.2 Taxpayer Identification Number	64
¶4.2.3 Address of notices and payments – change in address	67
¶4.2.4 Due date of return and payments	68
¶4.2.5 Making tax payments by mail	68
¶4.2.6 Date of payment	69
¶4.2.7 Timely-mailed, timely-filed rule	69
¶4.2.8 Illegible postmarks	70
¶4.2.9 Private delivery services	70
¶4.2.10 Timeliness when last day for performance falls on Saturday, *Sunday* or legal holiday	72
¶4.2.11 Requirements for filed returns	73
¶4.2.12 Refunds	73
¶4.2.13 Interest and penalties	74
¶4.2.14 Electronic filing of returns	74
¶4.2.15 Electronic payments	76
¶4.2.16 Tax preparer responsibilities with regard to electronic filing—penalties	78
¶4.2.17 Extension of time to file and pay	78
¶4.2.18 Good cause	78
¶4.2.19 Procedure for obtaining extensions to file (other than automatic extensions)	79
¶4.2.20 Automatic extensions	80

¶4.2.21 Extensions for Military Personnel	82
¶4.2.22 Failure to file, pay or protest by extended due date	82
¶4.2.23 Filing status	82
¶4.2.24 Name of spouse	82
¶4.2.25 Tentative returns not allowed	83
¶4.2.26 Requirements for reproduction of income tax forms and acceptance of computer generated forms	83
¶4.2.27 Requirements for tax return preparers—penalties	83
¶4.2.28 Amended returns	84
¶4.3 EXEMPTIONS FROM INCOME TAX	85
¶4.3.1 Employee compensation trust	85
¶4.3.2 Religious, educational, benevolent or other organizations not organized for profit	85
¶4.3.3 Income of a member of a NATO force	86
¶4.3.4 Income taxes applied to an individual on and income from a federal area	86
¶4.3.5 Income of member Indian nation, tribe, band, or pueblo	87
¶4.4 ESTIMATED TAX PAYMENTS	88
CHAPTER FIVE – RESIDENCY	**93**
¶5.1 RESIDENCY DEFINED	93
¶5.2 DOMICILE DEFINED	94
¶5.3 CREDIT FOR TAXES PAID TO ANOTHER STATE	96
¶5.4 NONRESIDENTS RECEIVING ROYALTY INCOME FROM NEW MEXICO	97
¶5.5 PART-YEAR RESIDENTS	98
¶5.6 EXAMPLE OF IMPACT OF RESIDENCY ON TAXATION OF INDIVIDUALS	99
CHAPTER SIX -MILITARY PERSONNEL – INCOME, FILING, RESIDENCY, AND DOMICILE	**101**
¶6.1 PREFERENTIAL INCOME TAX TREATMENT FOR MILITARY PERSONNEL	101
¶6.1.1 Income tax preferences	101

¶6.1.2 Military pay of an enrolled member of an Indian nation, tribe, or pueblo	102
¶6.1.3 Residency and domicile	103
¶6.2 RESIDENCY EXEMPTION FOR MILITARY SPOUSES	105
¶6.2.1 Dual residency issues and the Military Spouse Residency Relief Act	105
¶6.2.2 NM Resident who is a qualifying SM spouse in another state	106
¶6.2.3 Withholding exemption requirements	106
¶6.2.4 Tax Return Filing Requirement	107
¶6.3 FILING EXTENSIONS FOR MILITARY PERSONNEL	107
CHAPTER SEVEN - TAXABLE INCOME AND NET INCOME	**111**
¶7.1 OVERVIEW	111
¶7.2 ADJUSTED GROSS INCOME (AGI)	114
¶7.3 COMPUTING TAXABLE INCOME	115
¶7.3.1 Taxable income – tax return method	115
¶7.3.2 The Statutory Method – Computing net income, base income, lump sum amounts, and taxable income	115
¶7.3.2A Base income	116
¶7.3.2B Net income	117
¶7.3.2C Lump-sum amounts - defined	120
¶7.3.2D Taxable income	121
¶7.4 DEDUCTION OF PERSONAL EXEMPTIONS	122
¶7.4.1 New Mexico exemption deduction based on federal exemption deduction – Form PIT-1, line 13	122
¶7.4.2 Additional exemptions for low- and middle-income taxpayers- Form PIT-1, line 14	122
¶7.5 DEDUCTION OF UNREIMBURSED/UNCOMPENSATED MEDICAL EXPENSES	124
¶7.6 STATE AND LOCAL TAX ADD BACK	126
¶7.7 TAX ACCOUNTING RULES	128
¶7.7.1 Taxable years	128
¶7.7.2 Accounting Methods	128
¶7.8 COMMUNITY PROPERTY	129

CHAPTER EIGHT
ADJUSTMENTS TO ADJUSTED GROSS INCOME   **135**

¶8.1 OVERVIEW   135
¶8.2 NEW MEXICO ADDITIONS TO AGI ON SCHEDULE PIT-ADJ   135
¶8.2.1 Interest and dividends from federal tax-exempt
　　　bonds - line 1   135
¶8.2.2 Federal net operating loss carryover deduction -
　　　line 2   137
¶8.2.3 Contributions refunded when closing a
　　　NM-approved §529 account and certain
　　　contributions rolled out of a NM-approved §529 -
　　　line 3   137
¶8.2.4 Charitable deduction amount claimed on fed
　　　　Form 1040, Schedule A, for donation of land to
　　　private non-profit or public conservation agencies,
　　　for conservation, for which the NM Land
　　　Conservation Tax Credit was allowed - line 4   138
¶8.3 NEW MEXICO DEDUCTIONS AND EXEMPTIONS FROM AGI ON
　　　SCHEDULE PIT-ADJ   140
¶8.3.1 New Mexico tax-exempt interest and dividends -
　　　line 6   140
¶8.3.2 New Mexico net operating loss – line 7   141
¶8.3.3 Interest received on U.S. Government obligations -
　　　line 8   142
¶8.3.4 Taxable Railroad Retirement Act annuities
　　　and benefits, and taxable Railroad Unemployment
　　　Insurance Act sick pay - line 9   144
¶8.3.5 Income of a member of a NM federally-recognized
　　　Indian nation, tribe, or pueblo wholly earned on
　　　the lands of the reservation or pueblo of which the
　　　individual is an enrolled member while domiciled
　　　on that land, reservation, or pueblo - line 10   145
¶8.3.6 Income of persons age 100 years or older - line 11   145
¶8.3.7 Exemption for persons age 65 or older, or blind -
　　　line 12   145
¶8.3.8 Exemption for NM medical care

savings account- line 13 146
¶8.3.9 Deduction for contributions to a New Mexico-approved Section 529 college savings plan - line 14 148
¶8.3.10 Net Capital Gains Deduction - line 15 149
¶8.3.11 Armed forces active duty pay - line 16 150
¶8.3.12 Medical care expense exemption for persons age 65 years or older - line 17 151
¶8.3.13 Deduction for organ donation-related expenses - line 18 151
¶8.3.14 New Mexico National Guard member life insurance reimbursements exemption – line 19 152
¶8.3.15 Taxable refunds, credits, or offsets of state and local income taxes from line 10, Form 1040 - line 20 152
¶8.3.16 Non-resident U.S. Public Health Service members' active duty pay – line 21. 153

CHAPTER NINE
COMPUTING THE TAX ON TAXABLE INCOME **155**

¶9.1 OVERVIEW 155
¶9.2 INDIVIDUAL INCOME TAX RATE SCHEDULES AND TAX 155
¶9.2.1 Tax rate schedules 155
¶9.2.2 Tax tables 156
¶9.3 TAXPAYERS WITH INCOME FROM SOURCES BOTH WITHIN AND WITHOUT NEW MEXICO - SCHEDULE PIT-B 157
¶9.3.1 Allocation and apportionment of income – Schedule PIT-B 158
¶9.3.2 Uniform Division of Income for Tax Purposes Act (UDITPA) 161
¶9.3.3 Completing Schedule PIT-B 161
¶9.3.4 Allocation of income 162
¶9.3.5 Apportionment of business and farm income 172
¶9.3.6 Special rules for manufacturing and headquarters companies 175
¶9.3.7 Equitable adjustment of standard allocation or apportionment formula 178
¶9.3.8 Special industries 179

¶9.3.9 Allocation of community property and income … 179
¶9.4 LUMP SUM AMOUNTS … 180

CHAPTER 10 - CREDITS AGAINST THE INCOME TAX … 183

¶10.1 OVERVIEW … 183
¶10.2 CREDIT FOR TAXES PAID OTHER STATES (FORM PIT-1, LINE 20) … 185

CHAPTER ELEVEN – BUSINESS-RELATED CREDITS … 189

¶11.1 GENERAL … 189
¶11.2 AFFORDABLE HOUSING TAX CREDIT … 193
¶11.3 ANGEL INVESTMENT CREDIT … 196
¶11.4 AGRICULTURAL WATER CONSERVATION TAX CREDIT
    (EXPIRED EFFECTIVE JANUARY 1, 2013) … 202
¶11.5 ADVANCED ENERGY INCOME TAX CREDIT … 203
¶11.6 AGRICULTURAL BIOMASS INCOME TAX CREDIT … 209
¶11.7 BUSINESS FACILITY REHABILITATION CREDIT
    (NO LONGER OPERATIVE) … 212
¶11.8 BLENDED BIODIESEL FUEL CREDIT
    (EXPIRED AS OF DECEMBER 31, 2012) … 213
¶11.9 CANCER CLINICAL TRIAL TAX CREDIT
    (EXPIRES FOR TAX YEARS BEGINNING AFTER 12/31/2015) … 215
¶11.10 ELECTRONIC CARD READING EQUIPMENT TAX CREDIT … 218
¶11.11 GEOTHERMAL GROUND-COUPLED HEAT PUMP TAX CREDIT … 219
¶11.12 JOB MENTORSHIP TAX CREDIT … 222
¶11.13 LAND CONSERVATION INCENTIVES CREDIT … 224
¶11.14 PRESERVATION OF CULTURAL PROPERTY CREDIT … 228
¶11.15 RURAL JOB TAX CREDIT … 232
¶11.16 RURAL HEALTH CARE PRACTITIONER TAX CREDIT … 236
¶11.17 SOLAR MARKET DEVELOPMENT TAX CREDIT … 238
¶11.18 SUSTAINABLE BUILDING TAX CREDIT … 240
¶11.18.1 New sustainable building tax credit … 241
¶11.18.2 Sustainable Building Tax Credit (for tax
    years ending on or before Dec. 31, 2016) … 248
¶11.19 TECHNOLOGY JOBS (ADDITIONAL) TAX CREDIT … 253
¶11.19.1 Overview … 253
¶11.19.2 TJTC and TJRDTC … 254
¶11.19.3 Applying for and Claiming the Basic Credit … 258

¶11.19.4 Claiming the additional credit — 259
¶11.19.5 Taxpayers who can claim the credit — 260
¶11.19.6 Credit recapture and reporting — 261
¶11.19.7 Transition rules for the RDSBTC — 261
¶11.20 Veteran employment tax credit — 262
¶11.21 Film Production Credit — 264
¶11.22 Renewable energy production tax credit — 264
¶11.23 Venture Capital Investment Credit –
    The forgotten tax credit — 270

CHAPTER 12 - FILM PRODUCTION TAX INCENTIVES — 275

¶12.1 Overview — 275
¶12.2 Film and Television Tax Credit -- Principal Photography
    Commencing On or After January 1, 2016 — 276
¶12.2.1 Requirements for direct production and
    postproduction expenditures — 278
¶12.2.2 Direct production expenditures - definition — 278
¶12.2.3 Nonresident performing artists — 281
¶12.2.4 Limitation for performing artists — 283
¶12.2.5 Postproduction expenditures — 284
¶12.2.6 Film and audiovisual product requirements — 284
¶12.2.7 Residency requirement for purposes of the FTTC — 285
¶12.2.8 Requirement for taxable transaction for
    DPEs and PPEs — 285
¶12.2.9 Requirements to Contract with Certain Vendors — 285
¶12.2.10 Additional conditions for earning the FPTC — 287
¶12.3 Additional credit for use of qualified production
    facilities — 288
¶12.4 Additional Credit--Television Pilots and Series — 290
¶12.5 Additional Credit for Nonresident Industry Crew — 291
¶12.6 Qualifying for and Claiming the FTTC — 292
¶12.7 Payment of claim and aggregate amount of
    claims allowed — 294
¶12.7.1 Assignment of FTTC — 295
¶12.8 Reporting--accountability — 296
¶12.9 Film Production Tax Credit-- Principal Photography

COMMENCING PRIOR TO JANUARY 1, 2016	297
¶12.9.1 Overview	297
¶12.9.2 Requirements for direct production and postproduction expenditures	298
¶12.9.3 Direct production expenditures	299
¶12.9.4 Nonresident performing artists	302
¶12.9.5 Limitation on credit for performing artists	303
¶12.9.6 Postproduction Expenditures	303
¶12.9.7 Film and audiovisual product requirements	304
¶12.9.8 Residency requirement for purposes of the FPTC	304
¶12.9.9 Requirement for taxable transaction for DPEs and PPEs	305
¶12.9.10 Vendor requirements	305
¶12.9.11 Additional conditions for earning the FPTC	307
12.10 ADDITIONAL CREDIT FOR USE OF QPFS	308
¶12.11 ADDITIONAL CREDIT--TELEVISION PILOTS AND SERIES	310
¶12.12 QUALIFYING FOR AND CLAIMING THE FPTC	310
¶12.13 PAYMENT OF CLAIMS AND AGGREGATE AMOUNT OF CLAIMS ALLOWED	311
¶12.13.1 Overview	311
¶12.13.2 Assignment of FPTC	312

CHAPTER THIRTEEN
REFUNDABLE CREDITS AND REBATES   313

¶13.1 OVERVIEW	313
¶13.2 MODIFIED GROSS INCOME ("MGI")	314
¶13.3 LOW-INCOME COMPREHENSIVE TAX REBATE ("LICTR")	317
¶13.4 PROPERTY TAX REBATE FOR PERSONS 65 OR OLDER	319
¶13.5 ADDITIONAL LOW-INCOME PROPERTY TAX REBATE	323
¶13.6 NEW MEXICO DAY CARE CREDIT	325
¶13.7 REFUNDABLE MEDICAL CARE CREDIT FOR PERSONS 65 OR OLDER	329
¶13.8 SPECIAL NEEDS ADOPTED CHILD TAX CREDIT	332
¶13.9 WORKING FAMILIES TAX CREDIT	333

CHAPTER 14 - VOLUNTARY CONTRIBUTION OF REFUNDS   335

¶14.1 NEW MEXICO SYSTEM OF VOLUNTARY CONTRIBUTIONS	335

¶14.1.1 Share with Wildlife 336
¶14.1.2 Veterans' State Cemetery Fund 336
¶14.1.3 New Mexico Substance Abuse Education Fund ... 336
¶14.1.4 New Mexico Forest Re-Leaf Program 337
¶14.1.5 National Guard Member and Family Assistance ... 337
¶14.1.6 Kids 'N Parks Transportation Grant Program 337
¶14.1.7 Amyotrophic Lateral Sclerosis Research Fund ... 337
¶14.1.8 Vietnam Veterans Memorial State Park 338
¶14.1.9 New Mexico Political Parties 338
¶14.1.10 Veterans Enterprise Fund 338
¶14.1.11 Lottery Tuition Fund 338
¶14.1.12 Horse Shelter Rescue Fund 338
¶14.1.13 Animal Care and Facility Fund 339
¶14.1.14 Supplemental Senior Services 339

CHAPTER FIFTEEN - INTEREST AND PENALTIES 341

¶15.1 INTEREST ON DEFICIENCIES 341
¶15.2 INTEREST ON OVERPAYMENTS 344
¶15.3 CIVIL PENALTIES 346
¶15.3.1 Failure to pay tax or file a return. 346
¶15.3.2 Innocent Spouse Relief 350
¶15.3.3 Civil penalty for bad checks 352
¶15.3.4 Civil penalty--willful attempt to cause evasion
      of another's tax 353
¶15.4 CRIMINAL OFFENSES 353
¶15.4.1 Tax fraud 353
¶15.4.2 Other criminal violations 355
¶15.4.2.1 Penalty for attempts to evade or defeat tax ... 355
¶15.4.2.2 Interference with administration of
      revenue laws 355
¶15.4.2.3 Assault and battery of a TRD employee 356
¶15.4.2.4 Revealing information concerning taxpayers ... 356

CHAPTER SIXTEEN - AUDITS AND DISPUTES 357

¶16.1 AUDIT AND INSPECTION OF BOOKS OF TAXPAYERS 357
¶16.1.1 Notice of audit 357

¶16.1.2 Identification of auditors   357
¶16.1.3 Production of records and books of account   357
¶16.1.4 Reasonable hours   357
¶16.1.5 Records include governmental returns, documents, reports and other attachments   358
¶16.1.6 Notice of outstanding records   358
¶16.1.7 Taxpayer records in possession of another   358
¶16.1.8 Enforcement by subpoena   359
¶16.1.9 Managed audits   359
¶16.1.10 Federal audit adjustments   362
¶16.1.11 Closing agreements   363
¶16.2 DISPUTES   364
¶16.2.1 Exhaustion of administrative remedies   364
¶16.2.2 Election of remedies in disputing liabilities   364
¶16.2.3 Disputing liabilities – administrative protest   365
¶16.2.4 Informal conferences   366
¶16.2.5 Rules for formal hearings   367
¶16.2.6 Hearing officer   367
¶16.2.7 Evidence   369
¶16.2.8 Hearing record   369
¶16.2.9 Proposed findings, conclusions and briefs   369
¶16.2.10 Discovery   370
¶16.2.11 Failure to comply with orders   370
¶16.2.12 Prehearing conference   371
¶16.2.13 Motions   371
¶16.2.14 Appeals from hearing officer's decision   372
¶16.2.15 Conditions for refund or credit   372
¶16.2.16 Claimant remedies   376
¶16.2.17 Conclusiveness of court order on liability for payment of tax   377
¶16.2.18 Authority to make refunds or credits   378
¶16.2.19 Awarding of costs and fees   380

CHAPTER SEVENTEEN - TAX ADMINISTRATION   **383**

¶17.1 OVERVIEW   383
¶17.2 NEW MEXICO TAXPAYER BILL OF RIGHTS   383

¶17.3 Authorized Representative 385
¶17.4 Delegation of Authority Rules 385
¶17.5 Investigative Authority and Powers 387
¶17.5.1 Subpoenas and summons 387
¶17.6 Notice of Potential Eligibility Required 388
¶17.7 Confidentiality of Returns And Other Information ... 388

CHAPTER EIGHTEEN
RECORD RETENTION REQUIREMENTS — 399

¶18.1 Required Taxpayer Records 399
¶18.1.1 Insufficient records and alternative methods used to determine taxes due ... 399
¶18.1.2 Records reconstruction 400
¶18.2 Alternative Storage Media 400
¶18.3 Machine-Sensible Records 402
¶18.3.1 Electronic data interchange requirements. 403
¶18.3.2 Electronic Data Processing Systems Requirements 404
¶18.3.3 Business Process Information 404
¶18.3.4 TRD Access to machine-sensible records 405
¶18.3.5 Records maintenance requirements 405

CHAPTER NINETEEN - COLLECTION AND ENFORCEMENT — 407

¶19.1 Assessments of Tax 407
¶19.1.1 Methods of assessment 407
¶19.1.2 Delinquent taxpayers 408
¶19.1.3 Penalties and interest 409
¶19.1.4 Statutes of limitations on assessment or collection 409
¶19.1.5 Installment agreements 410
¶19.1.6 Jeopardy assessments 411
¶19.2 Tax liens 412
¶19.2.1 Assessment as lien 412
¶19.2.2 Notice of lien 412
¶19.2.3 Release or extinguishment of lien 413
¶19.2.4 Statute of limitation on actions to enforce lien 413
¶19.2.5 Foreclosure of lien 413
¶19.3. Levy of property 413
¶19.3.1 Seizure of property by levy for collection of taxes 413

¶19.3.2 Seizure of real property by levy ... 414
¶19.3.3 Surrender of property upon service of levy on a financial institution ... 414
¶19.3.4 Contents of warrant of levy ... 415
¶19.3.5 Successive levies ... 416
¶19.3.6 Surrender of property subject to levy—penalty ... 416
¶19.3.7 Stay of levy ... 417
¶19.3.8 Property exempt from levy ... 417
¶19.4 SALE OF PROPERTY ... 418
¶19.4.1 Notice of seizure and sale ... 418
¶19.4.2 Sale of indivisible property ... 418
¶19.4.3 Requirements of sale ... 418
¶19.4.4 Sale at auction, minimum prices ... 419
¶19.4.5 Redemption before sale ... 419
¶19.4.6 Documents of title and legal effect of sale ... 419
¶19.4.7 Proceeds of levy and sale ... 421
¶19.5 INJUNCTIONS AND SECURITY ... 421
¶19.5.1 Enjoining delinquent taxpayer from continuing business ... 421
¶19.5.2 Security for payment of tax ... 423
¶19.5.3 Sale of or proceedings against security ... 425
¶19.6 PERMANENCE OF TAX DEBT--CIVIL ACTIONS TO COLLECT TAX ... 425
¶19.7 ESTOPPEL AGAINST STATE ... 426
¶19.8 RECIPROCAL ENFORCEMENT OF TAX JUDGMENTS ... 426

APPENDIX ... 427

A.1 OBSOLETE PROVISIONS ... 427
A.1.1 Welfare-to-work tax credit (Obsolete) ... 427
A.1.2 2007 INDIVIDUAL INCOME TAX CREDIT ... 429
A.1.3 Tax rebate of property tax paid on property eligible for disabled veteran exemption ... 431
A.2 INFORMATION RETURNS ... 431
Automatic extension for 1099 information returns ... 432
Rents and royalties from oil and gas properties ... 432

INDEX ... 435

Key Dates

Filing Dates for Form PIT-1 for Calendar Year Taxpayers

- Paper returns with payment are due April 18, 2017.
- Electronic returns and payment (e-file and e-pay) are due May 1, 2017.
- The due date of New Mexico returns for taxpayers who have taken automatic extension of their federal return is October 16, 2017.
- The due date of Form RPD-41096 for taxpayers seeking a separate New Mexico filing extension is April 18, 2017.

Estimated Taxes

Estimated tax payments for 2016 are due as follows for calendar year taxpayers:

- April 18, 2016.
- June 15, 2016;
- September 15, 2016; and
- January 15, 2017.

Tax Rates for 2016

For married individuals filing separate returns

If the taxable income is:	The tax shall be:
Not over $4,000	1.7% of taxable income
Over $4,000 but not over $8,000	$68 plus 3.2% of excess over $4,000
Over $8,000 but not over $12,000	$196 plus 4.7% over $8,000
Over $12,000	384 plus 4.9% of excess over $12,000

For heads of household, surviving spouses and married individuals filing joint returns

If the taxable income is:	The tax shall be:
Not over $8,000	1.7% of taxable income
Over $8,000 but not over $16,000	$136 plus 3.2% of excess over $8,000
Over $16,000 but not over $24,000	$392 plus 4.7% of excess over $16,000
Over $24,000	$768 plus 4.9% of excess over $24,000

For single individuals and estates and trusts

If the taxable income is:	The tax shall be:
Not over $5,500	1.7% of taxable income
Over $5,500 but not over $11,000	$93.50 plus 3.2% of excess over $5,500
Over $11,000 but not over $16,000	$269.50 plus 4.7% of excess over $11,000
Over $16,000	$504.50 plus 4.9% of excess over $16,000

CHAPTER 1
INTRODUCTION TO THE NEW MEXICO PERSONAL INCOME TAX

¶ 1.1 Overview

When a state designs its tax system using federal adjusted gross income as a starting point, state lawmakers are often inclined to proclaim the simplicity of their income tax structure, and, in this regard, New Mexico is no exception. New Mexico state policymakers and administrators routinely describe the New Mexico Personal Income Tax (PIT) as easy for taxpayers to understand and to comply with since it is based upon the federal system.[1] To make this point, the PIT is explained in reductionist terms as starting with federal adjusted gross income, then making some adjustments to reach New Mexico taxable income, applying a tax rate against taxable income, and then reducing the liability by any available credits. Of course, the same conceptual model can be applied to the federal income tax, but starting instead with gross income, yet no one would argue that the federal tax code is easy to understand and comply with. Ideally, starting with a federally computed number should simplify matters, but the numerous adjustments and unique credits adopted by the state renders the New Mexico tax scheme anything but simple.

Specifically, although New Mexico bases the PIT on federal adjusted gross income (AGI), it has complicated its tax law by adding some twenty adjustments to AGI, as well as providing over twenty credits and rebates for social and economic development purposes. Taxpayers with income that is taxable outside New Mexico must go through an apportionment and allocation calculation that adds additional complexity to tax compliance. Moreover, in providing tax benefits to lower income taxpayers, the state has created a separate

---

[1] For example, see TRD, *2015 New Mexico Tax Expenditure Report*, p. 19, where it is stated: "Because it is based on a federal program, New Mexico's personal income tax ("PIT") is relatively simple for the taxpayer to comply with and the State to administer."

income calculation, known as modified gross income, to determine eligibility for these benefits. In effect, New Mexico has three different tax systems: the basic tax scheme for resident New Mexico taxpayers with no non-New Mexico source income and who are not low-income taxpayers, one for taxpayers with income outside New Mexico, and one for low-income taxpayers. Notably, the tax return form follows a method of computing taxable income that differs from that of the statute, although the end result is generally but not necessarily the same. Moreover, having two approaches to taxable income can be confusing to taxpayers trying to reconcile the tax return with the tax statute.

As a result of the above complexities, it is possible that taxpayers will find it more difficult to file a New Mexico return than a federal return. A low-income individual, for example, can often comply with the federal income tax simply by filing a one-page Form 1040EZ. However, if that individual wishes to claim one of the low-income rebates or credits available under the New Mexico PIT, he or she must make a modified gross income calculation and file Schedule PIT-RC, thereby making the completion of his or her New Mexico return more complicated than completing Form 1040 EZ. Similarly, in the case of economic development credits, it is often more complex to obtain the benefit of New Mexico credits than related federal credits. With regard to the federal research and development credit, for example, taxpayers do not have to obtain prior approval to be eligible for the credit. They simply indicate the amount of their qualified expenditures on their tax returns and take benefit of the credit. In New Mexico, however, prior approval is required before a taxpayer can claim the technology jobs and research and development tax credit. Many New Mexico tax credits require prior approval thereby making them more difficult to obtain than federal credits. For some of these credits, one wonders if the cost of obtaining approval and claiming the credit exceeds the benefit provided by the credit. In fact, some of the credits are rarely claimed.

New Mexico has a large Native American population and a member's income is exempt by federal law if earned on the lands of the Indian nation, tribe, or pueblo where the Indian is an enrolled member. The tax situation of enrolled tribal members and their spouses, however, is complicated by such factors as income earned

Introduction to the New Mexico Personal Income Tax

outside Indian lands, retirement or pension income earned while working off of tribal lands, or, in some situations, income earned from military service.

New Mexico also has a large military population and in appreciation of their service New Mexico does not tax active duty pay. Moreover, there are special residence rules for the servicemember and his or her spouse that have been made applicable by the federal Military Spouses Residence Relief Act.[2]

Finally, because New Mexico is a community property state, difficulties arise in determining the income of spouses filing separately. Moreover, in some cases, separate income of a spouse must be determined even when a joint return is filed, such as in the case of a taxpayer claiming the exemption for taxpayers 100 years of age or older.

The above complexities have made it more difficult than has been suggested to comply with and administer the PIT. The Tax and Revenue Department (TRD), which is responsible for administering the PIT, has done a very good job of creating forms, instructions, and publications that lead taxpayers through the complex network of applicable laws, regulations and guidance, and much useful information can be found on the TRD website.[3] However, as is the case of tax administrators all over the world, their best efforts at simplification and clarity are limited by the complexity of laws they have to administer. Thus, the need for a book such as this one.

¶ 1.2 History of the personal income tax

New Mexico became a state 1912 and enacted an income tax only several years later in 1919. The constitutionality of the tax was soon attacked, but the income tax prevailed and is now a permanent, integral, and essential part of the fiscal structure of the state, representing approximately 20% of state revenue. Although the state constitution explicitly provides some limits on property tax,[4] it does not place any restrictions on the imposition of an income tax. Further, no municipality in New Mexico imposes an income tax and none has

---

[2] Pub. L. No. 111-97, 123 Stat. 3007.
[3] http://www.tax.newmexico.gov.
[4] N.M. Const. art. VIII, §2.

the power to do so unless enabled by the state.[5]

¶ 1.2.1 Tax rate changes

Income tax rates in New Mexico have always been progressive, and initially ranged from .5% for taxable income of $5,000 through $10,000 and up to 3% for taxable income over $50,000. Over the years, the rates and ranges fluctuated, and by 2002 the rates ranged from a bottom rate of 1.7% to a top rate of 8.2% for single taxpayers with at least $65,000 in income ($100,000 in income for married taxpayers). The final changes occurred in 2003 when the top rates were significantly reduced. The 2003 Act gradually reduced the top rate over a period of years until reaching 4.9% for tax years beginning on or after January 1, 2008 for single taxpayers earning over $16,000 and married taxpayers earning over $24,000. At the low-end, single taxpayers with up to $4,000 of taxable income and married taxpayers with up to $8,000 in taxable income are taxed at a rate of 1.7%. While the income tax still remains progressive, the slope of the progressivity is now very gentle and is applicable only over a small band of income.

In addition to the rate reduction to 4.9%, high-income taxpayers also benefited from the enactment of a capital gain deduction in 2003. The amount of the deduction started at 10% in 2003 and gradually increased to 50% for years beginning in 2008. The tax rate reduction and the capital gain deductions were enacted as part of a drive to increase investment and bring higher-wage jobs to New Mexico.

Unfortunately, New Mexico has a dearth of high income individuals (it ranks 43rd in the nation in personal income) and this fact together with a low top tax rate results in lower income taxpayers paying a large proportion of the income tax; people earning $100,000 or less pay approximately 74% of the income tax.[6] These factors limit the amount of income tax New Mexico can collect and do not portend well for future increases in income tax revenue.

¶ 1.2.2 Benefits for low-income taxpayers

The regressive nature of the state's gross receipt tax, property tax, and various other taxes impact lower-income individuals most acutely. New Mexico has used the PIT to address this disproportionate result

---

[5] §3-18-2A NMSA 1978.
[6] TRD, *2015 New Mexico Tax Expenditure Report*, p. 22.

Introduction to the New Mexico Personal Income Tax

by providing several exemptions and credits for low-income taxpayers. These include the following:

- Refundable low-income comprehensive tax rebate (enacted in 1972),
- Low-income property tax rebate for Los Alamos or Santa Fe County (enacted in 1994),
- Property tax rebate for senior citizens (enacted in 1977),
- Exemption for low and middle income taxpayers (enacted in 2005),
- Refundable working families tax credit (enacted in 2007), and
- Child day care credit (enacted in 1981).

¶ 1.2.3 Adoption of federal adjusted gross income

An important change in the structure of the income tax occurred in 1961, when the state adopted federal adjusted gross income (AGI) as a starting point in determining state taxable income. This approach, which is common to many states, is known as "piggy-backing." Piggy-backing simplifies the computation of income, but it also takes away control of certain elements of the tax system from the state legislature and cedes it to the federal government, at least for those items affecting AGI. Any changes to the federal rules concerning income and deductions that affect AGI become the law of New Mexico, unless the state explicitly makes an adjustment to its taxable income calculation.

In addition to adopting AGI, New Mexico also adopts the taxpayer's marital status for federal purposes, the amount of federal itemized and standard deductions, the number of federal personal and dependency exemptions, and the amount of the federal exemption deduction.

¶ 1.2.4 Economic, Environmental, and Social Objectives

Over the years, the legislature has actively utilized New Mexico's tax system as a tool to promote economic, environmental, and social policy objectives. There are now thirty or so personal income tax credits, as well as about twenty New Mexico adjustments to AGI designed to reflect such goals. The addition of these credits and adjustments greatly increase the intricacy of the tax law. For example, as mentioned above, the computation of the low-income comprehensive tax rebate (LICTR) requires a second income computation, known as modified gross income (MGI), which is entirely different from federal AGI, federal taxable income or even New Mexico taxable income. Furthermore, the pre-approval of business-related credits, often require taxpayers to comply with the lengthy and complex rules of the agencies responsible for prequalification, so that taxpayers have the burden of not only meeting the requirements of the tax law, but also the requirements of a qualifying agency. These agency rules are often more demanding than the tax law that created the credit.

The amount of credits provided under a statute may be limited in the total amount that can be granted all taxpayers, and agencies must dole out credits in accordance with these limitations. This quota system often leaves taxpayers unsure if they will receive the credit for which they have otherwise met the statutory and agency requirements.

¶ 1.2.5 Withholding and Estimated Tax

In order to improve compliance and generate a more reliable flow of revenue, the state enacted a withholding tax on wages in 1961. In addition, as income other than wages increased in importance, the state adopted estimated tax rules, in 1997, that are similar to and as complex as the federal rules.

¶ 1.2.6 The Personal Income Tax Today

The PIT has become not only an important revenue source, but also an important tool for accomplishing state economic, environment, and social policy objectives. Although the effectiveness of using the tax law for these purposes is subject to debate, there is no doubt that the legislature will continue to use the law in this manner, giving rise to a high level of complexity and taxpayer anxiety that this book, hopefully, will help to alleviate.

¶ 1.3 Structure of this book

This book explains and organizes the New Mexico PIT law in a manner that makes it easy for taxpayers and tax professionals to understand, and therefore to plan for and to comply with. Since ultimately the tax law is reflected in the personal income tax return, this book organizes itself as much as possible using the path laid out by the New Mexico tax returns. When helpful, references are made to the appropriate tax form and line, and to the instructions of such

Introduction to the New Mexico Personal Income Tax

forms. The following table explains the content of each chapter.

Chapter	Subject
1	An **introduction** to the book and a description of the history of the New Mexico personal income tax law from tax statehood to modern times
2	A **step-by-step overview** of the law so that a taxpayer or professional can quickly gain an understanding of the key features of the tax law and become familiar with the state's tax forms
3	A **reference tool** that provides a snapshot of the key tax forms so that taxpayers and advisers can quickly and easily see how all the pieces of the tax law fit into the tax return
4	The **filing requirements** with regard to New Mexico income tax returns.
5	The rules for determining **residency,** the determination of which is important in many cases, but especially with regard to how income earned outside the state is taxed in New Mexico
6	The special rules with regard to **military personnel**
7	Computation of taxable income
8	Adjustments to AGI
9	Computing the **tax on taxable income**.
10	Credits against the tax
11	Business-related credits
12	Film production incentives
13	Refundable credits and rebates
14	Voluntary contribution of refunds
15	Interest and penalties
16	Procedures regarding **audits and disputes**
17	Tax administration
18	Record retention requirements
19	Collection and enforcement

¶ 1.4 References to Federal and New Mexico Income Tax Forms and to Websites

Any references in this book to New Mexico and federal income tax forms or instructions are to the latest forms available at the time of the publication of this book, unless otherwise indicated. Any references to federal Form 1040, may also include Form 1040A and 1040EZ, unless otherwise indicated. All citations to websites are as of the date of last viewing as indicated in the text.

CHAPTER 2
THE NEW MEXICO PIT IN TEN EASY STEPS

This section provides a step-by-step overview of the New Mexico personal income tax system. By reading through the next few pages, the reader should gain an understanding of the key concepts of the New Mexican tax law, how deductions and credits are applied, and how the taxpayer's income tax liability is determined. As is the structure of most of this book, this chapter follows along the path of Form PIT-1, the New Mexico personal income tax return. It would be helpful to read this chapter together with the outline of Form PIT-1 shown in the next chapter

¶ 2.1 Step 1: Enter AGI and other federal information

A great deal of the information necessary for completing Form 2016 PIT-1 comes directly from Form 1040. Because the New Mexico tax system piggy backs the federal system, federal AGI is the starting point for determining New Mexico taxable income. Other information required to complete Form PIT-1, such as the taxpayer's marital status, the number of personal exemptions (including dependents), and the personal exemption deduction is also carried over from the federal return. In addition, either the standard deduction or itemized deductions, whichever is applicable, and the federal deduction for state and local taxes (nondeductible in New Mexico), all come directly from federal Form 1040 or 1040A, and are entered on Form PIT-1. The following is a table of this information, indicating where it comes from on the applicable Form 1040 and where it is entered on the Form PIT-1.

New Mexico Personal Income Tax Guide

Tax Item	Federal return	New Mexico Return
Filing status	Forms 1040 and 1040A, check boxes 1 to 5 or Form 1040 EZ, single or joint return	Form PIT-1, Box 7
Number of personal and dependency exemptions	Forms 1040 or 1040A, line 6d	Form PIT-1, line 5
List of dependents	Forms 1040 or 1040A, line 6c	Form PIT-1, line 8
Federal exemption deduction	From 1040, line 42 or Form 1040A, line 26	PIT-1, line 13
AGI	Form 1040, line 38; Form 1040A, line 22; or Form EZ, line 4	Form PIT-1, line 9
Itemized or standard deduction	Form 1040, line 40; Form 1040A, line 24; or Form 1040 EZ, line 5	PIT-1, line 12
State and local tax income or sales tax deduction if taxpayer itemized	Form 1040, Schedule A, line 5	Form PIT-1, line 10

¶ 2.2 Step 2: Make adjustments to federal AGI on Schedule PIT-ADJ.

AGI is only the first step on the road to taxable income. In addition to the reductions in income allowed for either of the federal itemized or standard deductions, and for the personal and dependency exemptions described in Step 1, New Mexico requires other adjustments to be made. Some of these adjustments are necessary for constitutional reasons or by application of federal law. Others arise because New Mexico chooses not to allow some benefits the federal government allows, or because the benefits that New Mexico allows differ in amount from federal benefits, or because New Mexico provides benefits that the federal government does not provide.

Most of these adjustments are made on Schedule PIT-ADJ, and these are summarized in the table below. The total adjustments that increase income is entered on Form PIT-1, line 11, and the total adjustments the decrease income is entered on Form PIT-1, line 15. A few adjustments are made directly on Form PIT-1 and these are discussed in Step 3.

The New Mexico PIT in Ten Easy Steps

ADD/DEDUCT	Item	Reason	PIT-ADJ Line No.
ADD	State/local interest/dividends from federal tax-exempt obligations	NM does not provide a tax exemption for these income items unless they are generated from New Mexico (see line 6).	1
ADD	Federal NOL carryover	NM has different NOL carryover rules than the federal government.	2
ADD	Contributions refunded on closing a NM-approved 529 plan or rolled over to a non-NM-approved 529 plan	Prior tax deducted contributions are recaptured on non-qualifying distributions.	3
ADD	Fed. charitable deduction for donation of land for conservation purposes for which a NM land conservation credit was received	NM does not allow both a deduction and a credit for land donations for conservation purposes.	4
DEDUCT	Interest and dividends that are tax-exempt in NM	Interest and dividends from investments in NM state and local government bonds, and from obligations of US territories are tax-exempt in NM.	6
DEDUCT	New Mexico NOL carryover deduction.	NM allows a NOL carryover deduction but not a carryback deduction, as is allowed under federal rules.	7
DEDUCT	Interest or dividends received on US government obligations	Interest/dividends from investment in federal obligations may not be taxed by a state.	8
DEDUCT	Railroad Retirement Act annuities and benefits and Railroad Unemployment Insurance Act sick pay included in federal taxable income.	The Railroad Retirement and Railroad Unemployment Insurance Acts exempt these benefits from state income taxes. 45 U.S.C. 231m.	9

New Mexico Personal Income Tax Guide

ADD/DEDUCT	Item	Reason	PIT-ADJ Line No.
DEDUCT	Income of a member (and/or spouse) of an Indian nation, tribe, or pueblo wholly earned on Indian lands where the individual is an enrolled member while domiciled there.	NM exempts such income earned by an enrolled member of an Indian, nation, tribe, or pueblo.	10
DEDUCT	Income of persons age 100 years or older	NM exempts centenarians, not a dependent of another, from the PIT.	11a and 11b - Spouse
DEDUCT	Exemption for persons 65 or older, or blind	Persons 65 or older or blind are entitled to an exemption from income of up to $8,000 depending on their AGI.	12
DEDUCT	Exemption for NM Medical Care Savings Account	Contributions to or distributions from a NMMCSA that are included in federal AGI are exempt from NM tax.	13
DEDUCT	Contribution to a NM-approved Section 529 College Savings Plan	NM allows a deduction for contributions to approved 529 plans, but the federal government does not.	14
DEDUCT	Net capital gains deduction	NM allows a deduction of 50% of net capital gain (or 100% of up to $1,000 in gain if greater).	15
DEDUCT	Armed Forces active duty pay	Active duty pay is exempt and may be deducted if included in AGI.	16
DEDUCT	Medical care expense exemption for persons aged 65 or older	$3,000 exemption is allowed for persons 65 or older if unreimbursed medical expenses reach $28,000.	17
DEDUCT	Deduction for organ-donation-related expenses	Organ donation expenses not exceeding $10,000 are deductible.	18

The New Mexico PIT in Ten Easy Steps

ADD/ DEDUCT	Item	Reason	PIT-ADJ Line No.
DEDUCT	NM National Guard member life insurance reimbursements tax exemption	Reimbursement from the National Guard Life Insurance Reimbursement Fund are exempt.	19
DEDUCT	Taxable refunds, credits, or offsets of state and local income taxes from federal Form 1040, line 10	A deduction is allowed for state and local income tax refund amounts entered on Form 1040, line 10 if the taxpayer itemized deductions and included these amounts received as refunds, credits, or offsets on a prior year Form 1040, schedule A.	20
DEDUCT	Nonresident US Public Health Service members' active-duty pay	NM exempts the active day pay of nonresident US Public Health Service members.	21

¶ 2.3 Step 3: Deduct:

a) additional exemption amount for low- and middle-income taxpayers, and
b) unreimbursed medical expenses.

As previously noted, not all adjustments are made on Schedule PIT-ADJ. In addition to the adjustments derived from the federal return noted in Step 1 (itemized and standard deductions, the personal and dependency exemption deduction, and state and local taxes) and those entered on Schedule PIT-ADJ and set forth in Step 2 above, taxpayers are entitled to the following deductions from AGI which are entered directly on Form PIT-1.

New Mexico low- and middle-income tax exemption. An additional amount of income tax exemption is provided for low- and middle-income taxpayers. All taxpayers meeting the income requirements, including residents, part-year residents, first-year residents, and nonresidents may claim this exemption.

The maximum exemption is $2,500 for each qualified exemption for federal income tax purposes. The amount varies according to the taxpayers' filing status and AGI. To qualify for the exemption, AGI must be equal to or less than the following amounts:

- $36,667 (if single)
- $27,500 (if married filing separately)
- $55,000 (if married filing jointly, qualified widow(er), or head of household)

See ¶ 7.4.2 for details.

Unreimbursed medical expenses. A deduction is allowed for unreimbursed medical care expenses, which is computed as a percentage of medical care expenses paid during the tax year. The percentage allowed is based on the taxpayer's filing status and AGI. The percentage deduction is applied only to unreimbursed and uncompensated medical expenses that are not included in the itemized deduction amount on the federal Form 1040, Schedule A. Unreimbursed medical care expenses may qualify if they are not included in the federal itemized deduction amount because they were part of the federal AGI floor amounts of 10% or 7.5%, as applicable. See ¶ 7.5 for details.

¶ 2.4 Step 4: Calculate taxable income

Now that we have AGI and all additions and allowable deductions, we can compute taxable income. This is an easy step. We simply take AGI, increase it by the positive adjustments and reduce it by the deductions from the previous steps. The resulting total is entered on Form PIT-1, line 17.

We are almost ready to apply the New Mexico tax tables, except first we have to talk about the allocation and apportionment of income and the residency of taxpayers.

¶ 2.5 Step Five: Determine residency

Up to this point, Form PIT-1 through line 17 is completed in the same manner for residents and nonresidents, but things change when it is necessary to allocate income. Taxpayers with income taxable within and without the state must allocate and apportion their income between New Mexico and other jurisdictions. After computing the amount of tax on the taxpayer's total taxable income, the taxpayer's tax on New Mexico taxable income is determined by multiplying this tax by the taxpayer's percentage of total income from New Mexico sources. Essentially then, but perhaps not precisely, New Mexico only taxes income that is allocated and apportioned (that is sourced) to New Mexico.

As will become apparent in the next step, the allocation rules are dependent upon whether a taxpayer is resident or nonresident. In general, a resident is an individual who is domiciled in New Mexico during any part of the tax year, or who is physically present in New Mexico for 185 days or more during the tax year regardless of domicile. See Chapter 5 for further discussion.

Special residency rules apply to military personnel and their spouses (see ¶ *6.1.3 - 4*) and to Native Americans living on Indian land (see ¶ *4.3.5*).

¶ 2.6 Step Six: Allocate and apportion income

As mentioned in Step 5, those taxpayers with income taxable within and without New Mexico must allocate and apportion their income. One might think that it is appropriate to allocate and apportion income before computing taxable income, but that is not how it works in New Mexico. The purpose of the allocation and apportionment process is not to determine the amount of income subject to tax but instead to determine the percentage of the tax computed on total taxable income that should be paid to New Mexico. Nonbusiness income is allocated and business and farm income is apportioned.

Residency status affects the extent to which income is allocated to New Mexico. Some of the principal rules of allocation and apportionment are as follows.

- Residents have all their wages, interest, dividends, and retirement income allocated to New Mexico, whereas nonresidents have wages from services in the state allocated to New Mexico, but do not have interest, dividends, and retirement income allocated to the state.

- Residents and nonresidents have rents, royalties, and gains from the sales of property allocated to the state based on the

location of the property that gave rise to the income.
- Residents and nonresidents have their business income apportioned to the state using a formula generally comprised of apportionment fractions consisting of sales, property, and wages inside and outside the state; but a special single factor formula involving only sales may be elected by headquarters and manufacturing businesses; manufacturing businesses may take advantage of this formula beginning 2018, but a gradual transition to this single factor formula is provided for earlier years.
- Partial-year residents are taxed as residents only for the part of the year that they are residents.

Allocation and apportionment are accomplished on Schedule PIT-B, which is also used to calculate the taxpayer's tax on total income and the amount that is payable to New Mexico.

¶ 2.7 Step Seven: Calculate tax on taxable income and on lump sum amounts

The New Mexico income tax is calculated separately for taxable income and lump sum amounts, which are amounts from a retirement plan. First, let's look at taxable income. There are three ways to calculate the New Mexico tax on taxable income: the tax tables, Schedule PIT-B, and Schedule CC.

Tax tables. The default method of calculating taxes is to use the tax tables from the Form PIT-1 instructions. These tables calculate the tax based on income and the filing status of the taxpayer. The tax amount is entered on Form PIT-1, line 18.

Schedule PIT-B. Taxpayers with income from sources within and without New Mexico use Schedule PIT-B to allocate nonbusiness income and to apportion business and farm income between states. To calculate the tax on New Mexico income, the tax on total taxable income (Form PIT-1, line 17) is first determined using the rate tables. Then the additional tax on lump sum distributions is added in at this point.

Next, the sum of these two tax amounts is multiplied by the percentage that New Mexico income bears to total income (Schedule PIT-B, line

14), and the tax so calculated is entered on Form PIT-1, line 18. No entry is made on line 19 for lump sum distributions.

The alternative tax of Schedule CC. Schedule CC provides an alternative tax calculation for taxpayers who are involved only in sales in New Mexico. To qualify the taxpayer must have no business activities in New Mexico other than sales, cannot own or rent real estate in New Mexico, and have annual gross sales in or into New Mexico of $100,000 or less. In this case, Schedule CC provides a tax based only on gross sales at a rate of .75%. The tax is entered on PIT-1, line 18.

Lump-sum amounts. A separate tax calculation is made for lump-sum distributions. Taxpayers that have received a lump-sum payment from a retirement plan and are using the special federal 10-year tax option on federal Form 4972, use New Mexico's 5-year averaging method. The tax computed using this method is entered on Form PIT-1, line 19 and added to the tax on taxable income computed using the rate tables. For taxpayers using Schedule PIT-B, the tax on lump-sum distributions is added to the tax on taxable income and the total is multiplied by the New Mexico percentage of total income.

¶ 2.8 Step 8: Claim non-refundable credits for taxes paid to another state and business-related tax credits

New Mexico has two kinds of credits: refundable and nonrefundable. Nonrefundable credits reduce the tax liability, but not below zero. In this step we calculate the nonrefundable credit for taxes paid to another state and the total of non-refundable business-related income tax credits (Form PIT-1, line 21). By subtracting the total of these credits from the tax computed in Step 6, the Net New Mexico Income Tax (Form PIT-1, line 22) is obtained. As noted, the tax liability so computed cannot be less than zero.

Credit for taxes paid to another state. A resident who is taxed by another state upon income from sources outside New Mexico but which is allocated or apportioned to New Mexico is entitled to a credit for the amount of the tax paid to the other state with regard to that income. This credit is entered on Form PIT-1, line 20. See ¶ 10.2 for more details.

Business-related tax credits. These non-refundable credit items are entered on Schedule PIT-CR and are described in the following table.

New Mexico Personal Income Tax Guide

Form/ Line #	Credit Item	Description
PIT-1/ line 18	NM tax on NM Taxable Income	See Step 6
PIT-1/ line 19	Additional amount for tax on lump- sum distributions	See Step 7
PIT-1/ line 20	Credit for taxes paid to another state	A NM resident who must pay tax to another state on income that is also taxable in NM may take a credit against New Mexico tax for tax paid to the other state but not more than the NM tax paid on that income.
PIT-1/ line 21	Non-refundable business-related Income Tax Credits	To claim one of the business-related income tax credits listed, Schedule PIT-CR must be completed and the amount claimed entered on Form PIT-1, line 21.
PIT-CR	Affordable housing tax credit	For approved projects, the Mortgage Finance Authority (MFA) issues an investment voucher to taxpayers who made an investment in land, buildings, materials, cash, or services for an affordable housing project. The vouchers are good for up to 50% of the investment. The taxpayer may apply the credit against PIT liabilities among other taxes.
PIT-CR	Angel investment credit	Investors may claim a credit for 25% of the qualifying investment in a high- technology or manufacturing business. The maximum investment in a business for which a credit may be allowed is $62,500 per investment round (offering) for no more than five qualified businesses per tax year. The unused credit may be carried forward by the taxpayer for five years.
PIT-CR	Cancer clinical trial tax credit (expired)	A tax credit is provided to an oncologist who conducts a cancer clinical trial beginning on or after January 1, 2012 and before January 1, 2016. A tax credit of $1,000 is allowed for each participating patient, but the total credit must not exceed $4,000 for all cancer clinical trials conducted by that physician during the tax year.

The New Mexico PIT in Ten Easy Steps

Form/ Line #	Credit Item	Description
PIT-CR	Agricultural water conservation tax credit	This credit is for expenses incurred for improvements in irrigation systems or water management methods. The credit equals 50% of eligible expenses, but the total credit allowed may not exceed $10,000 in a tax year. Eligible expenses are for improvements primarily designed to substantially conserve water on NM land used to produce agricultural products, harvest or grow trees, or sustain livestock. The credit was repealed effective January 1, 2013, but the unused credit may be carried forward five years.
PIT-CR	Land conservation incentives credit	Persons who donate land or an interest in land to private or public conservation agencies for conservation purposes may claim a credit equal to 50% of the fair market value of the land transferred up to a fair market value of $250,000.
PIT-CR	Advanced energy tax credit	A taxpayer holding an interest in a qualified electric generating facility located in NM may be eligible for the advanced energy tax credit. The credit equals 6% of the eligible generation plant costs. The aggregate amount of tax credit that may be claimed with respect to a qualified generating facility is limited to $60,000,000.
PIT-CR	Agricultural biomass tax credit	A credit is available for a taxpayer who owns a dairy or feedlot equal to $5 per wet ton of agricultural biomass transported from the dairy or feedlot to a facility that uses agricultural biomass to generate electricity or to make biocrude or other liquid or gaseous fuel for commercial use.
PIT-CR	Business facility rehabilitation credit	The business facility rehabilitation credit equals 50% of pre-approved costs of restoration, rehabilitation, or renovation of a qualified business facility within a NM enterprise zone. The facility must be suitable for manufacturing, distribution, or the service industry immediately after work is complete. The credit may not exceed $50,000.

New Mexico Personal Income Tax Guide

Form/ Line #	Credit Item	Description
PIT-CR	Preservation of cultural properties credit	A credit for the preservation of cultural property may be claimed for 50% of the approved eligible costs of restoration, rehabilitation, or preservation of property listed on the NM Register of Cultural Properties. The credit is limited to $25,000, except for property located within a state- or municipally-certified arts and cultural district, in which case the maximum credit is $50,000.
PIT-CR	Rural job tax credit	Employers in rural areas of NM who qualify for the Job Training Incentive Program (JTIP) may claim a maximum rural job tax credit for each qualifying job created. The credit equals 6.25% of the first $16,000 in wages for each qualifying job for no more than four qualifying periods (12 months) in a Tier 1 area and two qualifying periods in a Tier 2 area.
PIT-CR	Technology jobs and research and development tax credit	A taxpayer who conducts qualified research at a qualified facility in NM may obtain a non-income tax credit equal to 5% of qualified R&D expenditures. If annual payroll is increased by at least $75,000 for every $1 million in qualified expenditures in a tax year, an additional 5% credit is available, which is taken against the income tax. These credits double for businesses in rural areas. This tax credit is partially refundable for small businesses. Note: This credit replaces the Technology Jobs Credit which was repealed effective January 1, 2016; any unused carryforward credits are combined into the new credit.
PIT-CR	Electronic card-reading equipment tax credit	A one-time $300 income tax credit is provided for businesses that purchase electronic identification card readers for age verification. A business may claim this credit if it is licensed to sell cigarettes, tobacco products, or alcoholic beverages and the business has purchased and is using equipment that electronically reads identification cards to verify age. The credit is available at each business location using electronic identification card readers.

The New Mexico PIT in Ten Easy Steps

Form/ Line #	Credit Item	Description
PIT-CR	Job mentorship tax credit	A NM business owner may claim a job mentorship tax credit for employing qualified students who take part in a school-sanctioned career-preparation education program. The credit equals 50% of gross wages paid to a maximum of 10 qualified students, on the first 320 hours of employment for each qualified student during the tax year. A taxpayer may not claim a credit for one qualified individual for more than three tax years. The maximum credit for one tax year is $12,000.
PIT-CR	Solar market development tax credit	This credit, which may not exceed $9,000, is available for up to 10% of the purchase and installation costs of a qualified photovoltaic or solar thermal system. The photovoltaic or solar thermal system must be purchased and installed before December 31, 2016.
PIT-CR	Blended biodiesel fuel tax credit	Beginning January 1, 2007, but not after December 31, 2012, a rack operator or supplier who is required to pay the special fuel excise tax and who files a NM personal or corporate income tax return may claim a credit against the tax due on the return for each gallon of blended biodiesel fuel on which the rack operator or supplier paid the special fuel excise tax in the tax year. Although the blended biodiesel tax credit is not refundable and is not available for tax years beginning on or after January 1, 2013, a carryforward of the credit can be claimed for five years.
PIT-CR	Film and television tax credit	The film and television tax credit provides a credit for an eligible film production company. The credit is equal to 25% of direct production and direct postproduction expenditures made in NM. An additional 5% is added for qualifying television series and pilots filmed in NM and for the use of qualified production facilities. An additional 15% credit is available for wages, fringe benefits, and per diem paid to nonresident industry crew meeting statutory requirements.

Form/ Line #	Credit Item	Description
PIT-CR	New sustainable building tax credit	A credit is available for construction of a sustainable building, for renovation of a building into a sustainable building, or for permanent installation of manufactured housing that is a sustainable building. To qualify for the credit, the building must have achieved a silver or higher certification level in the LEED green building rating system or the Build Green NM rating system. Note: The new sustainable building credit is effective January 1, 2017. For both the pre-existing credit and the new credit, the rate of the credit varies with a number of factors. In addition, the range of rates has changed with the adoption of the new credit.
PIT-CR	Rural health care practitioners tax credit	A health care practitioner providing health care services in an underserved rural area in NM may claim a credit up to the following amounts: • $5,000 for eligible physicians, osteopathic physicians, dentists, clinical psychologists, podiatrists, and optometrists; and • $3,000 for dental hygienists, physician assistants, certified nurse-midwives, certified registered nurse anesthetists, certified nurse practitioners, and clinical nurse specialists. The practitioner must have provided health care in an approved rural health care underserved area during a tax year for at least 2,080 hours to qualify for the full credit amount and at least 1,040 hours, but less than 2,080 hours, to qualify for one-half of the full credit amount.
PIT-CR	Geothermal ground-coupled heat pump tax credit	A credit is available for a taxpayer who has purchased and installed a geothermal ground-coupled heat pump. The credit is available for up to 30% of the purchase and installation costs, but may not exceed $9,000. The pump must be installed in a residence, business, or agricultural enterprise that is owned by the taxpayer or a partnership or other business association of which the taxpayer is a member.

The New Mexico PIT in Ten Easy Steps

Form/ Line #	Credit Item	Description
PIT-CR	Veteran employment tax credit	A taxpayer employing a qualified military veteran may be eligible for a credit for up to $1,000 for wages paid. The credit is only allowed if the veteran: 1) was not previously employed by the taxpayer before deployment; 2) was hired within two years of receipt of an honorable discharge; and 3) is employed full time. If the veteran is employed for less than a full year, the credit is reduced proportionally. The credit be may be claimed only for one year from the date of hire.
PIT-CR	Renewable energy production tax credit	Taxpayers receive a credit for producing electricity by solar light or heat, wind, or biomass for up to 10 consecutive years beginning on the date the qualified energy generator begins producing electricity. The credit is generally $.01 per kilowatt-hour of the first 400,000 megawatt hours produced.
PIT-CR/ line A; PIT/ line 21	Total Business related credits	
PIT/ line 22	Net New Mexico Income Tax	Add lines 18 and 19, then subtract lines 20 and 21. Cannot be less than zero.

¶ 2.9 Step 9: Subtract refundable low-income rebates and credits and refundable credits due all taxpayers

In addition to the business-related nonrefundable credits, New Mexico has two types of refundable credits, those for low-income taxpayers and those for all taxpayers regardless of income. Refundable tax credits are treated as cash payments to the taxpayer, and thus may be paid back to the taxpayer in excess of the taxpayer's liability. Low-income taxpayers may subtract the following additional credits:

New Mexico Personal Income Tax Guide

Form/ Line #	Rebate/Credit Item	Description
PIT-1/ line 24	Total claimed of the following rebates and credits from schedule PIT-RC, line 25.	NM provides several rebates and refundable credits for low-income taxpayers. Eligibility is generally based on the taxpayer's level of Modified Gross Income (MGI).
PIT-CR/ line 14	Low income comprehensive tax rebate	To qualify, taxpayers must have a MGI of $22,000 or less. The amount of the rebate depends on the level of the taxpayers MGI and the number of taxpayer exemptions. The maximum rebate is $450.
PIT-CR/ line 17c	Property Tax Rebate for Persons 65 or Older	A rebate is provided for property tax billed or rent paid during the tax year on a principal place of residence in NM. The rebate cannot exceed $250 or, $125 for a married taxpayer filing a separate return. To qualify the taxpayer must be age 65 or older on the last day of the tax year and have a MGI of $16,000 or less and meet certain other criteria.
PIT-RC/ Line 18c	Additional Low Income Property Tax Rebate for Los Alamos or Santa Fe County	A property tax rebate is provided for property tax paid during the tax year on a principal place of residence in Los Alamos or Santa Fe County. The maximum rebate is $350 or, for a married taxpayer filing a separate return, $175. The amount of rebate varies with the taxpayer's level of MGI. Taxpayers with a MGI of more than $24,000 are not eligible. Additional criteria apply to determine eligibility. Taxpayers do not have to be 65 or older to obtain this rebate.
PIT-RC/ line 22	NM child day care credit.	A gainfully employed taxpayer with MGI of $30,160 or less may claim a child day care credit equal to 40% of the compensation paid to a caregiver for the care of a qualifying dependent, but the credit may not exceed $480 for each qualifying dependent or a total of $1,200 for all qualifying dependents for a tax year ($600 for married taxpayers filing separate returns). For purposes of computing the credit, compensation paid to a caregiver may not exceed $8.00 per day for each qualifying dependent.

The New Mexico PIT in Ten Easy Steps

Refundable credits. All taxpayers, regardless of income can subtract these credits; and if, the credit exceeds the taxpayer's tax liability he or she may obtain a refund:

Form/ Line #	Refundable Credit	Description
PIT-RC/ line 23	Refundable medical care credit for persons 65 or older	Taxpayers or their spouses who are 65 years of age or older that have unreimbursed and uncompensated medical care expenses of $28,000 or more during the tax year, may claim a tax credit of $2,800 ($1,400 for married couples filing separate returns).
PIT-RC/ Line 24	Special needs adopted child tax credit	A taxpayer who adopts a special needs child may claim a tax credit against the income tax in the amount of $1,000. A taxpayer may claim the credit for each year that the child may be claimed as a dependent for federal taxation purposes. Married individuals who file separate tax returns are entitled to one-half the applicable credit.
PIT-1/ line 24	Total credits from Schedule RC	
PIT-1/ line 25	Working families tax credit	A NM resident who files a NM income tax return may claim a working families tax credit in an amount equal to 10% of the federal earned income tax credit for which the individual is eligible for the same tax year under §32 of the IRC.
PIT-1/ line 26	Refundable business-related income tax credits from Schedule PIT-CR, line B	The renewable energy production tax credit is refundable if the energy generator first produces electricity on or after October 1, 2007; certain amounts of the technology jobs and research and development (additional) tax credit are refundable to small businesses; and the film and television tax credit is refundable subject to annual limits.

53

¶ 2.10 Step 10: Subtract withholding and estimated tax and add any interest and penalties to determine tax due or amount of refund

After deducting the refundable credits in Step 9, the following payments are deducted from the Net Mexico Income Tax.

- income tax withheld,
- income tax withheld from oil and gas proceeds,
- income tax withheld from a pass-through entity,
- estimated income tax payments, and
- other payments (e.g., payments made using Form PIT-PV, and extension payments using Form PIT-EXT).

Interest and penalties, if any, are then added to determine tax, interest and penalty due or the amount to be refunded. The amount to be refunded can be paid to the taxpayer or applied either to voluntary contributions or estimated tax.

That's all there is!

CHAPTER 3
OUTLINE OF THE NEW MEXICO PERSONAL INCOME TAX RETURN (FORM PIT-1)

¶ 3.1 Overview of Form 2016 PIT-1

This section provides a snapshot of the New Mexico tax system from the vantage point of Form PIT-1, the New Mexico personal income tax return. Ultimately every item of income, deduction, or credit, and every issue of income tax treatment must be reflected in this form. By reviewing the outline below, the reader can obtain an overall perspective on both the form and the workings of the New Mexico tax system.

Form PIT-1 is deceptively simple because the computation of the many adjustments and credits of the New Mexico income tax takes place on supplemental schedules, the results of which are then entered on the Form PIT-1. For example, adjustments to AGI are recorded on Schedule PIT-ADJ, refundable rebates are recorded on Schedule PIT-RC, and business-related credits are recorded on Schedule PIT-CR. That being the case, the following outline not only illustrates and annotates Form PIT-1 but also incorporates the adjustment and credit schedules as well.

What follows is an outline of the Form PIT-1 for instructional purposes and is not an actual picture of the form, and thus the reader will find structural differences between the outline below and the actual form.

¶ 3.2 Outline of Form 2016 PIT-1

New Mexico Personal Income Tax Guide

Line	Outline of 2016 Form PIT-1 and PIT-ADJ, PIT-CR and PIT-RC		
1.	Taxpayer name, SSN, Blind ☐, Age 65 ☐, Residency status (R, N, F, P), DOB		
2.	Spouse's name, SSN, Blind ☐, Age 65 ☐, Residency status (R, N, F, P), DOB		
3b.	Address (check 3a –☐ if new address)	4.	Deceased taxpayer refund payment info:
5.	Number of qualified exemptions:	6.	Extension filed? ☐ Extension date:
7.	Filing status (from federal return): Single ☐, Married ☐, Married filing separately ☐, Head of household ☐, Qualifying widow(er) with dependent child ☐		
8.	Dependents (as listed on federal return); PIT-S is used for dependents > 5		
9.	FEDERAL AGI; If negative, fed. NOL entered on line 9a		
	ADDITION/ DEDUCTIONS TO/FROM AGI – lines 10 to 16		
10.	+	State and local tax deduction claimed on Form1040	
11.	+	Total additions to AGI from PIT-ADJ, line 5.	
		PIT-ADJ, line 1	Interest and dividends from federal tax-exempt bonds
		PIT-ADJ, line 2	Federal NOL carryover
		PIT-ADJ, line 3	Contributions refunded on closing NM-approved 529 plan or rolled-over to a non-NM-approved 529 plan
		PIT-ADJ, line 4	Federal charitable deduction for land donation for which a NM Land Conservation Tax Credit was allowed
		PIT-ADJ/line 5	PIT-ADJ ADDITIONS -enter on PIT-1, line 11
12.	−	Federal standard or itemized deduction amount (check 12a - ☐ if itemizing);Form 1040EZ filers enter line 5 from that form	
13.	−	Federal exemption amount – 1040, line 42; 1040A, line 26; 1040 EZ, no entry	
14.	−	NM low- and middle-income tax exemption	
15.	−	Total deductions and exemptions from AGI from PIT-ADJ, line 22	
		PIT-ADJ, line 6	NM tax-exempt interest and dividends
		PIT-ADJ, line 7	NM net operating loss.
		PIT-ADJ, line 8	Interest received on U.S. Government obligations
		PIT-ADJ, line 9	Taxable RR Act annuities/benefits, and taxable Railroad Unemployment Insurance Act sick pay
		PIT-ADJ, line 10	Income of a member of a NM federally-recognized Indian nation, tribe, or pueblo wholly-earned on the reservation or pueblo of which the individual is enrolled and domiciled

Outline of the New Mexico Personal Income Tax Return

		PIT-ADJ, line 11	Income of persons age 100 years or older
		PIT-ADJ, line 12	Exemption for persons age 65 or older, or blind
		PIT-ADJ, line 13	Exemption for NM medical care savings account.
		PIT-ADJ, line 14	Deduction for contributions to a NM 529 savings plan
		PIT-ADJ, line 15	Net capital gains deduction
		PIT-ADJ, line 16	Armed Forces active duty pay
		PIT-ADJ, line 17	Medical care expense exemption for persons age ≥ 65
		PIT-ADJ, line 18	Deduction for organ donation-related expenses
		PIT-ADJ, line 19	NM Nat'l Guard life insur. reimbursement exemption
		PIT-ADJ, line 20	Taxable refunds, credits, or offsets of state/local income taxes
		PIT-ADJ, line 21	Nonresident U.S. Pub. Health Service active duty pay
		PIT-ADJ, line 22	PIT-ADJ DEDUCTIONS AND EXEMPTIONS
16.	−	Medical care expense deduction; in box 16a: enter amount of unreimbursed and uncompensated medical care expenses	
17.	=	NM TAXABLE INCOME: lines 9+10+11, less lines 12+13+14+15+16. but less than zero.	
18.		NM TAX ON TAXABLE INCOME: 18a - from rate table $\boxed{R}$: from PIT-B $\boxed{B}$ (allocation and apportionment of income within and without NM); or $\boxed{Y}$ for nonresidents electing special gross income method for royalty income.	
19.	+	Additional amount for lump sum distributions (but not if using PIT-B).	
20	−	Credit for taxes paid another state. Must be resident for all or part of the year	
21.	−	Non-refundable business-related income tax credits − from PIT-CR, line A	
		PIT-CR Code A01	*Affordable housing tax credit:* A credit of up to 50% of an investment in an affordable housing project.
		PIT-CR Code A02	*Angel investment credit:* 25% of an investment in a high technology or manufacturing business.
		PIT-CR Code A03	*Agricultural water conservation tax credit:* 50% of costs of water conservation for crops or livestock.
		PIT-CR Code A04	*Advanced energy tax credit:* A credit of 6% of costs of a facility using advance energy technologies.
		PIT-CR Code A05	*Agricultural biomass tax credit:* $5 per ton of wet biomass to generate electricity or produce biofuels.
		PIT-CR Code B01	*Business facility rehabilitation credit:* 50% of costs of rehabilitating, restoring, or renovating a EZ facility.
		PIT-CR Code B02	*Blended biodiesel fuel credit:* A credit for each gallon on which the special fuel excise tax has been paid.

New Mexico Personal Income Tax Guide

		PIT-CR Code C01	*Cancer clinical trial tax credit:* a $1,000 credit per patient participating in a clinical trial.
		PIT-CR Code E01	*Electronic card-reading equipment credit:* $300 on the purchase of ID card readers for age verification.
		PIT-CR Code G01	*Geothermal ground-coupled heat pump tax credit:* 30% of cost of pump.
		PIT-CR Code J01	*Job mentorship tax credit:* 50% of wages of students participating in career preparation programs.
		PIT-CR Code L01	*Land conservation incentives credit:* 50% of the value of an interest in land donated for conservation use.
		PIT-CR Code P01	*Preservation of cultural property credit:* A credit of 50% of cost of improvement of cultural property.
		PIT-CR Code R01	*Rural job tax credit.* A credit of 6.25% of first $16,000 in wages for each qualifying job created.
		PIT-CR Code R02	*Rural health care practitioners credit:* $5000 for doctors ($3000 for others) in underserved rural areas.
		PIT-CR Code S01	*Solar market development tax credit.* Up to 10% of the cost of a solar photovoltaic or thermal system.
		PIT-CR Code S02	*Sustainable building credit:* A credit for creating sustainable buildings.
		PIT-CR Code T01	*Technology jobs & R&D tax credit.* 5% credit (10% in rural areas) for increased R&D expenditures
		PIT-CR Code V01	*Veteran employment tax credit:* Up to $1,000 for wages paid by an employer who hires a veteran.
		PIT-CR line A	TOTAL BUSINESS RELATED TAX CREDITS
22/23	=	NET NEW MEXICO INCOME TAX – Cannot be less than zero.	
		CREDITS AND REBATES AGAINST NET NM INCOME TAX	
24.	–	Total claimed on rebate and credit schedule - from PIT-RC, line 25	
		PIT-RC, line 14	Low income comprehensive rebate
		PIT-RC, line 17c	Property tax rebate for persons 65 or older.
		PIT-RC, line 18c	Additional low income property tax rebate for Los Alamos or Santa Fe county
		PIT-RC, line 22	New Mexico child day care credit
		PIT-RC, line 25	TOTAL REBATES AND CREDITS CLAIMED
25.	–	Working families credit. Line 25a: enter federal earned income credit (EIC)	
26.	–	Refundable business-related income tax credits from PIT-CR, line B.	
		PIT-CR Code F01	*Film and television tax credit:* A credit of 25% for direct and indirect production costs, plus 5% for qualifying productions and a separate 15% credit for nonresident industry crews.
		PIT-CR Code T02	*Technology jobs & R&D credit:* Refundable 5% credit if payroll increases for small businesses; the credit doubles in rural areas.
		PIT-CR Code R03	*Renewable energy production credit.* A credit based upon the amount of renewable energy produced.
		PIT-CR, line B	Total refundable business-related credits

Outline of the New Mexico Personal Income Tax Return

27.	−	NM income tax withheld
28.	−	NM income tax withheld from oil and gas proceeds
29.	−	NM income tax withheld from a pass-through entity
30.	−	Estimated income tax payments for the tax year
31.	−	Other Payments (e.g., using Form PIT-PV, and 7Form PIT-EXT)
32.	=	TOTAL PAYMENTS AND CREDITS: (lines 24 through 31)
33.		TAX DUE (Only if line 23 is greater than line 32)
34.	+	Penalty on underpayment of estimated tax
35.	+	Special method allowed for calculating estimated tax penalty
36.	+	Penalty
37.	+	Interest
38.	=	TAX, PENALTY, AND INTEREST DUE (lines 33, 34, 36, and 37)
39.		OVERPAYMENT (if line 23 is less than line 32)
40.	−	Refund voluntary contributions (attach PIT-D)
41.	−	Amount applied to estimated tax
42.	−	AMOUNT TO BE REFUNDED (Line 39 minus lines 40 and 41)

New Mexico Personal Income Tax Guide

¶3.3 Filling out the form

The instructions to Form PIT-1 provide for a number of conventions to be applied in filling out the form. Some of these are as follows:

- Round all numbers and enter only whole dollar amounts. For example, enter $10.49 as $10 and $10.50 as $11.
- To show a loss on PIT-1, line 9, place a minus sign (-) immediately to the left of the loss amount. Do not use brackets or parentheses.
- Do not use dollar signs ($), decimal points (.), or any punctuation marks or symbols other than a comma (,).

  For example, if the federal AGI is negative $23,742.48, the money field entry for a loss on the PIT-1, line 9 would look like this:

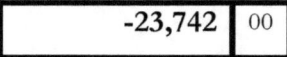

CHAPTER 4
FILING REQUIREMENTS, EXEMPT STATUS, AND ESTIMATED TAXES

¶ 4.1 Imposition of Tax on Individuals

The New Mexico individual income tax rules are found in the state's Income Tax Act, which is generally referred to as the ITA. The ITA imposes a progressive tax on the net income of individuals: income in the lowest bracket is taxed at 1.7% and income in the top bracket is taxed at 4.9%. Although residents and nonresidents report all of their worldwide income and compute their taxable income in an identical manner, New Mexico only intends to tax income that is allocated and apportioned to New Mexico. To reach this result, the ITA provides a credit equal to the tax on a taxpayer's total taxable income multiplied by the percentage of that income that is allocated and apportioned to sources outside the state.[1] For some administrative reason, however, this credit does not appear anywhere on New Mexico income tax forms. Instead, Schedule PIT-B produces the same effect in determining a taxpayer's tax liability by multiplying the amount of tax on a taxpayer's worldwide income by the percentage of income allocated and apportioned to New Mexico. The above-discussed credit should not be confused with the credit given to residents who are taxed by another state on income from sources outside New Mexico but which is allocated or apportioned to New Mexico.

> *Example.* Michelle Smith is a California resident that earns consulting income in New Mexico. Her worldwide taxable income (Form PIT-1, line 17) is $80,000 and the percentage of her income allocated and apportioned to sources outside New Mexico is 80%. Filing single, her tax on $80,000 from the tax tables is $3,643. Since 80% of her income is from sources outside New Mexico, she is entitled to a credit of $2,914 (.8 x

---

[1] §7-2-11C NMSA 1978.

$3,643) producing a net tax of $729. However, Schedule PIT-B ignores this credit and directly computes the tax by multiplying Ms. Smith's tax on worldwide taxable income of $3,643 by 20% (the percentage allocated and apportioned to New Mexico), producing a tax of $729. This is the same the result as using the credit mechanism of the ITA.

Residency is a very important aspect of New Mexico taxation because of the differences it produces in the allocation of income. For example, all wages of a resident are allocated to New Mexico, while only wages earned in New Mexico are allocated to New Mexico for a nonresident.[2] Additionally, interest and dividend income and retirement income are allocated to New Mexico in the case of a resident, while none of such income is allocated to New Mexico in the case of a nonresident. Special rules apply to military personnel and to the apportionment of business income, as well as to other types of income.

The actual allocation and apportionment of income is accomplished on Schedule PIT-B, which also computes the New Mexico tax on taxable income for residents and nonresidents that have taxable income from sources both within and without the state. The rules of allocation and apportionment are complex and are discussed in greater detail in ¶ 9.3 et seq.

¶ 4.2 Taxpayer requirements for filing returns and payment of tax

¶4.2.1 Individuals required to file

A resident individual who is required to file a federal income tax return must file a New Mexico income tax return. Nonresidents who derive income from any business transaction, property, or employment within the state and who are required to file a federal income tax return must also file a New Mexico tax return.[3] The returns must be complete and in form and content as prescribed by the Secretary of the TRD. Both residents and nonresidents do not have to file if they are

---

[2] §7-2-3 NMSA 1978.
[3] §7-2-3 NMSA 1978.

Filing Requirements, Exempt Status, and Estimated Taxes

statutorily exempt.[4] Residency is discussed in Chapter 5.

A military servicemember who moves out of state on military service will still have to file a return as a resident if he or she was a resident of New Mexico at the time of enlistment and has not changed his or her legal residence for purposes of withholding state income tax from military pay. However, military servicemembers may claim a deduction for military active duty pay included in AGI. If a servicemember has established domicile in another state and changed legal residence for withholding state income tax, his or her military pay is not subject to New Mexico income tax.

The income of Indians from work on lands of the Indian nations, tribes, or pueblos of which they are enrolled members and where they live is exempt from New Mexico PIT. If such income is the entire income of the Indian nation or tribe member, he or she does not have to file an income tax return. The income of a spouse or a dependent from work within the boundaries of member's nation, tribe, or pueblo is also exempt.

See ¶ 4.3.4 for a discussion of the taxation of the items of income of enrolled members of Indian nations, tribes, or pueblos.

Individuals who are not required to file a New Mexico income tax return may in any event file one in order to obtain a refundable credit or rebate. In this case, the TRD recommends that individual complete a federal return or a "dummy" or pro forma federal return because the federal AGI figure on that form is needed to claim New Mexico rebates and credits.[5]

An "individual" includes not only a natural person, but an estate, a trust or a fiduciary acting for a natural person, trust or estate.[6] Occasionally, the ITA uses the term "person" without modifying it, as above, with the word "natural." For example, the ITA allows the TRD to require any person doing business in the state to submit information reports to the TRD.[7] The definition of person without the natural modifier is quite broad and includes any individual, estate, trust,

---

[4] §7-2-12A NMSA 1978.
[5] See TRD, Brochure #2, *Tax Information for New Mexico's Low-Income Filers* (Rev. 7/2014).
[6] §7-2-20A NMSA 1978.
[7] §7-2-2R NMSA 1978.

receiver, cooperative association, club, corporation, company, firm, partnership, limited liability company, joint venture, syndicate or other association; person also means, to the extent permitted by law, any federal, state or other governmental unit or subdivision or agency, department or instrumentality thereof. This book only deals with natural persons and does not describe the taxation of estates, trusts, fiduciaries, or any other persons other than natural persons.

¶ 4.2.2 Taxpayer Identification Number

Taxpayers must enter their name and Social Security Number on all forms, schedules, and correspondence sent to the TRD. The TRD will not accept a return without a valid identification number. New Mexico requires taxpayers to use the same name and taxpayer identification number as required by the IRS.

A tax identification number issued by the IRS to individuals not qualified to be issued a Social Security Number will be accepted by the TRD in lieu of the Social Security Number in all cases in which reporting a Social Security Number is required. Resident or non-resident foreign nationals who do not have and who are not eligible to obtain a Social Security Number may obtain a federal Individual Taxpayer Identification Number (ITIN). An individual may obtain an ITIN by filing federal Form W-7 with the IRS. The ITIN must be entered in place of a Social Security Number everywhere the Social Security Number is required.

Filing Requirements, Exempt Status, and Estimated Taxes

What is an ITIN?
An Individual Taxpayer Identification Number (ITIN) is a tax processing number issued by the IRS to help individuals comply with the U.S. tax laws. The IRS issues ITINs to individuals who have federal tax reporting or filing requirements but who do not have, and are not eligible to obtain a Social Security Number (SSN). ITINs do not qualify the individual to work in the United States, nor do they create eligibility for Social Security benefits or the Earned Income Credit. An ITIN is used for tax reporting purposes only and serves no other purpose. ITINs are issued regardless of immigration status. Specifically, an ITIN is a nine-digit number that always begins with the number 9 and has a range of 70-88 in the fourth and fifth digit. Effective April 12, 2011, the range was extended to include 900-70-0000 through 999-88-9999, 900-90-0000 through 999-92-9999 and 900-94-0000 through 999-99-9999.
Source: IRS website: https://www.irs.gov/Individuals/General-ITIN-Information

Pass-through entities use their Federal Employer Identification Number for identification when filing a pass-through entity return, but generally, are not subject to New Mexico income tax.[8]

---

[8] §3.1.1.13 NMAC.

> **In Practice:** New Mexico defines pass-through entities (PTEs) in the negative. A PTE is any business or a personal service business or that is *not*
>
> - a sole proprietorship, or an estate or trust that does not distribute income to beneficiaries;
>
> - a corporation, limited liability company, partnership or other entity not a sole proprietorship taxed as a corporation for federal income tax purposes for the tax year;
>
> - a partnership that is organized as an investment partnership in which the partners' income is derived solely from interest, dividends and sales of securities;
>
> - a single-member limited liability company that is treated as a disregarded entity for federal income tax purposes; or
>
> - a publicly-traded partnership as defined in Subsection(b) of Section 7704 of the Internal Revenue Code.
>
> A PTE generally files an annual information return known as Form PTE, *New Mexico Information Return for Pass-through Entities*, using its federal tax identification number. That is not to say that the PTE is not subject to other taxes for which a New Mexico registration number would be required such as the New Mexico gross receipts tax.
>
> In New Mexico, S corporations, so designated for federal purposes, file a sort of hybrid return between the pass-through and corporate returns. S corporations file Form S-Corp, *New Mexico Sub-Chapter S Corporate Income & Franchise Tax Return*, using their federal identification number. The return provides information about income and deductions passed through to owners as well as any information regarding income for which the corporation is subject to tax. If the entity is not subject to income tax, it is subject to a minimum franchise tax of $50. An S corporation will likely need to obtain a New Mexico registration number if it is subject to the gross receipts tax.

Filing Requirements, Exempt Status, and Estimated Taxes

The TRD has established a system for the registration and identification of taxpayers, which in addition to state tax compliance, facilitates the exchange of information with other states and aids in statistical computations.[9] The filing of a tax return containing a Social Security Number constitutes registration for this purpose.[10]

A person who meets the definition of taxpayer under the ITA, but who has not registered or been identified, is nonetheless a taxpayer subject to the provisions of the Tax Administration Act (TAA).[11] A "taxpayer" is a person liable for payment of any tax, a person responsible for withholding and payment or for collection and payment of any tax, or a person to whom an assessment has been made, if the assessment remains unabated or the amount thereof has not been paid.[12]

¶ 4.2.3 Address of notices and payments – change in address

Any required notice that is effective if mailed or served may be mailed to or served at the last address shown on the records of the TRD. When a notice, return, application or payment is required or authorized to be delivered to the Secretary or the TRD by mail, it must be addressed to the Secretary of TRD, Santa Fe, New Mexico or in any other manner which the Secretary directs by regulation or instruction.[13]

A taxpayer must include his or her correct mailing address on all required notices, returns, or applications and must promptly advise the TRD in writing of any changes. Form RPD-41260, *Personal Income Tax Change Of Address Form*, may be used to notify the TRD of a change in address; but if the required information is contained in a change of address form or notice of the United States Postal Service, that form may be used in lieu of the TRD form.[14]

If a taxpayer notifies the United States Postal Service (USPS) of a change in mailing address, and the USPS gives this information to the

---

[9] §7-1-12 NMSA 1978. This provision also requires state registration for businesses subject to various state tax programs including but not limited to the Gross Receipts, Compensating, Withholding, or Worker's Compensation taxes.
[10] §3.1.1.15 NMAC.
[11] §3.1.1.13 NMAC.
[12] §7-1-3AA NMSA 1978.
[13] §7-1-9A NMSA 1978.
[14] §3.1.4.9A NMAC.

TRD either voluntarily or upon the TRD's request, the taxpayer is deemed to have fulfilled the obligation to notify the TRD of a change in mailing address. Unless the taxpayer specifically notifies the TRD that the change of mailing address does not apply to mailings from the TRD to the taxpayer, the notice to the USPS of a change in the taxpayer's mailing address and given by the USPS to the TRD applies to mailings from the TRD.[15]

¶ 4.2.4 Due date of return and payments

A taxpayer is liable for tax as soon as the taxable event occurs, but payment is not due until on and after the date established by statute for the payment of tax.[16]

Under statute, the return, along with the tax imposed, is due, and payment required on or before the 15th day of the 4th month following the end of the tax year.[17] Payment of the total amount due must precede or accompany the return. Delivery of a check that is not paid upon presentment does not constitute payment.[18]

Under a recent tax law amendment, New Mexico conformed it filing deadlines for the personal and corporate income with federal deadlines. Specifically, the new law amends the filing deadlines in the ITA and the Corporate Income Tax Act. It does not amend the pass-through entity informational filing deadlines as those rules already conform to federal law. Since New Mexico filing deadlines for the PIT generally follow federal deadlines this conformity rule should not have much impact.[19]

¶ 4.2.5 Making tax payments by mail

The instructions to Form PIT-1 offer these rules for paying by mail.

- If taxpayers owe one dollar or more, they should complete the Form PIT-PV payment voucher.
- Full payment should be included with the voucher and a check or money order should be made payable to New Mexico Taxation and Revenue Department.

---

[15] §3.1.4.9B NMAC.
[16] §3.1.4.10 NMAC.
[17] §7-2-12 NMSA 1978.
[18] §7-1-13D NMSA 1978.
[19] Chapter 15 [HB-249 (Section 1)].

Filing Requirements, Exempt Status, and Estimated Taxes

- The taxpayer should write his or her social security number and the tax year of the return, for example "2016 PIT-1" on the payment.[20]
- Taxpayers should never send cash.
- A payment voucher should be submitted only if a check or money order payment is included.
- Only high-quality printed, original vouchers may be used. Photocopy vouchers are not acceptable.

The instructions also provide requirements for printed vouchers in order to allow accuracy with their high-speed scanner. Electronic payments are discussed below.

¶ 4.2.6 Date of payment

The payment of any tax or the filing of any return may be accomplished by mail, except if regulation, ruling, order or instruction of the Secretary provides otherwise. When the filing of a tax return or payment of a tax is accomplished by mail, the date of the postmark is considered the date of submission of the return or payment.[21]

¶ 4.2.7 Timely-mailed, timely-filed rule

All notices, returns, applications or payments that are authorized or required to be made or given by mail are timely filed if mailed on or before the date on which they are required.[22] Mailings are considered timely if the USPS postmark on the envelope bears the date on or before the last date prescribed for filing the notice, return or application, or for making the payment. The date affixed on an envelope by a postage meter stamp will be considered the postmark date if it is not superseded by a USPS postmark. If the postmark does not bear a date on or before the last date prescribed for filing the notice, return or application, or for making the payment, the notice, return, application, or payment will be presumed to be late. The sender assumes the responsibility that the postmark will bear a date on or before the last date prescribed for filing the notice, return or

---

[20] 2016 PIT-1, Personal Income Tax Return Instructions, p. 36.
[21] §7-1-13B NMSA 1978.
[22] §7-1-9B NMSA 1978.

application, or for making the payment.[23]

If a mailing is not received by the TRD, the mailing is not timely. If an envelope is improperly addressed and is returned to the sender by the post office, there has been no timely mailing. The postmark date on an improperly addressed envelope will not be deemed the date of receipt.[24]

A facsimile transmittal of a notice, return, or application will be considered timely filed only if it is received by the due date for filing, *and* the original is delivered by the due date, or, if mailed, it is postmarked on or before the due date.[25]

¶ 4.2.8 Illegible postmarks

If the postmark on an envelope is illegible, but the contents are received by the TRD by the second business day following the due date, the filing of the return, payment, or other action will be considered timely. If the contents are received by the TRD after the second business day following the due date, the person who is required to file the notice, return or application, or make payment, has the burden of proving the time when the postmark was made.[26]

¶ 4.2.9 Private delivery services

Generally, if a taxpayer sends or delivers the notice, return, application or payment by any means other than by mailing with the United States postal service, it must be received by the TRD on or before the due date for filing.[27] An exception is made with regard to certain private delivery services.

A delivery to a private delivery service (PDS) designated by the Secretary of the Treasury[28] is considered a timely mailing if the date recorded or marked by the PDS is on or before the date by which mailing is required. Of course, the delivery must be made during the time the designation by the Secretary of Treasury is in effect.[29] The

---

[23] §3.1.4.10C(1) NMAC.
[24] §3.1.4.10C(2) NMAC.
[25] §3.1.4.10C(3) NMAC.
[26] §3.1.4.10D(1) NMAC.
[27] §3.1.4.10D(3) NMAC.
[28] Under 26 USCA §7502.
[29] §3.1.4.16 NMAC. This rule applies to deliveries to a designated private delivery service after June 30, 1999.

Filing Requirements, Exempt Status, and Estimated Taxes

following are the PDSs that have been designated by Treasury as qualifying for the timely mailing, timely filing/paying rule.[30]

FedEx:

- Fed Ex First Overnight
- FedEx Priority Overnight
- FedEx Standard Overnight
- FedEx 2 Day
- FedEx International Next Flight Out
- FedEx International Priority
- FedEx International First
  FedEx International Economy

UPS:

- UPS Next Day Air Early AM
- UPS Next Day Air
- UPS Next Day Air Saver
- UPS 2nd Day Air
- UPS 2nd Day Air A.M.
- UPS Worldwide Express Plus
- UPS Worldwide Express

DHL:

- DHL Express 9:00
- DHL Express 10:30
- DHL Express 12:00
- DHL Express Worldwide
- DHL Express Envelope
- DHL Import Express 10:30
- DHL Import Express 12:00
- DHL Import Express Worldwide

---

[30] Notice 2016-30, which added eight new DHL delivery services to the list of designated delivery services effective April, 11, 2016.

¶ 4.2.10 Timeliness when last day for performance falls on Saturday, Sunday or legal holiday

If the last date for filing notices, returns or applications or for the payment of taxes falls on a Saturday, Sunday, or a legal state or national holiday, the filing or the payment is considered timely if postmarked on the next day which is not a Saturday, Sunday, or state or national holiday.[31] The due date for income tax returns for the 2016 calendar tax year is April 18, 2017.[32]

Legal public holidays and their dates in New Mexico are:

- New Year's day, January 1;
- Martin Luther King, Jr.'s birthday, third Monday in January;
- Washington's and Lincoln's birthday, President's day, third Monday in February;
- Memorial day, last Monday in May;
- Independence day, July 4;
- Labor day, first Monday in September;
- Columbus day, second Monday in October;
- Armistice day and Veterans' day, November 11;
- Thanksgiving day, fourth Thursday in November; and
- Christmas day, December 25.[33]

Whenever the New Mexico state government observes a state legal holiday on a day other than that specified above, the day upon which the holiday is observed is deemed to be a "legal state holiday."[34] This rule is relevant with regard to President's day. Although the third Monday in February is a legal holiday, state offices are traditionally open, and state government observes the holiday on the Friday following Thanksgiving. Therefore, any notices, returns, applications or payments due on that Friday may be made the following Monday.

---

[31] §7-1-77 NMSA 1978; §3.1.4.10E NMAC.
[32] April 15, 2017 falls on a Saturday, and the filing date would appear to be Monday, April 17. But the District of Columbia celebrates Emancipation Day on April 16 and the IRS treats that day as a federal holiday. Since that day is a Sunday, the holiday is observed on Monday, April 17, which is why federal and New Mexico returns are due Tuesday, April 18.
[33] §12-5-2 NMSA 1978.
[34] §3.1.4.10F(1) NMAC.

Filing Requirements, Exempt Status, and Estimated Taxes

Because the third Monday in February is a state and national legal holiday, any notices, returns, applications or payments due on that date may be made the following day, even though state offices are open on President's Day.[35]

¶ 4.2.11 Requirements for filed returns

The ITA, TRD regulations, and TRD forms and instructions provide requirements for completing and filing a return. Returns are considered complete and timely filed when these requirements are met.[36]

Form PIT-1 must be filed using official state forms that are either provided by or approved by the TRD. If a taxpayer uses computer software products with tax forms, the TRD must preapprove these forms.[37] When using a computer-generated Form PIT-1, the printing and legibility requirements of the software company must be complied with. If a printer can clearly print a logo, it can print a quality tax form.[38]

¶ 4.2.12 Refunds

A taxpayer who is entitled to a refund may choose to receive a check or have the refund deposited directly into a checking or savings account.

But, if a taxpayer owes the TRD other taxes, the TRD may keep all or part of the overpayment and apply it to the liability. If a taxpayer owes money for past due child support, educational assistance loans, unemployment compensation, medical support, public assistance or food stamp overpayments, fines, workers compensation fees, or fees and costs owed to district, municipal, magistrate, or metropolitan courts, the TRD must transfer all or part of the overpayment for those purposes.[39] If the taxpayer wishes to protest the transfer to an agency, the instructions to Form PIT-1 provide the contact information for the appropriate agency.

---

[35] §3.1.4.10F(2) NMAC.
[36] §3.1.4.8A NMAC.
[37] 2016 PIT-1, Personal Income Tax Return Instructions, p. 7.
[38] 2016 PIT-1, Personal Income Tax Return Instructions, p. 7.
[39] 2016 PIT-1, Personal Income Tax Return Instructions, p. 36.

¶ 4.2.13 Interest and penalties

A taxpayer is liable for interest if a tax is not paid when due. If the failure to file a report or to make a payment when due is a result of the negligence of the taxpayer or the taxpayer's representative, the taxpayer is liable for a penalty. It is immaterial to liability for the payment of tax that an individual has not registered as a taxpayer.[40] See Chapter 15 for full discussion of interest and penalties.

¶ 4.2.14 Electronic filing of returns

New Mexico taxpayers may file their income tax returns either in paper format or use computers to electronically file returns and make tax payments. The TRD encourages taxpayers and tax preparers to file electronically whenever possible. According to the TRD, E-filing provides the fastest turnaround for a refund and it saves tax dollars.

Any notice, return, and application that is authorized or required to be made or given by electronic transmission is timely if electronically transmitted to the TRD *and* accepted on or before the last date prescribed for filing. The sender assumes the responsibility to provide the TRD with proof that the electronic transmission to the TRD was initiated on or before the last date prescribed for filing.[41]

If a calendar year taxpayer both files a return and pays the tax due electronically, the filing deadline is extended to April 30 (May 1, 2017 for the 2016 calendar year).[42]

The TRD has authorized Form PIT-1 for electronic filing and encourages electronic filing for the following reasons:

- Electronic filing is fast and secure
- Taxpayers will receive refunds faster.
- The state saves tax dollars in processing costs.
- Filing is free on the TRD website.
- E-filing minimizes errors and delays associated with manual handling and data entry of tax forms.
- The electronically transmitted return cannot be lost in the mail.
- Electronic returns have a much higher accuracy rate because

---

[40] §3.1.4.10A NMAC.
[41] 3.1.4.10B(1) NMAC.
[42] §7-2-12 NMSA 1978.

Filing Requirements, Exempt Status, and Estimated Taxes

the software alerts the preparer to obvious errors.
- Taxpayers who both file and pay electronically receive an extension of their payment and filing deadline to May 1, 2017 for 2016 calendar year tax returns.[43]

All information supplied electronically by taxpayers is protected using encryption and fire walls. However, the TRD also reminds taxpayers to be careful about refund fraud, which has recently become more prevalent.

The TRD offers two ways to file electronically, either through the TRD website or through the Federal/State Electronic Filing Program. The TRD website can be accessed at Taxpayers' Access Point (TAP): *https:tap.state.nm.us*. However, the website cannot be used if any of the following is true:

The taxpayer is a fiscal year filer.
The taxpayer files as married filing jointly, and his or her spouse is the dependent of another taxpayer.
The taxpayer has income from sources inside and outside New Mexico and is claiming an additional amount of tax on a lump-sum distribution by filing federal Form 4972 and Schedule PIT-B.

In these situations, the taxpayer must file on paper or electronically with an alternative software solution.[45]

The Fed/State program, which is administered by the IRS, allows a taxpayer to electronically file his or her federal and state tax returns together or separately. The taxpayer can file a Fed/State return through an online home tax-filing program on a personal computer or through a professional tax preparer. This method requires Internet access where a taxpayer can reach companies that offer Fed/State e-file services and tax preparation software. A taxpayer can also buy over-the-counter software to file taxes online.[46]

The IRS has partnership agreements with many companies and the IRS website lists companies that provide tax preparation software and

---

[43] 2016 PIT-1, Personal Income Tax Return Instructions, p. 7; TRD, *2016 Tax Preparer's Guide for Income Tax Returns*, p. 16.
[45] 2016 PIT-1, Personal Income Tax Return Instructions, p. 7-8.
[46] See www.irs.gov/filing/e-file-options.

Fed/State e-file opportunities. The IRS e-file provider page lists the companies that participate in free Internet filing for low income and other qualified individuals. The Fed/State electronic filing service is also available through tax professionals who meet IRS and TRD qualifications for acceptance into the Fed/State program.

When paid preparers, Electronic Return Originators, or other third-party transmitters electronically transmit a personal income tax return, they are required to complete Form PIT-8453, *2016 Individual Income Tax Declaration for Electronic Filing and Transmittal.* Form PIT-8453 authorizes electronic transmission of the tax return, authenticates the electronic part of the return, and under certain circumstances provides a transmittal for additional supporting documentation. This form can only be submitted to the TRD in paper format.

Generally, a taxpayer will not have to file Form PIT-8453, but if the electronically filed tax return requires documentation that cannot be submitted electronically, such documents must be submitted separately with Form PIT-8453. The instructions to Form PIT-8453 lists the supporting documentation that should be included if not submitted electronically. Copies of Form PIT-1 or Schedules PIT-S, PIT- ADJ, PIT-RC, PIT-B, PIT-D, or PIT-CR are not required to be submitted with Form PIT 8453. Individuals electronically filing their own return through the New Mexico WebFile application are instructed by the program when to complete and submit Form PIT-8453.

This form may also be used to submit backup documentation for amended returns. For an amended return, a taxpayer must submit corrected annual information returns and statements of withholding, and, if required, applicable federal forms and schedules, and letters of explanation.

¶ 4.2.15 Electronic payments

Payments that are authorized or required to be made or given by electronic payment are timely if the payment is electronically transmitted to the TRD and accepted on or before the last date prescribed for making the payment. The sender assumes the responsibility to provide the TRD with proof that the electronic transmission was initiated on or before the last date prescribed for making payment.[47] In addition, the sender assumes the

---

[47] §3.1.4.10 I(1) NMAC.

Filing Requirements, Exempt Status, and Estimated Taxes

responsibility that the funds were available to the TRD on or before the last date prescribed for making the payment.[48]

On the TRD website, a taxpayer may pay by electronic check at no charge. The electronic check authorizes the TRD to debit the taxpayer's checking account in the amount and on the date specified.

Taxpayers may use any of these credit cards: Visa, MasterCard, American Express, or Discover Card for online payment. A fee of 2.40% is applied when using a credit card. New Mexico uses this fee to pay charges from the credit card companies.[49]

When electronically sent funds have been received by the fiscal agent designating the TRD as the payee with sufficient information to identify the taxpayer, neither the TRD nor the fiscal agent of New Mexico may refuse to accept the funds or to reverse transactions. The TRD or the fiscal agent may refuse to accept a payment or to cause the reversal of the transaction only when the transaction is not successful in making the funds available or in identifying the taxpayer. The TRD and the fiscal agent may refuse to accept electronic payments tendered by means other those described above.

When an electronic payment transaction is reversed through the taxpayer's action or when the taxpayer's financial institution dishonors a check, neither the TRD nor the fiscal agent is obligated to resubmit the transaction or check for payment. If the reversal or dishonoring causes the final payment of taxes to be untimely, then interest will begin to run, if applicable.[50]

An "electronic payment" is defined as a payment made by automated clearinghouse deposit, any funds wire transfer system, or a credit card, debit card, or electronic cash transaction through the Internet.[52] An "automated clearinghouse transaction" means an electronic credit or debit transmitted through an automated clearinghouse payable to the state treasurer and deposited with the fiscal agent of New Mexico.[53]

---

[48] §3.1.4.10 I(2) NMAC.
[49] 2016 PIT-1, Personal Income Tax Return Instructions, p. 36.
[50] §7-1-67 NMSA 1978.
[52] §7-1-3C NMSA 1978.
[53] §7-1-3A NMSA 1978.

¶ 4.2.16 Tax preparer responsibilities with regard to electronic filing — penalties

A tax return preparer who prepares over 25 New Mexico personal income tax returns for a tax year must ensure that each return is submitted to the TRD by TRD-approved electronic media. A tax return preparer must pay to the TRD a penalty not to exceed $5.00 for each tax return filed in violation of this electronic filing requirement.[54] However, the taxpayer may elect to waive the preparer's requirement to file by electronic media. The preparer must have the taxpayer complete a signed Form RPD- 41338, *Taxpayer Waiver for Preparer's Electronic Filing Requirement*, and keep it on file. The preparer must mark the box in the paid preparer's use only section of the return indicating that Form RPD-41338 is on file for the taxpayer.[55]

¶ 4.2.17 Extension of time to file and pay

If there is good cause, the TRD may extend for a particular taxpayer or a class of taxpayers the due date for the filing of any return or the payment of tax. But the extension or extensions granted a taxpayer cannot be more than a total of 12 months. An extension does not prevent the accrual of interest, but it does eliminate any late payment penalties. When a federal extension has been granted a taxpayer for filing federal Form 1040, 1040A, or 1040EZ that extension serves to extend the time for filing New Mexico income tax returns, but a copy of any approved federal extension must be attached to the New Mexico income tax return. To ensure the collection of the tax, the TRD may require, as a condition of granting any extension, that the taxpayer furnish security.[57]

¶ 4.2.18 Good cause

"Good cause" is strictly construed and good cause extensions are granted only where the taxpayer shows a good faith effort to comply with the statute. The regulations provide the following examples of how good cause is interpreted.

- If the taxpayer operates a multistate business and the filing of

---

[54] §7-1-71.4 NMSA 1978.
[55] TRD, *2016 Tax Preparer's Guide for Income Tax Returns*, p. 7.
[57] §7-1-13E NMSA 1978.

Filing Requirements, Exempt Status, and Estimated Taxes

the New Mexico returns at the due date would result in unreasonable bookwork and recordkeeping, an extension will be given favorable consideration.
- If the taxpayer is temporarily disabled because of injury or prolonged illness and is unable to procure the services of a person to complete the return, an extension will be given favorable consideration.
- If the taxpayer's business has been substantially impaired due to the disability of a principal officer, physical damage to the business, or similar impairments making the taxpayer unable to compute taxes before the due date, an extension of time will be given favorable consideration.
- If the taxpayer's accountant has suddenly died or become disabled and the taxpayer is unable either to complete the return or to procure the services of a person to complete the return before the due date, an extension will be given favorable consideration.
- If the taxpayer is awaiting the outcome of a court or administrative proceeding or the action of the IRS on a federal tax claim, an extension will be given favorable consideration provided that the extension does not contravene the time limits established by New Mexico statute or federal statute.[58]

¶ 4.2.19 Procedure for obtaining extensions to file (other than automatic extensions)

A taxpayer may request an extension of time in which to file a tax return by filing Form RPD-41096, *Application for Extension of Time to File*. The request must be must be received by the TRD on or before the date that the tax is due. On the form, the applicant must set forth:

1. the tax or tax return to which the extension would apply;
2. a clear statement of the reasons for the extension; and
3. the signature of the taxpayer or an authorized representative.[59]

The extension will not be granted unless the reason is satisfactory to the TRD. If the taxpayer is unable to sign the application because of illness, absence, or other good cause, any person in a close personal

---

[58] §3.1.4.12A NMAC.
[59] §3.1.4.12B NMAC.

or business relationship to him or her may sign. However, the signer must state the reason for his or her signature and the relationship to the taxpayer.[60]

An approved extension will ordinarily be granted for a period not to exceed 60 days. A request for longer extensions will not be granted unless sufficient need for the additional time is shown. Additional extensions or a longer extension may be granted by TRD for up to a maximum aggregate extension of 12 months. The following two examples are taken and modified (for the sake of clarity) from TRD regulations.

> *Example 1.* Patricia is a tax preparer who realizes that she will be unable to complete all of her customers' tax returns by the due date because of the great volume of her business. She submits a request for an extension on behalf of each customer whose return she is unable to complete. However, the request will be denied. It is irrelevant whether Patricia's request states a good cause because an extension will not be granted unless the *taxpayer's* personal necessity is the basis of the request.[61]

> *Example 2.* On April 20, 20XX, the TRD grants Tom a 30-day extension for payment of March, 20XX taxes due April 25, 20XX. On May 20, 20XX, Tom, showing good cause, requests a further extension of 12 months. The TRD will not grant Tom the 12-month extension because the payment or filing date may not be extended by more than 12 months, and the TRD will not grant a series of extensions that in aggregate exceed 12 months. The maximum extension that the TRD could grant to Tom is until April 25 of the year following 20XX.[62]

¶ 4.2.20 Automatic extensions

New Mexico generally follows federal rules and taxpayers are allowed an automatic extension of time to file their New Mexico income tax return if they have obtained an automatic federal extension. The IRS grants an automatic extension for six months on the filing of Form

---

[60] See Form RPD 41096 (Rev. 6/2016), Application for Extension of Time to File Instructions.
[61] §3.1.4.12B NMAC.
[62] §3.1.4.12B NMAC.

Filing Requirements, Exempt Status, and Estimated Taxes

4868, *Application for Automatic Extension of Time To File U.S. Individual Income Tax Return*. The extension is considered granted by the IRS unless the taxpayer receives a denial notice. New Mexico by statute limits its automatic extensions as well to six months.[63] Under federal law, an automatic extension does not excuse late payment of taxes and penalties and interest can be assessed. However, pursuant to New Mexico rules, an automatic extension precludes the imposition of late payment penalties, but interest starts running as of the original due date. To avoid interest accruing, a payment can be made with the filing of Form PIT-EXT.

If it is necessary to submit a form to the IRS to claim an automatic extension, such as Form 4868, then a copy of that form must be attached to the taxpayer's New Mexico income tax return which will serve as the basis for extending the time for filing. If it is not necessary to submit a form to the IRS to claim an automatic extension for filing the federal return, then the due date for filing the New Mexico income tax return is extended automatically to the same date as the extension for the federal return. As an example, an automatic extension to file of two months is granted without filing a form in the case of taxpayers who are out of the country when the return is originally due. Taxpayers who use this extension can receive an additional four-month extension by filing Form 4868, for a total of 6 months of extension. If the federal extended date is more than six months from the original due date, the automatic extended due date for the New Mexico return remains six months after the original due date.

If the taxpayer needs additional time beyond the date granted as an automatic extension, the request must be made by filing Form RPD-41096 prior to the expiration of the extended federal date. If it was necessary to submit a form to the IRS to claim an automatic extension for filing the federal return, then a copy of the federal form requesting the automatic extension for filing the federal return must accompany the taxpayer's request for additional time to file the New Mexico income tax return beyond the extended federal date. The total combined extensions for filing the New Mexico return may not exceed

12 months beyond the actual due date for that return.[64]

If an extension of time to file a federal income tax return is invalidated for any reason for federal income tax purposes, it is also invalidated for New Mexico income tax purposes.[65]

¶ 4.2.21 Extensions for Military Personnel

In addition to the extensions discussed above, there are two additional circumstances under which extensions are allowed to military personnel.[66] See ¶ 6.3 for a discussion of these situations.

¶ 4.2.22 Failure to file, pay or protest by extended due date

The "extended due date" is the latest date to which the due date for filing the New Mexico income tax return has been extended by an extension granted either by the IRS or the TRD.[67] To avoid becoming delinquent, a taxpayer must either file the required return and pay any taxes due or file a protest in accordance with administrative procedures by the extended due date.[68]

¶ 4.2.23 Filing status

A taxpayer filing a New Mexico income tax return must use the same filing status for New Mexico purposes as is used for federal purposes for the tax year. Spouses using the status "married filing jointly" for federal purposes must use the same status for New Mexico purposes; those using the status "married filing separately" for federal purposes must do likewise for New Mexico.[69]

¶ 4.2.24 Name of spouse

Spouses who report income to the federal government for income tax purposes using different last names, whether they report jointly or separately, must report their income to New Mexico using the same names as used on the federal return. Spouses who report to the United States under one surname must also report to New Mexico under the

---

[64] §3.1.4.12E NMAC.
[65] §3.1.4.12F NMAC.
[66] See FYI-311, *Military Extensions for New Mexico Personal Income Tax Filers* (Rev. 5/2014).
[67] §3.1.4.12G NMAC.
[68] See §7-1-24 NMSA 1978.
[69] §3.3.12.12A NMAC.

Filing Requirements, Exempt Status, and Estimated Taxes

same surname.[70]

¶4.2.25 Tentative returns not allowed

The filing of a "tentative" return is not allowed. "Tentative" is not defined in the statute, but one dictionary defines the term as "of the nature of or made or done as a trial, experiment, or attempt; experimental."[71]

However, a prepayment of a tax liability will be accepted. A prepayment of a taxpayer's tentative or estimated tax liability prior to the due date of the return is made with Form PIT-ES, *Personal Income Estimated Tax Payment Voucher*.[72]

¶4.2.26 Requirements for reproduction of income tax forms and acceptance of computer generated forms

Privately printed and computer generated income tax forms are accepted by the TRD. Regulation §3.3.12.9 of the New Mexico Administrative Code provides the requirements for the acceptance of reproduced or privately printed New Mexico individual income tax return forms. Regulation §3.3.12.10 provides the requirements for the acceptance of computer-generated New Mexico individual income tax return forms.

¶ 4.2.27 Requirements for tax return preparers—penalties

A return preparer must sign and furnish the preparer's identification number with each income tax return or claim of refund that the preparer completes. A tax return preparer's identification number is one of the following: the preparer's department-issued CRS identification number, the preparer's social security number, or the preparer's IRS-issued practitioner's tax identification number (PTIN).[73]

To "sign" a return or claim for refund means to affix a name or cause it to be attached using one of the following methods: handwritten; rubber stamp; mechanical device (such as a mechanical pen); computer software program; or any other method of signature acceptable under the Internal Revenue Code.[74]

Any tax return preparer who is required to sign a return or claim

---

[70] §3.3.12.12B NMAC.
[71] See Dictionary.com at http://www.dictionary.com/browse/tentative.
[72] §3.3.12.11 NMAC.
[73] §7-1-71.1A and B NMSA 1978; §3.1.1.18 NMAC.
[74] §3.1.1.7 NMAC.

for refund or to furnish an identification number and fails to do so must pay a penalty of $25.00 for such failure unless it is shown that the failure is due to reasonable cause and not due to willful neglect.[75]

Any tax return preparer who endorses or otherwise negotiates a warrant (i.e., a check) issued to a taxpayer, either directly or through an agent, must pay a penalty of $500 with respect to each such warrant. This penalty does not apply with respect to the deposit by a bank, savings and loan association, credit union or other financial corporation of the full amount of the warrant in the taxpayer's account for the benefit of the taxpayer.[76]

Any of the above penalties is considered to be a tax due.[77]

A "tax return preparer" is defined as a person who prepares for others for compensation or who employs one or more persons to prepare for others for compensation any return of income tax, a substantial portion of any return of income tax, any claim for refund with respect to income tax or a substantial portion of any claim for refund with respect to income tax. A person is not a tax return preparer merely because a person: (1) furnishes typing, reproducing or other mechanical assistance; (2) is an employee who prepares an income tax return or claim for refund with respect to an income tax return of the employer, or of an officer or employee of the employer, by whom the person is regularly and continuously employed, or (3) prepares as a trustee or other fiduciary an income tax return or claim for refund with respect to income tax for any person.[78]

¶ 4.2.28 Amended returns

When there is a change to a taxpayer's New Mexico taxable income, credits, or rebates, an amended return must be made for that year generally by filing New Mexico Form PIT-X.

For tax years beginning on or after January 1, 2016, but not after December 31, 2016, a taxpayer must file an amended return using Form 2016 PIT-X, *Personal Amended Income Tax Return*. For tax years beginning on a date after January 1, 2005 but before December 31,

---

[75] §7-1-71.1C NMSA 1978.
[76] §7-1-71.1D NMSA 1978.
[77] §7-1-71.1E NMSA 1978.
[78] §7-1-3Z NMSA 1978.

Filing Requirements, Exempt Status, and Estimated Taxes

2010, a taxpayer must file an amended return on the PIT-X form specific to the tax year of the original return. For tax years beginning before January 1, 2005, amended returns are filed using the form for the appropriate tax year. In this case, the amended box should be marked, or if the form does not have that box, "Amended" should be written at the top of the form. An amended return for those years should not be filed on a PIT-X form even if indicated in the instructions for the tax year. The TRD warns that it cannot accept a return filed on a PIT-X return for a year before January 1, 2005.[79]

See ¶ 16.1.10 as to when an amended return must be filed with regard to federal return changes. When an amended return is required in this case it must be filed within 180 days of the final determination of the adjustment, together with the payment of any additional tax due.[80]

¶ 4.3 Exemptions from Income Tax

Certain income, organizations, and individuals (as that term is defined by the ITA) are exempt from the individual income tax. In addition, certain individuals may claim exemptions and deductions reducing income, except that a person may not claim combined exemptions and deductions for more than 100% of income.

¶ 4.3.1 Employee compensation trust

Income tax is not imposed on trusts organized or created in the United States and forming part of an employer stock bonus, pension or profit-sharing plan for the exclusive benefit of employees or their beneficiaries, and which are exempt from taxation under the Internal Revenue Code.[81]

¶ 4.3.2 Religious, educational, benevolent or other organizations not organized for profit

No income tax is imposed upon the income of religious, educational, benevolent, or other organizations not organized for profit that are exempt from taxation under the Internal Revenue Code except to the extent that such income is subject to federal taxation as unrelated

---

[79] 2016 PIT-1, Personal Income Tax Return Instructions, p. 11.
[80] §7-1-13C NMSA 1978.
[81] §7-2-4 NMSA 1978.

business income.[82]

¶4.3.3 Income of a member of a NATO force

The salary, fringe benefits, and other emoluments received by a member of a NATO force with respect to employment by or membership in the NATO force are not subject to New Mexico income tax pursuant to Article X, Section 1 of the North Atlantic Treaty. However, income of a member of a NATO force from sources within New Mexico, other than from the member's employment by or membership in the NATO force, are subject to tax.

"NATO force" means any NATO signatory's military unit or force or civilian component thereof present in New Mexico in accordance with the North Atlantic Treaty. A "NATO signatory" is a nation, other than the United States, that is a contracting party to the North Atlantic Treaty.[83] A "member of a NATO force" includes the military and civilian personnel of the NATO force and their dependents. This provision applies to tax years beginning on or after January 1, 1995.[84]

¶ 4.3.4 Income taxes applied to an individual on and income from a federal area

An individual that resides within a federal area is not exempt from income tax, nor is the income earned from transactions occurring or from work or services performed in such area.[85] Although the ITA does not define the term "federal area," a federal statute defines it as follows: "any lands or premises held or acquired by or for the use of the U. S. or any department, establishment, or agency of the United States; and any Federal area, or any part thereof, which is located within the exterior boundaries of any State, shall be deemed to be a Federal area located within such State."[86]

¶ 4.3.5 Income of member Indian nation, tribe, band, or pueblo

Income earned by a member of a New Mexico federally recognized Indian nation, tribe, band, or pueblo, and his or her spouse or dependent, who is

---

[82] §7-2-4 NMSA 1978.
[83] The North Atlantic Treaty, signed Apr. 4, 1949, created NATO, which now has a membership of 28 countries. The original purpose was to deter aggression by the Soviet Union. Under the treaty, an armed attack on any member is considered an attack against all.
[84] §3.3.4.8 NMAC.
[85] §7-2-10 NMSA 1978.
[86] 4 USC §110(e).

Filing Requirements, Exempt Status, and Estimated Taxes

a member of a New Mexico federally recognized Indian nation, tribe, band, or pueblo, is exempt from state income tax if –

1. the member, spouse or dependent lives within the boundaries of the Indian member's or the spouse's reservation or pueblo grant or within the boundaries of lands held in trust by the United States for the benefit of the member or spouse or his nation, tribe, band, or pueblo, subject to restriction against alienation imposed by the United States, and
2. the income is earned from work performed within such lands.[87]

A member of an Indian nation whose entire income is exempt as described above does not have to file a New Mexico income tax return.[88]

Retirement or pension income for an Indian member living within the boundaries of his or her nation, tribe, or pueblo is exempt only when the retirement or pension is the result of employment on the member's Indian nation, tribe, or pueblo.[89] Retirement or pension income from employment off the lands of the nation, tribe, or pueblo is not exempt.

The military pay of an enrolled member of an Indian nation, tribe, or pueblo is exempt from New Mexico tax when his or her home of record is on the lands of that Indian nation, tribe, or pueblo and the legal residence of that member has not been changed.[90] In addition, pension income from an enrolled member's service in the United States armed forces is exempt to the extent that is derived from service during the time that his or her home of record was his or her tribal territory, or, during marriage, the tribal territory of the spouse; or is from service while stationed on his or her the tribal territory, or, during marriage, the spouse's Indian nation, tribe or pueblo.[91]

¶ 4.4 Estimated tax payments

Under New Mexico's estimated tax rules, an individual who is required to file a state income tax return must pay a "required annual payment" (RAP)

---

[87] §7-2-5.5 NMSA 1978,
[88] 2016 PIT-1, Personal Income Tax Return Instructions, p. 3.
[89] 3.3.4.12A. See 2016 PIT-1, Personal Income Tax Return Instructions, p. 3.
[90] 3.3.19E(8). See 2016 PIT-1, Personal Income Tax Return Instructions, p. 3.
[91] §3.3.4.14B NMAC.

either through estimated tax payments or employment withholding.[92] There is a penalty for underpayment or non-payment of estimated tax, unless exceptions apply. Generally, four equal installments of the RAP are due each year, with employment withholding generally counting as quarterly payments. For taxpayers whose income is received disproportionately, such as seasonally, during the year, the amount of estimated tax payments may be adjusted to reflect the disproportionality. The estimated tax rules do not apply to first-year residents.[93]

For taxpayers reporting on a calendar year basis, estimated payments of the RAP are due on or before April 15, June 15 and September 15 of the tax year and January 15 of the following tax year. For the 2016 calendar tax year, the due dates of estimated tax payments are April 18, 2016, June 15, 2016, September 15, 2016 and January 15, 2017. For taxpayers reporting on a fiscal year other than a calendar year, the due dates for the installments are the 15th day of the fourth, sixth and ninth months of the fiscal year and the 15th day of the first month following the fiscal year.[94]

Sometimes a due date for an estimated payment falls on a Saturday, Sunday, or state or national legal holiday. The estimated payment is timely when the postmark bears the date of the next business day.[95] Delivery by a private delivery service is timely if the date recorded or marked by the private delivery service is on or before the date by which mailing is required.[96]

The amount of tax deducted and withheld with respect to a taxpayer under the Withholding Tax Act[97] or the Oil and Gas Proceeds and Pass-Through Entity Withholding Tax Act[98] is deemed a payment of estimated tax.[99] A remitter or pass-through entity that is subject to the PIT and has an obligation to pay estimated taxes, may not credit the

---

[92] §7-2-12.2A NMSA 1978.
[93] §7-2-12.2M NMSA 1978. Query, If a first-year resident had been paying estimated tax in prior years because of income derived from the State, is that taxpayer entitled to an exemption if he or she becomes a resident? Perhaps the exemption would only apply to that income that is included in New Mexico taxable income as a result of residency.
[94] §7-2-12.2D NMSA 1978.
[95] §7-1-77 NMSA 1978.
[96] §3.1.4.16 NMAC. See ¶4.2.9.
[97] §7-3-1 NMSA 1978.
[98] §7-3A-1. 8j NMSA 1978.
[99] §7-2-12.2F NMSA 1978.

Filing Requirements, Exempt Status, and Estimated Taxes

amounts it withheld from payments to remittees or owners against its own estimated tax liability.[100]

An equal part of the amount of withheld tax is deemed paid on each due date for the tax year unless the taxpayer establishes the dates on which all amounts were actually withheld. In that case, the amounts withheld are deemed payments of estimated tax on the dates on which the amounts were actually withheld.[101]

The amount of estimated tax payments due is based upon the RAP, which is the lesser of:

1. 90% of the tax shown on the return for the tax year or, if no return is filed, 90% of the tax for the tax year; or
2. 100% of the tax shown on the return for the preceding tax year if the preceding tax year was a tax year of 12 months and the taxpayer filed a tax return for that year.[102]

If a taxpayer is not liable for estimated tax payments on March 31, but becomes liable thereafter, a calendar year taxpayer makes estimated tax payments as follows (to avoid penalties):

- if the taxpayer first becomes required to pay estimated tax after March 31 and before June 1, 50% of the RAP must be paid on or before June 15, 25% on September 15, and 25% on or before January 15 of the following tax year;
- if the taxpayer first becomes required to pay estimated tax after May 31, but before September 1, the taxpayer must pay 75% of the RAP on or before September 15 and 25% on or before January 15 of the following tax year; and
- if the taxpayer first becomes required to pay estimated tax after August 31, the taxpayer must pay 100% of the RAP on or before January 15 of the following tax year.[103]

A rancher or farmer who expects to receive at least 2/3rds of his or her gross income for the tax year from ranching or farming, or who has received at least 2/3rds of gross income for the previous tax year from ranching or farming, may pay the RAP for the tax year in one

---

[100] §3.3.12.15 NMAC.
[101] §7-2-12.2F NMSA 1978.
[102] §7-2-12.2B NMSA 1978.
[103] §7-2-12.2C NMSA 1978.

installment on or before January 15 of the following tax year, or file a return for the tax year and pay in full the amount computed as payable on the return on or before March 1 of the following tax year.[104]

An underpayment penalty would not to be imposed unless the rancher or farmer underpays the tax by more than $1/3^{rd}$. If a joint return is filed, a rancher or farmer must consider the spouse's gross income in determining whether at least $2/3^{rds}$ of gross income is from ranching or farming.[105]

In the case of an underpayment of the RAP, a penalty is added to the tax. The penalty is calculated in the form of interest that accrues at the same rate as interest on the underpayment of tax.[106] The penalty is computed on a daily basis with the interest rate applied to the amount of the underpayment for the period of the underpayment. The amount of the underpayment is the excess of the amount of the RAP over the amount, if any, paid on or before the due date for the installment. The period of the underpayment runs from the due date for the installment to the earlier of the 15th day of the 4th month following the close of the tax year; or with respect to any portion of the underpayment, the date on which the portion was paid. A payment of estimated tax is credited against unpaid or underpaid installments in the order in which the installments are required to be paid.[107]

A penalty is not imposed for any tax year in any of the following situations:

1. there us a difference of less than $1,000 between the tax shown on the return for the tax year, or, when no return is filed, the tax for the tax year, and any amount withheld under the provisions of the Withholding Tax Act or the Oil and Gas Proceeds and Pass-Through Entity Withholding Tax Act for that tax year;
2. the taxpayer's preceding tax year was a tax year of 12 months, the taxpayer did not have a tax liability for the preceding tax year, and the taxpayer was a resident of New Mexico for the

---

[104] §7-2-12.2E NMSA 1978.
[105] §7-2-12.2E(2) NMSA 1978.
[106] It is the same rate as the one established for individual income tax purposes by the Internal Revenue Code.
[107] §7-2-12.2G NMSA 1978.

Filing Requirements, Exempt Status, and Estimated Taxes

       entire tax year;
3. through either withholding or estimated tax payments, the taxpayer paid the RAP as defined; or
4. the TRD determines that the underpayment was not due to fraud, negligence or disregard of rules and regulations.[108]

If on or before January 31 of the following tax year a calendar year taxpayer files a return for the tax year and pays in full the amount computed on the return as payable, then a penalty will not be imposed on an underpayment of the fourth required installment for the tax year.[109]

These penalties are also applicable to tax years of less than 12 months and to taxpayers reporting on a fiscal year other than a calendar year.

In the case of a decedent, for a tax year that ends before two years after the date of death, the estimated tax rules do not apply to the estate of the decedent. In addition, the estimated tax rules do not apply to a trust all of which was treated by the Internal Revenue Code as owned by the decedent[110] and to which the residue of the decedent's estate will pass under the decedent's will, or, if no will is admitted to probate, the decedent's trust is primarily responsible for paying debts, taxes and expenses of administration.[111]

---

[108] §7-2-12.2H NMSA 1978.
[109] §7-2-12.2I NMSA 1978.
[110] See 26 USC 671 et seq. regarding grantor trusts.
[111] §7-2-12.2L NMSA 1978.

CHAPTER 5
RESIDENCY

¶ 5.1 Residency defined

Residency is an important concept in the New Mexico scheme of taxation. Residency does not impact the calculation of a taxpayer's taxable income. But it does impact how the tax on taxable income is calculated. A taxpayer's tax on taxable income is determined by how much of his or her income is allocated or apportioned to New Mexico. The allocation and apportionment process relies greatly on whether a taxpayer is a resident or nonresident. The allocation and apportionment rules are discussed in ¶ 9.3 et. seq.

Individual taxpayers must declare their residency on Form PIT-1, line 1e, by indicating whether they are a resident (R), first-year resident (F), part-year resident (P), or nonresident (NR). A "resident" is an individual who is domiciled in New Mexico during any part of the tax year, or who is physically present in New Mexico for 185 days or more during the tax year regardless of domicile. A "nonresident" is an individual who is not domiciled in New Mexico for any part of the year and who was not physically present in New Mexico for at least 185 days.

The days spent in New Mexico do not have to be consecutive to count towards residency, but partial days do not count. In determining days of residency only those days in which a person spends 24 hours in New Mexico count as a day towards the 185-day standard. The instructions to 2016 Form PIT-1 (page 4) give an example of a worker who lives in Texas but works in New Mexico and was present in New Mexico for 185 partial days during the year. Since the worker was not in New Mexico 24 hours on any day, she was not resident for New Mexico income tax purposes.

> *Example.* An actress who is a resident of California, comes to New Mexico on three separate occasions in 2004 to work on a movie, but does not intend to remain in New Mexico, and when

the movie is completed, returns to her home in California. She is physically present in New Mexico for 200 days in 2004. Because she was physically present for at least 185 days, she must file as a full-year resident of New Mexico for tax year 2004.[1]

¶ 5.2 Domicile defined

The ITA does not define the term "domicile" but the regulations do. According to the regulations, every individual has a domicile somewhere, and each individual has only one domicile at a time.[2] The individual's domicile is the place where the individual has a true, fixed home. It is the permanent establishment to which the individual intends to return after an absence, and is where the individual has voluntarily fixed habitation of self and family with the intention of making a permanent home.

Once an individual establishes a domicile, it does not change until the individual moves to a new location with the intention of making that location his or her permanent home.

There is no change in domicile when an individual leaves the state intending to stay away only for a limited time, no matter how long, including:

- for a period of rest or vacation;
- to complete a particular transaction, perform a contract or fulfill an engagement or obligation, but intending to return to New Mexico whether or not the transaction, contract, engagement, or obligation is completed; or
- to accomplish a particular purpose, but not intending to remain in the new location once the purpose is accomplished.

To determine domicile, due weight is given to an individual's declaration of intent. However, those declarations are not conclusive

---

[1] Based upon §3.3.1.9E, Ex. (4) NMAC.

[2] It is likely that this is not intended to be a philosophical statement, but a directive that the TRD will determine a domicile for each taxpayer, regardless of whether that person believes he or she has a domicile in New Mexico may conflict with the life style choice of some people. Some full-time RVers, for example, may believe they have no domicile, but the TRD will determine that they do. This raises an interesting tax question: does a US citizen or resident have to have a domicile in a state? Is not possible to have no domicile?

Residency

where they are contradicted by facts, circumstances and the individual's conduct. In particular, the following factors are considered in determining whether an individual is domiciled in New Mexico (this list is not exclusive and is in no particular order):

- homes or places of abode owned or rented (for the individual's use) by the individual, their location, size and value; and how they are used by the individual;
- where the individual spends time during the tax year and how that time is spent; e.g., whether the individual is retired or is actively involved in a business, and whether the individual travels and the reasons for traveling, and where the individual spends time when not required to be at a location for employment or business reasons, and the overall pattern of residence of the individual;
- employment, including how the individual earns a living, the location of the individual's place of employment, whether the individual owns a business, extent of involvement in business or profession and location of the business or professional office, and the proportion of in-state to out-of-state business activities;
- home or place of abode of the individual's spouse, children, and dependent parents, and where minor children attend school;
- location of domicile in prior years;
- ownership of real property other than residences;
- location of transactions with financial institutions, including the individual's most active checking account and rental of safety deposit boxes;
- place of community affiliations, such as club and professional, and social organization memberships;
- home address used for filing federal income tax returns;
- place where individual is registered to vote;
- state of driver's license or professional licenses;
- resident or nonresident status for purposes of tuition at state schools, colleges and universities, fishing and hunting licenses, and other official purposes; and
- where items or possessions that the individual considers "near

and dear" to his or her heart are located, e.g., items of significant sentimental or economic value (such as art), family heirlooms, collections or valuables, or pets.

The TRD evaluates questions regarding domicile on a case-by-case basis and no one of the above factors is conclusive. Factors such as the state issuing the taxpayer's driver's license, place of voter registration, and home address may be given less weight, depending on the circumstances, because they are relatively easy to change.[3]

> *Example.* A college graduate was born and raised in New Mexico but leaves in December 2003 to pursue a two-year master's degree program in Spain. She intends to return to New Mexico when she completes her studies. During her absence she keeps her New Mexico driver's license and voter registration. Because New Mexico remains her domicile, she must file returns for tax years 2003, 2004 and 2005 as a full-year New Mexico resident.[4]

¶ 5.3 Credit for Taxes Paid to Another State

When a resident individual is taxed by another state upon income derived from sources outside New Mexico but which is also income allocated or apportioned to New Mexico, the individual receives a credit in the amount of the tax paid to the other state with regard to that income. The credit may not exceed the amount of the taxpayer's New Mexico income tax liability on the portion of income allocated or apportioned to New Mexico on which the tax payable to the other state was determined. This credit does not apply to taxes paid to any municipality, county or other political subdivision of a state.[5] The amount of the credit is determined using a worksheet contained in the instructions to Form PIT-1 and is entered on line 20 of that form. See ¶ 10.2 for a further discussion of the calculation.

An example of where this credit may come into play is where a resident has compensation for services performed outside the state. The state where the services are performed will likely tax the compensation from these services, but New Mexico will, too, since the

---

[3] §3.3.1.9C NMAC.
[4] Based upon §3-3.1.9E, Ex. (3), NMAC.
[5] §7-2-13 NMSA 1978.

Residency

taxpayer is a resident. In this case, the compensation is from income from sources outside New Mexico but which are allocated to New Mexico because of the taxpayer's residency. To alleviate double taxation, New Mexico provides a credit in the amount of tax paid to the other state on such compensation, limited to the New Mexico tax liability on that amount.

The application of the credit may also arise in cases of dual residency. A taxpayer may be resident in New Mexico because he or she is in the state for 185 days, but may have a domicile in another state. In the case of investment income, each state may have a claim of taxation because each claims the taxpayer as a resident. Schedule PIT-B states that in the case of investment income, New Mexico provides a credit for taxes paid to another state.[6]

¶ 5.4 Nonresidents receiving royalty income from New Mexico

A nonresident who has less than $5,000 of royalty income from New Mexico, and has no other income from New Mexico sources, can elect to calculate the amount of his or her tax due using gross royalty income. Instead of filing a complete Form PIT-1 and Schedule PIT-B, the taxpayer skips lines 9 through 16a and then enters the gross royalty income from New Mexico sources on line 17, and enters a "Y" in box 18a of Form PIT-1. The tax is computed by applying the tax rate tables to the gross royalty income.[7] The instructions to Form PIT-1 give the following guidance.

> To complete Form PIT-1 using this election do the following:
> - Complete lines 1 through 8.
> - Leave lines 9 through 16a blank.
> - On line 17, enter your total **gross** royalty income from New Mexico sources.
> - Using the instructions, complete lines 18, 22 and 23 and then lines 27 through 42.

The instructions note that a taxpayer cannot reduce income by the

---

[6] 2016 PIT-B Schedule of New Mexico Allocation and Apportionment of Income Instructions, p. 5B.
[7] §3.3.11.8 NMAC.

standard deduction or exemption amounts or any credits when tax is computed using this method.[8]

¶ 5.5 Part-Year Residents

An individual who is domiciled in New Mexico for only part of the tax year, and who is physically present in New Mexico for fewer than 185 days, is a part-year resident.[9] There are three categories of part-year residents, described below.

> **First-year residents.** An individual who moves into New Mexico with the intention of making New Mexico his or her permanent domicile is a first-year resident. During the first tax year in which an individual is domiciled in New Mexico, but physically present for less than 185 days, the individual is a nonresident of New Mexico for the period prior to establishing domicile. The regulations provide that a first-year resident reports any income earned prior to moving into New Mexico as nonresident income even if physically present in New Mexico for 185 days or more.[10]
>
>> *Example.* A life-long Texas resident accepts a job in New Mexico and moves there on December 5, 2003 with the intention of making it her permanent home. As a result, she has established domicile in New Mexico during the 2003 tax year, but because she was physically present in New Mexico for fewer than 185 days during that year, she files as a part-year resident, and she will be treated as a resident for personal income tax purpose only for that period after she establishes a New Mexico domicile.[11]
>
> **Leaving residents.** If an individual is physically present in New Mexico for less than 185 days during the tax year and changes his or her domicile from New Mexico during a tax year, with the intention of continuing to live permanently outside New Mexico, the individual is not a resident after the change of domicile.[12]

---

[8] Form 2016 PIT-1, Personal Income Tax Return Instructions, p. 5.
[9] §3.3.1.9B(1) NMAC
[10] §3.3.1.9B(1)(a), B(2) NMAC. This regulation appears to be odds with the rule that anyone in the state for 185 days is a resident.
[11] Based upon §3-3.1.9E, Ex. (1) NMAC.
[12] §7-2-2S NMSA 1978; §3.3.1.9B(1)-(2) NMAC.

Residency

Residents who come and go. If an individual moves to New Mexico with the intention of creating a permanent home, but after a few months, and within the same tax year, moves elsewhere, the individual is a part-year resident. In this case, if the individual has not been physically in the state 185 days during the year, he or she is taxed as a resident only during the period during which he or she actually had a domicile in New Mexico.

> *Example.* A resident of Arizona makes several weekend visits to New Mexico in the early months of 2004 but on July 1, 2004, he moves to New Mexico with the intention of making it his permanent home. Family matters call him back to Arizona on August 1, 2004, and he soon determines that he must remain in Arizona. He was domiciled in New Mexico during the thirty days he spent in this state with the intention of making it his permanent home. Because he was physically present in this state for fewer than 185 days in 2004, he files as a part-year resident for that tax year. For personal income tax purposes he is be treated as a resident of New Mexico only from July 1 to August 1, 2004.[13]

See Chapter 6 for residency issues involving military personnel.

¶ 5.6 Example of impact of residency on taxation of individuals

To allow the reader a better understanding of how residency affects New Mexico taxation, it is useful to see how the residency rules operates in an real-world example, and one that may have relevance to New Mexico's development objectives.

> *Doris Roberts, Actress.* Doris Roberts is successful movie actress who has lived in Texas her entire life. As a result of her career earnings, she has amassed an investment portfolio of $10 million dollars that earned $500,000 in interest and dividends in 2016. In 2016 she accepted the lead role in a movie shot in Santa Fe, and had to reside in Santa Fe for 186 full days in order to complete the movie. She also accepted a part in a mini-series to

---

[13] Based upon §3.3.1.9E, Ex. (2) NMAC.

be shot in Texas, which required her to spend 150 days in Dallas. She earned $4 million for the movie and $2 million for the mini-series. Doris had no other income in 2016.

New Mexico taxation. Doris is a New Mexico resident in 2016 because she lived in New Mexico for more than 185 full days during the year. As a result of being a resident, all her compensation is allocated to New Mexico. In addition, all her investment income is allocated to New Mexico. Therefore, her income of $7.5 million is subject to New Mexico taxation.

Alternative scenario. This tax result is quite a shock to Doris who lives in Texas where there is no income tax. She thought that she would pay tax on her movie compensation, but not on the mini-series or her investment earnings. Fortunately, she hired a New Mexico CPA who advised her of these consequences and how to avoid it. The CPA explained that only full-days in New Mexico count towards residency. Therefore, if Doris flew out of New Mexico to Texas several days during shooting and returned the next day, she would be under the 185 standard. Doris took this advice, and, as a result, was not a New Mexico resident in 2016. Only her $4 million income from shooting the movie in New Mexico was allocated to New Mexico and subject to New Mexico tax.

CHAPTER 6
MILITARY PERSONNEL - INCOME, FILING, RESIDENCY, AND DOMICILE

¶ 6.1 Preferential income tax treatment for military personnel

Military personnel are given preferential federal and state income tax treatment in respect for their contribution to our country. For its part, New Mexico has special rules regarding income and residency for military personnel and their spouses.

¶ 6.1.1 Income tax preferences

Regular duty pay is taxable by the federal and New Mexico governments, but pay from active duty service in the armed forces is exempt from state income taxation.[1] A resident serviceman must file a return and claim a deduction for military active duty pay that is included in federal AGI. (See ¶ 8.3.11 for further discussion of the tax return treatment of active duty pay.) Combat pay is excluded from federal AGI and is not subject to New Mexico tax to extent it is so excluded.[2]

The ITA does not define "active duty," but the following definition is given by federal statute and is cited by the instructions to Schedule PIT-ADJ.

> The term "active duty" means full-time duty in the active service of a uniformed service, and includes full-time training duty, annual training duty, full-time National Guard duty, and attendance, while in the active service, at a school designated as a service school by law or by the Secretary concerned..[3]

Apparently, the term active duty does not include service with the

---

[1] §7-2.5.11 NMSA 1978.
[2] TRD, FYI-311, *Military Extensions for New Mexico Personal Income Tax Filers* (Rev. 9/12).
[3] 37 USC §101(18), which is cited by Schedule PIT-ADJ Instructions, p. 6A.

United States Public Health Service. Although such service may qualify if a person is detailed to the army or navy.[4]

Military compensation includes many allowances, some of which are not included in federal AGI. For example, basic allowances for housing and subsistence, death allowances, moving allowances, travel allowances, and various other allowances are excluded from AGI. To the extent these allowances are excluded from AGI, they are not subject to New Mexico's PIT.[5]

The federal government forgives the unpaid tax liability of a person who at the time of death is a military or civilian U.S. employee and who dies from wounds or injury incurred while a U.S. employee in a terrorist or military action regardless of where the military or terrorist action occurred. New Mexico does not excuse the state PIT liability in this case.[6]

Compensation for service in the armed forces is subject to personal income tax only in the state of the servicemember's domicile. Compensation for military service does not include compensation for off-duty employment, or military retirement income.[7]

¶ 6.1.2 Military pay of an enrolled member of an Indian nation, tribe, or pueblo

The military pay of an enrolled member of an Indian nation, tribe, or pueblo is exempt from New Mexico tax when his or her home of record is on the lands of that Indian nation, tribe, or pueblo and the legal residence of that member has not been changed.[8] See ¶ 4.3.5 for a discussion of the exemption of Native American income. See *Example 4* below regarding a change in residency.

---

[4] §3.3.1.9D(5) NMAC. A TRD hearing officer ruled that the pay of a member of United States Public Health Service was not exempt from income tax because the member was not detailed to the army or navy. In The Matter of the Protest of Thomas & Leslie Hammack To Assessments Issued Under Letter Id Nos. L12048697296, L1504781776, L0967910864, L1576867280, & L1039996368, Decision 15-02 of Hearing Officer of TRD. See further discussion in ¶8.3.11.
[5] IRS, Armed Services Tax Guide (2014), p. 14; TRD, FYI-311, Military Extensions for New Mexico Personal Income Tax Filers (Rev. 5/2014).
[6] 26 USC §692(c).
[7] §3.3.1.9D(4) NMAC.
[8] 3.3.1.9E(8) NMAC. See 2016 PIT-1, Personal Income Tax Return Instructions, p. 3.

Military Personnel

¶ 6.1.3 Residency and domicile

A resident of New Mexico who is a member of the United States armed forces does not lose New Mexico residence or domicile, or gain residency or domicile in another state, solely because the servicemember left the state in compliance with military orders.[9] The instructions to Form PIT-1 states –

> "...you must file a resident return if both of the following are true:
>
> - You were a resident of New Mexico at the time of enlistment.
>
> - You have not changed your legal residence for purposes of withholding state income tax from military pay."[10]

A resident of another state who is a member of the United States armed forces does not acquire residence or domicile in New Mexico solely because the servicemember is in New Mexico in compliance with military orders.[11] Likewise, a resident of another state who is a member of the United States armed forces does not become a resident of New Mexico solely because the service person is in this state for 185 or more days in a tax year.[12]

A nonresident servicemember must continue to allocate non-military income from services performed to the state where the income was earned.[13]

With regard to determining residency, the term "armed forces" means all members of the army of the United States, the United States navy, the marine corps, the air force, the coast guard, all officers of the public health service detailed by proper authority for duty either with

---

[9] §3.3.1.9D(1) NMAC.
[10] 2016 PIT-1, Personal Income Tax Return Instructions, p. 2.
[11] 3.3.1.9D(2) NMAC.
[12] 3.3.1.9D(3) NMAC.
[13] 2016 PIT-1, Personal Income Tax Return Instructions, p. 2.

New Mexico Personal Income Tax Guide

the army or the navy, reservists placed on active duty, and members of the national guard called to active federal duty.

The income earned by a nonresident in New Mexico for active duty in the United States Public Health Service is exempt and deducted on PIT-ADJ, line 21. The instructions to that form do not indicate that the nonresident has to be detailed to the army or navy.

> **Example 1.** A resident of New Mexico joins the army and since joining the military, has been stationed in various places around the world. Although he has not been back to New Mexico in the ten years since he joined the army, he continues to vote in New Mexico and holds a current New Mexico driver's license. He must file as a full-year resident of New Mexico.[15]

> **Example 2.** Same facts as above, except that in August 2015, while stationed in Georgia, he retires from the military. Instead of returning to New Mexico, he moves to Florida where he intends to spend his retirement. For tax year 2015, he must file as a part-year resident, because he was not physically present in the state for 185 days or more. He is a resident of New Mexico until August 2015, when he moves to Florida with the intent of making that his permanent home.[16]

> **Example 3.** A resident of Texas is an air force officer and in March 2015 he moves to New Mexico to begin a two-year assignment at Kirtland Air Force Base. He is registered to vote in Texas and holds a Texas driver's license. He is not a resident of New Mexico in 2015. During the second year of his assignment, he registers to vote in New Mexico, obtains a New Mexico driver's license, and enrolls his son in a New Mexico university paying resident tuition. Although his presence in New Mexico under military orders is not sufficient to establish New Mexico residency or domicile, his conduct in 2015 is sufficient to establish domicile. In 2015 he must file as a part-year resident of New Mexico. He will be treated as a nonresident for income tax purposes for that period of 2015 prior to establishing

---

[15] Adapted from §3.3.1.9E(5) NMAC.
[16] Adapted from §3.3.1.9E(6) NMAC.

Military Personnel

domicile in New Mexico.[17]

Example 4. A Native American lives and works on his tribe's pueblo in New Mexico. Federal law prohibits the state from taxing income earned by a Native American who lives and works on his tribe's territory. He joins the marines and is stationed outside New Mexico. Because his domicile remains unchanged during his military service, his income from military service is treated as income earned on the tribe's territory by a tribal member living on the tribe's territory, and is not taxable by New Mexico.[18]

See ¶ 9.3.4 for an explanation of the allocation of the compensation of nonresident military personnel.

¶ 6.2 Residency Exemption for Military Spouses

¶ 6.2.1 Dual residency issues and the Military Spouse Residency Relief Act

Dual residency issues can arise for spouses of military servicemembers who move to New Mexico to be with their spouses who are in New Mexico because of military service. This problem was addressed in the federal Military Spouse Residency Relief Act (MSSRA),[19] which overturned New Mexico rules of residency with regard to military spouses.

Beginning with the tax year 2009, if a military servicemember (SM) moves to New Mexico because of military orders, and his or her spouse moves to New Mexico solely to be with the SM, the spouse may keep his or her out-of-state residency status and may source non-military wages, salaries, tips, etc., and other income from services performed to the state of residence. In effect, the SM spouse is not taxed on service income in New Mexico if he or she has a residency elsewhere. Under guidance issued by the TRD, in order for the exception to apply, the SM must have declared legal residence for purposes of withholding state income taxes from military pay in

---

[17] Adapted from §3.3.1.9E(7) NMAC.
[18] Adapted from §3.3.19E(8) NMAC. See 2016 PIT-1, Personal Income Tax Return Instructions, p. 3. See ¶4.3.5 for a further discussion of the exemption of Native American income.
[19] Military Spouse Residency Relief Act, Pub.L. No. 111-97, 123 Stat. 3007 (Nov. 11, 2009).

another state.[20]

Nevertheless, a qualifying military spouse in this situation still has to pay New Mexico income taxes on income other than services, where such income in the case of nonresidents is sourced to New Mexico. Thus, for example, the income from New Mexico rental property or the sale of property located in New Mexico is taxable in New Mexico.

¶ 6.2.2 New Mexico Resident who is a qualifying SM spouse in another state

A resident of New Mexico who is a qualifying SM spouse living in another state, should complete PIT-1 as a resident of New Mexico and allocate wages, salaries, tips, and other income from services performed on Schedule PIT-B as if from New Mexico sources even if earned in another state.[21]

In the case of a qualifying SM's spouse who becomes an actual resident of New Mexico, income from services performed in New Mexico is allocated to New Mexico during periods of residency.[22]

¶ 6.2.3 Withholding exemption requirements

A qualifying SM spouse may claim exempt New Mexico withholding status based upon the MSSRA by submitting Form RPD-41348, *Military Spouse Withholding Tax Exemption Statement*, to an employer or payor responsible for withholding New Mexico income tax. The statement for exempt status applies only for one tax year and Form RPD-41348 must be completed annually. The form should be submitted prior to the beginning employment or performing services and by the first day of each subsequent tax year.

The employer or payor is required to verify eligibility. Once verified, the income is reported on the federal forms W2 or 1099 to the state of domicile declared by the spouse.

The employee or payee must provide at least one document from each of three groups of verification.[23]

---

[20] Form RPD 41348 (Rev. 7/2010), Military Spouse Withholding Tax Exemption Statement Instructions.
[21] 2016 Form PIT-1, Personal Income Tax Return Instructions, p. 3.
[22] 2016 Form PIT-1, Personal Income Tax Return Instructions, p. 3.
[23] See Form RPD 41348 (Rev. 7/2010), Military Spouse Withholding Tax Exemption Statement, Instructions.

Military Personnel

Group 1 – Verification of Marriage
• Employee's military ID card indicating that the employee is the spouse of the SM.
• Marriage license.
Group 2 – Verification of SM's Domicile
• SM's current Leave and Earnings Statement indicating that the SM has declared legal residence for purposes of withholding state income taxes from military pay in another state.
• SM's recent W-2
Group 3 – Verification of Spouse's Domicile – Documents spouse may have showing that the spouse was domiciled in another state. These documents must be issued to the spouse as a resident of the other state.
• Spouse's voter registration card
• Spouse's driving license
• Marriage license, unless provided as verification in Group 1
• Divorce decree
• Children's birth records
• Professional license
• Documentation showing that the spouse qualifies for in-state tuition
• Proof of employment

¶ 6.2.4 Tax Return Filing Requirement

A nonresident who qualifies as a SM's spouse living in New Mexico must nevertheless file a New Mexico Form PIT-1 as a nonresident taxpayer. Income from services performed in New Mexico should be allocated on Schedule PIT-B to the state of the spouse's residence.

¶ 6.3 Filing Extensions for military personnel

In addition to the filing extensions available to all taxpayers (see Chapter 4), New Mexico provides two additional exceptions for servicemembers.

New Mexico follows the federal rule that allows an automatic extension of at least 180 days following cessation of specified military activities of servicemembers. Here is a description of these qualifying activities from the IRS publication, *Armed Forces Tax Guide*.[24]

---

[24] IRS Publication 3, *Armed Forces Tax Guide*, p. 24 (2015).

> The deadline for filing tax returns, paying taxes, filing claims for refund, and taking other actions with the IRS is automatically extended if either of the following statements is true.
>
> You serve in the Armed Forces in a combat zone or you have qualifying service outside of a combat zone.
>
> You serve in the Armed Forces on deployment outside the United States away from your permanent duty station while participating in a contingency operation. A contingency operation is a military operation that is designated by the Secretary of Defense or results in calling members of the uniformed services to active duty (or retains them on active duty) during a war or a national emergency declared by the President or Congress.

The length of the of the extension is described as follows:

> Your deadline for taking actions with the IRS is extended for 180 days after the later of:
>
> The last day you are in a combat zone, have qualifying service outside of the combat zone, or serve in a contingency operation (or the last day the area qualifies as a combat zone or the operation qualifies as a contingency operation), or the last day of any continuous qualified hospitalization (defined later) for injury from service in the combat zone or contingency operation or while performing qualifying service outside of the combat zone.
>
> In addition to the 180 days, your deadline is extended by the number of days that were left for you to take the action with the IRS when you entered a combat zone (or began performing qualifying service outside the combat zone) or began serving in a contingency operation. If you entered the combat zone or began serving in the contingency operation before the period of time to take the action began, your deadline is extended by the entire period of time you have to take the action. For example, you had $3^{1/2}$ months (January 1– April 15, 2014) to file your 2013 tax return. Any days of this $3^{1/2}$ month period that were left when you entered the combat zone (or the entire $3^{1/2}$ months if you entered the combat zone by January 1, 2014) are added to the 180 days when determining the last day allowed for filing your 2013 tax return.

The term "qualified hospitalization" is defined as the hospitalization as the result of an injury received while serving in a combat zone or a contingency operation and which is outside the United States, or up to 5 years of hospitalization in the United States.[25]

---

[25] IRS Publication 3, *Armed Forces Tax Guide*, p. 24-35 (2015).

Military Personnel

Interest only applies to any tax unpaid as of the extended due date of the return. There is no penalty during the extension period.[26]

To claim the extension, the taxpayer indicates the extension date and marks the extension box on the New Mexico return. In addition, the taxpayer should write "combat zone" in red across the top the New Mexico return.

The second additional extension for military personnel is an extension that New Mexico offers armed service personnel who are New Mexico residents and who have been called to active duty, deployed, and serving between April 3, 2003 and the date the United States declares that emergency call-up is terminated. In this case, residents are allowed extensions of one year after they return to the state for filing a tax return if the original filing date occurs while the member is on active duty or deployed.

There is no penalty during the extension period. Interest applies to any tax unpaid as of the original due date of the return. Taxpayers who qualify for this extension may also qualify for an extension of time to pay under the federal extension discussed above.

To claim the extension, the taxpayer should indicate the extension date on the front of the return, mark the extension box, write "deployment" in red on the top of the return, and attach a copy of Federal DD Form 214, *Discharge Papers and Separation Documents*.[27]

---

[26] IRS Publication 3, *Armed Forces Tax Guide*, p. 23 (2015).
[27] TRD, FYI-311, Military Extensions for New Mexico Personal Income Tax Filers (Rev. 5/2014).

CHAPTER 7
TAXABLE INCOME AND NET INCOME

¶ 7.1 Overview

The ITA imposes an income tax upon the *net income* of every resident individual and upon the net income of every nonresident individual employed or engaged in the transaction of business in, into or from the state or deriving any income from any property or employment within the state.[1] The use of term "net income" by the statute may create some confusion because although the PIT is a tax on net income, this term does not appear on Form PIT-1 and is invisible to those who prepare any of the New Mexico tax forms. Instead, the PIT tax forms focus on *taxable income,* which Form PIT-1 determines by starting with AGI and then adding or subtracting statutory adjustments, without ever mentioning net income. Under the statutory approach, taxable income equals net income less any lump sum amounts. Under both approaches, the amount of taxable income is the same; only the method of getting there differs. The TRD chose to avoid the statutory approach because determining taxable income using the concept of net income is complex, as shown in the sections below. Therefore, for the sake of clarity and simplicity, the tax forms ignore this concept and get directly to taxable income without mentioning several of the important statutory terms. The following table shows how taxable income and the resulting tax liability are determined both on the Form PIT-1 (the "tax return method") and by statute (the "statutory method").

---

[1] §7-2-3 NMSA 1978.

New Mexico Personal Income Tax Guide

	A. Statutory Method of Determining Tax Due	B. Tax Return Method Determining Tax Due	Notes
1	AGI	AGI	
2	**Plus:** Adjustments (federal NOL deduction, interest on state and local bonds, 529 plan adjustments, fed. charitable deduction for land donation for which a NM credit is obtained, and income not in AGI but taxed by fed gov.)	**Minus:** PIT-1, lines 12 (std. or itemized deductions), 13 (fed. exemption amount, 14 (additional exempt. for low/middle income taxpayers), and 16 (med. care expense ded.); **Plus:** state and local tax deds. for itemizers	
3	**Plus:** Lump sum amounts (not included in AGI)		Base income includes federally taxed income not included in AGI.
4	**Equals:** Base Income		A statutory, but not a tax return concept.
5	**Minus:** Adjustments (See ¶ 7.31.B)	**Plus/minus:** adjustments (PIT-1, lines 11 and 15)	
6	**Equals:** Net income		A statutory, but not a tax return concept.
7	**Less:** Lump sum amounts		
8	**Equals:** NM Taxable income	**Equals:** NM Taxable income	
9	**Tax on NM taxable income**	**Tax on NM taxable income**	**Tax on taxable income** using tax tables or Schedule B (PIT-1, line 18).
10	**Tax** on lump sum amounts	**Tax** on lump sum amounts	**Tax on lump sum amounts** (special averaging rule) (PIT-1, line19).
11	**Tax** on net income (9A + 10A)		Not a tax return concept.
12	**Business related credits and credit for taxes paid to another state**	**Business related credits and credit for taxes paid another state** (PIT-1, lines 20, 21)	**Cannot reduce tax due below zero.**
13		Net NM income tax: 9B + 10B less 12B (PIT-l, line 22)	Net NM income tax is not a statutory term.
14	**Refundable credits and rebates, withholdings, estimated taxes**	**Refundable credits and rebates, withholdings, estimated taxes**	
15	**Tax Due or refund:** 11A less 12A and 14A	**Tax Due or refund:** 13B less 14B	**15A and 15B are equivalent.**

Taxable Income and Net Income

Another confusing feature of the PIT is that the statutory tax rate schedules and the TRD's tax tables are applied against *taxable income,* not net income. Since statutorily the income tax is imposed on net income, it would seem appropriate for the tax rate schedules to be applied against net income. However, this is not necessary, because the tax on net income is composed of the tax on taxable income plus the tax on lump sum amounts, which are separately determined and then aggregated. The tax on taxable income is determined using the tax tables and the tax on lump sum amounts is determined using a special averaging rule (See ¶ 9.4).[2]

On Form PIT-1, the tax on taxable income is reported on line 18 and the tax on lump sum amounts is reported on line 19. If these two lines were added together on the form, the sum would equal the tax on net income. However, these two amounts are never totaled on the form to produce the tax on net income. Instead line 18, line 19, and the credits on lines 20 and 21 are combined to determine Net New Mexico Income Tax on line 22. This is not a statutory term, but Net New Mexico Income Tax is equivalent to the amount of tax on net income (the tax on taxable income plus the tax on lump sum amounts), less the credits on lines 21 and 22, and this equivalence means that the tax return method and the statutory method both lead to the same tax due.

AGI is always the starting point for taxable income, whether it is being determined under the tax return or the statutory method. Under the tax return method, taxable income is determined by starting with AGI, from which a number of positive and negative adjustments are made to get to taxable income. The statutory method is a little more complex. It starts with AGI and then certain positive adjustments are made to get to "base income." From base income, negative adjustments are made to get to net income. From net income, lump sum amounts are deducted to get to taxable income. These concepts and adjustments are discussed in ¶ 7.3.1 et. seq.

In computing taxable income, community property rules (See ¶ 7.7) and tax accounting rules (See ¶ 7.6) must be observed.

---

[2] §§7-2-2B, 7-2-2N, 7-2-2X and 7-2-7.1 NMSA 1978.

¶ 7.2 Adjusted gross income (AGI)

AGI is defined by IRC §62, as amended or renumbered. Therefore, as the definition of AGI changes for federal purposes, it also changes for the PIT. On Form PIT-1, line 9, taxpayers enter AGI as reported on line 38 of federal Form 1040, line 22 of federal Form 1040A, or line 4 from federal Form 1040EZ, as applicable. In general, AGI equals federal gross income, less statutory deductions, as shown in the following table:

Deductions Allowed From Federal Gross Income
• self-employed individual's trade or business expenses, including one-half self-employment tax and self-employed health insurance;
• deduction for foreign housing costs;
• certain business expenses of performing artists as employees;
• certain expenses of an official as an employee of a state or local government compensated on a fee-basis for his or her services;
• teacher's classroom expenditures;
• travel expenses of National Guard or reservists while away from home to attend meetings or training sessions;
• losses from the sale or exchange of property;
• deductions attributable to the rental or royalty of property;
• depreciation or depletion allowed a life tenant or income beneficiary;
• contributions to a self-employed individual's profit-sharing, pension or annuity (qualified retirement plan);
• contributions to IRAs for taxpayers or non-working spouses;
• penalties on premature withdrawals from savings accounts;
• alimony payments;
• amortization or reforestation expenses;
• required repayments of supplemental unemployment benefits;
• jury duty pay remitted to employer;
• moving expenses;
• student loan interest;
• contribution to Archer MSAs and contributions to HSAs;
• tuition and fees deduction for post-secondary education;
• attorney fees and costs associated with unlawful discrimination claims or whistleblower awards; and
• domestic production deduction associated with a trade or business.

Taxable Income and Net Income

¶ 7.3 Computing taxable income

As noted above, taxable income may be computed using a statutory method and a tax return method. These two methods are discussed in the following sections.

¶ 7.3.1 Taxable income – tax return method

The tax return method of computing taxable income is relatively straightforward. Starting with AGI, one makes four negative adjustments directly on Form PIT-1. These adjustments are the federal standard or itemized deduction, line 12, the federal deduction for personal and dependency exemptions, line 13 (see ¶ 7.4.1), the additional deduction for personal exemptions, line 14 (see ¶ 7.4.2), and the deduction for unreimbursed medical expenses, line 16 (see ¶ 7.5). In addition, for taxpayers who itemize, the amount deducted for state and local taxes paid is added back to AGI on line 10. Then, positive and negative adjustments from Schedule PIT-ADJ are added and subtracted to arrive at taxable income. (See Chapter 8.) This book for the most part follows the tax return method because this is what we see when view the tax forms, and to follow the statutory approach would create a disconnect between the text and the forms. See Chapter 2 for an overview of the steps involved in computing taxable income.

¶7.3.2 The Statutory Method – Computing net income, base income, lump sum amounts, and taxable income

The ITA statutes were created in the context of the statutory method, not the tax return method, and to understand the statutes and the regulations thereunder, one has to understand the statutory scheme. Under the statutory method, there are two taxable elements: taxable income and lump sum amounts, each of which are taxed differently. Taxable income is defined as net income less any lump-sum amounts, and so it is first necessary to determine net income in order to determine taxable income.[7] Net income is determined by making adjustments to base income. Base income equals AGI plus certain positive adjustments. From base income a number of statutory deductions are made to reach net income.

---

[7] §7-2-2X NMSA 1978.

¶ 7.3.2A Base income

The starting point, then, for determining statutory net income is base income. Base income is determined by starting with federal AGI, and then adding certain adjustments. The adjustments to determine base income are as follows.

1. Begin with AGI (see inset above), and add, for tax years beginning on or after January 1, 1991, the amount of the NOL deduction allowed by IRC §172(a), and taken by the taxpayer for that year.

2. Add any other income of the taxpayer not included in AGI, but upon which a federal tax is calculated for income tax purposes, except pursuant to IRC §55 (alternative minimum tax).

3. Add interest received on a state or local bond.[8] Expenses related to such interest are deductible to the extent they have not been deducted in determined federal taxable income.[9]

4. Add an amount deducted for payments to an education trust fund in a prior tax year if:

    a. such amount is transferred to another qualified tuition program, as defined in IRC §529, not authorized in the

---

[8] A "state or local bond" is a bond issued by a state *other* than New Mexico or by a local government other than one of New Mexico's political subdivisions, the interest from which is excluded from income for federal income tax purposes under IRC§ 103. §7-2-2V NMSA 1978. A "state" means any state of the United States, the District of Columbia, the commonwealth of Puerto Rico, any territory or possession of the United States or any political subdivision of a foreign country. §7-2-2U NMSA 1978. In apparent contradiction with the statute, the tax regulations provide that the term "state or local bond" does not include any obligation of the Commonwealth of Puerto Rico or of territories or possessions of the United States the income from which New Mexico is prohibited from taxing by the laws of the United States. §3.3.1.12E NMAC. Bonds issued by Indian governments are not "state or local bonds" under the ITA. In addition, the term "state" does not include Indian nations, tribes or pueblos or their governments. The tax regulations note that the term "local government" is not defined by the ITA but is commonly used to mean political subdivisions of states and that Indian nations, tribes and pueblos are not political subdivisions of states. §3.3.1.12F NMAC. As a result, to the extent that the Internal Revenue Code treats interest from bonds issued by Indian governments as if it were interest from "state or local bonds", such interest is excluded from AGI and therefore initially excluded from New Mexico base income as well. Because bonds issued by Indian governments are not "state or local bonds" for purposes of the ITA, interest income with respect to such bonds is not required to be added to AGI in determining New Mexico base income.

[9] §3.3.1.12D(2) NMAC.

Taxable Income and Net Income

>>b. a distribution or refund is made for any reason other than to pay for qualified higher education expenses, as defined IRC §529, or upon the beneficiary's death, disability or receipt of a scholarship.[10]

> 5. Add any charitable deduction amount claimed on federal Form 1040, Schedule A, for a donation of land to private non-profit or public conservation agencies, for conservation purposes, from the taxpayer that was allowed the New Mexico land conservation tax credit.

Under the statutory method, lump sum amounts (defined in ¶ 7.3.1C) move through a circuitous path. They are not included in AGI under federal rules, but they are then added to AGI under New Mexico rules to reach base income. Under the ITA, items are added to AGI to reach base income if they are not included in AGI but a federal tax is otherwise imposed upon them, except in the case of the federal alternative minimum tax.[11] A lump-sum amount is not included in federal AGI if the ten-year-averaging option had been elected, but at the same time it is subject to federal tax. Therefore, although a lump sum amount is excluded from AGI, it is nevertheless included in base income, with the net effect that the lump sum amount is included in net income. (See ¶ 9.4 for a discussion of the tax on lump sum amounts.)

¶7.3.2B Net income

Once base income is determined, deductions are made to reach net income. The following deductions are taken to reach net income.

> 1. Standard deduction. The amount of the standard deduction allowed the taxpayer under the Internal Revenue Code (IRC §63(c)) is deducted.

> 2. Itemized deductions. Itemized deductions deductible by the taxpayer under the Internal Revenue Code (as determined by IRC §63(d)) are deductible from net income to the extent allowed for the tax year, less the amount of the standard

---

[10] §7-2-2B NMSA 1978.
[11] IRC §55.

deduction allowed (excluded by paragraph 1), and less the amount of state and local income and sales taxes included in the taxpayer's itemized deductions.

3. Personal exemptions. The exemption amount allowed under federal rules for the tax year[12] multiplied by the number of personal exemptions allowed for federal income tax purposes is excluded.

4. Interest from US obligations. Income from obligations of the United States of America less, expenses incurred to earn that income, is excluded.[13]

5. Other exempt amounts. Other amounts that the state is prohibited from taxing because of the laws or constitution of New Mexico or the United States is excluded. This includes, for example, income earned on any obligation of the commonwealth of Puerto Rico or of territories or possessions of the United States.[14]

6. NOL (pre-1991). The net operating loss (NOL) deduction for a tax year that began prior to January 1, 1991 is excluded in an amount equaling the sum of NOL carryback deductions to that year from tax years beginning prior to January 1, 1991, and NOL carryover deductions to that year.

7. NOL (1991 to 2012). A carryover deduction for tax years beginning on or after January 1, 1991 and prior to January 1, 2013 is excluded as follows:

    a. in the tax year immediately following the tax year for which the return is filed for a timely filed return; or

    b. in the first tax year beginning after the date on which

---

[12] The exemption amount is determined by IRC §151. Each dependent claimed as an exemption for New Mexico purposes must meet the dependency tests of IRC §152. The taxpayer must provide the name of each dependent and the social security number for any dependent who is two years of age or older as required by the instructions to the New Mexico income tax return. The failure to provide this information may result in the loss of the exemption claimed. §3.3.1.11 NMAC.
[13] The tax regulations provide that to the extent that such expenses have been deducted in determining federal taxable income, the amount must be added back to net income. §3.3.1.12D(1) NMAC.
[15] §7-2-2N(9) NMSA 1978

Taxable Income and Net Income

       the return or amended return establishing the NOL is filed for an amended return or an original return not timely filed; and

    c. in either case, if the NOL carryover exceeds net income (exclusive of the NOL carryover) for the tax year to which the exclusion first applies, in the next four succeeding tax years until exhausted, but never after the 4th tax year.

8. NOL (after 2012). NOL deduction for tax years beginning on or after January 1, 2013, equal to the sum of any NOL deductions to that year claimed and allowed; provided that the amount of any NOL carryover is excluded as follows:

    a. in the tax year immediately following the tax year for which the return is filed for a timely filed return; or

    b. in the first tax year beginning after the date on which the return or amended return establishing the NOL is filed in the case of an amended return or an original return not timely filed; and

    c. in either case, if the NOL carryover exceeds net income (exclusive of the NOL carryover) for the tax year to which the exclusion first applies, in the next 19 succeeding tax years until exhausted; but a carryover from a tax year beginning: 1) prior to January 1, 2013 may not be excluded after the 4th tax year beginning after the tax year to which the exclusion first applies; or 2) on or after January 1, 2013 may not be excluded after the 19th tax year beginning after the tax year to which the exclusion first applies.

9. Refund of state and local income and sales taxes. For tax years beginning on or after January 1, 2011, the amount included in AGI that represents a refund of state and local income and sales taxes that were deducted for federal tax purposes in tax years beginning on or after January 1, 2010 is excluded.[15]

10. Unreimbursed medical expenses. See ¶ 7.5.

---

[15] §7-2-2N(9) NMSA 1978

11. Other deductions listed in Schedule PIT-ADJ (see Chapter 8), including the following:
    a. New Mexico tax-exempt interest and dividends.
    b. Taxable Railroad Retirement Act annuities and benefits, and taxable Railroad Unemployment Insurance Act sick pay.
    c. Income of a member of a New Mexico federally-recognized Indian nation, tribe, or pueblo that was wholly earned on the lands of the reservation or pueblo of which the individual is an enrolled member while domiciled on that land, reservation, or pueblo.
    d. Income of persons age 100 years or older.
    e. Exemption for persons age 65 or older, or blind.
    f. Exemption for New Mexico medical care savings account.
    g. Deduction for contributions to a New Mexico-approved Section 529 college savings plan.
    h. Net capital gains deduction.
    i. Armed Forces active duty pay.
    j. Medical care expense exemption for persons age 65 years or older.
    k. Deduction for organ donation-related expenses.
    l. New Mexico National Guard member life insurance reimbursements tax exemption.
    m. Non-resident U.S. Public Health Service members' active duty pay.

¶ 7.3.2C Lump-sum amounts – defined

Under federal tax rules a lump-sum amount is a distribution in one tax year of the balance of a plan participant from all of his or her employer's qualified plans of one kind (such as pension, profit-sharing, or stock bonus plans). Distributions from nonqualified plans do not qualify as lump sum distributions subject to the special income tax averaging calculation.

Taxable Income and Net Income

A plan participant born before January 2, 1936, who received a lump-sum distribution from a qualified employee plan or qualified employee annuity may be able to elect optional methods of figuring the tax on the distribution. The portion of the lump sum payment derived from active participation in the plan before 1974 may qualify as capital gain subject to a 20% tax rate. The part attributable to participation after 1973 (and any part from participation before 1974 that is not reported as capital gain) is ordinary income and a taxpayer may use a 10-year tax averaging option to compute tax on the ordinary income portion.[16]

The 10-year tax option is a special formula used to figure a separate tax on the ordinary income part of a lump-sum distribution. The tax is paid only once, in the year in which a distribution is received. Form 4972 is used to elect the 10-year tax option.

For New Mexico purposes a "lump-sum amount" means an amount that was not included in federal AGI but for which the taxpayer elected the federal 10-year option. The statute also provides that a lump-sum amount is one for which a five-year option is elected, but the federal five year option was repealed for tax years beginning in 2000.[17] In addition, the Worksheet for Calculating Tax on Lump-Sum Distributions found in the instructions to Form PIT-1 treats capital gain amounts as lump-sum amounts, although the statute does not appear to authorize this treatment.[18]

Lump-sum amounts are taxed in New Mexico using a five-year averaging method, which is discussed in ¶ 9.4

¶ 7.3.2D Taxable income

Taxable income under the tax return and the statutory methods are equivalent. Under the statutory method, taxable income equals net income less lump-sum amounts. The tax return method starts with AGI and then makes all the adjustments that are also made under the statutory method in computing base income and net income. In both methods the tax rate tables are applied to taxable income, and the tax

---

[16] The special rules applicable to lump sum amounts under IRC §402 are applied without regard to community property laws. §IRC §402(e)(4)(D)(iii)
[17] See §1401(b)(2) of the Small Jobs Protection Act of 1996, Pub. L. No. 104-188 (August 20, 1996).
[18] Form 2016 PIT-1, Personal Income Tax Return Instructions, p. 28.

on lump-sum amounts is separately computed.

¶ 7.4 Deduction of personal exemptions

¶ 7.4.1 New Mexico exemption deduction based on federal exemption deduction – Form PIT-1, line 13

The Internal Revenue Code provides a deduction for personal and dependency exemptions, and New Mexico provides a personal and dependency exemption deduction equivalent to that obtained on federal Forms 1040 and 1040A. The federal exemption deduction is based upon the number of the federal personal and dependency exemptions, and the Internal Revenue Code generally allows a deduction of $4,000 per taxpayer, spouse, and dependent (annually adjusted for inflation). However, as a taxpayer's income increases this amount is gradually phased-out, leaving very high income taxpayers with no deduction for personal exemptions.

The number of claimed federal exemptions is reported on line 6D of Form 1040 and Form 1040A. This number is then reported on Form PIT-1, line 5.

The federal deduction for exemptions is reported on line 42 of Form 1040 and line 26 of Form 1040A. This amount is then reported on PIT-1, line 13.

If a taxpayer files federal Form 1040EZ, line 13 is left blank. The deduction for personal exemption in this case is included in the amount on line 12, which is transferred from Form 1040EZ, line 5, which includes both the federal personal exemption and standard deduction.

¶ 7.4.2 Additional exemptions for low- and middle-income taxpayers- Form PIT-1, line 14

In addition to the personal exemption deduction discussed in the prior subsection, New Mexico provides an additional tax exemption deduction for low-and middle-income taxpayers. All taxpayers who meet the statute's income requirements, including residents, part-year residents, first-year residents, or non-residents, may claim this additional exemption deduction. The amount of the exemption deduction varies according to filing status and AGI, but the maximum exemption deduction is $2,500 for each federal exemption. To qualify for the exemption, the taxpayer's federal AGI (amount on line 9, Form

Taxable Income and Net Income

PIT-1) must be equal to or less than:
- $36,667, if single;
- $27,500, if married filing separate, or
- $55,000, if married filing joint, qualified widow(er), or head of household.[21]

The amount of the exemption is determined as follows.

For a married individual filing a separate return with AGI up to $27,500:
1. if the AGI is not over $15,000, the amount of the exemption is $2,500 for each federal exemption; and
2. if AGI is over $15,000, but not over $27,500, the amount of the exemption for each federal exemption is calculated as follows:
   a. $2,500; less
   b. 20% of the amount obtained by subtracting $15,000 from AGI.

For single individuals with AGI up to $36,667:
1. if the AGI is not over $20,000, the amount of the exemption is $2,500 for each federal exemption; and
2. if the AGI is over $20,000, but not over $36,667, the amount of the exemption for each federal exemption is calculated as follows:
   a. $2,500; less
   b. 15% of the amount obtained by subtracting $20,000 from the AGI.

For married individuals filing joint returns, surviving spouses or for heads of households with AGI up to $55,000:
1. if AGI is not over $30,000, the amount of the exemption is $2,500 for each federal exemption; and
2. if the adjusted gross income is over $30,000 but not over $55,000, the amount of the exemption for each federal exemption is be calculated as follows:
   a. $2,500; less

---

[21] §7-2-5.8 NMSA 1978.

b. 10% of the amount obtained by subtracting $30,000 from adjusted gross income.[22]

¶ 7.5 Deduction of unreimbursed or uncompensated medical care expenses – PIT-1, line 16

A taxpayer may deduct from net income[23] a portion of "medical care expenses" paid during the tax year. The deduction is available for medical care expenses of the taxpayer, the taxpayer's spouse, or a dependent, as long as the expenses are not reimbursed or compensated by insurance or otherwise and have not been included in the taxpayer's federal itemized deductions[24] for the tax year.[25] However, medical care expenses that comprise either the federal 10%, or 7.5% floor, as applicable, qualify for this deduction.[26]

The deduction may be claimed for tax years beginning on or after January 1, 2015 and prior to January 1, 2025.

The deduction is claimed on Form PIT-1, line 16 in an amount equal to the following percentage of medical care expenses paid during the tax year, based on the taxpayer's filing status and AGI:

---

[22] 7-2-5.8B-D NMSA 1978.
[23] Here is an example of where the statute specifies that a deduction is from net income and not from AGI. As noted at the beginning of the chapter, this terminology can be confusing because the tax forms do not mention net income.
[24] As defined in §63 of the IRC.
[25] ¶7-2-37 NMSA 1978.
[26] Form 2016 PIT-1, Personal Income Tax Return Instructions, p. 27.

Taxable Income and Net Income

Surviving spouses and married individuals filing joint returns	
If AGI is:	Percent of medical care expenses paid may be deducted:
Not over $30,000	25%
More than $30,000 but not more than $70,000	15%
Over $70,000	10%
Single individuals and married individuals filing separate returns	
If AGI is:	Percent of medical care expenses paid may be deducted:
Not over $15,000	25%
More than $15,000 but not more than $35,000	15%
Over $35,000	10%
Heads of household	
If AGI is:	Percent of medical care expenses that may be deducted:
Not over $20,000	25%
More than $20,000 but not more than $50,000	15%
Over $50,000	10%

Important terms

Medical care expenses are the amounts paid for:

- the diagnosis, cure, mitigation, treatment or prevention of disease or for the purpose of affecting any structure or function of the body, excluding cosmetic surgery, if provided by a physician or in a health care facility;
- prescribed drugs or insulin;
- qualified long-term care services (as defined in §7702B(c) of the IRC);
  insurance covering medical care, including amounts paid as premiums under Part B of Title 18 of the Social Security Act or for a qualified long-term care insurance contract (as defined in §7702B(b) of the IRC), if the insurance or other amount is paid from income included in the taxpayer's AGI for the tax year;
- nursing services, regardless of where the services are rendered, if provided by a practical nurse or a professional nurse licensed to practice in the state pursuant to the Nursing Practice Act;

- specialized treatment or the use of special therapeutic devices if the treatment or device is prescribed by a physician and the patient can show that the expense was incurred primarily for the prevention or alleviation of a physical or mental defect or illness; and
- care in an institution other than a hospital, such as a sanitarium or rest home, if the principal reason for the presence of the person in the institution is to receive the medical care available; provided that if the meals and lodging are furnished as a necessary part of such care, the cost of the meals and lodging are medical care expenses.

A "health care facility" is a hospital, outpatient facility, diagnostic and treatment center, rehabilitation center, free-standing hospice or other similar facility at which medical care is provided.

A "physician" is a medical doctor, osteopathic physician, dentist, podiatrist, chiropractic physician, or psychologist licensed or certified to practice in New Mexico.

A "prescribed drug" is a drug or biological that requires a prescription of a physician for its use by an individual.

The term "dependent" is as defined under federal rules.[27]

¶ 7.6 State and local tax add back

New Mexico allows a deduction from AGI for the amount of itemized deductions or standard deduction that was claimed on the federal return.[28] See Form PIT-1, line 12. However, for itemizers this deduction is reduced by the amount of state and local income and sales taxes that are reported on the federal return (Schedule A, line 5) and these taxes are added back on Form PIT-1, line 10.[29]

The instructions to Form PIT-1 add the following qualifications:

- The amount cannot be below the standard deduction amount you would have qualified for if you had not elected to or if you were required to itemize your deductions on your federal

---

[27] See §152 of the IRC.
[28] §7-2-2N(1)- (2) NMSA 1978.
[29] §7-2-2N(2) NMSA 1978.

Taxable Income and Net Income

return.

- If the amount of the itemized deductions allowed on your federal return is limited because your federal adjusted gross income exceeds certain thresholds, your state and local tax deduction add-back is also reduced. The add-back is reduced by a percentage equal to the itemized deductions allowed and the total itemized deductions reported on federal Form 1040, Schedule A, before the limitation is applied.

The instructions provide a worksheet to help compute the add-back, which is replicated in the following table.

Worksheet for Computing the Amount on Line 10 of the PIT-1 Return	
1. Enter the state and local income tax deduction you claimed on federal form 1040, Schedule A, line 5	$
2. Enter your total itemized deductions from federal form 1040, line 40. Also enter this amount on PIT-1, line 12, and mark the box on line 12a.	$
3. Enter the sum of the amounts you reported of federal Form 1040, Schedule A, lines 4, 9, 15,19, 20, 27, and 28.	$
4. Divide line 2 by line 3. Round to 4 decimal places.	
5. Multiply line 4 by line 1.	$
6. Enter the standard deduction amount you could have claimed on federal Form 1040, line 40, if you had not itemized you federal allowable deductions.	$
7. Subtract line 6 from line 2. If less than zero, enter zero.	$
8. Enter the lesser of lines 4 and 7. Also enter this amount on PIT-1, line 10.	$

¶ 7.7 Tax accounting rules

¶ 7.7.1 Taxable years

The PIT is imposed on a taxable year basis. A taxable year (or tax year, as used synonymously in this text) is the calendar year or fiscal year upon the basis of which the net income of the taxpayer is computed under the ITA and includes, in the case of the return made for a fractional part of a year, the period for which the return is made.[30] A fiscal year means any accounting period of twelve months ending on the last day of any month other than December.[31] Any individual who files a federal return on the basis of a fiscal year must report income for the New Mexico personal income tax on the same basis.[32]

¶ 7.7.2 Accounting Methods

A taxpayer must use the same accounting methods for New Mexico income tax purposes as are used in reporting income for federal income tax purposes.[33] A taxpayer engaged in more than one business may use a different method of accounting for each business.[34]

A taxpayer must obtain the consent of the TRD prior to changing the method of accounting in keeping books and records for tax purposes unless a change is required by law. If consent is not secured, the TRD may upon audit require the taxpayer to compute the amount of tax due on the basis of the accounting or reporting method earlier used.[35]

There is no requirement that the method of accounting for one type of state tax be the same method of accounting for another type of state tax. For example, a taxpayer may account for and report the taxpayer's gross receipts tax on the cash basis, while accounting for and reporting the taxpayer's income tax on an accrual basis.[36]

---

[30] §7-2-2Y NMSA 1978.
[31] §7-2-2G NMSA 1978.
[32] §7-2-21 NMSA 1978.
[33] §7-2-21.1 NMSA 1978.
[34] §7-1-10B NMSA 1978.
[35] §7-1-10C-D NMSA 1978.
[36] §3.1.5.10 NMAC.

Taxable Income and Net Income

¶ 7.8 Community property

New Mexico is a community property state, one of 12 in the country. In a community property state, the manner in which income is reported by a married couple for federal tax purposes may depend upon whether the income is from separate property or community property or whether earned income is considered separate income or community income. Since New Mexico bases its personal income tax on federal AGI, many of the allocations of community income and deductions made for federal purposes are automatically incorporated in the New Mexico tax return. Nevertheless, there are circumstances where community property and income have a separate impact on New Mexico taxation.

IRS Publication 555, *Community Property*, Table 1,[37] as reproduced in the inset below, provides a summary of the general rules concerning community property and income and separate property and income. These are only general rules and New Mexico rules may vary, especially in complex situations. For example, New Mexico does not recognize community property rights of registered domestic partners, while several other states do.[38]

---

[37] IRS, Publication 555, *Community Property* (Rev. Feb. 2016), p. 4.
[38] See TRD, FYI-310, Community Property Divorce, Separation, and Your New Mexico Income Tax (Rev. 5/2014).

Table 1. General Rules – Property and Income: Community or Separate?	
Community property. Generally, community property is property: • That you, your spouse (or your registered domestic partner), or both acquire during your marriage (or registered domestic partnership) while you and your spouse (or your registered domestic partner) are domiciled in a community property state. • That you and your spouse (or your registered domestic partner) agreed to convert from separate to community property. • That cannot be identified as separate property.	**Separate property.** Generally, separate property is: • Property that you or your spouse (or your registered domestic partner) owned separately before your marriage (or registered domestic partnership). • Money earned while domiciled in a noncommunity property state. • Property that you or your spouse (or your registered domestic partner) received separately as a gift or inheritance during your marriage (or registered domestic partnership). • Property that you or your spouse (or your registered domestic partner) bought with separate funds, or acquired in exchange for separate property, during your marriage (or registered domestic partnership). • Property that you and your spouse (or your registered domestic partner) converted from community property to separate property through an agreement valid under state law. • The part of property bought with separate funds, if part was bought with community funds and part with separate funds.

Taxable Income and Net Income

Community income. Generally, community income is income from:<ul><li>Community property.</li><li>Salaries, wages, and other pay received for the services performed by you, your spouse (or your registered domestic partner), or both during your marriage (or registered domestic partnership) while domiciled in a community property state.</li><li>Real estate that is treated as community property under the laws of the state where the property is located.</li></ul>	**Separate income.** Income from separate property is the separate income of the spouse (or the registered domestic partner) who owns the property.

Note: New Mexico does not recognize community rights of registered domestic partners.

When married people file joint returns, community property laws generally do not result in any special treatment or adjustments for federal purposes. In this case, all income, whether separate or community income is included in joint income and no allocation of income has to be made between the parties. Since New Mexico follows federal rules regarding marriage status and income there is generally no special treatment for New Mexico income tax as well, but for two exceptions, which are as follows:

- when one person of a married couple claims the exemption for income of persons 100 years or older.
- when one spouse is a resident and the other is not and the couple has income from sources both in and out of New Mexico, then the apportionment process under Schedule PIT-B must consider the community property and income rules.

In the case of the centenarian, only the income of the centenarian is eligible for the exemption related to taxpayers 100 years or older, and an allocation must be made of community and separate income that is related to the centenarian.

When one spouse is resident and the other is not, then the

allocation or apportionment of income under Schedule PIT-B might be impacted by community property rules, even when there is no impact for federal purposes. For example, if one spouse is a nonresident of New Mexico, then his or her share of community interest income might be allocated outside of New Mexico, while for the spouse that is a resident of New Mexico, his or her share of interest income would be allocated to New Mexico. See ¶ 9.3.7 for a discussion of the allocation of community property income.

The reporting of income under federal rules is impacted by community income when married taxpayers file separately. In such cases, it is necessary to determine the amount of income allocable to each spouse under community property rules. IRS Form 8958, *Allocation of Tax Amounts between Certain Individuals in Community Property States*, is essentially a worksheet that allows taxpayer to break down community income between spouses for these purposes. This worksheet should be provided with Form 1040 to the New Mexico return. Spouses are taxed only on the community income that is allocated to each of them. New Mexico automatically follows federal rules with regard to this allocation since such allocations are reflected in AGI. In some cases, however, such as with regard to federal interest income that is not taxed by New Mexico or interest from state and local obligations that are taxed by New Mexico but not by the federal government, the adjustment taxpayers must make to AGI on the New Mexico Form PIT-1 must take into account the appropriate allocations under community property rules. Similarly, the deduction for capital gains must be allocated based on community property rules.

Under federal rules, interest, dividends, and rents from community property are community income and are evenly split. Gains and losses from the disposition of property are classified as community or separate depending on how the property is held. Distributions from IRAs are deemed to be separate property, even if the funds in the account would otherwise be community property, and such distributions are wholly taxable to the spouse whose name is on the account, who is also liable for any penalties and additional taxes on the distributions. Generally, distributions from pensions are characterized as community or separate income, depending on the respective periods of participation in the pension while either married and domiciled in a community property state or in a noncommunity property state. If an

Taxable Income and Net Income

interest is held in a partnership, and income from the partnership is attributable to the efforts of either spouse, the partnership income is community property. Community income that is exempt from federal tax generally keeps its exempt status for both spouses.

In addition to splitting up community income, under federal rules married couples must also appropriately allocate their deductions. New Mexico has incorporated these allocations in its tax system by the adoption of federal AGI and the federal itemized deductions. When taxpayers file separate returns, the allocation of deductions generally depends on whether the expenses involve community or separate income. Expenses incurred to earn or produce community business or investment income are generally divided equally between spouses. Each spouse is entitled to deduct one-half of the expenses on their separate returns. Expenses associated with separate business or investment income are deductible by the spouse who earns the income.[39] Deductions for IRA contributions are not split between spouses. The deduction for each spouse is figured separately and without regard to community property laws. Expenses that are paid out of separate funds, such as medical expenses, are deductible by the spouse who pays them. If these expenses are paid from community funds, the deduction is divided equally between spouses. The deductible portion of the self-employment tax is split only when the spouses split the self-employment income. With regard to net income from a trade or business (other than a partnership) that is community income, self-employment tax is imposed on the spouse carrying on the trade or business. All of the distributive share of a married partner's income or loss from a partnership trade or business is attributable to the partner for computing any self-employment tax, even if a portion of the partner's distributive share of income or loss is community income or loss that is attributable to the partner's spouse for income tax purposes. If both spouses are partners, any self-employment tax is allocated based on their distributive shares.

There is a federal exception to the community property rules when spouses live apart for a tax year and one or both have earned income that is community income. If such individuals are married to each other at any time during a calendar year and do not file a joint return, any community income of such individuals for the calendar year is treated as income of the spouse who earned the income if the spouses

---

[39] Other limits may apply to the deductibility and allocation of business and investment expenses. See IRS Publication 535, *Business Expenses* (2016), Publication 550, *Investment Income and* Expenses (2015), and Publication 555, *Community Property* (2016).

live apart at all times during the year and no portion of such earned income is transferred (directly or indirectly) between them during the year.[40] This rule applies in New Mexico as well.

An individual may be relieved of reporting community income if he or she does not file a joint return for any tax year, does not include in gross income an item of community income that is properly includible, but which pursuant to federal allocation rules (see IRC §879(a))[41] would be treated as income attributed to the other spouse, establishes that he or she did not know of, and had no reason to know of, such item of community income, and, taking into account all facts and circumstances, it is inequitable to include such item of community income in such individual's gross income. In this case, such income is included in the gross income of the other spouse.[42] In addition, if under all the facts and circumstances, it is inequitable to hold an individual liable for any unpaid tax or any deficiency (or any portion of either) attributable to any item for which relief is not available under the above rule, the Secretary of the Treasury may relieve such individual of such liability.

Moreover, the application of the community property rules may be disallowed if a taxpayer acted as if he or she was solely entitled to an item income and did not notify his or her spouse of the nature and amount of the income before the due date (including extensions) for filing the return for the tax year in which the income was derived.[43] In this case, the taxpayer will have to report all of the community income for that item for the tax year.

---

[40] IRC §66(a).
[41] For example, IRC §879(a)(1) assigns earned income to the spouse who rendered the personal services and IRC §879(a)(2) in dealing with trade or business gross income and deductions cross references IRC §1402(a)(5) which allocates income and deduction to the spouse who carries on the trade or business, except if they carry on the business jointly, in which case income and deductions are allocated according to distributive shares.
[42] IRC §66(c).
[43] IRC §66(b).

CHAPTER 8
ADJUSTMENTS TO ADJUSTED GROSS INCOME

¶ 8.1 Overview

As discussed elsewhere in this text, New Mexico taxable income is determined on Form PIT-1 by starting with AGI and then making adjustments that reflect New Mexico tax policies and US constitutional limits on New Mexico's taxing power. Five adjustments to AGI are made directly on Form PIT-1 (and described in Chapter 7) and the remainder are made on Schedule PIT-ADJ. The adjustments on Schedule PIT-ADJ, which are the subject of this chapter, are categorized as either additions to AGI or deductions and exemptions from AGI. In determining these adjustments, taxpayers must take into account the impact of the community property rules in New Mexico when computing the amount of adjustment for each spouse of a married couple when they are filing separate returns. See ¶ 7.8 for a discussion of community property rules. The following discussion of the adjustments to AGI follows the format of Schedule PIT-ADJ.

¶ 8.2 New Mexico additions to AGI on Schedule PIT-ADJ

The sum of additions to AGI discussed in ¶¶ 8.2.1 to 8.2.4 is entered on line 5 of Schedule PIT-ADJ and then transferred to Form PIT-1, line 11.

¶ 8.2.1 Interest and dividends from federal tax-exempt bonds - line 1

Unlike the federal tax rules which exempt income earned on or received from certain state and local obligations, New Mexico taxes the income from investments in state and local bonds. If excluded from federal AGI, such federally exempt interest income is entered on line 1 of Schedule PIT-ADJ, as a New Mexico addition to AGI.[1] Apparently, the term "state or local bond" includes any obligation of the Commonwealth of Puerto Rico or of territories or possessions of the United States.[2] Although New Mexico is prohibited from taxing the income from such obligations by the laws of the United States, the income from such obligations are deducted on line 6. Since they are added to AGI on line 1 and subtracted from AGI on line 6, the net result is that such income is not taxable in New Mexico.

Income from state or local bonds is to be included in income in the year it is actually received without regard to federal tax treatment of the income, except that:

- the taxpayer may elect to report this income for New Mexico purposes on an accrual basis; and
- income is earned or accrued ratably, by assigning an equal amount of income to each day of the accrual period.[5]

Bonds issued by Indian tribal governments are not "state or local bonds" under the ITA. The term "state" does not include Indian nations, tribes or pueblos or their governments. The term "local government" is not defined by the ITA but is commonly used to mean political subdivisions of states. Indian nations, tribes and pueblos are not political subdivisions of states.

To the extent that the Internal Revenue Code treats interest from bonds issued by Indian tribal governments as if it were interest from "state or local bonds", such interest is excluded from AGI. Because bonds issued by Indian tribal governments are not "state or local bonds" for purposes of the ITA, interest income with respect to such bonds is not required to be added to AGI in determining New Mexico

---

[1] §7-2-2V NMSA 1978. The instructions for Line 1 of Schedule PIT-ADJ differs from the statutory rule. Under §7-2-2V a state and local obligation *does not* include an obligation of the state of New Mexico or a subdivision and interest from such obligation should not be added back to AGI. Nevertheless, the instructions to Line 1 require that interest on a New Mexico obligation be added back to AGI. The TRD makes up for this by allowing a taxpayer to deduct the interest income from such obligations on line 6. See Chapter 7, n. 8 for more details.

[2] Guam, 48 USC 1423a: Puerto Rico, 48 USC 745: Virgin Islands, 48 USC 1403: Northern Mariana Islands, 48 USC 1681(c).

[5] §3.3.1.12E NMAC.

Adjustments to Adjusted Gross Income

taxable income.[6]

Since income from state and local bonds is subject to New Mexico taxation, expenses related to earning this income are deductible. To the extent that such expenses have not been deducted in determining federal taxable income, the tax regulations provide that these amounts may be subtracted from net income. The instructions to Schedule PIT-ADJ do not explain how to obtain this deduction. Perhaps a taxpayer can reduce the amount of state and local bond income that is entered on line 1 by the amount of these expenses.[7]

¶8.2.2 Federal net operating loss carryover deduction - line 2

The rules for applying a net operating loss deduction to New Mexico taxable income differ from the federal rules. In order to put the New Mexico rules in effect, the federal net operating loss carryover deduction is added back on Schedule PIT-ADJ, line 2 and the New Mexico net operating loss carryover deduction is entered on PIT-ADJ, line 7. See the discussion related to line 7 for more details.

¶8.2.3. Contributions refunded when closing a New Mexico-approved §529 account and certain contributions rolled out of a New Mexico-approved §529- line 3

Unlike the federal government, New Mexico allows a deduction for contributions to a Section 529 college savings plan. As a result, unqualified withdrawals or withdrawals spent for nonqualified higher education expenses, as well as refunds from the New Mexico Education Trust Fund account, are subject to tax in the year in which they are received and entered on line 3 to the extent not included in federal AGI.

> *In Practice:* Income on contributions to a 529 plan is permitted to be accumulated tax-free for federal income tax purposes, and remains so provided that the distributions when made are used for qualified education expenses. To the extent distributions and withdrawals are not so qualified the income earned on the contributed amounts will be included in federal AGI. Thus, for state tax purposes, these amounts should not be included in the New Mexico adjustment. See ¶ 8.3.9 for a discussion of New Mexico taxation of §529 plans.

---

[6] See Chapter 7, n.8.
[7] §3.3.1.12D(2) NMAC.

¶ 8.2.4 Charitable deduction amount claimed on federal Form 1040, Schedule A, for a donation of land to private non-profit or public conservation agencies, for conservation purposes, for which the New Mexico Land Conservation Tax Credit was allowed - line 4.

Taxpayers who claim a federal charitable tax deduction for a contribution for which the New Mexico land conservation tax credit is also claimed, must reduce their New Mexico itemized deductions by the amount of the federal deduction. See discussion at ¶ 11.4. The Schedule PIT-ADJ instructions provide the following worksheet to help compute the amount of the adjustment, which is entered on Schedule PIT-ADJ, line 4.

Adjustments to Adjusted Gross Income

Worksheet for computing the Charitable Deduction Amount claimed on Federal Form 1040, Schedule A, from which you were allowed the New Mexico Land Conservation Tax Credit	
1. Enter the charitable deduction you claimed on federal Form 1040, for a donation of land to private non-profit or public conservation agencies for conservation purposes from which you were allowed the New Mexico Land Conservation Tax Credit.	$
2. Enter your total itemized deductions from federal Form 1040, line 40.	$
3. Enter the sum of the amounts you reported on federal Form 1040, Schedule A, lines 4, 9, 15, 19, 20, 27, and 28.	$
4. Divide line 2 by line 3. Round to 4 decimal places.	%
5. Multiply line 4 by line 1.	$
6. Enter the standard deduction amount you could have claimed on federal Form 1040, line 40, if you had not itemized your federal allowable deductions.	$
7. Add the amount entered on Form PIT-1, line 10, if any, to line 6 and enter the result here; otherwise, enter the amount from line 6.	$
8. Subtract line 7 from line 2. If less than zero, enter zero.	$
9. Enter the lesser of lines 5 and 8. **Also enter this amount on PIT-ADJ, line 4.**	

¶ 8.3 New Mexico deductions and exemptions from AGI on Schedule PIT-ADJ

The sum of the deductions and exemptions discussed below in ¶¶ 8.3.1 to 8.3.16 is entered on line 22 of Schedule PIT-ADJ and transferred to Form PIT-1, line 15.

¶ 8.3.1 New Mexico tax-exempt interest and dividends - line 6

The instructions to Schedule PIT-ADJ lists interest income from the following types of investments as tax exempt and require that they be entered on line 6:

- State and local bonds exempt from New Mexico taxable income, including the State of New Mexico or its agencies, institutions, instrumentalities, or political subdivisions;
- Obligations of the Commonwealth of Puerto Rico, Guam, Virgin Islands, American Samoa, or Northern Mariana Islands other territories or possessions of the United States;[8]
- Federally taxable bonds issued by the State of New Mexico;[9] and
- Mutual funds, unit investment trusts, or simple trusts invested in obligations of the State of Mexico or its agencies, institutions, instrumentalities, or political subdivisions, or from the Commonwealth of Puerto Rico, Guam, Virgin Islands, American Samoa, or Northern Mariana Islands. [10] See Table 8.1 for description of excluded income from mutual funds.[11]

The instructions to line 1 state that if line 6 is greater than line 1, an explanation should be attached to the return. This circumstance may occur if interest income from a New Mexico obligation is taxable for federal purposes but exempt for New Mexico purposes. The federal government taxes certain private activity bonds, arbitrage bonds, and unregistered bonds and the interest from these bonds are not added on line 1 because they are not excluded from AGI. Since the state does not have the same limitations on taxability as does the federal

---

[8] §3.3.1.12B NMAC.
[9] The statutory authority for this exemption is not obvious to the author.
[10] N.M. Const. art. VIII, §3
[11] See 2016 PIT-ADJ New Mexico Schedule of Additions, Deductions, and Exemptions Instructions, p. 2A.

Adjustments to Adjusted Gross Income

government, the taxable interest from New Mexico bonds that are taxed federally and included in AGI would be deducted on line 6.[12] Therefore, in this case the amount on line 6 would be greater than the amount on line 1.

¶ 8.3.2 New Mexico net operating loss – line 7

There are a number of differences between the computation of the New Mexico NOL and the federal NOL. For example, New Mexico allows net operating losses (NOLs) to be carried forward and deducted in years after the loss occurred; but carrybacks of NOLs are not allowed as they are under federal rules. Another difference involves interest earned on obligations of the United States. Because such interest income is not taxable in New Mexico, any such exclusion of interest income may serve either to increase or create[13] a New Mexico NOL.

A New Mexico NOL incurred in tax years after January 1, 2013 cannot be carried back but may be carried forward for 19 years or until the total amount of the loss carryover has been used, whichever occurs first. A New Mexico NOL incurred in tax years after 1990, but before December 31, 2012, may only be carried forward for five years. For tax years beginning prior to January 1, 1991, a NOL could be carried forward or carried back to any other tax year beginning prior to January 1, 1991, in accordance with the provisions of the Internal Revenue Code.[14]

In order to deduct an NOL, a taxpayer must establish the NOL for the year of loss by the filing of a return for that year, either original or amended, within the time period allowed for filing.[15]

The first year a New Mexico NOL can be applied is the year following the loss (if the return was filed on time) or the first tax year that begins after the date the return establishing the loss is filed.

---

[12] IRC §103.
[13] If the exclusion of income from obligations of the United States results in a negative amount of New Mexico net income, the resulting negative amount may be deemed to be a NOL for that tax year. §3.3.1.13A(2) NMAC.
[14] §3.3.1.13E(1) NMAC.
[15] See subsections B, C and E of §7-1-26 NMSA 1978 for applicable time periods.

The NOL deduction is reflected in the Schedule PIT-ADJ as follows:

- On PIT-ADJ, line 2, the amount of the federal NOL deduction is added to AGI.[16]
- On PIT-ADJ, line 7, the New Mexico NOL deduction is subtracted from AGI.[17]

The New Mexico NOL is calculated by adding the federal NOL and any interest received on U.S. government obligations less related expenses reported on the New Mexico tax return for the tax year of the loss. From this total is subtracted any loss used in earlier tax years. The calculation of the amount of the NOL for a particular year and the amount of carry forward is calculated on Form RPD-41369, *New Mexico Net Operating Loss Carryforward Schedule for Personal Income Tax*, which is attached to the return.

The NOL carryover of an unincorporated business acquired by the taxpayer, or otherwise included in the taxpayer's return for a tax year, as for example through a change in reporting method, may be deducted from New Mexico income only to the extent that a deduction for that tax year would be permitted under federal rules.[18]

¶ 8.3.3 Interest received on U.S. Government obligations – line 8

Income from obligations issued by the United States are not includable in income and are entered on line 8.[19] These obligations include –

- U.S. savings bonds
- Treasury bills
- Notes issued by the Federal Home Loan Banks (but not dividends)
- U.S. government obligations from the taxpayer's share of income from partnerships, S corporations, or limited liability companies, or

---

[16] §7-2-2B(2) NMSA 1978. Technically, the add back is made to AGI to reach base income. See ¶7.3.1.
[17] §§7-2-2N(7) and (8) NMSA 1978. Technically, the deduction is made from base income to reach net income. See ¶7.3.1.
[18] §3.3.1.13C NMAC.
[19] §3.3.1.12A(1) NMAC.

Adjustments to Adjusted Gross Income

a distribution from a unit investment or simple trust

In case of income from mutual funds, see Table 8.1.

However, the following *are not* obligations of the United States, and the income from these arrangements are includable in income:

- financial instruments guaranteed by the federal national mortgage association ("Fannie Maes"), the government national mortgage association ("Ginnie Maes"), the federal national home loan association ("Freddie Macs") and any similar organization the income from which states are not prohibited by federal law from subjecting to income taxation;
- financial instruments issued by the College Construction Loan Insurance Corporation or the National Consumer Cooperative Bank;
- agreements ("repo's") to sell and repurchase United States government obligations; and
- agreements ("reverse repo's") to purchase and resell United States government obligations.[20]

---

[20] §3.3.1.12A(2) NMAC. This paragraph is retroactively effective for tax years beginning on or after January 1, 1991. §3.3.1.12A(3) NMAC.

Table 8.1 – Exclusion of income from mutual funds or trusts
Income from investments in investment funds (including dividends) may be deducted where the following conditions are met:
1. The fund is a mutual fund, unit investment trust, or simple trust,
2. The income is from obligations of – • the United States; • the state of New Mexico or any of its agencies, institutions, instrumentalities or political subdivisions; • the commonwealth of Puerto Rico, the income from which obligations states are prohibited from taxing by the laws of the United States; and • Guam, the Virgin Islands, American Samoa, Northern Mariana Islands or other territories or possessions of the United States, the income from which obligations states are prohibited from taxing by the laws of the United States; and
3. The mutual fund provides the investor an annual statement of the income, by source, which was distributed to the individual investor; and the trust provides to the beneficiary an annual statement of the income by source and that the income received by the beneficiary retains the same character as that income had when earned by the trust. Only that amount of income may be deducted which is shown on the statement as flowing through to the investor.[21]

Investment expenses relating to the exempt interest income may not be deducted from income. If such expenses have been deducted in determining federal taxable income, the amount must be added back.[22]

Expenses related to the earning of income from investments in state or local bonds other than New Mexico, made directly or through mutual funds, unit investment trusts or simple trusts, are deductible in determining income. To the extent that such expenses have not been deducted in determining federal taxable income, these amounts may be deducted.

¶8.3.4 Taxable Railroad Retirement Act annuities and benefits, and taxable Railroad Unemployment Insurance Act sick pay - line 9

Federal law exempts Railroad Retirement Act benefits from state taxation. If Railroad Retirement Act annuities and benefits, or taxable

---

[21] §3.3.1.12C NMAC.
[22] §3.3.1.12D NMAC.

Adjustments to Adjusted Gross Income

Railroad Unemployment Insurance Act sick pay are part of a taxpayer's federal taxable income, the total of those amounts is entered in line 9.[23]

Taxpayers should attach any Forms RRB-1099 and RRB- 1099-R to the return.

¶ 8.3.5 Income of a member of a New Mexico federally-recognized Indian nation, tribe, or pueblo that was wholly earned on the lands of the reservation or pueblo of which the individual is an enrolled member while domiciled on that land, reservation, or pueblo - line 10

The income earned by a member of a New Mexico federally recognized Indian nation, tribe, band or pueblo, and his or her spouse or dependent, who is a member of a New Mexico federally recognized Indian nation, tribe, band or pueblo, is exempt from state income tax in certain cases.[24] See ¶ 4.3.5.

The amount of qualifying exempt income is entered on line 10.

¶8.3.6 Income of persons age 100 years or older - line 11

The income of an individual who is one hundred years of age or older and who is not a dependent of another individual is exempt from state income tax.[25] If the individual is married, the taxpayer must determine the amount of his or her community and separate income, as only the income of centenarian qualifies for the exemption. See ¶ 7.8 for a discussion of community property and income.

If a taxpayer reports an exemption for more or less than 50% of total joint income, a statement in support must be attached to the return showing a correct division of community property along with separate income and payments.[26]

¶ 8.3.7 Exemption for persons age 65 or older, or blind - line 12

As presented in the table below, an individual who is either sixty-five

---

[23] 2016 PIT-ADJ New Mexico Schedule of Additions, Deductions, and Exemptions Instructions, p. 4A.
[24] §7-2-5.5 NMSA 1978.
[25] §7-2-5.7 NMSA 1978.
[26] 2016 PIT-ADJ New Mexico Schedule of Additions, Deductions, and Exemptions Instructions, p. 5A.

New Mexico Personal Income Tax Guide

years of age or older or blind for federal income tax purposes may claim an additional exemption amount determined by the level of the taxpayer's AGI and marital status. The exemption may not exceed $8,000 per individual.[27] Both the husband and wife can claim the exemption on a joint return if they are both 65 or older or blind on the last day of the tax year. One exemption is allowed per person and one person cannot take exemptions for being both 65 or older and blind. Individuals having income both within and without the state must apportion this exemption.[28]

TABLE 1. Exemptions for Persons 65 or Older or Blind (see line 12 instructions)						
Married Filing Jointly, Head of Household, Qualifying Widow(er)		**Single**		**Married Filing Separately**		**Amount for each taxpayer 65 or older, or blind, for federal income tax purposes**
Adjusted Gross Income PIT-1 Return, Line 9		Adjusted Gross Income PIT-1 Return, Line 9		Adjusted Gross Income PIT-1 Return, Line 9		
$	But not Over	$	But not Over	$	But not Over	
0	$30,000	0	$18,000	0	$15,000	--------$ 8,000
30,001	33,000	18,001	19,500	15,001	16,500	-------- 7,000
33,001	36,000	19,501	21,000	16,501	18,000	-------- 6,000
36,001	39,000	21,001	22,500	18,001	19,500	-------- 5,000
39,001	42,000	22,501	24,000	19,501	21,000	-------- 4,000
42,001	45,000	24,001	25,500	21,001	22,500	-------- 3,000
45,001	48,000	25,501	27,000	22,501	24,000	-------- 2,000
48,001	51,000	27,001	28,500	24,001	25,500	-------- 1,000
51,001	-----------	28,501	-----------	25,501	-----------	-------- 0

Source: Schedule PIT-ADJ, instructions

The instructions to Schedule PIT-ADJ provide the following examples.

> *Example:* A married couple files jointly. Both are 65 or older. Their federal adjusted gross income is $35,000. According to g
>
> If the same couple was also blind, the exemption is still $12,000.
>
> *Example:* A married couple files jointly. The primary taxpayer is 65. The spouse is 45 and blind. Their federal adjusted gross income is $28,000. According to the table above, the exemption

---

[27] §7-2-5.2 NMSA 1978.

[28] For tax years beginning on or after January 1, 1990, apportionment of the deduction is accomplished through the process of determining the tax due pursuant to § 7-2-11C NMSA 1978. Accordingly, the regulations provide that no separate apportionment process is necessary. §3.3.4.9 NMAC. However, see ¶9.3.1 for a discussion of a different view of allocation and apportionment of deductions and exemptions.

Adjustments to Adjusted Gross Income

is $16,000 or $8,000 x 2.

¶ 8.3.8 Exemption for New Mexico medical care savings account- line 13

Employers, including self-employed individuals, may establish a medical care savings account program (NMMSA) that will –

- provide a qualified higher deductible (individual or family) health plan (HDHP) for the benefit of employees;
- contribute to medical care savings accounts for employees; and
- appoint an account administrator to administer the savings accounts.[29]

The governing instrument must provide that only cash contributions will be accepted, and that a contribution, when added to previous contributions to the trust for the calendar year, must not exceed 75% of the highest annual limit deductible permitted.[30]

The funds from the NMMSA are used to pay employee's unreimbursed medical care expenses. Any principal contributed to and interest earned on a NMMSA and money paid or distributed for eligible medical expenses are exempt from taxation.[31] Any amounts advanced interest free to an employee by an employer for medical care payments in excess of the employee's balance in his or her account are also exempt if the employee agrees to repay the advance from future installments or when he or she ceases to be an employee or a participant in the program.[32]

An "eligible medical expense" means an expense paid by the employee for medical care that is deductible for federal income tax purposes (as described in §213(d) of the IRC) to the extent that those amounts are not compensated for by insurance or otherwise.[33]

Generally, if an employee withdraws money from the employee's NMMSA that is not used exclusively to pay eligible medical expenses of the employee or a dependent, it is included in the gross income of

---

[29] §59A-23D-4 NMSA 1978.
[30] §59A-23D-2I NMSA 1978.
[31] §7-2-5.6 NMSA 1978.
[32] §59A-23D-5D NMSA 1978; §7-2-5.6 NMSA 1978.
[33] §59A-23D-2F NMSA 1978.

the employee for taxation purposes. However, an employee may withdraw money without penalty from his medical care savings account for a purpose other than payment of eligible medical expenses when the employee attains the age to receive medical benefits under the Social Security Act (as specified in §1811 of the Social Security Act). An employee may also withdraw money without penalty for payment of coverage for:

- a health plan during any period of continuation coverage required under any federal law;
- a qualified long-term care insurance contract (as defined by §7702B(6) of the IRC; or
- a health plan during a period in which the person is receiving unemployment compensation under any federal or state law.

An exemption from New Mexico taxable income may not be claimed if a qualified contribution, earnings, or distribution is excluded, exempted or deducted from federal taxable income.[35] Otherwise there would be a double benefit to taxpayers. Conversely, a taxpayer qualifies for a deduction if exempt amounts have been included in federal taxable income. Exempt amounts included in federal taxable income may be deducted and reported on line 13.

The exemption does not apply to excess contributions, unqualified distributions, or money rolled over into another medical savings account.

¶ 8.3.9 Deduction for contributions to a New Mexico-approved Section 529 college savings plan - line 14

New Mexico has established the New Mexico Education Trust Fund to allow New Mexico taxpayers to take advantage of IRC Section 529, under which savings for education may earn income that is federally tax-exempt.[36] Since the tax-exempt income from a Section 529 plan is excluded from AGI, such income is also not taxed in New Mexico. In the case of payments to such a trust, they are not deductible for federal tax purposes, but they are deductible under the New Mexico PIT.[37]

---

[35] 2016 PIT-ADJ New Mexico Schedule of Additions, Deductions, and Exemptions Instructions, 5A.
[36] §21-21K-3 NMSA 1978.
[37] §7-2-32 NMSA 1978. See TRD, Brochure #6, New Mexico Income Tax and Your

Adjustments to Adjusted Gross Income

This difference in treatment is why the amount of the contribution must be entered as a deduction on line 14.

The amount of payments made for any one beneficiary may not exceed in the aggregate the cost of attendance at the applicable institution of higher education, as determined by the Education Trust Board.

A taxpayer and spouse who file separate returns may each claim one-half of the deduction allowed on a joint return.

A tax deductible contribution includes the principal and earnings of amounts rolled over to a New Mexico-approved Section 529 college savings plan account from a non-New Mexico-approved Section 529 college savings plan.

Individuals having income both within and without this state must apportion this deduction in accordance with regulations of the TRD.[38]

¶ 8.3.10 Net Capital Gains Deduction - line 15

To encourage capital investment in New Mexico, the state provides a tax deduction for net capital gain.[39] In defining net capital gain, New Mexico adopts the definition used in the federal tax code, which defines net capital gain as the excess of the net long-term capital gain for the tax year over the net short-term capital loss for such year.[40]

A taxpayer may claim a deduction from net income in an amount equal to the greater of:

1. The taxpayer's net capital gain income for the tax year for which the deduction is being claimed, but not to exceed $1,000; or
2. The following percentage of the taxpayer's net capital gain income for the tax year for which the deduction is being claimed:
    a. for a tax year beginning in 2003, 10%;
    b. for a tax year beginning in 2004, 20%;
    c. for a tax year beginning in 2005, 30%;

---

[38] Education Trust (529) Plan (Rev. 4/14).
No such regulations currently exist. See ¶9.3.1 for a discussion of allocation and apportionment of deductions..
[39] Enacted into law in 2003.
[40] IRC §1222(11).

d. for a tax year beginning in 2006, 40%; and
e. for tax years beginning on or after January 1, 2007, 50%.[41]

A husband and wife who file separate returns for a tax year in which they could have filed a joint return may each claim only one-half of the deduction that would have been allowed on the joint return.

A taxpayer who has claimed the venture capital investment credit may not also claim the capital gain deduction.[42]

¶ 8.3.11 Armed forces active duty pay - line 16

New Mexico exempts from state income taxation the salary paid by the United States to a taxpayer for active duty service in the armed forces of the United States.[43] If a taxpayer's wages, or salaries for U.S. Armed Forces active duty service were included in AGI, that amount included is entered as a deduction on line 16.

The Armed forces includes the Army, Navy, Air Force, Marine Corps, and Coast Guard. As described in ¶ 6.1.1, active duty means full-time duty in active service and includes the following:

- Full-time training duty
- Annual training duty
- Full-time National Guard duty
- Attendance, while in active service, at a school designated as a service school by law or by the Secretary of the service.[44]

This exemption applies to residents and to non-residents of New Mexico.

As noted in ¶ 6.1.1, the TRD has ruled that the tax exemption applicable to active armed services personnel does not apply to members of the United States Public Health Service.[46] In support of this ruling, the hearing officer cited the definition of armed services

---

[41] §7-2-34 NMSA 1978.
[42] §7- 2D-8.1 NMSA 1978.
[43] §7-2-5.11 NMSA 1978.
[44] 37 USC 101. See 2016 PIT-ADJ New Mexico Schedule of Additions, Deductions, and Exemptions Instructions, p. 6A.
[46] In The Matter of The Protest Of Thomas & Leslie Hammack To Assessments Issued Under Letter Id Nos. L12048697296, L1504781776, L0967910864, L1576867280, & L1039996368, Decision 15-02 of Hearing Officer of TRD.

Adjustments to Adjusted Gross Income

found in the TRD regulations regarding residency, which included only servicemembers of the USPHS that were detailed to the army and navy.[47] However, the New Mexico income from active duty service of a *nonresident* servicemember of the USPHS is exempt from New Mexico tax. See discussion of line 21, below.

See Chapter 6 for a discussion of the New Mexico tax treatment of military personnel.

¶ 8.3.12 Medical care expense exemption for persons age 65 years or older - line 17

An individual 65 or older is entitled to a $3,000 income exemption (to be entered on line 17) if the individual pays medical care expenses exceeding $28,000 for the individual or the individual's spouse or dependent during the tax year,[48] and if these expenses are unreimbursed by insurance or otherwise.

The term "medical care" has the same meaning that is applicable with regard to the deduction for unreimbursed or uncompensated medical care expenses on Form PIT-1, line 16. See ¶ 7.5.

The definition of "dependent" is the same as that used for federal tax purposes.[49]

Taxpayers eligible for this exemption are also eligible to claim the refundable medical care credit for persons 65 or older. See ¶ 13.7.

¶8.3.13 Deduction for organ donation-related expenses - line 18

A taxpayer may deduct from income organ donation-related expenses in an amount not to exceed $10,000. Organ donation-related expenses include lost wages, lodging expenses and travel expenses incurred during the tax year by the taxpayer or the taxpayer's dependent as a result of the taxpayer's or dependent's donation of a human organ to another person for transfer of that human organ to the body of another person.[50] A "human organ" is all or part of a heart, liver, pancreas, kidney, intestine, lung or bone marrow. The meaning of the

---

[47] §3.3.1.9D(5) NMAC.
[48] 7-2-5.9 NMSA 1978.
[49] IRC §152.
[50] §7-2-36 NMSA 1978.

term "dependent" is the same as under federal rules.[51]

A husband and wife who file separate returns for a tax year in which they could have filed a joint return may each claim only one-half of the deduction that would have been allowed on a joint return.

¶8.3.14 New Mexico National Guard member life insurance reimbursements tax exemption – line 19

An individual who receives a reimbursement from the Service Members' Life Insurance Reimbursement Fund may claim an exemption of the amount of the reimbursement by entering that amount on line 19.[52]

The "Service Members' Life Insurance Reimbursement Fund" is a nonreverting fund in the state treasury consisting of: legislative appropriations to the fund; gifts, grants, donations and bequests to the fund; and income from investment of the fund. The fund is administered by the Department of Military Affairs, and money in the fund is appropriated for the purpose of reimbursing eligible members of the New Mexico national guard for premiums paid for benefits under the Service Members' Group Life Insurance Program.[53]

The New Mexico Office of Military Affairs issues the reimbursement and sends each recipient a Form 1099-MISC, which should be attached to the income tax return.

¶ 8.3.15 Taxable refunds, credits, or offsets of state and local income taxes from line 10, federal Form 1040 - line 20

Taxpayers who itemize deductions on their federal returns receive a similar New Mexico tax deduction on Form PIT-1, line 12, except that state and local income and sales taxes are not deductible, and must be added back on line 10. See ¶ 7.6. When an itemizing taxpayer receives a refund of state and local taxes, that refund is included in federal AGI, on Form 1040, line 10. Since New Mexico itemizers do not receive the benefit of a deduction of state and local taxes, it would be inequitable to have them include in income the amount of the refund of such taxes.

---

[51] IRC §152.
[52] §7-2-5.10 NMSA 1978.
[53] §20-4-7.3 NMSA 1978.

Adjustments to Adjusted Gross Income

Accordingly, New Mexico allows a deduction that equals the amount included in AGI that represents a refund of state and local income and sales taxes that were deducted for federal tax purposes. The deduction has been available starting with taxable years beginning on our after January 1, 2011.[54] The instructions to Schedule PIT-ADJ state that to qualify, a taxpayer must have itemized deductions and included the refunds, credits, or offsets in AGI on a prior year federal Form 1040, Schedule A.[55] See ¶ 7.6 a further discussion of the calculation of the deduction.

¶8.3.16 Non-resident U.S. Public Health Service members' active duty pay - line 21.

The income earned by a nonresident in New Mexico for active duty in the United States Public Health Service is exempt and is entered on line 21 unless it has been excluded from AGI. See ¶ 6.1.3 for a discussion of residency issues concerning military personnel.

If the taxpayer has income from within and without the state, Schedule PIT-B must be completed. In completing that schedule the taxpayer must exclude from line 1, columns 1 and 2, any military wages or salary earned that was included in federal AGI. In this case the total income on line 11, column 1 may be less than the federal AGI reported on Form PIT-1, line 9. The instructions to Schedule PIT-B note that this is not an error.[57]

---

[54] §7-2-2N(9) NMSA 1978.
[55] 2016 PIT-ADJ New Mexico Schedule of Additions, Deductions, and Exemptions Instructions, p.7A
[57] 2015 PIT-B, Instructions, p. 4B.

CHAPTER 9

COMPUTING THE TAX ON TAXABLE INCOME

¶ 9.1 Overview

The ITA provides tax rate schedules to determine a taxpayer's New Mexico income tax liability. There are three schedules that are organized in accordance with federal filing status (which is entered on Form PIT-1, line 7). The three tables are as follows: 1) for married taxpayers filing jointly, surviving spouses and heads of households; 2) for taxpayers filing as single individuals; and 3) for married people filing separate returns. Whereas there are four federal tax rate schedules, New Mexico has only three, as there is no separate table for taxpayers filing as the head of household.

The tax rates from tax rate schedules are applied against taxable income. However, if a taxpayer has income that is taxable within and without New Mexico, then Schedule PIT-B, discussed below, is used to compute the tax. Schedule PIT-B uses the same ITA rate schedules but effectively provides a credit for the tax related to income from sources outside New Mexico by computing the New Mexico tax liability on a proportionate basis.

Lump sum amounts received by the taxpayer from a qualified retirement plan are treated separately and are taxed based on a five-year averaging convention. The taxpayer's total liability is the combination of the tax on taxable income and the tax on the taxpayer's lump sum amount, if any.

¶ 9.2 Individual income tax rate schedules and tax

¶ 9.2.1 Tax rate schedules

The rates of the tax schedules are graduated, starting out at 1.7% and topping out at a maximum rate of 4.9%. However, the band of progressivity is very narrow as the top rate is reached at $24,000 for married couples filing jointly, $16,000 for single people, and $12,000 for those who are married filing separately. The following are the ITA tax rate schedules for tax years beginning on or after January 1, 2008:

For married individuals filing separate returns:

If taxable income is:	The tax is:
Not over $4,000	1.7% of taxable income
Over $4,000 but not over $8,000	$68.00, plus 3.2% of the excess over $4,000
Over $8,000 but not over $12,000	$196, plus 4.7% of the excess over $8,000
Over $12,000	$384, plus 4.9% of the excess over $12,000.

For heads of household, surviving spouses, and married individuals filing joint returns:

If taxable income is:	The tax is:
Not over $8,000	1.7% of taxable income
Over $8,000 but not over $16,000	$136, plus 3.2% of the excess over $8,000
Over $16,000 but not over $24,000	$392, plus 4.7% of the excess over $16,000
Over $24,000	$768, plus 4.9% of the excess over $24,000

The terms "head of household"[1] and "surviving spouse"[2] have the meanings given to those terms for federal income tax purposes.

For single individuals and for estates and trusts:

If taxable income is:	The tax is:
Not over $5,500	1.7% of taxable income
Over $5,500 but not over $11,000	$93.50, plus 3.2% of the excess over $5,500
Over $11,000 but not over $16,000	$269.50, plus 4.7% of the excess over $11,000
Over $16,000	$504.50 plus 4.9% of the excess over $16,000.

¶ 9.2.2 Tax tables

The tax rates from the ITA tax schedules have been incorporated in

---

[1] §7-2-2H NMSA 1978. See IRC §2(b).
[2] §7-2-2W NMSA 1978. See IRC §2(a).

Computing the Tax on Taxable Income

tax rate tables published by the TRD, which provide a taxpayer's tax liability for each $100 of incremental New Mexico taxable income up to $96,000. A taxpayer who files a personal income tax return on a calendar-year basis is required to use these tables. The tables are included in the TRD's instructions for the personal income tax form PIT-1 for each calendar year.[3]

If line 17, taxable income, is over $96,000, taxpayers must use the following table to compute their tax.

Filing Status	Tax is	Plus	of taxable income in excess of
Single	$4,422.00	4.9%	$96,000
Married filing jointly	$4,294.00	4.9%	$96,000
Married filing separately	$4,498.00	4.9%	$96,000
Head of household	$4,294.00	4.9%	$96,000

¶9.3 Taxpayers with income from sources both within and without New Mexico - Schedule PIT-B

Taxpayers with income from sources both within and without New Mexico must compute their tax using Schedule PIT-B. Schedule PIT-B first calculates a taxpayer's tax on total New Mexico taxable income on Form PIT-1, line 17 using the standard rate tables, and then calculates the tax related to income from New Mexico sources.[4] It calculates the New Mexico tax by multiplying the tax on income from everywhere by a fraction consisting of New Mexico source income in the numerator and total income in the denominator.

Taxpayers determine their New Mexico source income by allocating and apportioning their total income in accordance with the rules set out in the instructions to Schedule PIT-B. A taxpayer's residency status is essential to the allocation process. This process is described below.

When Schedule PIT-B is used to calculate the New Mexico tax liability on Form PIT-1, and the taxpayer also computes a tax on a lump-sum distribution on Form PIT-1, line 19 (see ¶ 9.4), lines 18 and

---

[3] §7-2-7.1 NMSA 1978, §3.3.7.9A NMAC.
[4] §7-4-3 NMSA 1978.

19 are not added together when computing the taxpayer's net New Mexico income tax on Form PIT-1, line 22, as instructed on line 22. Rather, on Schedule PIT-B, the tax on the lump sum distribution is added to the tax on total taxable income and then the sum of the two is subject to the New Mexico percentage calculation. Therefore, it is only necessary to subtract lines 20 and 21 from line 18 on Form PIT-1 and to determine the net New Mexico tax liability on line 22.

¶ 9.3.1 Allocation and apportionment of income– Schedule PIT-B

When income is taxable both within and without New Mexico, net income must be allocated and apportioned between New Mexico sources and non-New Mexico sources. A taxpayer is taxable in another state if he or she is subject to a net income tax, a franchise tax measured by net income, a franchise tax for the privilege of doing business, or a corporate stock tax, or if that state has jurisdiction to subject the taxpayer to a net income tax, regardless of whether it does.[5]

Allocation is the method by which **nonbusiness income** is determined to be from sources within or without New Mexico.[6] Apportionment is the method by which **business income** is determined to be from sources within or without New Mexico.[7]

The upshot of the allocation and apportionment rules is essentially that New Mexico only taxes New Mexico source income. In computing the tax on New Mexico source income, the statute and the TRD take different paths, although both paths lead to the same amount of tax, with exception for how income is allocated and apportioned, as discussed below. To add to the confusion this creates, the tax return instructions to Schedule PIT-B make reference to a credit, while the form itself does not..[8] However, taxpayers are safe by

---

[5] §7-4-4 NMSA 1978.
[6] §7-4-5 NMSA 1978.
[7] §7-4-10 NMSA 1978.
[8] A paragraph on Page 1B of the instructions to 2016 PIT-B states the following:
PIT-B is for taxpayers with income from sources both inside and outside New Mexico. Schedule PIT-B provides a credit against New Mexico tax equal to the New Mexico source income divided by total income everywhere.
This sentence does not make any sense as it only produces a ratio of New Mexico source income to non-New Mexico source income but does not produce an actual amount of credit.

Computing the Tax on Taxable Income

simply following the calculations of the form.

Under the statutory approach, taxpayers calculate the New Mexico income tax that would be due on their total income, and then are given a credit equal to that amount multiplied by the non-New Mexico percentage.[9] The non-New Mexico percentage is determined by dividing the difference between the taxpayer's net income and the sum of the amounts allocated or apportioned to New Mexico by that net income.[10] As noted previously in Chapter 7, although the ITA imposes a tax on net income, the TRD tax forms do not refer to or calculate net income. The exclusion of this key concept may be one reason that the tax form does not calculate a credit in determining the tax due.

> **The Schedule PIT-B Credit Bypass**
>
> Schedule PIT B does not use a credit mechanism to reach the amount of tax due on New Mexico income as is directed by statute. Instead, the form requires the taxpayer to multiply the amount of total tax by the New Mexico percentage (instead of the non-New Mexico percentage) to determine the New Mexico tax on New Mexico income. In this manner, a credit is not needed because the New Mexico tax on New Mexico income is directly calculated. Therefore, although the statute and the instructions to Schedule PIT-B mention a credit, there is no such credit on the New Mexico tax forms. There should be no difference in result, except for the confusion to those who are looking for the credit on the tax return that is described by the statute and instructions.

As indicated in the note above, Schedule PIT-B does not follow the statutory scheme with regard to providing a credit for taxes related to income from non-New Mexico sources. But this is not the only way in which Schedule PIT-B does not follow the ITA. The ITA requires the allocation and apportionment of *net income*.[11] But Schedule PIT-B does not allocate and apportion net income; instead it allocates and apportions on the basis of AGI. By using AGI instead of net income as the basis for allocation and apportionment, deductions and exemptions that reduce AGI are not taken into account in determining New Mexico and non-New Mexico source income. Since deductions and exemptions may be allocated or apportioned differently than AGI, the result followed by the Schedule PIT-B could yield a different result than that required by the statute. For example, the deduction for

---

[9] §7-2-11C NMSA 1978.
[10] §7-2-11B NMSA 1978.
[11] §7-2-11A(6) NMSA 1978.

159

medical care expense, the low- and middle-income exemption, and adjustments to AGI from Schedule PIT-ADJ might be allocable to New Mexico in a different percentage in determining New Mexico net income than the percentage of New Mexico AGI compared to total AGI. The instructions to Schedule PIT-B and the schedule itself states that residents must allocate all income *and* deductions on lines 1, 2, 3, and 7 fully to New Mexico, but it appears that this allocation only impacts deductions that are involved in calculating AGI and not deductions to reach net income. One can draw this conclusion from Schedule PIT-B, line 11, which states that total income must be equal to or greater than AGI. Therefore, it appears that any deductions that reduce income below AGI are not to be taken into account.

The regulations do address the apportionment of the standard and itemized deductions and personal exemptions and try to resolve the issue by stating that apportionment is accomplished in the process of determining the tax due and the amount of the credit available, and that no separate process is necessary to apportion the standard and itemized deductions and exemption.[12] Apparently the regulations are assuming that the use of AGI for allocation is correct and that the apportionment of the standard and itemized deductions are automatically handled by multiplying the total tax (the calculation of which includes these deductions) by either the New Mexico or non-New Mexico percentage. The regulations only mention apportionment and not allocation, and it is unclear if this is an oversight or intended.

Moreover, the regulations do not address any other deductions or adjustments, and it must be assumed that the approach of the TRD with respect to other deductions and adjustments would be the same as for the standard and itemized deductions and personal exemptions. It should be noted that the ITA gives the Secretary great leeway in setting forth rules for allocation and apportionment of deductions and exemptions. The ITA provides that "other deductions and exemptions allowable in computing net income and not specifically allocated in the Uniform Division of Income for Tax Purposes Act shall be equitably allocated or apportioned in accordance with instructions, rulings or regulations of the secretary."[13] Perhaps this language gives the Secretary the authority to handle allocation and apportionment as

---

[12] §§3.3.11.9; 3.3.4.9; and 3.3.11.10 NMAC.
[13] §7-2-11A(6) NMSA 1978.

Computing the Tax on Taxable Income

provided in Schedule PIT-B.

Of course, taxpayers are safe in following the path of Schedule PIT-B, but planning opportunities and controversy may arise for those who attempt to apportion and allocate on the basis of net income instead of AGI.

¶ 9.3.2 Uniform Division of Income for Tax Purposes Act (UDITPA)

New Mexico has adopted the Uniform Division of Income for Tax Purposes Act (UDITPA) for the purpose of allocating and apportioning income, and the rules of UDITPA govern except where New Mexico statute provides explicit rules or in cases where the UDITPA does not provide any rule.[14] In 1957 the Uniform Law Commission[15] approved UDITPA as a model act. UDITPA provides a uniform method of division of income between states for tax purposes to minimize the likelihood that a taxpayer would be subject to multiple state taxation on his or her income. UDITPA has been adopted by 23 states and the District of Columbia: Alabama, Alaska, Arizona, Arkansas, California, Colorado, District of Columbia, Hawaii, Idaho, Kansas, Kentucky, Maine, Michigan, Minnesota, Missouri, Montana, New Mexico, North Dakota, Oregon, Pennsylvania, South Dakota, Texas, Utah, Washington.

When a New Mexico law describes the treatment of a particular item, that statute overrules UDITPA. In addition, not every item of income is allocated or apportioned by that Act, in which case the item is allocated or apportioned in accordance with New Mexico statute, regulations, instructions, forms, or rulings. Therefore, the New Mexico allocation and apportionment rules are found in the aggregate of these sources.

¶ 9.3.3 Completing Schedule PIT-B

Before Schedule PIT-B can be completed, a taxpayer must first complete PIT-1 through line 17 in order to determine New Mexico taxable income. Schedule PIT-B consists of 14 lines, and 2 columns. One column is for the amount of federal income reported for an item and the second column is for the appropriate amount of New Mexico income for such item. A summary of how each line of the form is

---

[14] §7-4-1 NMSA 1978.
[15] http://www.uniformlaws.org/Default.aspx

completed is described in the following table.

Schedule PIT-B Allocation and Apportionment of Income		
Objective	Line No.	Action
Allocate nonbusiness income	1 to 7	Use rules described in the text below to determine NM source of nonbusiness income
Apportion business income	8	Apportion business income to NM using the apportionment percentage which is determined using three apportionment factors (or the special apportionment factors for manufacturing and headquarters companies) per the worksheet on the second page of the form
Calculate total income and total NM source income	9	Lines 1 to 7 and line 8 are totaled to arrive at total income and total NM source income
Apportion federal adjustments to income	10	Federal adjustments to income (form 1040, line 36, or 1040A, line 20) are entered and apportioned to NM using ratio of NM income to total income on line 9
Compute total income	11	Total income and total NM income are computed by subtracting line 9 from line 10
Determine percentage of NM source income	12	NM source percentage of total income is determined by dividing the NM source income on line 11 by the total income on line 11
Enter tax on NM taxable income	13	The tax on NM taxable income (PIT-1, line 17) is calculated and entered
Enter tax applying NM source percentage	14	NM tax on New Mexico taxable income is determined by multiplying the tax on line 13 by the NM percentage on line 12.

Standard deductions, itemized deductions, and personal exemptions do not enter into the allocation and apportionment process. Since New Mexico taxable income is computed taking into account deductions and exemptions, these deductions are in effect allocated and apportioned and no separate allocation and apportionment of deductions and exemptions is deemed necessary by the TRD. However, the statutory approach is somewhat different than that of Schedule PIT-B, and may produce a different result. See ¶ 9.3.1.

¶ 9.3.4 Allocation of income

Nonbusiness income is aptly defined as income that is not business

Computing the Tax on Taxable Income

income.[16] The appropriate source of nonbusiness income is determined by the process of allocation. The allocation process is simply a designation of income as being sourced to New Mexico or outside New Mexico in accordance to the rules of the statute or other authority. Residency is an important factor in the application of the allocation rules. Most nonbusiness income is sourced to the taxpayer's state of residence. For example, for residents, interest income is allocated to New Mexico while for nonresidents interest income is allocated to sources outside New Mexico.[17] The following is a discussion that describes the allocation rules for various forms of income. The discussion corresponds to the line numbers of page 1 of Schedule PIT-B.

Line 1. Compensation earnings

Compensation received while a New Mexico resident is allocated to New Mexico whether or not such compensation is earned from employment in or outside the state.[18] Compensation of a nonresident is allocated to New Mexico if the compensation is for activities, labor or personal services performed within the state. For nonresidents whose job is located in New Mexico but requires temporary assignment outside of New Mexico, the TRD provides the PIT-110 worksheet, *Adjustment to New Mexico Income*. In addition, New Mexico provides the following three exceptions for allocating the income of nonresidents to New Mexico:

1. *Fifteen-day rule.* If the activities, labor or services are performed in New Mexico no more than 15 days during the tax year, the compensation may be allocated to the taxpayer's state of residence.
2. *Twenty-mile manufacturing rule.* If the compensation is for activities, labor or services performed for a manufacturing business in New Mexico that is located within 20 miles of the Mexico border, has at least 5 full-time employees who are residents of New Mexico, is not receiving development training funds,[19] and qualifies under one of the following four items, the compensation may be allocated to the taxpayer's

---

[16] §7-4-2E NMSA 1978.
[17] §7-2-11A(1) NMSA 1978.
[18] §3.3.11.11 NMAC.
[19] See § 21-19-7 NMSA 1978.

state of residence:

- the business had no payroll in New Mexico during the previous calendar year;
- the business had a payroll in New Mexico for less than the entire previous calendar year, and the first payroll of the new calendar year includes payments to New Mexico residents exceeding the highest monthly payroll for such residents in the previous calendar year;
- the business had a payroll in New Mexico for the entire previous calendar year, and the first payroll of the new calendar year includes payments to New Mexico residents exceeding by at least 10% both the payroll for all employees in January 2001 and the payroll for New Mexico residents 12 months prior to the commencement of the new calendar year; or
- the business had a payroll in New Mexico for the entire prior calendar year, but had no payroll in New Mexico within one year prior to January 1, 2001, and the first payroll of the new calendar year includes payments to New Mexico residents exceeding by at least 10% the payroll for such residents 12 months earlier.

3. *Disaster or emergency-related activities.* If the activities, labor or services are performed in New Mexico for disaster or emergency-related critical infrastructure work in response to a declared state of emergency during a disaster relief period as defined in the Tax Administration Act,[20] the taxpayer's compensation may be allocated to the state of residence.[21]

When completing Schedule PIT-B, nonresident military personnel, including members of the U.S Public Health Service, with income within and without the state, exclude any military wages or salary that was included in federal AGI (and reported on Form PIT-1, line 9) from line 1, columns 1 and 2.[23] These deductions for PIT-B, line 1 may make total income on line 11, column 1 less than the federal AGI on PIT-1,

---

[20] See §7-1-83E(4) NMSA 1978.
[21] §7-2-11A[4] NMSA 1978
[23] 2016 PIT-B New Mexico Allocation and Apportionment of Income Schedule Instructions, p. 4B.

Computing the Tax on Taxable Income

line 9. The instructions to Schedule PIT-B advise that this is not an error.[24]

Line 2. Interest and dividends.

In the case of a resident, interest and dividends are allocated to New Mexico. In the case of a nonresident without a commercial domicile in the state, interest and dividends are not allocated to New Mexico.[25] On Schedule PIT-B, column 1, the total amount of interest and dividends is entered, and the amount allocated to New Mexico is entered in column 2. The instructions to Schedule PIT-B provide the following description of how to allocate interest and dividends.

Column 1
To calculate interest and dividends, follow these steps: 1. Start with the amount of federal taxable dividends and interest on federal Form 1040, 1040A, or 1040EZ. 2. If you have municipal bond income, subtract the New Mexico tax-exempt interest and dividends reported on PIT-ADJ, line 6, from the amount of federal tax-exempt dividends and interest reported on PIT-ADJ, line 1. 3. Add the amounts from steps 1 and 2 and enter the result in line 2, column 1.
Column 2
Resident. Enter the same amount you entered in column 1. …. Nonresident. If you are a nonresident with no commercial domicile (the principal place from where you direct or manage a trade or business) in New Mexico, enter zero. If you operate a business with a commercial domicile in New Mexico, allocate to New Mexico any non-business interest and dividend income from your New Mexico operations.

Line 3. Retirement income (Pensions, annuities, social security, and lump-sum distributions.)

Under federal law, a state may not impose an income tax on any retirement income (see text box below for the definition of retirement income)[26] of an individual who is not a resident or domiciliary of the

---

[24] 2016 PIT-B New Mexico Allocation and Apportionment of Income Schedule Instructions, p. 8B.
[25] §7-4-8 NMSA 1978.
[26] 4 U.S.C. §114(a).

state (as determined under the laws of the state).

The ITA treats retirement income as compensation and in the case of a resident is fully allocable to New Mexico, regardless of the source of the retirement income, where it is paid from, or whether the resident was a resident of New Mexico at the time of the employment which gave rise to the income. Retirement income received by a first-year resident after becoming a resident of New Mexico is allocable to New Mexico. Retirement income of a nonresident is allocable to the nonresident's state of residence regardless of the fact that the income is paid by or derived from a source in New Mexico or the employment giving rise to the income took place in New Mexico. Retirement income received by a first-year resident before the first-year resident becomes a resident of New Mexico is not allocable to New Mexico. [27]

In completing Schedule PIT-B, line 3, residents and nonresidents enter the total amount of pensions, annuities, social security, and lump-sum distributions from the federal return in Column 1. The ordinary income reported on federal Form 4972 is included. In Column 2 residents enter the same amount as in Column 1 and nonresidents enter zero.

---

[27] §3.3.11.13 NMAC.

Computing the Tax on Taxable Income

> **Retirement income** is any income from—
> - a qualified trust under IRC §401(a) and tax exempt under §501(a);
> - a simplified employee pension (IRC §408(k));
> - an annuity plan (IRC §403(a));
> - an annuity contract (IRC §403(b));
> - an individual retirement plan (IRC §7701(a)(37));
> - an eligible deferred compensation plan (IRC §457);
> - a governmental plan (IRC §414(d));
> - a trust described in IRC §501(c)(18);
> - any plan, program, or arrangement described in IRC §3121(v)(2)(C) (or if in writing, providing for retirement payments in recognition of prior service to be made to a retired partner, and is in effect immediately before retirement begins), if such income
>   - is part of a series of substantially equal payments (not less frequently than annually which may include income described above for—
>   - the life or life expectancy of the recipient (or the joint lives or joint life expectancies of the recipient and designated beneficiary; or
>   - a period of not less than 10 years;
> - a payment received after termination of employment and under a plan, program, or arrangement (to which such employment relates) maintained solely for the purpose of providing retirement benefits in excess of the limitations imposed by one or more of IRC §§401(a)(17), 401(k), 401(m), 402(g), 403(b), 408(k), or 415 or any other limitation on contributions or benefits.
>
> Retirement income includes any retired or retainer pay of a member or former member of a uniform service computed under chapter 71 of title 10, United States Code.[28]

Line 4. Rents and royalties.

Net rents and royalties from real property that is located in New Mexico (including rents and royalties from oil and gas interests) are allocated to the state.[29]

Net rents and royalties from tangible personal property are either

---

[28] 4 U.S.C. §114(b)(1).
[29] §7-4-6A NMSA 1978.

partially allocable to the state to the extent that the property is utilized in the state, or in their entirety if the taxpayer's commercial domicile[30] is in the state and the taxpayer is not organized under the laws of or taxable in the state in which the property is utilized.[31]

The utilization of tangible personal property in a state is determined by multiplying the rents and royalties by a fraction, the numerator of which is the number of days the property is physically located in the state during the rental or royalty period in the tax year and the denominator of which is the number of days the property is physically located everywhere during all rental or royalty periods in the tax year. If the physical location of the property during the rental or royalty period is unknown or unascertainable by the taxpayer, tangible personal property is deemed utilized in the state in which the property was located at the time the rental or royalty payer obtained possession.[32]

The instructions to Schedule PIT-B provide the following example.

> **Example.** An out-of-state taxpayer rents a drilling rig to a New Mexico taxpayer. The drilling rig is in New Mexico for 90 days. The rig is rented for a total of 270 days during the tax year in several states. The total rents and royalties everywhere are $25,000,000. The calculation for the line 4, column 2 entry is computed as follows: 90 days located in NM ÷ 270 total days everywhere = 33.3% percent of time in NM x $25,000,000 rents/royalties everywhere. The result is the rent and royalty income allocable to New Mexico. Enter this amount on line 4, column 2.

Royalties from intangibles (copyrights, patents, franchises, trademarks, and licenses) are allocable to New Mexico if and to the extent they are utilized by the payer in the state. In addition, residents allocate income to the state from intangible and tangible personal property used in another state if the resident is not subject to tax on

---

[30] Commercial domicile means the principal place from which the trade or business of the taxpayer is directed or managed. §7-4-2B NMSA 1978.
[31] §7-4-6B NMSA 1978.
[32] §7-4-6C NMSA 1978. The instructions to Schedule PIT-B state it differently. If a taxpayer does not know the extent to which property was located in New Mexico during the rental period, the entire rental or royalty income from those to whom the property was delivered in New Mexico is allocated to New Mexico.

Computing the Tax on Taxable Income

the income in the other state. Similarly, nonresidents with a commercial domicile in New Mexico allocate income from intangible property used elsewhere to the state if the nonresident is not taxed in the state where the property is being used. A patent is utilized in a state to the extent that it is employed in production, fabrication, manufacturing, or other processing in the state or to the extent that a patented product is produced in the state. A copyright is used in New Mexico when printing or other production takes place in New Mexico.

If the basis for earnings from intangibles used in New Mexico and elsewhere does not permit allocation to a definite state, or if accounting procedures do not clearly show the state or states where the intangible was used, the total income from all intangibles is allocated to New Mexico in the case of a resident or a nonresident business with a commercial domicile in New Mexico.[33]

In completing the form, taxpayers enter the amount of rental and royalty income from federal Schedule E in Column 1 on line 4 of Schedule PIT-B. If income from real property, tangible personal property, or intangibles is reported on federal Schedule C or similar business income schedules, that income should be treated as business income and apportioned on Schedule PIT-B, line 8, and not allocated on line 4.[34]

Line 5. Gains or losses from the sale or exchange of property

Income or loss from the sale or exchange of property is allocated on Schedule PIT-B, line 5, based on the location of the income-earning property or activity. The net amount of gains or losses from the sale or exchange of property reported on Form 1040 or 1040A is entered in column 1.[35]

In column 2, taxpayers enter the net amount of a gain or loss from the sale or exchange of any of the following:

---

[33] 2016 PIT-B New Mexico Allocation and Apportionment of Income Schedule Instructions, p. 6B.
[34] 2016 PIT-B New Mexico Allocation and Apportionment of Income Schedule Instructions, p. 6B.
[35] Although the form describes rows 1 to 7 as the allocation of nonbusiness income, the instructions to the form on page 6B state that all taxpayers with income from the sale and exchange of property should allocate *and* apportion the income and loss on line 5. It is unclear why the instructions instruct taxpayers to apportion their income while the form itself requires taxpayer only to allocate income.

- real property located in New Mexico;
- tangible personal property located in New Mexico at the time of sale;
- tangible personal property located in another state at the time of sale, if the taxpayer is a New Mexico resident;
- tangible personal property of a business located in another state at the time of sale when the taxpayer is not subject to tax in that state, the taxpayer's commercial domicile is in New Mexico, and the income is not subject to apportionment; or
- intangible personal property, if the taxpayer is a New Mexico resident, part-year resident, or has a commercial domicile in New Mexico, and the income is not subject to apportionment.[36]

Line 6. Income or losses from pass-through entities

Income or losses from pass-through entities and trusts are allocated on Schedule PIT-B, line 6. Pass-through entities include partnerships, S corporations, and limited liability companies and other entities electing to be taxed as partnerships. A taxpayer's distributive share of an unincorporated business entity's nonbusiness income is allocated in accordance with the allocation rules described above for nonbusiness income. The instructions to Schedule PIT-B note that federal Schedules E and K-1 may include income from both business and nonbusiness sources.

If the unincorporated business entity fails to provide the taxpayer with information distinguishing nonbusiness income from business income, the entire distribution from the unincorporated business entity must be considered business income and none of the income will be subject to allocation.

> **In Practice:** In some cases it would be beneficial if the entire distribution from an unincorporated business would be treated as business income subject to apportionment rather than nonbusiness income subject to allocation.

A taxpayer's distributive share of an unincorporated business

---

[36] §7-4-7 NMSA 1978.

Computing the Tax on Taxable Income

entity's business income is apportioned to New Mexico by multiplying the taxpayer's distributive share times the New Mexico apportionment percentage determined by application of UDITPA to the entire business income of the entity.

If the entity does not provide the taxpayer with the necessary New Mexico apportionment percentage or information sufficient to enable the taxpayer to calculate the percentage, the taxpayer's entire distributive share of business income is apportioned as if all of the entity's activities, property, payroll and sales were in New Mexico.[37]

In column 1, the taxpayer enters from federal Schedule E the taxpayer's share of income or losses from pass-through entities. In column 2 the taxpayer enters the portion of column 1 income that is allocated to New Mexico using the pass-through entity allocation rules.

Line 7. All other income not included elsewhere in Schedule PIT-B

In column 1 of line 7 of Schedule PIT-B, taxpayers must enter the total of all other income shown on federal Form 1040, 1040A, or 1040EZ, and not reported in another section of Schedule PIT-B. Net operating loss carryforwards are not entered on PIT- B, line 7.

Residents must allocate all other income to New Mexico and must enter in column 2 the same amount entered in column 1. Nonresidents enter the portion of column 1 earned from sources in New Mexico. The following describes several special cases.

- *Gambling winnings.* Residents must allocate all their gambling winnings to New Mexico. Gambling winnings of a nonresident are allocated to New Mexico if the gambling winnings arose from a source within the state. The instructions to Schedule PIT-B state that a taxpayer may not offset income from gambling winnings from a New Mexico source with gambling losses on Schedule PIT-B.
- *Income from unemployment compensation.* Income from unemployment compensation is allocated to the recipient's state of residence at the time the payment was received, regardless of which state is paying the unemployment compensation benefit.

---

[37] §3.3.11.12 NMAC.

- *Income from trading securities for one's own account.* Income of an individual, other than a dealer holding securities for sale to customers in the ordinary course of the dealer's trade or business, from the purchase or sale of securities for the individual's own account or from the writing of securities option contracts for the individual's own account is deemed to be income other than income from engaging in a trade or business.[38] The income is allocable to the individual's state of residence. The income of an investment entity from the purchase or sale of securities for the entity's own account or from the writing of securities option contracts for the entity's own account is not income from a trade or business. The income attributable to the entity's owners is allocable to the owners' state of residence.[39] An investment entity is a pass-through entity meeting the following criteria: the entity is not a securities dealer; each of the entity's owners is an individual; and 90% or more of the entity's income during the tax year is from the purchase or sales of securities or from writing of securities option contracts.[40]

¶ 9.3.5 Apportionment of business and farm income

Whereas nonbusiness income is allocated, business income is *apportioned* on Schedule PIT-B between New Mexico and non-New Mexico sources. Apportionment is handled according to the rules of the UDITPA, except in the cases of manufacturing and headquarters companies, which are apportioned in accordance with special formulas (¶ 9.3.6), and in cases where the standard apportionment rules do not fairly represent the extent of the taxpayer's business activity in the state (¶ 9.3.7).

"Business income" is defined as income arising from transactions and activity in the regular course of the taxpayer's trade or business and includes income from tangible and intangible property if the acquisition, management, and disposition of the property constitute integral parts of the taxpayer's regular trade or business operations.[41]

---

[38] §3.3.11.14A NMAC
[39] §3.3.11.14B NMAC.
[40] §3.3.11.14C NMAC.
[41] §7-4-2A NMSA 1978; UDITPA §1(a).

Computing the Tax on Taxable Income

As such, business income includes farm income, which is apportioned on Schedule PIT-B, line 8.

Business income is apportioned to New Mexico is accordance with what is known as the three-factor formula. The taxpayer's total business income is multiplied by a fraction, the numerator of which is the sum of the property factor, the payroll factor, and the sales factor, and the denominator of which is the number three.[42]

- *Property factor.* The property factor is a fraction, the numerator of which is the average value of the taxpayer's real and tangible personal property owned or rented and used in New Mexico during the tax period and the denominator of which is the average value of all of the taxpayer's real and tangible personal property owned or rented and used during the tax period.[43] Property owned by the taxpayer is valued at its original cost. Property rented by the taxpayer is valued at eight times the net annual rental rate. The net annual rate is the annual rental paid by the taxpayer less any annual rental rate received by the taxpayer from subrentals.[44] The average value of property is determined by averaging the values at the beginning and ending of the tax period, but the TRD may require the averaging of monthly values during the tax period if reasonably required to properly reflect the average value of the taxpayer's property.[45]
- *Payroll factor.* The payroll factor is a fraction, the numerator of which is the total amount paid in the state during the tax period by the taxpayer for compensation, and the denominator of which is the total compensation paid everywhere during the tax period.[46] Compensation is paid in the state if: 1) the individual's service is performed entirely within the state; 2) the individual's service is performed both within and without the state, but the service performed without the state is incidental to the individual's service within the state; or 3) some of the service is performed in the state and the base of operations; or, if there

---

[42] §7-4-10 NMSA 1978.
[43] §7-4-11 NMSA 1978.
[44] §7-4-12 NMSA 1978.
[45] §7-4-13 NMSA 1978.
[46] §7-4-14 NMSA 1978.

is no base of operations, the place from which the service is directed or controlled, is in the state; or the base of operations or the place from which the service is directed or controlled is not in any state in which some part of the service is performed, but the individual's residence is in this state.[47]

- *Sales factor.* The sales factor is a fraction, the numerator of which is the total sales of the taxpayer in the state during the tax period, and the denominator of which is the total sales of the taxpayer everywhere during the tax period.[48] Sales of tangible personal property are deemed to have occurred in the state for purposes of inclusion in the sales factor under the following circumstances:
    - the property is delivered or shipped to a purchaser other than the United States government within the state regardless of the f. o. b. point or other conditions of the sale; or
    - the property is shipped from an office, store, warehouse, factory or other place of storage in the state and
        - the purchaser is the United States government; or
        - the taxpayer is not taxable in the state of the purchaser and did not make an election for apportionment of business income available to manufacturers or headquarters companies.[49]

Sales, other than sales of tangible personal property, are deemed to have occurred in New Mexico if the income-producing activity is performed in this state, or the income-producing activity is performed both in and outside the state and a greater proportion of the income-producing activity is performed in New Mexico than in any other state, based on costs of performance.[50]

Schedule PIT-B provides the following worksheet for determining the apportionment decimal fraction, which is entered on line 5 of the worksheet. The business income amount on line 8, column 1 on page

---

[47] §7-4-15 NMSA 1978.
[48] §7-4-16 NMSA 1978.
[49] §7-4-17 NMSA 1978.
[50] §7-4-18 NMSA 1978

Computing the Tax on Taxable Income

1 of Schedule PIT-B is multiplied by this decimal fraction and the result is entered on line 8, column 2 on page 1 of Schedule PIT-B. If there is more than one business the process is repeated for each business and total income apportioned to New Mexico is entered on column 2 of line 8.

WORKSHEET FOR APPORTIONMENT OF BUSINESS AND FARM INCOME
Complete a worksheet for each business or farm.
See worksheet instructions for definitions relating to the apportionment factors below.

		Column 1 Total Everywhere	Column 2 New Mexico
1.	PROPERTY FACTOR		
a.	Average value of real and tangible personal property owned or rented by the taxpayer and used during tax period	1a [ ] 00	[ ] 00

			Column 3 Factor
b.	DIVIDE column 2 by column 1. (Compute to 3 decimal places)		1b [_ . _ _ _]
2.	PAYROLL FACTOR		
a.	Compensation paid by taxpayer	2a [ ] 00 [ ] 00	
b.	DIVIDE column 2 by column 1. (Compute to 3 decimal places)		2b [_ . _ _ _]
3.	SALES FACTOR		
a.	Total sales excluding nonbusiness income	3a [ ] 00 [ ] 00	
b.	DIVIDE column 2 by column 1. (Compute to 3 decimal places)		3b [_ . _ _ _]
4.	Total of lines 1b, 2b and 3b		4 [_ . _ _ _]
5.	DIVIDE line 4 by the number of factors used and enter here. (Compute to 3 decimal places)		5 [_ . _ _ _]

MULTIPLY the amount on line 8, column 1 on page 1 of Schedule PIT-B by the decimal amount on line 5 of this worksheet. Enter the result on line 8, column 2 on page 1 of Schedule PIT-B. If you have more than one business or farm, complete a worksheet for each business or farm, compute the result for each business or farm and enter the sum of the results on line 8, column 2. Attach the worksheet for each business or farm with your PIT-1 return and Schedule PIT-B.

¶ 9.3.6 Special rules for manufacturing and headquarters companies

To attract employers to New Mexico, the state has provided optional apportionment formulas for manufacturers and headquarters companies. A taxpayer whose principal business activity in New Mexico is manufacturing may elect to have business income apportioned to the state using the apportionment fractions presented in the following table.[51]

---

[51] §7-4-10B NMSA 1978.

Taxable year	Apportion business income to New Mexico by:
In the taxable year beginning on or after January 1, 2014 and prior to January 1, 2015	Multiplying the income by a fraction, the numerator of which is 2X the sales factor plus the property factor plus the payroll factor and the denominator of which is 4
In the taxable year beginning on or after January 1, 2015 and prior to January 1, 2016	Multiplying the income by a fraction, the numerator of which is 3X the sales factor plus the property factor plus the payroll factor and the denominator of which is 5
In the taxable year beginning on or after January 1, 2016 and prior to January 1, 2017	Multiplying the income by a fraction, the numerator of which is 7X the sales factor plus 1.5X the property factor plus 1.5X the payroll factor and the denominator of which is 10;
In the taxable year beginning on or after January 1, 2017 and prior to January 1, 2018	Multiplying the income by a fraction, the numerator of which is 8X the sales factor plus the property factor plus the payroll factor and the denominator of which is 10
In taxable years beginning on or after January 1, 2018	Multiplying the income by a fraction, the numerator of which is the total sales of the taxpayer in New Mexico during the tax year and the denominator of which is the total sales of the taxpayer from any location within or outside of the state during the tax year.

The term "manufacturing" means combining or processing components or materials to increase their value for sale in the ordinary course of business, but does not include:

- construction;
- farming;
- power generation, except for electricity generation at a facility other than one for which both location approval and a certificate of convenience and necessity are required prior to commencing construction or operation, pursuant to the Public Utility Act, or
- processing natural resources, including hydrocarbons.[52]

---

[52] §7-4-10E(2) NMSA 1978.

Computing the Tax on Taxable Income

A taxpayer whose principal business activity in New Mexico is a headquarters operation may elect to have business income apportioned to New Mexico by multiplying the income by a fraction, the numerator of which is the total sales of the taxpayer in New Mexico during the tax year and the denominator of which is the total sales of the taxpayer from any location within or outside of the state during the tax year.[53]

A "headquarters operation" is defined as the center of operations of a business in either of two cases –

1. involving centralized business activities:
   - where corporate staff employees are physically employed;
   - where centralized functions are performed, including administrative, planning, managerial, human resources, purchasing, information technology and accounting, but not including operating a call center;
   - the function and purpose of which is to manage and direct most aspects and functions of the business operations within a subdivided area of the United States;
   - from which final authority over regional or subregional offices, operating facilities and any other offices of the business are issued; and
   - including national and regional headquarters if the national headquarters is subordinate only to the ownership of the business or its representatives and the regional headquarters is subordinate to the national headquarters;[55] or

2. involving centralized management authority:
   - the function and purpose of which is to manage and direct most aspects of one or more centralized functions; and
   - from which final authority over one or more centralized functions is issued.[56]

To elect these optional apportionment methods, the taxpayer must provide the TRD with written notification of the election no later than the date on which the taxpayer files the return for the first tax year to

---

[53] §7-4-10C NMSA 1978.
[55] §7-4-10E(1)(a) NMSA 1978.
[56] §7-4-10E(1)(b) NMSA 1978.

177

which the election will apply. The election applies to that tax year and to each tax year thereafter until the taxpayer provides the TRD written notification that the election is terminated. The election may not be terminated until the elected method has been used by the taxpayer for at least three consecutive tax years, including a total of at least 36 calendar months.[57]

¶ 9.3.7 Equitable adjustment of standard allocation or apportionment formula

The ITA provides that if the standard allocation and apportionment provisions do not fairly represent the extent of the taxpayer's business activity in the state, the taxpayer may utilize without prior approval or the TRD may require if reasonable, in respect to all or any part of the taxpayer's business activity, the following methods:

- separate accounting;
- the exclusion of any one or more of the factors;
- the inclusion of one or more additional factors which will fairly represent the taxpayer's business activity in the state; or
- the employment of any other method to effectuate an equitable allocation and apportionment of the taxpayer's income.

A departure from the standard allocation and apportionment provisions is permitted only in limited and specific cases where the standard apportionment and allocation produce incongruous results.[58]

In addition, in circumstances where the standard apportionment formula does not fairly represent the taxpayer's business activity in the state and in other circumstances where the revenues of the state would not be adversely affected, the Secretary may to enter into an agreement in writing with any person with respect to apportionment and allocation of that person's income. Unless there is a showing of fraud or misrepresentation of a material fact or a change in statutory law, such agreement is conclusive. Such agreement may be terminated by either party by written notice to the other party at least 90 days before the beginning of the tax year to which the termination applies.[59]

---

[57] §7-4-10D NMSA 1978.
[58] §7-4-19 NMSA 1978; §3.5.19.8 NMAC; 2016 PIT-B, New Mexico Allocation and Apportionment of Income Schedule Instructions, p. 10B.
[59] §7-4-20 NMSA 1978.

Computing the Tax on Taxable Income

¶ 9.3.8 Special industries

In the case of industries such as air transportation, rail transportation, ship transportation, trucking, television, radio, motion pictures, and various types of professional athletics, the standard apportionment factors may not provide an equitable result. In this case, the TRD may establish appropriate procedures for determining the apportionment factors for each such industry, and such procedures must be applied uniformly. The regulations do provide adjustment to the apportionment factors for many industries and the rules with regard to these industries may be found in the income tax regulations.[60]

¶ 9.3.9 Allocation of community property and income

Additional complications arise when one spouse, but not both, is a resident of a community property state. In this case, the following allocation must be made:

1. The community income of the spouse who is a resident of a community property state is equally divided between both spouses, and

2. 100% of the separate income is treated as if it was the income of the spouse who owns the property.

The allocation and apportionment rules are applied to each type of income for each spouse based on each spouse's New Mexico residency status.[61]

> ***Example 1.*** A New Mexico full-year resident and a Colorado resident are married and file a joint return. Colorado is not a community property state. The New Mexico resident has wage income from employment in Texas. Because New Mexico is a community property state and the resident spouse is domiciled in New Mexico, the resident spouse's wage income is community property. Half the wage income from employment in Texas is the property of each spouse. The instructions to Schedule PIT-B, line 1 require that half of the New Mexico resident's wage income be allocated in full to New Mexico, even

---

[60] See §3.5.19.12 et seq. NMAC.
[61] Examples 1 to 4 are adopted and modified from the instructions to 2016 PIT-B, New Mexico Allocation and Apportionment of Income Schedule Instructions, p. 2B.

if the income was not earned in New Mexico. The non-resident spouse's share of the community wage income is not allocated to New Mexico, because the income is not from services performed in New Mexico.

Example 2. The facts are the same as Example 1, except that the wage income is the separate income of the New Mexico resident spouse due to a separation agreement. All wage income is allocated to New Mexico, because the spouse who is entitled to the entire amount of wage income is a New Mexico resident. The New Mexico resident must allocate this wage income to New Mexico according to the Schedule PIT-B, line 1 instructions for a resident taxpayer.

Example 3. The facts are the same as Example 1, except that the non-resident spouse is domiciled in Texas and earned the wages from employment in Texas. Texas is a community property state. Because the non-resident spouse is domiciled in a community property state, the wage income is community property. The resident spouse's half of the community income is allocated to New Mexico based on the Schedule PIT-B, line 1 instructions. The other half is not allocated to New Mexico, based on the Schedule PIT-B instructions with regard to the non-resident spouse's share of the community income.

Example 4. If both spouses are residents of New Mexico, all community wage income is allocated to New Mexico.

¶ 9.4 Lump Sum Amounts

Taxpayers who receive a lump-sum payment from a retirement plan may elect to use a special federal 10-year tax averaging computation option as computed on federal Form 4972, *Tax on Lump Sum Distributions*. If this election is made, the taxpayer must use New Mexico's special 5-year averaging method to compute the tax due on the lump sum distribution.[62] See ¶ 7.3.2C for a definition of lump sum

---

[62] The instructions to Form PIT-1 state that if the federal averaging option is used a taxpayer *may* use the New Mexico 5-year averaging. but the statute appears to make this mandatory rather than optional. The instructions also indicate that the New Mexico 5-year averaging can be used if the taxpayer makes a capital gain election on Form 4792, but the statute does not provide for this. §7-2-2K NMSA 1978.

Computing the Tax on Taxable Income

amounts.

The averaging method works as follows. The tax on any lump-sum amounts is equal to five times the difference between:

1. the amount of tax due on the taxpayer's taxable income; and
2. the amount of tax that would be due on an amount equal to the taxpayer's taxable income and twenty percent of the taxpayer's lump-sum amounts included in net income.[63]

The tax is paid once, in the year the lump sum amount is received. The tax computed using this method is entered on Form PIT-1, line 19 and added to the tax on taxable income computed using the rate tables. For taxpayers using Schedule PIT-B, the tax on lump sum income is added to the tax on taxable income and the total is multiplied by the New Mexico percentage of income.

The instructions to Form 2016 PIT-1 provides a worksheet for computing the tax on lump-sum distributions.

---

[63] §7-2-7 NMSA 1978.

CHAPTER 10
CREDITS AGAINST THE INCOME TAX

¶ 10.1 Overview

An income tax credit is a statutory device that allows taxpayers to reduce the amount of their income tax liability to the state. Tax credits are more valuable than deductions because rather than reduce the tax base, as in the case of deductions, they reduce the actual liability. A credit reduces an income tax liability dollar for dollar. An income tax credit of $100, for example, reduces a taxpayer's income tax liability by $100.

Credits may be either refundable or non-refundable. Non-refundable credits may be used against existing tax liabilities only. Any excess credits may be carried forward for a set period of years as prescribed by statute.[1] A refundable credit is one that may be refunded to taxpayers under certain circumstances. Only three of New Mexico's business-related credits are refundable: the film production credit, the technology jobs and research and development tax credit (beginning 2017) in certain circumstances, and the renewable energy production credit. Most nonbusiness-related credits are refundable. Several business-related credits are transferrable, meaning that they may be sold or exchanged as a business asset.

The New Mexico government has used the tax credit mechanism to fulfill a wide variety of social and economic objectives, including the following:

- to encourage individuals and companies to invest in New Mexico and to create jobs in the state;
- to provide financial assistance to low-income and elderly taxpayers;

---

[1] Some jurisdictions allow taxpayer to carry their credits back to prior years, but New Mexico does not allow for this.

- to attract particular industries to the state;
- to encourage the use of environmentally friendly energy generation methods and construction techniques; and
- to prevent inequitable double taxation in the case of income taxed in another state that is also taxed in New Mexico.

The ITA provides about 30 different income tax credits, which may be categorized as follows:

- *Credit for taxes paid to another state.* A very important credit is the credit for taxes paid to another state, as it provides relief to taxpayers who are taxed in two states on the same income. This credit figures prominently in Form PIT-1 as is it entered directly on line 20. This credit is discussed in ¶ 10.2.
- *Business-related credits.* There are twenty-one business related credits and these are entered on Schedule PIT-CR, *New Mexico Business-Related Income Tax Credit Schedule*, and the total from this form is then entered on Form PIT-1, line 21. As noted above, the business-related credits are non-refundable with three exceptions. These refundable business credits are entered on Part B of Schedule PIT-CR and then on Form PIT-1, line 26. These credits are discussed in Chapter 11.
- *Refundable credits and rebates.* There are six nonbusiness-related refundable credits and rebates that are reported on their own schedule, Schedule PIT-RC, *New Mexico Rebate and Credit Schedule*. Rebates are income tax credits which are in part compensation for property taxes and other state and local taxes paid by lower income taxpayers. The total from this schedule is entered on Form PIT-1, line 24. Since they are refundable, New Mexico will send a check to the taxpayer if they create an overpayment. These credits and rebates are discussed in Chapter 13.
- *Working families credit.* In addition to the credits and rebates that are entered on Schedule PIT-RC, the working families credit is another refundable nonbusiness-related credit, which is entered directly on Form PIT-1, line 25. This credit is discussed in ¶ 13.9.

Credits Against the Income Tax

Pre-approval of credits

Many of the statutes authorizing credits require taxpayers to obtain pre-approval from specified government agencies before being entitled to claim a credit. Sometimes, it is necessary to obtain pre-approval from both an administrative agency as well as the TRD before claiming a credit. If a taxpayer requests approval of a statutory tax credit but the request is not granted or denied within 180 days of the date filed, the taxpayer is deemed to have received approval. However, the TRD is not prevented from auditing taxes paid or from assessing taxes owed, including any tax resulting from tax credits found not to be valid.[2]

Three-year time limitation for claiming credits and tax rebates

A credit or tax rebate is disallowed if the claim is first made after the end of the third calendar year following the calendar year in which the return upon which the credit or tax rebate was first claimable was initially due. This rule does not apply to the credit for income taxes paid to another state.[3]

¶ 10.2 Credit for taxes paid other states (Form PIT-1, line 20)

The potential for a double tax situation exists when a New Mexico resident pays tax to another state on income derived from activities outside New Mexico, but which is also allocated or apportioned to New Mexico. For example, compensation of a resident earned outside New Mexico may be taxed in the state where earned but would also be allocated to New Mexico. New Mexico provides a tax credit for this situation. The ITA provides that when a resident pays income tax to another state, the individual is entitled to a tax credit if the item of income subject to tax is also "income allocated or apportioned to New Mexico."[4] If income is allocated or apportioned outside New Mexico on PIT-B, the taxes paid to another state on such income do not

---

[2] §7-1-29.2 NMSA 1978.
[3] §§7-2-12.1, 7-2-13 NMSA 1978.
[4] §7-2-13 NMSA 1978.

qualify for the credit for taxes paid to another state.[5]

The credit equals the amount of tax paid to the other state with respect to the income allocated or apportioned to New Mexico.[6] However, the amount of the credit may not exceed the amount of the taxpayer's New Mexico income tax liability on that portion of income that is also taxed in the other state.[7]

The credit is for the amount of tax that another state imposes on any part of income that by law is included in New Mexico income. Therefore, the allowable credit does not include withholding taxes in the other state, as such withholding taxes are advance payments on the tax imposed.

A state is any state of the United States, the District of Columbia, the Commonwealth of Puerto Rico, any territory or possession of the United States, or any political subdivision of a foreign country, but does not include the central governments of foreign countries.[8]

The credit does not apply to or include income taxes paid to any municipality, county or other political subdivision of a state.[9]

The instructions to Form PIT-1 provide the following examples:

> **Example 1.** A New Mexico resident's interest earned from an investment in Arizona is allocated to New Mexico on PIT-B, column 2. The resident can claim the credit for taxes paid to another state when the interest income is:
>
> • Required to be allocated to New Mexico and
>
> • Taxed in Arizona
>
> **Example 2.** A New Mexico resident allocates rental income from property located outside of New Mexico on PIT-B to sources outside of New Mexico. The resident cannot claim the credit for tax paid to another state because the resident did not

---

[5] 2016 PIT-1, Personal Income Tax Return Instructions, p. 29.
[6] §7-2-13 NMSA 1978.
[7] §7-2-13 NMSA 1978.
[8] §7-2-2U NMSA 1978.
[9] §7-2-13 NMSA 1978.

Credits Against the Income Tax

include that income on PIT-B, column 2.[10]

Evidence of the payment to the other state must be filed to receive the credit. Typically, this means attaching a copy of the return filed with the other state to the New Mexico return.

The amount of the credit is entered on Form PIT-1, line 20. The instructions to that form contain a worksheet for computing the credit.

---

[10] 2016 PIT-1, Personal Income Tax Return Instructions, p. 29.

CHAPTER 11
BUSINESS-RELATED CREDITS

¶ 11.1 General

There are twenty-one business related credits. In order to claim a credit, the amount claimed must be entered in Schedule PIT-CR, which gives each credit an identifying code. Listed below are each credit and the code that has been assigned to it:

Non-Refundable Credits

A01	Affordable housing tax credit
A02	Angel investment credit
A03	Agricultural water conservation tax credit
A04	Advanced energy income tax credit
A05	Agricultural biomass income tax credit
B01	Business facility rehabilitation credit
B02	Blended biodiesel fuel tax credit
C01	Cancer clinical trial tax credit
E01	Electronic card-reading equipment tax credit
G01	Geothermal ground-coupled heat pump tax credit
J01	Job mentorship tax credit
L01	Land conservation incentives credit
P01	Preservation of cultural property tax credit
R01	Rural job tax credit
R02	Rural health care practitioners tax credit

S01   Solar market development tax credit

S02   Sustainable building tax credit

T01   Technology jobs (additional) tax credit

V01   Veteran employment tax credit

Venture Capital Investment Credit (the forgotten credit, which has not been assigned a code)

Refundable Credits

F01   Film production and television tax credit

R03   Renewable energy production tax credit

T02   Technology jobs and research and development (additional) tax credit.

Many of the business-related credits require the approval of a government agency before the credit can be claimed with the TRD. For example, a taxpayer must obtain a certificate of eligibility from the New Mexico Environment Department to enable the requester to claim an advanced energy income tax credit. Likewise, a taxpayer must apply for certification of eligibility for the angel investment credit from the New Mexico Economic Development Department (EDD). So, a taxpayer must meet not only the criteria of the applicable statute, but also the qualifying criteria set out by the agencies that determine eligibility for the credit.

Some of the business-related credits are limited in the overall amount that the state can grant each year. For example, the film and television tax credit is limited to $50 million in total credits in any year and such credits are allocated on a first come first serve basis. Generally, if a taxpayer cannot utilize all the credit claimed because his or her tax liability is not great enough, the surplus can be carried over to a future year. But the number of years for which a carryover is available differs by credit. The following table describes the attributes of each of the business-related credits.

Business-related Credits

Attributes of Business-related Credits							
Credit	Agency Giving Pre OK	Annual max credit per taxpayer	Annual limit all taxpayers	Carry-forward years	Transfer Allowed	Recapture	Refundable
Affordable housing	MFA		$1.85 x state population	5	Yes	No	No
Angel investment	EDD	$62k per investment for up to 5 investments per year	$2 million	5	No		No
Agricultural Water conservation expenses (expired)	Dept. of Agric.	$10,000	None	5	No	No	No
Advanced Energy	NMED	None	$60 million per facility	10	No	Yes	No
Agricultural Biomass	ENMRD	None	$5 million	4	Yes	No	No
Business facility rehab. (no longer operative)	NM EZ Program Officer	$50,000 per project	None	4	No	No	No
Blended biodiesel fuel (expired)	None	None	None	5	No	No	No
Cancer clinical trial (expired)	None	$4,000		0	No	No	No
Electronic card reading equipment	None	None	None	0	No	No	No
Film and Television	Film Division		$50 million	No	Yes	No	Yes
Geothermal heat pumps	EMNRD	$9,000	$2 million	10	No	No	No
Job Mentorship	School principal	$12,000	None	3	No	No	No
Land Conservation	EMNRD	$250,000 per conveyance	None	20	Yes	No	No
Preservation of cultural property	Cultural Property Review Comm.	$25,000/ $50,000 per property	None	4	No	No	No

191

New Mexico Personal Income Tax Guide

Attributes of Business-related Credits							
Credit	Agency Giving Pre OK	Annual max credit per taxpayer	Annual limit all taxpayers	Carry-forward years	Transfer Allowed	Recap-ture	Refund-able
Rural jobs	TRD	$1,000	None	3	Yes	No	No
Rural health care practitioner	Dept. of Health	$5000 for doctors/ $3,000 for others		3	No	No	No
Solar market development	EMNRD	$9,000 per system	$2 million for solar thermal and $3 million for solar PV	10	No	No	No
New sustainable building	EMNRD		$5 million	7	Yes	No	No
Technology jobs (additional) tax credit	TRD	No	No	3	No	Yes	Yes, in part
Veteran employment	TRD	$1,000		3	No	No	No
Renewable energy production	EMNRD	Limit on total creditable megawatts	Limit on total creditable megawatts	5 - if production began prior to 2008	No	No	Yes
Venture Capital Investment		50% of federal tax paid		Until used	No	No	No

The following sections describe each of the business-related credits, the qualifying criteria, the process for claiming the credit, any cap on the total amount of credits claimed and other essential credit attributes.

¶ 11.2 Affordable Housing Tax Credit

To promote an increase in the supply of affordable housing for low-income residents, New Mexico enacted the Housing Tax Credit Act in 2006, which provides a tax credit for investments in affordable housing. The credit is eponymously known as the affordable housing tax credit (AHTC), which is administered by the New Mexico Mortgage Finance Authority (MFA).[1] Pursuant to this credit program, persons who invest in affordable housing projects are given an investment voucher that equals 50% of the amount of their investment. The investment may be in the nature of land, buildings, materials, cash or services.[2] This voucher can then be submitted to the TRD in order to claim an income tax credit equal to the value of the voucher.[3] Alternatively, the vouchers may be sold or transferred. The required investment is in the form of a donation to an affordable housing development that has been approved by the MFA.[4] It is considered a donation by the MFA because the transfer is irrevocable and the transferor cannot receive any consideration for the investment. Once a project is approved and donations secured, investment vouchers are issued to the donors. The MFA will certify to the TRD its approval of an affordable housing project for which an investment voucher is issued within twenty days of issuance of the voucher.[5]

The minimum donation permitted to an affordable housing project is $200 and the maximum is $1,000,000.[6] The MFA may not issue vouchers in excess of the following annual aggregate limitation:

---

[1] §7-9I-1 NMSA 1978. The MFA's website provides this description of its functions:
The New Mexico Mortgage Finance Authority is a quasi-public entity that provides financing for housing and other related services to low- to moderate-income New Mexicans at no cost to taxpayers. As the state's official housing agency, MFA administers more than 30 programs, initiatives and funding mechanisms that allow MFA to build affordable rental communities, offer emergency shelter, rehabilitate aging homes and provide rental assistance and subsidies. MFA partners with lenders, realtors, nonprofit organizations, local governments and developers throughout the state to make its programs and services available to all eligible New Mexicans. http://www.housingnm.org/about/what-we-do, last viewed February 11, 2016.
[2] §7-9I-3A NMSA 1978.
[3] §7-9I-3A NMSA 1978.
[4] §7-9I-3A NMSA 1978; http://housingnm.org/developers/new-mexico-state-affordable-housing-tax-credit, last viewed October 14, 2016.
[5] §7-9I-4 NMSA 1978.
[6] http://www.housingnm.org/developers/new-mexico-state-affordable-housing-tax-credit, last viewed October 14, 2016.

1. $200,000 for calendar years beginning on January 1, 2006;
2. $500,000 for calendar years beginning on January 1, 2007; and
3. for calendar years beginning on January 1, 2008 and each subsequent calendar year, the state population multiplied by a base rate of $1.85, adjusted annually for inflation.[7] The population for 2016 is estimated at 2.09 million.

Any limitation on the issuance or approval of investment vouchers for a calendar year does not apply to an investment voucher issued by the MFA during that calendar year that was approved during a previous calendar year.[8]

Since there is a limit on the aggregate amount of vouchers, the MFA has adopted a reservation system, described as follows:

> ...Sponsors whose projects are designated as eligible affordable housing projects under the State Tax Credit Program will receive a reservation of available tax credits for a given program year. This reservation will enable the project sponsor to solicit donations to pay for eligible costs for the Affordable Housing Project. Upon acceptance of evidence of donations and valuation and satisfaction of readiness and other program requirements for the project, MFA will issue investment vouchers to the donor.[9]

The MFA awards affordable housing tax credit reservations on a first-come first-serve basis. An investment voucher issued by the MFA is numbered for identification and may be sold, exchanged, or otherwise transferred, but only once, in whole or in part, to one or more persons. The parties to such a transaction must notify the TRD and the MFA of the sale, exchange, or transfer within 10 days of the sale, exchange or transfer by submitting a completed *Affordable Housing Tax Credit Transfer Form*.[10]

A pass-through entity may not claim the AHTC, but the credit may be transferred to the owners of a pass-through entity by the filing of

---

[7] §7-9I-3B NMSA 1978.
[8] §7-9I-3C NMSA 1978.
[9] New Mexico Affordable Housing Tax Credit Program Notice of Funding Availability Approved by the MFA Board of Directors April 21, 2010 (Effective July 1, 2010), Amended May 15, 2013.
[10] §7-9I-3E NMSA 1978.

Business-related Credits

the tax credit transfer form. The new holder will receive notification of approval of the transfer and a new voucher number will be issued for that portion of the balance that was transferred to the entity owner.

The TRD will allow a tax credit in an amount not to exceed the value of the investment voucher during the tax year if the MFA certifies to the TRD:

1. completion of a service for which an investment voucher has been issued; or
2. approval by the MFA or completion of an affordable housing project for which a land, building or cash donation has been made and for which an investment voucher has been issued.[11]

A holder of an investment voucher may apply all or a portion of the affordable housing tax credit against the holder's personal income tax liability by filing Form RPD-41301, *Affordable Housing Tax Credit Claim Form*, with Form PIT-1. Any balance of the credit claimed may be carried forward for up to five years from the calendar year during which the MFA certifies to the TRD approval of the affordable housing project for which the investment voucher used to claim the AHTC is issued.[12]

When a credit is transferred, the transfer form will identify the original voucher date. The original voucher date is the date the original investment voucher was issued for the affordable housing project. Upon receipt of the approved transfer form, the new holder may apply the AHTC against future returns, but may not carry forward any credit for more than 5 years from the calendar year in which the original investment voucher was issued.[13]

The instructions to Form RPD-41301 provide this example.

> ***Example.*** For example, if an affordable housing project was approved and later certified by MFA, and the resulting original investment voucher was issued to holder Z on January 15, 2006, Z may not claim the affordable housing tax credit for any unused balance of the investment voucher after December 31, 2011. If all or a portion of the investment voucher balance is

---

[11] §7-9I-5A NMSA 1978.
[12] §7-9I-5B NMSA 1978.
[13] Form RPD-41301, Affordable Housing Tax Credit Claim Form (Rev. 9/2016).

subsequently transferred to holder X, X may not claim the tax credit for the transferred balance after December 31, 2011. The original voucher date for the original investment voucher issued to Z and the transfer investment voucher issued to X is January 15, 2006.

The MFA also allows tax credits for donations made directly to the New Mexico Affordable Housing Charitable Trust for affordable housing projects approved by the MFA. The MFA website describes the following tax benefits that flow from contributions to the Trust:

Assumptions: Combined federal and state tax rate: 40% Amount donated: $1,000	
Donation:	$1,000
Less:	
State tax credit:	500
Deduction for donation on federal and state returns:	400
Out of pocket funds:	$100

Important terms

An "affordable housing project" means land acquisition, construction, building acquisition, remodeling, improvement, rehabilitation, conversion or weatherization for residential housing that is approved by the MFA and that includes single-family housing or multifamily housing.[14]

A "person" is an individual, tribal government, housing authority, corporation, limited liability company, partnership, joint venture, syndicate, association or nonprofit organization.[15]

¶ 11.3 Angel investment credit

An angel investor or "angel" is an affluent individual who provides capital for a business start-up in exchange for convertible debt or ownership equity.[16] Angel investing has been an important source of capital and mentoring for high-tech start-ups in Silicon Valley, often providing needed financing when traditional venture capital firms

---

[14] §7-9I-2A NMSA 1978.
[15] §7-9I-2E NMSA 1978.
[16] https://en.wikipedia.org/wiki/Angel_investor

Business-related Credits

refuse to participate. In order to encourage angels to invest in New Mexico high-technology research and manufacturing start-ups, New Mexico offers an angel investment credit. An accredited investor who makes a qualified investment may claim an angel investment credit not to exceed 25% of the qualified investment, subject to limitations; the credit allowed for each qualified investment may not exceed $62,500 for tax years beginning on or after January 1, 2015. (For prior years, the credit was limited to 25% of not more than $100,000 of the qualified investment.) An "accredited investor" is a person who is an accredited investor within the meaning of Rule 501 issued by the federal Securities and Exchange Commission (SEC) pursuant to the federal Securities Act of 1933 (See inset below).[17] The credit is applicable only for an investor who files a New Mexico income tax return and is not a dependent of another taxpayer. A claim for the credit may not be made or allowed with respect to any investment made before January 1, 2007, or after December 31, 2025.[18]

---

[17] §7-2-18.17K(1) NMSA 1978.
[18] §7-2-18.17C NMSA 1978; Form RPD-41320, *Angel Investment Credit Claim Form* (Rev. 9/2016).

Accredited investors under 7 CFR 302.501(a) includes these individuals:

(5) Any natural person whose individual net worth, or joint net worth with that person's spouse, exceeds $1,000,000.
   (i) Except as provided in paragraph (a)(5)(ii) of this section, for purposes of calculating net worth under this paragraph (a)(5):
      (A) The person's primary residence shall not be included as an asset;
      (B) Indebtedness that is secured by the person's primary residence, up to the estimated fair market value of the primary residence at the time of the sale of securities, shall not be included as a liability (except that if the amount of such indebtedness outstanding at the time of sale of securities exceeds the amount outstanding 60 days before such time, other than as a result of the acquisition of the primary residence, the amount of such excess shall be included as a liability); and
      (C) Indebtedness that is secured by the person's primary residence in excess of the estimated fair market value of the primary residence at the time of the sale of securities shall be included as a liability;
   (ii) Paragraph (a)(5)(i) of this section will not apply to any calculation of a person's net worth made in connection with a purchase of securities in accordance with a right to purchase such securities, provided that:
      (A) Such right was held by the person on July 20, 2010;
      (B) The person qualified as an accredited investor on the basis of net worth at the time the person acquired such right; and
      (C) The person held securities of the same issuer, other than such right, on July 20, 2010.
(6) Any natural person who had an individual income in excess of $200,000 in each of the two most recent years or joint income with that person's spouse in excess of $300,000 in each of those years and has a reasonable expectation of reaching the same income level in the current year.
(See Rule 501 of Regulation D for all categories of qualified investors.)

A qualified investment (QI) must be made in cash, in a qualified business in exchange for equity (defined below). A QI does not include an investment where the taxpayer, a member of the taxpayer's immediate family, or an entity affiliated with the taxpayer receives compensation from the business in exchange for services provided to the business within one year of the investment.[19]

A taxpayer may not claim the angel investment credit for more than one QI per investment round and for no more than five qualified

---

[19] §7-2-18.17K(7) NMSA (1978).

Business-related Credits

businesses per tax year.[20]

A husband and wife who file separate returns for a tax year in which they could have filed a joint return may each claim only one-half of the credit that would have been allowed on a joint return.[21]

A "qualified business" is a business that has New Mexico as its hub. The business must carry out the following activities in New Mexico: 1) engage in qualified research or manufacturing activities, 2) maintain its principal place of business, 3) employ a majority of its full-time employees (if any), and 4) have a majority of its tangible assets (if any). The business must have no more than 100 employees (calculated on a full-time-equivalent basis) at the time of the investment and cannot have had gross revenues in excess of $5,000,000 in any fiscal year ending on or before the date of the investment. The business is not qualified if it has engaged in any of the following security law activities or requirements: 1) issued securities registered pursuant to Section 6 of the federal Securities Act of 1933; 2) issued securities traded on a national securities exchange; 3) is subject to reporting requirements of the federal Securities Exchange Act of 1934; or 4) is registered pursuant to the federal Investment Company Act of 1940, at the time of the investment.

A business is not qualified if it is primarily engaged in or primarily organized as any of the following types of businesses:

- credit or finance services, including banks, savings and loan associations, credit unions, small loan companies or title loan companies;
- financial brokering or investment;
- professional services, including accounting, legal services, engineering and any other service the practice of which requires a license;
- insurance;
- real estate;
- construction or construction contracting;
- consulting or brokering;
- mining;

---

[20] §7-2-18.17B NMSA (1978).
[21] §7-2-18.17I NMSA (1978).

- wholesale or retail trade;
- providing utility service, including water, sewerage, electricity, natural gas, propane or butane;
- publishing (including publishing newspapers or other periodicals);
- broadcasting; or
- providing internet operating services.[22]

The term "qualified research" has the same meaning as that term is used in IRC §41, which provides a federal credit for research activities. The term qualified research in that section means:

1. research with respect to which expenditures may be treated as expenses (under IRC §174),
2. which is undertaken for the purpose of discovering information which is technological in nature,
3. the application of which is intended to be useful in the development of a new or improved business component of the taxpayer, and
4. substantially all of the activities of which constitute elements of a process of experimentation for purposes relating to
    a. (i) a new or improved function,
    b. (ii) performance, or
    c. (iii) reliability or quality, but not for a purpose related to style, taste, cosmetic, or seasonal design factors.

"Manufacturing" is the activity of combining or processing components or materials to increase their value for sale in the ordinary course of business, but does not include construction, farming, processing natural resources, including hydrocarbons, or preparing meals for immediate consumption, on- or off-premises.[23]

Certification of eligibility

A taxpayer must apply for certification of eligibility for the angel investment credit from the New Mexico Economic Development Department (EDD). In addition, the qualified business must submit or have on file at the EDD, an Angel Investment Qualified Business Application form identifying the names of qualified investors and the

---

[22] §7-2-18.17K(6) NMSA (1978).
[23] §7-2-18.17K(5) NMSA (1978).

Business-related Credits

amounts invested.[24]

If the EDD determines that the taxpayer is an accredited investor and the investment is a QI, it will issue a dated certificate of eligibility. The certificate will include a calculation of the amount of the credit for which the taxpayer is eligible.[25]

The EDD may issue a certificate of eligibility only if the total amount of angel investment credits represented by certificates of eligibility issued by the EDD in any calendar year would not exceed $2,000,000 (prior to January 1, 2015, the total amount of credits issued in a calendar year could not exceed $750,000). If the applications for certificates of eligibility for angel investment credits represent an aggregate amount exceeding $2,000,000 for any calendar year, certificates will be issued in the order that the applications were received. The excess applications that would have been certified, but for the limit, will be certified, subject to the same limit, in subsequent calendar years.[26]

Claiming the credit

To claim the angel investment credit, the taxpayer must provide the TRD with a certificate of eligibility and any other information the TRD may require to determine the amount of the credit. If the requirements of the credit have been complied with, the TRD will approve the claim for the credit.[27]

A taxpayer who otherwise qualifies for and claims a credit for a QI made by a partnership or other business association of which the taxpayer is a member may claim a credit only in proportion to the taxpayer's interest in the partnership or business association.[28]

The angel investment credit may only be deducted from the taxpayer's income tax liability. Any portion of the tax credit that remains unused at the end of the taxpayer's tax year may be carried

---

[24] See https://gonm.biz/business-resource-center/edd-programs-for-business/finance-development/angel-investment-tax-credit/. Last viewed October 14, 2016.
[25] For assistance regarding this credit, contact the EDD at 505-827-0300 or email angel.investment@state.nm.us.
[26] §7-2-18.17E NMSA 1978.
[27] §7-2-18.17G NMSA 1978.
[28] §7-2-18.17H NMSA 1978.

forward for five consecutive years.[29]

A taxpayer claiming the credit must file a completed Form RPD-41320, *Angel Investment Credit Claim Form,* and a copy of the certificate of eligibility with the TRD no later than one year following the end of the calendar year in which the qualified investment was made. Form RPD-41320 should be attached to the New Mexico personal income tax return for the year in which the angel investment credit is taken.

A claim for the credit may not be made or allowed with respect to any investment made after December 31, 2025.

Additional important terms

For purposes of the credit, "equity" is the common or preferred stock of a corporation, a partnership interest in a limited partnership, or a membership interest in a limited liability company, including debt subject to an option in favor of the creditor to convert the debt into common or preferred stock, a partnership interest or a membership interest.[31]

A "business" is a corporation, general partnership, limited partnership, limited liability company or other similar entity, but excludes an entity that is a government or a nonprofit organization designated as such by the federal government or any state.[32]

An "investment round" means an offer and sale of securities and all other offers and sales of securities that would be integrated with such offer and sale of securities under Regulation D issued by the federal Securities and Exchange Commission pursuant to the federal Securities Act of 1933, as amended.[33]

¶ 11.4 Agricultural water conservation tax credit (Expired effective January 1, 2013)

A tax credit had been available for agricultural water conservation expenses incurred for improvements in irrigation systems or water management methods. The improvements had to be designed primarily to substantially conserve water on land used to produce

---

[29] §7-2-18.17I NMSA 1978.
[31] §7-2-18.17K(3) NMSA 1978.
[32] §7-2-18.17K(2) NMSA 1978.
[33] §7-2-18.17K(4) NMSA 1978.

Business-related Credits

agricultural products, harvest or grow trees, or sustain livestock. The credit amount was 35% of eligible expenses incurred in calendar year 2008 and 50% of expenses in subsequent years through December 31, 2012, when the credit expired.[34] The maximum annual credit allowed was $10,000.

Although the credit expired effective January 1, 2013, excess credits may be carried forward for five consecutive years from the tax year in which the qualified eligible expenses were incurred. Form RPD-41319, *Agricultural Water Conservation Tax Credit Claim Form*, must be attached to the return to claim the carryover credits.

¶11.5 Advanced energy income tax credit

A taxpayer holding an interest in a qualified generating facility (QGF) located in New Mexico may claim an advanced energy income tax credit (AEITC) in an amount equal to 6% of the development and construction costs ("eligible generation plant costs") of the QGF. A claimed tax credit must be verified and approved by the New Mexico Environment Department (NMED) and may be claimed only by an individual who files a New Mexico income tax return.[35]

The eligible generation plant costs are the expenses incurred for the development and construction of a qualified generating facility and include expenses related to –

- permitting;
- site characterization and assessment;
- engineering;
- design;
- carbon dioxide capture, treatment, compression, transportation and sequestration;
- site and equipment acquisition; and
- fuel supply development used directly and exclusively in a QGF.[36]

The value of eligible generation plant costs equals the adjusted basis

---

[34] §7-2-18.20 NMSA 1978
[35] §7-2-18.25 NMSA 1978.
[36] §7-2-18.25L(3) NMSA 1978.

established for the QGF under the Internal Revenue Code.[37]

A QGF is a facility that begins construction not later than December 31, 2015, and is:

- a solar thermal electric generating facility that begins construction on or after July 1, 2007 and which may include an associated renewable energy storage facility;
- a solar photovoltaic electric generating facility that begins construction on or after July 1, 2009 and which may include an associated renewable energy storage facility;
- a geothermal electric generating facility that begins construction on or after July 1, 2009;
- a recycled energy project if that facility begins construction on or after July 1, 2007; or
- a new or repowered coal-based electric generating facility and an associated coal gasification facility.[38]

An "interest in a QGF" includes –

- the title to a QGF;
- a leasehold interest in a QGF;
- an ownership interest in a business or entity that is taxed for federal income tax purposes as a partnership that holds title to or a leasehold interest in a QGF; or
- an ownership interest, through one or more intermediate entities that are each taxed for federal income tax purposes as a partnership, in a business that holds title to or a leasehold interest in a QGF.[39]

Applying for the credit

An "entity" (defined below as including an individual) that holds an interest in a QGF may request a certificate of eligibility from the NMED to enable the requester to apply for an AEITC. The NMED must:

1. determine if the facility is a QGF;

---

[37] Form RPD-41333, Advanced Energy Tax Credit Application Instructions (Rev. 12/2015), p. 2.
[38] §7-2-18.25L(8) NMSA 1978.
[39] §7-2-18.25L[6] NMSA 1978.

Business-related Credits

2. require that the requester provide the NMED with the information necessary to assess whether the requester's facility meets the criteria to be a QGF;
3. issue a certificate to the requester stating that the facility is or is not a QGF within 180 days after receiving all information necessary to make a determination;
4. issue a schedule of fees in which no fee exceeds $150,000, and deposit these fees in the state air quality permit fund;[40] and
5. report annually to the appropriate interim legislative committee information that will allow the legislative committee to analyze the effectiveness of the AEITC.[41]

Taxpayers holding less than 100% of the interest in the QGF must designate an individual to submit the application, the eligible generation plant costs incurred during the calendar year, and the relative interest of those costs attributed to each eligible interest holder.

Once the NMED issues the certificate of eligibility, the claimant should submit Form RPD-41333, *Advanced Energy Tax Credit Application*, to the TRD for approval. The certificate of eligibility should be attached to the application, along with the certificate showing the claimant's interest in the QGF, and information required to establish the amount of the tax credit. This application should be submitted within one year after the end of the calendar year in which the eligible generation plant costs are incurred.

A taxpayer may be allocated the right to claim the AEITC without regard to the taxpayer's relative interest in the QGF, if:

1. the business entity making the allocation provides notice of the allocation and the taxpayer's interest in the QGF to the NMED;
2. allocations to the taxpayer and all other taxpayers allocated a right to claim the AEITC do not exceed 100% of the AEITC allowed for the QGF; and
3. the taxpayer and all other taxpayers allocated a right to claim the AEITCs collectively own at least a 5% interest in the

---

[40] Created pursuant to §74-2-15 NMSA 1978.
[41] §7-2-18.25C NMSA 1978.

QGF.[42]

A taxpayer allocates the right to claim all or a portion of the AEITC by completing the *Notice of Allocation of Right to Claim Advanced Energy Tax Credit* and attaching it to Form RPD-41333. A Pass-Through Entity (PTE) may not claim the AEITC. To allocate the right to claim the credit to the pass-through entity owners, the PTE must complete and attach it to Form RPD-41333.

Once approved by TRD, the claimant may apply all or part of the credit against the personal or corporate income tax due, the gross receipts, compensating, or withholding tax. A completed Form RPD-41334, *Advanced Energy Tax Credit Claim Form*, should be attached to the PIT-1 or any other returns to which the credit would be applied, and the claim should specify the amount of credit intended to apply to each return.

A husband and wife who file separate returns for a tax year in which they could have filed a joint return may each claim only one-half of the AEITC that would have been allowed on a joint return.[43]

The aggregate amount of all advanced energy tax credits claimed with regard to any QGF may not exceed $60,000,000.[44]

Expenditures for which a taxpayer claims an AEITC are ineligible for credits under the Investment Credit Act or any other credit against personal income tax, corporate income tax, compensating tax, gross receipts tax or withholding tax.[45]

If the AEITC exceeds the amount of the taxpayer's tax liabilities in the tax year in which it is claimed, the balance of the unpaid credit may be carried forward for ten years. The AEITC is not refundable or transferrable.[46]

Recapture of credit

If the NMED issues a certificate of eligibility, and the taxpayer does not sequester or control CO_2 emissions as required by January 1, 2017, or 18 months after the commercial operation date of the QGF, the

---

[42] §7-2-18.25D NMSA 1978.
[43] §7-2-18.25G NMSA 1978.
[44] §7-2-18.25K NMSA 1978.
[45] §7-2-18.25J NMSA 1978.
[46] §7-2-18.25I NMSA 1978.

Business-related Credits

NMED will revoke the certification and the taxpayer must refund the tax credits granted. But if the taxpayer demonstrates that to the extent feasible every effort had been made to sequester or control CO_2 emissions and the inability to meet the sequestration requirements was beyond the facility's control, the NMED will determine, after a public hearing, the amount of the credit to be refunded. The NMED will consider the facility's environmental performance and the extent to which the inability to meet the sequestration requirements was in the taxpayer's control. The recapture amount determined by NMED must be paid within 180 days following a final order.[47]

Other important terms

A "coal-based electric generating facility" is a new or repowered generating facility and an associated coal gasification facility, if any, that uses coal to generate electricity and that meets the following specifications:

1. emits the lesser of: a) what is achievable with the best available control technology; or b) .035 pound per million BTUs of sulfur dioxide, .025 pound per million BTUs of oxides of nitrogen and .01 pound per million BTUs of total particulates in the flue gas;
2. removes the greater of: a) what is achievable with the best available control technology; or b) 90% of the mercury from the input fuel;
3. captures and sequesters or controls carbon dioxide emissions so that by the later of January 1, 2017 or 18 months after the commercial operation date of the coal-based electric generating facility, no more than 1,100 pounds per megawatt-hour of carbon dioxide is emitted into the atmosphere;
4. all infrastructure required for sequestration is in place by the later of January 1, 2017 or 18 months after the commercial operation date of the coal-based electric generating facility;
5. includes methods and procedures to monitor the disposition of the carbon dioxide captured and sequestered from the coal-based electric generating facility; and

---

[47] Form RPD-41333, Advanced Energy Tax Credit Application Instructions (Rev. 2/2015), p. 2.

6. does not exceed a name-plate capacity of 700 net megawatts.[48]

A "geothermal electric generating facility" is a facility with a name-plate capacity of one megawatt or more that uses geothermal energy to generate electricity, including a facility that captures and provides geothermal energy to a preexisting electric generating facility using other fuels in part.

"Name-plate capacity" means the maximum rated output of the facility measured as alternating current or the equivalent direct current measurement.[49]

"Recycled energy" is energy produced by a generation unit with a name-plate capacity of not more than fifteen megawatts that converts the otherwise lost energy from the exhaust stacks or pipes to electricity without combustion of additional fossil fuel.[50]

"Sequester" means to store, or chemically convert, carbon dioxide in a manner that prevents its release into the atmosphere and may include the use of geologic formations and enhanced oil, coalbed methane or natural gas recovery techniques.[51]

A "solar photovoltaic electric generating facility" is an electric generating facility with a name-plate capacity of one megawatt or more that uses solar photovoltaic energy to generate electricity.[52]

A "solar thermal generating facility" is an electric generating facility with a name-plate capacity of one megawatt or more that uses solar thermal energy to generate electricity, including a facility that captures and provides solar energy to a preexisting electric generating facility using other fuels in part.[53]

An "entity" is defined as an individual, estate, trust, receiver, cooperative association, club, corporation, company, firm, partnership, limited liability company, limited liability partnership, joint venture, syndicate or other association or a gas, water or electric utility

---

[48] §7-2-18.25L(2) NMSA 1978.
[49] §7-2-18.25L(5) NMSA 1978.
[50] §7-2-18.25L(9) NMSA 1978.
[51] §7-2-18.25L(10) NMSA 1978.
[52] §7-2-18.25L(11) NMSA 1978.
[53] §7-2-18.25L(12) NMSA 1978.

Business-related Credits

owned or operated by a county or municipality.[54]

¶ 11.6 Agricultural biomass income tax credit

In order to encourage the sale and use of agricultural biomass as a fuel, New Mexico provides a tax credit for the transfer of agriculture biomass to a facility that uses agricultural biomass to generate electricity or make biocrude or other liquid or gaseous fuel for commercial use. A taxpayer who owns a dairy or feedlot may apply for an agricultural biomass income tax credit equal to $5.00 per wet ton of agricultural biomass transported from the taxpayer's dairy or feedlot to a facility that uses agricultural biomass to generate electricity or make biocrude or other liquid or gaseous fuel for commercial use.[55] To qualify for the credit an individual must own a dairy or feedlot and file a New Mexico income tax return for a tax year beginning on or after January 1, 2011 and ending prior to January 1, 2020.

A taxpayer who claims an agricultural biomass personal income tax credit may not also claim an agricultural biomass corporate income tax credit for transportation of the same agricultural biomass.[56]

The New Mexico Energy, Minerals and Natural Resources Department ("EMNRD") must limit the annual combined total of all agricultural biomass income tax credits and all agricultural biomass corporate income tax credits allowed to a maximum of $5,000,000. Applications for the credit are considered in the order received.[57]

---

[54] §7-2-18.25L(4) NMSA 1978.
[55] §7-2-18.26 NMSA 1978. As a result of the lack of specificity in the statute, it appears that as long as the taxpayer filed a tax return during that period, the taxpayer could receive the credit even after January 1, 2020. It is unlikely that this is the intent of the drafters. However, the regulations specify that certificates of transportation may be issued by the department for agricultural biomass transported during tax years beginning on or after January 1, 2011 and ending prior to January 1, 2020. §3.3.33.8 NMAC.
[56] §7-2-18.26G NMSA 1978.
[57] §7-2-18.26H NMSA 1978.

Qualifying for the credit

To obtain the credit, taxpayers must first apply for it. They can do that by submitting an application package to the EMNRD, which determines the quantity of agricultural biomass transported and used for the allowed purpose. If the EMNRD approves the application package, it will issue the facility owner a certificate of transportation.[58] A "certificate of transportation" is a document issued by the ENMRD to the applicant and the TRD, enumerated with a unique system certification number and certifying the number of wet tons of agricultural biomass transported to a qualified facility during a specified tax year. The purpose of this document is to certify the number of wet tons of biomass qualifying for the biomass personal income tax credit.[60]

Once the certificate is issued by EMNRD, the owner of the facility must promptly submit Form RPD-41362, *Agricultural Biomass Tax Credit Approval*, to the TRD with a copy of the certificate. After approving a credit, the TRD will furnish the applicant a numbered and dated document indicating the amount of credit granted.[61]

Claiming the credit

Once approval is received, the taxpayer claims the credit by submitting Form RPD-41361, *Agricultural Biomass Tax Credit Claim Form*, with the taxpayer's New Mexico personal income tax return. Any portion of the agricultural biomass income tax credit that remains unused in a tax year may be carried forward for up to four consecutive tax years following the tax year in which the credit originates until fully expended.[62]

Alternatively, the document provided by the TRD may be sold, exchanged or otherwise transferred to another taxpayer. The parties to such a transaction must notify the EMNRD of the sale, exchange or transfer within 10 days of the sale, exchange or transfer.[63] Form RPD-41363, *Notice of Transfer of Agricultural Biomass Tax Credit*, is used to report to TRD a transfer of approved credit to another taxpayer. The credit cannot be transferred to a pass-through entity.

---

[58] §3.3.33.10 NMAC.
[60] §3.3.33.7[G] NMAC.
[61] §7-2-18.26B NMSA 1978.
[62] §7-2-18.26C NMSA 1978.
[63] §7-2-18.26B NMSA 1978.

Business-related Credits

A taxpayer who otherwise qualifies and claims an agricultural biomass income tax credit with respect to a dairy or feedlot owned by a partnership or other business association of which the taxpayer is a member may claim the credit only in proportion to that taxpayer's interest in the partnership or business association. The total agricultural biomass income tax credits claimed in the aggregate with respect to the same dairy or feedlot by all members of the partnership or business association may not exceed the amount of the credit that could have been claimed by a single owner of the dairy or feedlot.[64] Notification of distribution of the credit from an owner of the facility that is a partnership or other business association passing all or a portion of the credit to its owners can be made at the time the credit is approved by EMNRD, by completing Section II on Form RPD-41362, *Agricultural Biomass Tax Credit Approval*.

A husband and wife who file separate returns for a tax year in which they could have filed a joint return may each claim only one-half of the credit that would have been allowed on a joint return.[65]

Important terms

"Agricultural biomass" means wet manure meeting specifications established by the EMNRD from either a dairy or feedlot commercial operation.[66]

"Biocrude" means a nonfossil form of energy that can be transported and refined using existing petroleum refining facilities and that is made from biologically derived feedstocks and other agricultural biomass.[67]

"Feedlot" means an operation that fattens livestock for market.[68]

"Dairy" means a facility that raises livestock for milk production.[69]

"Wet ton" means 2000 pounds of agricultural biomass qualifying for a certificate of transportation from the EMNRD. The number of wet tons qualifying for the certificate of transportation from a dairy

---

[64] §7-2-18.26D NMSA 1978.
[65] §7-2-18.26E NMSA 1978.
[66] §7-2-18.26I(1) NMSA 1978.
[67] §7-2-18.26I(2) NMSA 1978.
[68] §7-2-18.26I(3) NMSA 1978.
[69] §7-2-18.26I(4) NMSA 1978.

during a specific time period is the amount in tons transported from the agricultural biomass production facility calculated by adding:
1. the daily population of milking cows times 49 pounds of biomass per milking cow per day of apron scrape plus 70 pounds of biomass per day per milking cow of corral scrape; plus
2. the daily population of dry cows times 30 pounds of biomass per dry cow per day of apron scrape plus 45 pounds of biomass per day per dry cow of corral scrape; plus
3. the daily population of heifers times 17 pounds of biomass per heifer per day of apron scrape plus 26 pounds of biomass per day per heifer of corral scrape; plus
4. 13 pounds of biomass per milking cow per day pumped from the agricultural biomass production facility as greenwater for each day of the time period. If less than 100 percent of the biomass produced at the agricultural biomass production facility is transported to a qualified facility, the amount of calculated transported biomass qualifying for a certificate of transportation will be proportionally reduced by the percentage of each of the three categories (apron scrape, corral scrape and greenwater) of the biomass not transported to a qualifying facility during the time period.[70]

A "qualified facility" or "qualified energy producing facility" is a facility that the ENMRD has determined uses agricultural biomass to generate electricity or make biocrude or other liquid or gaseous fuel for commercial use.[71]

¶ 11.7 Business facility rehabilitation credit (no longer operative)

Although it remains on the books, this credit is no longer operative. It was enacted to support the Federal Enterprise Zone Program, which subsidized the renovation and rehabilitation of damaged or destroyed structures in enterprise zones. The Federal Enterprise Zone Program was discontinued, and after 2006 the New Mexico EDD listed the New

---

[70] §3.3.33.7V NMAC.
[71] §3.3.33.7Q NMAC.

Business-related Credits

Mexico Enterprise Zone Program as an inactive program.[72] Since there are no enterprise zones, the credit has no purpose.[73]

The statute provides a credit equal to 50% of the costs of the restoration, rehabilitation or renovation of qualified business facilities. A "qualified business facility" is a building located in a New Mexico enterprise zone that is suitable for use and is put into service by a person in the manufacturing, distribution or service industry immediately following the restoration, rehabilitation or renovation project. The building must have been vacant for the 24-month period immediately preceding the commencement of the project.[74]

Claims are limited to three consecutive years and may not exceed $50,000 for any single project. Any credit that remains unused at the end of the taxpayer's tax year may be carried forward for four consecutive years. Each claim for a credit must be accompanied by certification from the New Mexico Enterprise Zone Program Officer.[75]

¶ 11.8 Blended biodiesel fuel credit (expired as of December 31, 2012)

New Mexico has a special fuels supplier tax, which is an excise tax on suppliers for the privilege of receiving or using special fuel in New Mexico.[76] A special fuel is any diesel-engine fuel, bio diesel, blended bio-diesel, or kerosene used to propel a motor vehicle. There are exceptions and deductions, related to the imposition of the tax, listed in the statute.[77] The tax applies to the gallons of special fuel received in New Mexico and is owed either by the rack operator, if sold to a non-registered customer, or by the registered New Mexico supplier buying the special fuel. The tax is $0.21 per gallon, plus an additional petroleum products loading fee. The revenue is deposited in the Tax Administration Suspense Fund and distributed to the Local

---

[72] 2015 CIT-5, New Mexico Qualified Business Facility Rehabilitation Credit Instructions, p. 1. See also *FYI-106, Claiming Tax Credits for CRS and Business-Related Income*, p. 16 (Rev. 5/2016).
[73] §7-2-18.4 and §7-2A-15 NMSA 1978.
[74] §7-2-18.4G NMSA 1978.
[75] §7-2-18.4B NMSA 1978.
[76] §7-16A-3 NMSA 1978.
[77] §7-16A-2Q NMSA 1978. See §7-16A-10 NMSA 1978

Governments Road Fund and the State Road Fund.

In order to encourage the creation or expansion of blended biodiesel fuel facilities in the state, an income tax credit was established for the use of blended biodiesel fuel. A taxpayer who is liable for payment of the special fuel excise tax[78] and who files a New Mexico income tax return is eligible to claim a credit against income tax liability for each gallon of blended biodiesel fuel on which that person paid the special fuel excise tax in the tax year, or would have paid the special fuel excise tax in the tax year but was allowed deductions or the treaty exemption for North Atlantic Treaty Organization use.[79]

A "blended biodiesel" fuel is a diesel fuel that contains at least two percent biodiesel.[80] The credit equals the following amounts for the following periods:

- from January 1, 2007 until December 31, 2010, at a rate of three cents ($.03) per gallon;
- from January 1, 2011 until December 31, 2011, at a rate of two cents ($.02) per gallon; and
- January 1, 2012 until December 31, 2012, at a rate of one cent ($.01) per gallon.[81]

Consequently, this credit expired for periods after December 31, 2012. However, any unused credit may be carried over for five years. The credit could not be claimed with respect to the same blended biodiesel fuel for which a credit has been claimed pursuant to the Corporate Income and Franchise Tax Act or for which a credit or refund has been claimed in the case of special fuel destroyed by fire, accident or acts of God before retail sale.[82] The credit is neither refundable nor transferable.

A husband and wife who file separate returns for a tax year in which they could have filed a joint return may each claim only one-half of the credit that would have been allowed on a joint return.[83]

---

[78] See subsections A through D of §7-16A-2.1 NMSA 1978.
[79] §7-2-18.21 NMSA 1978. See §7-16A-10B-F NMSA 1978. See ¶4.3.3. for definition of North Atlantic Treaty Organization (or NATO).
[80] §7-2-18.21G(2) NMSA 1978.
[81] §7-2-18.21A NMSA 1978.
[82] §7-2-18.21B NMSA 1978. See §7-16A-13 NMSA 1978.
[83] §7-2-18.21D NMSA 1978.

Business-related Credits

A taxpayer who otherwise qualified for and claimed a credit for blended biodiesel fuel on which special fuel excise tax has been paid by a partnership or other business association of which the taxpayer is a member may claim a credit only in proportion to the taxpayer's interest in the partnership or business association. The total credit claimed in the aggregate by all members of the partnership or business association could not exceed the amount of credit otherwise allowed.[84]

To claim the credit, a taxpayer used Form RPD-41322, *Blended Biodiesel Fuel Tax Credit Application*, for reporting qualifying biodiesel fuel receipts to establish eligibility for the credit. A taxpayer could establish eligibility for all or a portion of a calendar year, but all approved credits from qualifying blended biodiesel fuel must have been claimed on the income tax return for the tax period in which the special fuels excise tax was due. A detailed schedule of the qualified gallons sold or deducted, or the treaty exemption for North Atlantic Treaty Organization use had to be attached.

Important terms

A "rack operator" is the operator of a refinery in New Mexico, any person who blends special fuel in the state or the owner of special fuel stored at a pipeline terminal in the state.[87]

"Diesel fuel" is any diesel-engine fuel used for the generation of power to propel a motor vehicle.[88]

"Biodiesel" is defined as renewable, biodegradable, monoalkyl ester combustible liquid fuel that is derived from agricultural plant oils or animal fats and that meets American society for testing and materials D 6751 standard specification for biodiesel B100 blend stock for distillate fuels.[89]

¶ 11.9 Cancer clinical trial tax credit (expires for tax years beginning after December 31, 2015)

In order to encourage New Mexico physicians to participate as clinical trial investigators by performing cancer clinical trials of new treatments

---

[84] §7-2-18.21C NMSA 1978.
[87] §7-16A-2L NMSA 1978.
[88] §7-2-18.21G(3) NMSA 1978.
[89] §7-2-18.21G(1) NMSA 1978.

and making cancer clinical trials more readily available to patients in the state, New Mexico provides a cancer clinical trial tax credit for tax years beginning on or after January 1, 2012, but before January 1, 2016.[90]

A taxpayer may claim a cancer clinical trial tax credit of $1,000 for each patient participating in a cancer clinical trial under the taxpayer's supervision, for a maximum credit of $4,000 for all cancer clinical trials conducted by that taxpayer during the tax year. To qualify, the taxpayer must be an oncologist who is a physician licensed pursuant to the Medical Practice Act and whose practice is located in rural New Mexico.[91] The taxpayer must file an individual New Mexico income tax return and not be a dependent of another taxpayer.[92]

A "cancer clinical trial" is a clinical trial:

1. conducted for the purposes of the prevention of or the prevention of reoccurrence of cancer or the early detection or treatment of cancer for which no equally or more effective standard cancer treatment exists;
2. that is not designed exclusively to test toxicity or disease pathophysiology and has a therapeutic intent;
3. provided in New Mexico as part of a scientific study of a new therapy or intervention and is for the prevention, prevention of reoccurrence, early detection, treatment or palliation of cancer in humans and in which the scientific study includes all of the following:
   a. specific goals;
   b. a rationale and background for the study;
   c. criteria for patient selection; specific direction for administering the therapy or intervention and for monitoring patients;
   d. a definition of quantitative measures for determining treatment response;
   e. methods for documenting and treating adverse reactions;

---

[90] Form RPD-41358 described the credit being available for tax years beginning before January 1, 2016, but §7-2-18.27 NMSA 1978 describes the credit as being available for tax years beginning before January 1, 2015. Since the credit is now expired and has never been used, this discrepancy is moot.
[91] §7-2-18.27A NMSA 1978. See §61-6-1 NMSA 1978.
[92] §7-2-18.27 NMSA 1978.

and
   f. a reasonable expectation that the treatment will be at least as efficacious as standard cancer treatment.
4. that is being conducted with approval of at least one of the following:
   a. one of the federal national institutes of health;
   b. a federal national institutes of health cooperative group or center;
   c. the Department of Defense;
   d. the Food and Drug Administration in the form of an investigational new drug application;
   e. the United States Department of Veterans Affairs; or
   f. a qualified research entity that meets the criteria established by the federal National Institutes of Health for grant eligibility.
5. that is considered part of a cancer clinical trial;
6. that has been reviewed and approved by an institutional review board that has an active federal-wide assurance of protection for human subjects; and
7. in which the personnel conducting the clinical trial are working within their scope of practice, experience and training and are capable of providing the clinical trial because of their experience, training and volume of patients treated to maintain their expertise.[93]

The cancer clinical trial tax credit may only be claimed for the tax year in which the physician participates as an investigator in a clinical trial[94] and may not be carried forward to another year, or refunded.

A partnership or business association in which one or more members qualifies for a cancer clinical trial tax credit may claim only one cancer clinical trial tax credit. The total cancer clinical trial tax credit allowed by the TRD for all the members of a partnership or business association may not exceed the amount of cancer clinical trial tax credit that could have been claimed by one physician conducting, supervising or participating in the cancer clinical trial for which the

---

[93] §7-2-18.27(G)(1) NMSA 1978.
[94] §7-2-18.27C NMSA 1978.

credit is allowed.[95]

A husband and wife who file separate returns for a tax year in which they could have filed a joint return may each claim only one-half of the cancer clinical trial tax credit that would have been allowed on a joint return.[96]

To claim the credit, a taxpayer must submit a completed Form RPD-41358, *Cancer Clinical Trial Tax Credit Claim Form*, with Form PIT-1.

Important term

"Rural New Mexico" means a class B county in which no municipality has a population of 60,000 or more according to the most recent federal decennial census and includes the municipalities within that county, and includes any location outside of Bernalillo, Santa Fe, Sandoval, Doña Ana, San Juan, Los Alamos and De Baca Counties.[97]

¶ 11.10 Electronic card reading equipment tax credit

A taxpayer who is licensed to sell cigarettes, other tobacco products, or alcoholic beverages and has purchased and uses equipment that electronically reads identification cards to verify age may claim a one-time credit in the amount of $300 for each business location such equipment is in use. To qualify, a taxpayer must file an individual New Mexico income tax return and not be a dependent of another individual.[99]

This credit may only be deducted from the taxpayer's New Mexico income tax liability for the tax year and cannot be refunded or carried over or carried back to another year.[100] In addition, the credit is not transferrable. A husband and wife who file separate returns for a tax year in which they could have filed a joint return may each claim only one-half of the credit that would have been allowed on a joint return.[101]

---

[95] §7-2-18.27D NMSA 1978.
[96] §7-2-18.27E NMSA 1978.
[97] §7-2-18.27G(2) NMSA 1978.
[99] §7-2-18.8A NMSA 1978.
[100] §7-2-18.8B NMSA 1978.
[101] §7-2-18.8C NMSA 1978.

Business-related Credits

A taxpayer who otherwise qualifies and claims a credit for equipment owned by a partnership or other business association of which the taxpayer is a member may claim a credit only in proportion to his or her interest. The total credit claimed by all members of the partnership or association may not exceed $300 in the aggregate for each business location for which the partnership or association has purchased equipment and has it in use.[102]

To claim the credit, individuals complete and submit Form RPD-41246, *Income Tax Credit for Electronic Identification Card Reader Purchase and Use Statement*, along with the Form PIT-1. Owners of pass-through entities may claim the credit on their personal income tax returns. Each owner of the pass-through entity that claims the credit must supply a schedule of the names, addresses, and the pro rata credit amounts of all other entity owners, which may not exceed $300 for a single business location.

¶11.11 Geothermal ground-coupled heat pump tax credit

Geothermal heating and cooling takes advantage of the fact that the ground is warmer than outside air in the winter and cooler in the summer. Inserting small pipes into the ground allows heat to be transferred to and from a home or business. Heat is not created in this process; rather it is transported, and therefore no fuel is burned. To encourage this alternative energy source, New Mexico provides a tax credit for the purchase and installation of a geothermal ground-coupled heat pump. A "geothermal ground-coupled heat pump" is a defined as a system that –

1. uses energy from the ground, water or, ultimately, the sun for distribution of heating, cooling or domestic hot water;
2. that has either a minimum coefficient of performance of 3.4 or an efficiency ratio of 16 or greater; and
3. that is installed by an accredited installer certified by the International Ground Source Heat Pump Association.[103]

A taxpayer may apply for a credit of up to 30% of purchase and installation costs of a geothermal ground-coupled heat pump, not to

---

[102] §7-2-18.8D NMSA 1978.
[103] §7-2-18.24G NMSA 1978.

exceed $9,000.[104] A tax credit is available to a taxpayer who files an individual New Mexico income tax return for a tax year beginning on or after January 1, 2010 and who purchases and installs a geothermal ground-coupled heat pump after January 1, 2010 and before December 31, 2020 in a New Mexico residence, business, or agricultural enterprise owned by the taxpayer.

The TRD will allow a geothermal ground-coupled heat pump tax credit only for geothermal ground-coupled heat pumps certified by the Energy, Minerals and Natural Resources Department ("EMNRD"). Regulations issued by the EMNRD provide guidance as to what systems qualify and how to determine the cost of the system.[105]

The EMNRD may allow a maximum annual aggregate of $2,000,000 in geothermal ground-coupled heat pump tax credits.[106]

A taxpayer who otherwise qualifies and claims a geothermal ground-coupled heat pump tax credit with respect to property owned by a partnership or other business association of which the taxpayer is a member may claim a credit only in proportion to that taxpayer's interest in the partnership or association. The total credit claimed in the aggregate by all members of the partnership or association with respect to the property may not exceed the amount of the credit that could have been claimed by a sole owner of the property.[108]

A husband and wife who file separate returns for a tax year in which they could have filed a joint return may each claim only one-half of the credit that would have been allowed on a joint return.[109]

Applying for the credit

To apply for the tax credit an applicant may obtain an application form from the EMNRD and submit a complete package. One application package is submitted for each geothermal ground-coupled heat pump system.[110]

The EMNRD considers applications in the order received,

---

[104] §7-2-18.24A NMSA 1978.
[105] §7-2-18.24C NMSA 1978. See §§3.3.32.7 – 3.3.32.14 NMAC.
[106] §7-2-18.24D NMSA 1978.
[108] §7-2-18.24E NMSA 1978.
[109] §7-2-18.24F NMSA 1978.
[110] §3.3.32.9 NMAC. See http://www.emnrd.state.nm.us/ECMD/RenewableEnergy/geothermal.html. Last viewed

Business-related Credits

according to the day they are received, but not the time of day. If the EMNRD approves applications received on the same day and the applications would exceed the annual cap, the EMNRD divides the available tax credit on a prorated system cost basis.

The EMNRD reviews the application package to calculate the tax credit and check the accuracy of the documentation and determines whether the EMNRD will certify the geothermal ground-coupled heat pump system. If an application fails to meet requirements, the EMNRD disapproves the application and issues a disapproval letter stating the reasons for the disapproval.

If the EMNRD finds that the application package meets the requirements for the credit and an amount of tax credit is available, the EMNRD certifies the applicant's geothermal ground-coupled heat pump system and documents the taxpayer as eligible for a tax credit. If a tax credit is not available in the tax year of certification of the geothermal ground-coupled heat pump system submitted in the application package, the EMNRD places the taxpayer on a waiting list for inclusion in the following tax year, if a tax credit remains available. The EMNRD provides approval through written notification to the applicant, which includes the taxpayer's contact information, social security number, system certification number, net system cost eligible for the tax credit, the tax credit amount, and, if applicable, waiting list status. The EMNRD provides the TRD a copy of its approval notification thereby enabling the TRD to verify, process, and distribute each tax credit.[111]

Claiming the credit

To claim the tax credit, a taxpayer who has been certified for the credit submits a completed claim Form RPD-41346, *Geothermal Ground-Coupled Heat Pump Tax Credit Claim Form*, and the certificate of eligibility issued by the EMNRD with his or her personal income tax return. The amount of credit is entered on the applicable line of Schedule PIT-CR.

If a portion of the geothermal ground-coupled heat pump tax credit remains unused in a tax year, the unused portion may be carried forward for a maximum of 10 consecutive tax years following the tax

---

October 14, 2016.
[111] §3.3.32.10 NMAC.

year in which the credit originates until the credit is fully expended.[112]

Federal credit

In addition to the state tax credit, the federal government provides a 30% federal tax credit for a geothermal ground-coupled heat pump system through 2016.[113]

¶ 11.12 Job mentorship tax credit

To encourage New Mexico businesses to hire youths that are participating in career preparation education programs, New Mexico offers a job mentorship tax credit to eligible taxpayers who hire qualified students. An eligible taxpayer may claim a credit equal to 50% of the gross wages paid to qualified students who are employed by the business during the tax year for which the return is filed. An eligible taxpayer is an individual who files a New Mexico income tax return, who is not a dependent of another, and who is an owner of a New Mexico business.[114] A "New Mexico business" is a partnership, limited partnership, limited liability company treated as a partnership for federal income tax purposes, S corporation or sole proprietorship that carries on a trade or business in New Mexico and employs in New Mexico fewer than 300 full-time employees at any one time during the tax year.[115]

A "qualified student" is a student who is at least 14 years of age, but not older than 21, who is attending an accredited New Mexico secondary school on a full time basis, and who is a participant in a career preparation education program sanctioned by the secondary school.[116] A "career preparation education program" is a work-based learning or school-to-career program designed for secondary school students to create academic and career goals and objectives and to find employment in a job meeting those goals and objectives.[117]

The credit may be claimed for each tax year in which a business employs one or more qualified students. The maximum aggregate

---

[112] §7-2-18.24B NMSA 1978.
[113] IRC §25D.
[114] §7-2-18.11A NMSA 1978.
[115] §7-2-18.11I(2) NMSA 1978.
[116] §7-2-18.11I(3) NMSA 1978.
[117] §7-2-18.11I(1) NMSA 1978.

Business-related Credits

credit allowable may not exceed 50% of the gross wages paid to not more than 10 qualified students employed by the business for up to 320 hours of employment for each student in each tax year. The credit may be claimed for a maximum of three tax years for each qualified student. A taxpayer may not claim a credit in excess of $12,000 in any tax year. The taxpayer must certify that hiring the qualified student does not displace or replace a current employee.[118]

To claim the credit, individual taxpayers must file Form PIT-1 and Schedule PIT-CR, and attach Form RPD-41281, *Job Mentorship Tax Credit Claim Form,* along with Form RPD-41280, *Job Mentorship Tax Credit Certificate,* for each student employed during the tax year for which the return is filed. Schedule A of Form RPD-41281, *Job Mentorship Tax Credit Claim Form,* is attached, as well, if the taxpayer has unused job mentorship tax credit available as a carry forward from prior years, or if the total available credit can be claimed by one or more owners, partners, or associates and an allocation of relative interests is required.

The TRD will issue Form RPD-41280 upon request to any accredited New Mexico secondary school that has a school-sanctioned career preparation education program. The maximum number of certificates that may be issued in a school year to any one school is equal to the number of qualified students in the school-sanctioned career preparation education program on October 15 of that school year, as certified by the school principal. To obtain the certificates, the school principal completes and submits Form RPD-41279, *New Mexico Job Mentorship Tax Credit Certificate Request Form,* to a local district tax office.[119]

A school principal then may execute a job mentorship tax credit certificate with respect to a qualified student and transfer the certificate to a New Mexico business that employs that student. By executing the certificate with respect to a student, the school principal certifies that the school has a school-sanctioned career preparation education program and the student is a qualified student. A certificate cannot be transferred to another business, another school year or another

---

[118] §7-2-18.11B NMSA 1978.
[119] §7-2-18.11C NMSA 1978.

qualified student.[120]

The job mentorship tax credit may only be deducted from the taxpayer's New Mexico income tax liability for the tax year. It is not refundable or transferable. Any portion of the maximum credit that remains unused at the end of the taxpayer's tax year may be carried forward for 3 consecutive tax years, but the total credits claimed in a single year may not exceed $12,000.[122]

A husband and wife who file separate returns for a tax year in which they could have filed a joint return may each claim only one-half of the credit that would have been allowed on a joint return.[123]

A taxpayer who otherwise qualifies for and claims a job mentorship tax credit for employment of qualified students by a partnership, limited partnership, limited liability company, S corporation or other business association of which the taxpayer is a member may claim a credit only in proportion to his interest in the partnership, limited partnership, limited liability company, S corporation or association. The total credit claimed by all members of the business may not exceed the maximum credit allowable.[124]

¶11.13 Land conservation incentives credit

At times, people who wish to preserve open space and achieve other environmental purposes sometimes find it beneficial to donate their property to either a governmental entity or a non-profit organization that will maintain the property for public use. To encourage this type of gifting, New Mexico provides an income tax credit equal to 50% of the fair market value of the land or interest in land that is conveyed for the purpose of open space, natural resource or biodiversity conservation, agricultural preservation, or watershed or historic preservation. The conveyance must be an unconditional donation in perpetuity by the landowner or taxpayer to a public or private conservation agency eligible to hold the land and interests therein for conservation or preservation purposes.[125] Only a person listed as an

---

[120] §7-2-18.11C-D NMSA 1978.
[122] §7-2-18.11F NMSA 1978.
[123] §7-2-18.11G NMSA 1978.
[124] §7-2-18.11H NMSA 1978.
[125] §7-2-18.10A NMSA 1978.

Business-related Credits

owner on the deed conveying the land or interest in land is eligible for the land conservation incentives tax credit.[126]

The fair market value of qualified donations must be substantiated by a qualified appraisal prepared by a qualified appraiser. A "qualified appraisal" is generally an appraisal of such property that is conducted by a qualified appraiser in accordance with generally accepted appraisal standards. A "qualified appraiser" is an individual who has earned an appraisal designation from a recognized professional appraiser organization or has otherwise met minimum education and experience requirements, regularly performs appraisals for which the individual receives compensation, and meets such other requirements set forth in IRS regulations or other guidance.[127]

The credit originates in the year the property is conveyed, which is determined by the date that the deed is recorded with the county clerk.[128] The credit claimed by a taxpayer may not exceed $100,000 for a conveyance made prior to January 1, 2008 and $250,000 for a conveyance made on or after that date. The amount of credit used in a year may not exceed the individual income tax otherwise due in the tax year. The unused tax credit may be carried over for a maximum of 20 consecutive tax years following the tax year in which the credit originated until fully expended. A taxpayer may claim only one tax credit per tax year.[129] For purposes of the credit, a "taxpayer" is a citizen or resident of the United States, a domestic partnership, a limited liability company, a domestic corporation, an estate, including a foreign estate, or a trust.[130]

"Qualified donations" include the conveyance in perpetuity of a fee interest in real property or a less-than-fee interest in real property, such as a conservation restriction, preservation restriction, agricultural preservation restriction or watershed preservation restriction, pursuant to the Land Use Easement Act,[131] provided that the less-than-fee interest qualifies as a charitable contribution deduction under federal

---

[126] §3.13.20.8B NMAC.
[127] §7-2-18.10 NMSA 1978 references IRC §170 for the definitions of qualified appraisal and qualified appraiser. Those definitions are found in IRC §§170(f)(11)(E) and the regulations thereunder. See also §3.13.20.7[P] and [Q] NMAC.
[128] §3.13.20.8I NMAC.
[129] §7-2-18.10H NMSA 1978.
[130] §7-2-18.10K(2) NMSA 1978.
[131] §7-2-18.10C NMSA 1978. See §47-12-1 NMSA 1978.

rules.[132] Dedications of land for open space for the purpose of fulfilling density requirements to obtain subdivision or building permits are not be considered as qualified donations pursuant to the Land Conservation Incentives Act.[133]

Qualified donations are eligible for the tax credit if the donations are made to the state of New Mexico, a political subdivision thereof or a tax-exempt charitable organization which is described in §501(c)(3) of the Internal Revenue Code and which meets the requirements of §170(h)(3) of that Code.[134]

If a taxpayer claims a federal charitable income tax deduction for any contribution for which the credit is claimed, the taxpayer's itemized deductions for New Mexico income tax is reduced by the amount of the deduction.[135] An applicant claiming a tax credit pursuant to the Land Conservation Incentives Act may not claim a credit pursuant to a similar law for costs related to the same donation.[136]

Applying for the credit

As a first step in obtaining the credit, the land or interests in land donated must be certified by the Secretary of Energy, Minerals and Natural Resources Department ("EMNRD") as fulfilling the purposes of §75-9-2 NMSA 1978, which are to encourage private landowners to be stewards of lands that are important habitat areas or contain significant natural, open space and historic resources, and to encourage the protection of private lands for open space, natural resources, biodiversity conservation, outdoor recreation, farmland and forest land preservation, historic preservation and land conservation purposes.

A taxpayer may apply for certification of eligibility for the tax credit from the EMNRD by submitting a Land Conservation Assessment Application. The EMNRD website lists its assessment date deadlines. The website states that all Assessment Applications received by the deadline will be reviewed by the Natural Lands Protection Committee and the EMNRD Cabinet Secretary at a Public Meeting and that

---

[132] See IRC §170(h).
[133] See §75-9-1 NMSA 1978.
[134] §7-2-18.10D NMSA 1978.
[135] §7-2-18.10J NMSA 1978. See ¶8.2.4.
[136] §3.13.20.8K NMAC.

Business-related Credits

eligibility certification will be determined at that time.[138]

Applicants approved for eligibility must complete the Certificate of Eligibility Application. The Certification Application is reviewed by the Land Conservation Program Specialist and forwarded to the New Mexico Tax and Revenue Property Appraisal Bureau for a complete review. If the appraisal is approved, a Certificate of Eligibility, including a calculation of the maximum amount of tax credit to which the taxpayer is entitled, is mailed from the EMNRD Cabinet Secretary to the applicant. This letter is required when applying for a tax credit.

If after applying for the certification of eligibility, the applicant changes a proposed donation, the donation assessment report, or, the public or private conservation agency to which the applicant is making the donation (in the case of a proposed donation), a new assessment application must be submitted and a new favorable finding received before the applicant can apply for the certification of eligibility.[139]

Claiming the credit

Once the certificate of eligibility is received from EMNRD, the taxpayer must complete Form RPD-41335, *Land Conservation Incentives Tax Credit Application*, and submit it to the TRD with a copy of the certificate of eligibility. Once approval is received from TRD, Form RPD-41282, *Land Conservation Incentives Tax Credit Claim Form*, should be attached to a completed Form PIT-1. For pass through entities, once approval is received from TRD, Form RPD-41282 should be attached to Form PTE. Either the entity or the member may claim the credit, but not both. If applicable, the entity must apportion the credit according to the percentage of each member's interest.[140]

The approval document from the TRD is numbered for identification purposes and declares its date of issuance and the amount of the tax credit allowed for the qualified donation.

A taxpayer may apply for the land conservation incentives tax credit and then amend his or her tax return for the year the property is conveyed as long as the applicant receives approval of the land

---

[138] http://www.emnrd.state.nm.us/SFD/LandConservationTaxCredit.html. Last viewed October 14, 2016.
[139] §3.13.20.10A NMAC.
[140] Form RPD-41282, Land Conservation Incentives Tax Credit Claim Form Instructions (Rev. 7/2016), p. 1.

conservation incentives tax credit and files the amendment within a three-year period.[141]

Transferring of the credit

The tax credit document made on or after January 1, 2008, or an increment of that tax credit, may be sold, exchanged or otherwise transferred. Credits may only be transferred in increments of $10,000 or more. A tax credit or increment of a tax credit may be transferred only once to any taxpayer. A taxpayer to whom a credit has been transferred may use the credit for the tax year in which the transfer occurred and any unused amounts may be carried forward to succeeding tax years, but in no event may the transferred credit be used more than 20 years after it was originally issued.[142]

A transfer of a tax credit must be take place through a "qualified intermediary." Within 10 days of the transfer, the taxpayer must complete and notarize Form RPD-41336, *Notice of Transfer of Land Conservation Incentives Tax Credit,* notifying the TRD of the transfer. The qualified intermediary must keep an account of the credits and have the authority to issue sub-numbers registered with the TRD and traceable to the original credit. A qualified intermediary does not include a person who has been previously convicted of a felony or who has had a professional license revoked, but rather is engaged in public practice pursuant to the Public Accountancy Act,[143] is identified as a real estate broker or salesman,[144] or any entity owned wholly or in part or employing any of the foregoing persons.[145]

¶ 11.14 Preservation of cultural property credit

New Mexico has a colorful and interesting cultural heritage that serves the state well not only through tourism but also by adding to the indefinable mixture of old and new that makes New Mexico a great place to live. In order to help preserve structures that are a part of that heritage, New Mexico provides an income tax credit for the costs of restoring, rehabilitating, or preserving cultural property. The credit is

---

[141] §3.13.20.8I NMAC. See §7-1-26 NMSA 1978.
[142] §7-2-18.10H NMSA 1978.
[143] §61-28B-3 NMSA 1978.
[144] According to §61-29-2 NMSA 1978.
[145] §7-2-18.10I NMSA 1978; §3.13.20.7R NMAC.

Business-related Credits

available to a taxpayer who owns a cultural property listed on the official New Mexico register of cultural properties, files an individual New Mexico income tax return, and is not the dependent of another.[146] Since the credit was enacted in 1984, more than 800 rehabilitation projects have been approved for homes, hotels, restaurants, theaters and businesses.[147]

The credit equals 50% of the cost of restoration, rehabilitation, or preservation of a cultural property that is listed on the official New Mexico register of cultural properties, but the credit cannot exceed a maximum of $25,000 for a particular property. Both commercial and residential buildings may be eligible for the program. The credit limit is increased to $50,000 if the property is located within an arts and cultural district certified by the state or a municipality pursuant to the Arts and Cultural District Act.[148]

The credit may be claimed for each tax year in which restoration, rehabilitation or preservation is carried out. But claims for the credit are limited to three consecutive years. The credit may only be deducted from the taxpayer's income tax liability. It is not refundable, but any portion of the tax credit that remains unused at the end of the tax year may be carried forward for four consecutive years.[149] Unlike some other New Mexico tax credits, this credit may be not transferred to other taxpayers

To claim the credit, the taxpayer must comply with a two-part application process that requires the taxpayer to take the following steps:

1. submit a plan and specifications for restoration, rehabilitation or preservation to the cultural properties review committee (CPRC);[150]
2. receive Part 1 approval from the CPRC for the plan and specifications prior to commencement of the work to insure

---

[146] §7-2-18.2A(1) NMSA 1978.
[147] See the tax credit guide of the New Mexico Historic Preservation Division: http://www.nmhistoricpreservation.org/assets/files/grants-loans-tax/State-Tax-Credit-Guide-8-2015.pdf. Last viewed October 14, 2016. This guide provides a great deal of practical information with regard to qualifying for and claiming the credit.
[148] §7-2-182A(1) and (2) NMSA 1978; See §15-5A-1 et seq. NMSA 1978.
[149] §7-2-18.2F NMSA 1978.
[150] Created under §18-6-4 NMSA 1978.

conformation with program standards (the Secretary of the Interior's Standards for Rehabilitation);
3. receive Part 2 approval, consisting of certification from the CPRC after completing the restoration, rehabilitation or preservation, or CPRC-approved phase, that the work conformed to the plan and specifications and preserved and maintained those qualities of the property that made it eligible for inclusion in the official register; and
4. complete the project within 24 months of the date the project is approved by the CPRC. [151]

Part 2 of the application (submitted upon completion of the proposed rehabilitation) must be received by the historic preservation division (HPD) of the office of cultural affairs division at least 14 days prior to the CPRC's meeting in which it will be reviewed and within 60 days after the completion of the work. In no event, may Part 2 of the application be received later than January 25 of the year following the tax year in which the credit is claimed. If a Part 2 application is submitted by the January 25 deadline, it will be reviewed by the CPRC at their February meeting. At this meeting, the HPD determines whether the information presented is complete and adequate. The property owner must submit accurate and complete documentation, including a summary sheet of expenditures along with invoices, canceled checks, receipts, or any documents requested by the CPRC of all expenses for which the property owner proposes to claim the credit.[152]

The project term expires 24 months from the date of the Part 1 approval. Expenses incurred before the approval date or after the expiration date are ineligible for the credit. However, a new Part 1 application may be submitted after the expiration date, for additional expenses.

Both Part 1 and Part 2 approvals are necessary before claiming the credit.[153] The Part 2 approval will specify the amount of credit that the taxpayer is entitled to and the years for which the credit may be claimed. Since expenses may be incurred in a year prior to obtaining

---

[151] §7-2-18.2B NMSA 1978.
[152] §4.10.9.9E NMAC.
[153] See Form PIT-4, New Mexico Preservation of Cultural Property Credit.

Business-related Credits

the Part 2 approval and a credit may be earned in such years, a taxpayer might have to file amended returns to claim credits for those earlier years if original returns have already been filed for the year of project completion.

After the CPRC issues a Part 2 approval, a signed copy of the Part 2 application is sent to the applicant along with a notification letter. The credit may be claimed by completing Form PIT-4, *New Mexico Preservation of Cultural Property Credit*, for each project and attaching this form, as well as the signed application and notification letter, to Form PIT-1. The claim must be submitted with the tax return for the year in which the restoration, rehabilitation or preservation is carried out. If applicable a certified statement from the state coordinator of New Mexico arts and cultural districts must also be attached.

A husband and wife who file separate returns for a tax year in which they could have filed a joint return may each claim only one-half of the credit that would have been allowed on a joint return.[154]

In the case of a joint-venture or part ownership, or partnership, owners may claim the credit only in proportion to their interest in the ownership or partnership. The term "owner" includes the owner of a leasehold interest in a registered cultural property if the term of the lease (without considering renewal periods) is at least five years.

A taxpayer may claim a credit on a restoration, rehabilitation or preservation project on property owned by a partnership of which the taxpayer is a member in proportion to the taxpayer's interest in the partnership. The total credit claimed by all members of the of business entity may not exceed $25,000, or $50,000 if the property is located in a certified arts and cultural district for any single project.[155]

The ITA requires the state historic preservation division to promulgate regulations for implementation of this cultural preservation credit and such regulations may be found in the New Mexico Administrative Code.[156]

The federal government also provides a rehabilitation tax credit for rehabilitation of historic, income-producing buildings that are

---

[154] §7-2-18.2D NMSA 1978.
[155] §3.3.13.10D NMAC.
[156] See §§4.10.9.1 NMAC - 4.10.9.14 NMAC.

"certified historic structures."[157] The credit equals 20% of qualifying expenses. A 10% credit is also available in the case of the rehabilitation of non-historic buildings placed in service before 1936. The building must be rehabilitated for income-producing use. In order to qualify, the rehabilitation must meet three criteria: at least 50% of the existing external walls must remain in place as external walls, at least 75% of the existing external walls must remain in place as either external or internal walls, and at least 75% of the internal structural framework must remain in place.[158] A taxpayer may claim both the state and federal credits if the qualifications for each are met.

For both the state and federal tax credits, the HPD is the portal for submission of applications and for general advice about the programs.[159] Both programs have adopted the Secretary of the Interior's Standards for Rehabilitation. For the state program, the decisions are made by the CPRC and for the federal Historic Tax Credit, the decisions are made by the NPS ("National Park Service") in Washington, DC.

¶11.15 Rural job tax credit

To encourage the start of new businesses and the hiring of employees in rural areas, New Mexico enacted a rural job tax credit.[160] Eligible employers can earn a tax credit equaling 6.25% of the first $16,000 in wages paid for a qualifying job in a qualifying period.[161]

A "qualifying period" is the twelve-month period beginning on the day an eligible employee begins working in a qualifying job or the period of twelve months beginning on the anniversary of the day an eligible employee began working in a qualifying job. A qualifying job is one that is filled by an eligible employee for 48 weeks in a 12-month qualifying period beginning on the day the employee starts work.[162] The credit can be claimed for each qualified job for each of four qualifying periods in a Tier One Area and two qualifying periods in a

---

[157] See IRC §47. The federal credit is subject to recapture.
[158] See https://www.nps.gov/tps/tax-incentives.htm
[159] See nmhistoricpreservation.org. Last viewed October 14, 2016. Forms and documents may be accessed on this site.
[160] §7-2E-1.1B NMSA 1978.
[161] §7-2E-1.1C NMSA 1978.
[162] §7-2E-1.1N(5) and (6) NMSA 1978.

Business-related Credits

Tier 2 Area.[163]

The maximum amount of the credit for each qualifying job is 25% of the first $16,000 of wages paid if the job is performed or based in a Tier One Area and 12.5% of the first $16,000 of wages paid if the job is performed or based in a Tier Two Area.[164]

An eligible employer is one who is eligible for the state's Job Training Incentive Program ("JTIP").[165] In order to be eligible for JTIP an employer's business must be in one of the qualifying categories. These include companies that manufacture or produce a product in New Mexico and non-retail service companies that export a substantial percentage of services out of state (50% or more of revenues and/or customer base).[166]

An "eligible employee" is any individual other than an individual who has a proscribed relationship with the employer. These proscribed relationships, essentially related party or control relationships, include an individual that owns 50% of the employer corporation, an individual who has a relationship with the employer specified in IRC §§152(a)(1) to (a)(8) (dealing with dependents),[167] and, if the employer entity is not a corporation, any individual who owns more than 50% of the capital and profits interests in the entity. If the employer is an estate or trust, the employee may not be a grantor, beneficiary or fiduciary of the estate or trust.

A job is not eligible for a rural job credit if it results from a reshuffling of jobs as a result of a reorganization of a business. Specifically, a job is not eligible for the credit if –

1. the job is created due to a business merger, acquisition or other change in organization;
2. the eligible employee was terminated from employment in

---

[163] §7-2E-1.1C NMSA 1978.
[164] §7-2E-1.1A NMSA 1978.
[165] §7-2E-1.1N(2) NMSA 1978 requires the employer to be eligible for in-plant training under §21-19-7 NMSA 1978. This program is known and JTIP or Job Training Incentive Program.
[166] See JTIP, *Job Training Incentive Program Policy/Procedures Manual*, Fiscal Year 2017 for more details on eligible companies, which can be found at https://gonm.biz/business-resource-center/edd-programs-for-business/job-training-incentive-program/. Last viewed October 14, 2016.
[167] This reference to the Internal Revenue Code is apparently to the 1954 Code and not the more recent 1986 Code.

New Mexico by another employer involved in the change in organization; and

3. the job is performed by either the person who performed the job or its functional equivalent prior to the change in organization, or a person replacing the person who performed the job or its functional equivalent prior to the change in organization.[168]

A job is not eligible for a rural job tax credit if the job is created due to an eligible employer entering into a contract or becoming a subcontractor to a contract with a governmental entity that replaces one or more entities performing functionally equivalent services for the governmental entity in New Mexico unless the job is a qualifying job that was not being performed by an employee of the replaced entity.[169]

Applying for the credit

To receive the rural job tax credit, an eligible employer must apply to the TRD on Form RPD-41238, *Application for Rural Job Tax Credit*. As part of this application, the employer must attach Form RPD-41247, *Certificate of Eligibility For The Rural Job Tax Credit* in which the employer certifies the amount of wages paid to each eligible employee during each qualifying period, the number of weeks during the qualifying period the position was occupied, and whether the qualifying job was in a Tier One or Tier Two area.[170] If all the requirements for the credit are met, the TRD returns the application as approved and provides a credit number for identification and an issuance date.

Claiming the credit

To claim the credit, the taxpayer completes Form RPD-41243, *Rural Job Tax Credit Claim Form,* and attaches it to Form PIT-1. The holder of the tax credit document may apply all or a portion of the rural job

---

[168] §7-2E-1.1K NMSA 1978. A qualifying job that was created by another employer and for which the rural job tax credit claim was received by the TRD prior to July 1, 2013 and is under review or has been approved remains eligible for the rural job tax credit for the balance of the qualifying periods for which the job qualifies by the new employer that results from a business merger, acquisition or other change in the organization. §7-2E-1.1L NMSA 1978.
[169] §7-2E-1.1M NMSA 1978.
[170] §7-2E-1.1D NMSA 1978.

Business-related Credits

tax credit granted by the document against the holder's modified combined tax liability, personal income tax liability, or corporate income tax liability. Any balance of the rural job tax credit granted by the document may be carried forward for up to three years from the date of issuance of the tax credit document. The rural job tax credit may not be applied against a gross receipts tax imposed by a municipality or county.[171]

Transferring the credit

The tax credit documents may be sold, exchanged or otherwise transferred.[172] Form RPD-41365, *Notice of Transfer of Rural Job Tax Credit*, must be used to report to the TRD a transfer or distribution of an approved rural job tax credit to another taxpayer. This notice must be signed by the holder of an approved credit or the authorized representative of the holder. The notice must be mailed to TRD within 10 days of a sale, exchange or other transfer.

Important terms

"Wages" includes all compensation paid through the employer's payroll system, including those wages the employee elects to defer or redirect, such as the employee's contribution to a §401(k) or cafeteria plan program, but not including benefits or the employer's share of payroll taxes.[173]

A "Tier One Area" is: (a) any municipality within a rural area if the municipality's population according to the most recent federal census is 15,000 or less; or (b) any part of the rural area that is not within the exterior boundaries of a municipality.[174]

A "Tier Two Area" is any municipality within a rural area if the municipality's population according to the most recent federal decennial census is more than 15,000.[175]

In describing rural and tiered areas, the instructions to Form RPD-41238 states as follows:

---

[171] §7-2E-1.1E NMSA 1978.
[172] §7-2E-1.1F NMSA 1978.
[173] §7-2E-1.1N(10) NMSA 1978. This definition is effective July 1, 2013.
[174] §7-2E-1.1N(8) NMSA 1978.
[175] §7-2E-1.1N(9) NMSA 1978.

A rural area *excludes* Albuquerque, Corrales, Farmington, Las Cruces, Los Alamos County, Los Ranchos, Rio Rancho, Santa Fe, or Tijeras, or any area within a ten-mile zone around any of these municipalities. A tier two area is within the cities of Alamogordo, Carlsbad, Clovis, Gallup, Hobbs, and Roswell. A tier one area is anywhere within New Mexico not listed above.

¶ 11.16 Rural health care practitioner tax credit

To encourage doctors and nurses to work in rural New Mexico, the state enacted the rural health care practitioner tax credit in 2007. An eligible healthcare practitioner who provides healthcare service in an underserved rural area in a tax year may claim a maximum income tax credit of either $5,000 in the case of doctors or $3,000 in the case of other healthcare professionals. The credit is only available to a taxpayer who files a New Mexico income tax return and who is not a dependent of another person.[176]

To qualify for the maximum $5,000 or $3,000 credit, an eligible health care practitioner must have provided health care during a tax year for at least 2,080 hours at a practice site located in an approved, rural health care underserved area. An eligible rural health care practitioner who provided such health care services for at least 1,040 hours but less than 2,080 hours is eligible for one-half of the maximum credit amount.[177] No credit is provided for those who do not meet the minimum of 1,040 hours. A "practice site" is a private practice, public health clinic, hospital, public or private nonprofit primary care clinic or other health care service location in a health care underserved area.[178]

A "health care underserved area" is a geographic area or practice location that the Department of Health ("DOH") has determined, through the use of indices and other standards, provides insufficient health care services.[179] A "rural" area is an area or location identified by the DOH as falling outside of an urban area.[180]

---

[176] §7-2-18.22A and B NMSA 1978.
[177] §7-2-18.22C NMSA 1978.
[178] §7-2-18.22F(3) NMSA 1978.
[179] §7-2-18.22F(2) NMSA 1978.
[180] §7-2-18.22F(4) NMSA 1978.

Business-related Credits

An "eligible health care practitioner" is one of the following professionals:

- a certified nurse-midwife licensed by the Board of Nursing as a registered nurse and licensed by the Public Health Division of the DOH to practice nurse-midwifery as a certified nurse-midwife;
- a dentist or dental hygienist licensed pursuant to the Dental Health Care Act;[181]
- an optometrist licensed pursuant to the provisions of the Optometry Act;[182]
- an osteopathic physician [183] or an osteopathic physician assistant licensed pursuant to the provisions of the Osteopathic Physicians' Assistants Act;[184]
- a physician or physician assistant licensed pursuant to the provisions of the Medical Practice Act;[185]
- a podiatrist licensed pursuant to the provisions of the Podiatry Act; [186]
- a clinical psychologist licensed pursuant to the provisions of the Professional Psychologist Act;[187] and
- a registered nurse in advanced practice who has been prepared through additional formal education[188] to function beyond the scope of practice of professional registered nursing, including certified nurse practitioners, certified registered nurse anesthetists and clinical nurse specialists.

The eligible health care practitioners that may receive the maximum $5,000 credit comprise all eligible physicians, osteopathic physicians, dentists, clinical psychologists, podiatrists and optometrists. Those that may receive a maximum credit of $3,000 comprise all eligible dental hygienists, physician assistants, certified nurse-midwives,

---

[181] §61-5A-1 NMSA 1978.
[182] §61-2-1 NMSA 1978.
[183] Licensed pursuant to the provisions of Chapter 61, Article 10 NMSA 1978.
[184] §61-10A-1 NMSA 1978.
[185] Licensed pursuant to the provisions of Chapter 61, Article 6 NMSA 1978.
[186] **Licensed pursuant to the provisions of the Podiatry Act 61-8-1 NMSA 1978.**
[187] Licensed pursuant to the provisions of the Professional Psychologist Act 61-9-1 NMSA 1978.
[188] As provided in §§61-3-23.2 through 61-3-23.4 of the Nursing Practice Act.

certified registered nurse anesthetists, certified nurse practitioners and clinical nurse specialists.[189]

Qualifying for the credit

Before an eligible health care practitioner may claim the rural health care practitioner tax credit, the practitioner must submit an application to the DOH that describes the practitioner's clinical practice and contains additional information that the DOH may require.[190] The Department , then, will determine whether an eligible health care practitioner qualifies for the rural health care practitioner tax credit, and will issue a certificate to each qualifying eligible health care practitioner. The DOH also provides the TRD with appropriate information for all eligible health care practitioners to whom certificates are issued.

Claiming the credit

A taxpayer claiming the credit must complete Form RPD-41326, *Rural Health Care Practitioner Tax Credit Claim Form*, and file it with Form PIT-1. A copy of the certificate issued by the DOH must be included.

If the amount of the credit claimed exceeds a taxpayer's tax liability for the tax year in which the credit is being claimed, the excess may be carried forward for 3 consecutive tax years.[191]

¶ 11.17 Solar market development tax credit

A 10% credit is offered for an individual who installs a solar thermal system or a photovoltaic system in a New Mexico residence, business or agricultural enterprise that is owned by that individual. The credit is named the solar market development tax credit and the 10% rate is applied to the purchase and installation costs of the system.[192] The total solar market development tax credit allowed for either a photovoltaic system or a solar thermal system may not exceed $9,000.[193] The system

---

[189] §7-2-18.22B NMSA 1978.
[190] The instructions to Form RPD-41326, *Rural Health Care Practitioner Tax Credit Claim Form* (Rev. 7/2015), advise the health practitioner to apply for certification of eligibility by contacting the DOH at (505) 841-5849, by sending an email to RHCP.TaxCredit@state.nm.us, or by visiting their website at www.health.state.nm.us. Last viewed October 14, 2016.
[191] §7-2-18.22E NMSA 1978.
[192] §7-2-18.14A NMSA 1978.
[193] §7-2-18.14B NMSA 1978.

Business-related Credits

has to be purchased and installed after January 1, 2006 but before December 31, 2016.

A "photovoltaic system" is an energy system that collects or absorbs sunlight for conversion into electricity. A "solar thermal system" is an energy system that collects or absorbs solar energy for conversion into heat for the purposes of space heating, space cooling or water heating.[194]

Solar market development tax credits are not allowed for a heating system for a swimming pool or a hot tub or for a commercial or industrial photovoltaic system other than an agricultural photovoltaic system on a farm or ranch that is not connected to an electric utility transmission or distribution system.[195]

The TRD will allow solar market development tax credits only for solar thermal systems and photovoltaic systems certified by the New Mexico Energy, Minerals and Natural Resources Department ("EMNRD").[196]

The TRD may allow a maximum annual aggregate of $2,000,000 in solar market development tax credits for solar thermal systems; and $3,000,000 in solar market development tax credits for photovoltaic systems.[197]

Certifying the system

To qualify for the credit, a taxpayer must complete the Solar System Certification Application Form, which may be downloaded from the EMNRD web site.[198] The web site also contains an application checklist of all items that must be included with the application. The required forms are sent to the EMNRD. Upon approval, the EMNRD will send a letter certifying the system and approving the tax credit.

---

[194] §7-2-18.14G NMSA 1978.
[195] §7-2-18.14C NMSA 1978.
[196] §7-2-18.14B NMSA 1978. For detailed regulations regarding the specifications of qualifying systems, the determination of system costs, and other requirements, see §§3.3.28.1 – 3.3.28.20 NMAC.
[197] §7-2-18.14D NMSA 1978.
[198] www.emnrd.state.nm.us/ecmd/CleanEnergyTaxIncentives/SolarTaxCredit.html. Last viewed October 14, 2016.

Claiming the credit

A taxpayer claims the tax credit by completing Form RPD-41317, *Solar Market Development Income Tax Claim*, and filing it with the taxpayer's Form PIT-1. A copy of the letter from EMNRD certifying the system and approving the taxpayer for the credit must be included with Form RPD-41317.

Any portion of the solar market development tax credit that remains unused in a tax year may be carried forward for a up to ten consecutive tax years following the tax year in which the credit originates, until fully expended.[199] In such case, Schedule A of Form RPD-41317 must be completed and included in the filing.

A federal tax credit of 30% is also available for solar electric systems and solar water heating systems.[200]

¶ 11.18 Sustainable building tax credit

Energy conservation is an important government priority in New Mexico, and one element of the state's conservation program is the promotion of green buildings.[201] A green building, which is also known as a sustainable building, is one that uses the latest energy saving practices in design and construction. As an incentive to the private sector to build or renovate buildings in an energy conscious manner, the state enacted the sustainable building tax credit ("SBTC") in 2007.[202] In 2013, the SBTC was modified, and then in 2015, a new credit, called the New Sustainable Building Credit ("NSBTC") was enacted, although this new credit looks a lot like the prior one.

¶ 11.18.1 New sustainable building tax credit

The NSBTC is effective for tax years beginning on or after January 1, 2017 for the construction of a sustainable building, the renovation of an existing building into a sustainable building, or the permanent installation of manufactured housing that is a sustainable building, regardless of where the housing is manufactured.[203] The credit is

---

[199] §7-2-18.4E NMSA 1978.
[200] §25D(a)(1) and (2).
[201] See Executive Order 2006-001, which set energy saving standards for government buildings.
[202] See §7-2-18.19 NMSA 1978.
[203] §7-2-18.29 NMSA 1978.

Business-related Credits

determined by multiplying the qualified occupied square footage of a sustainable building by the tax credit amount provided for each square foot. The amount of the tax credit per square foot depends on the level of energy conservation that the building has achieved. The NSBTC may not be claimed for a building for the personal income tax if the NSBTC provided for in the Corporate Income and Franchise Tax Act has been claimed with respect to the same building.[204]

An important term is "sustainable building" which is defined as either a sustainable commercial building or a sustainable residential building. The terms sustainable commercial building and sustainable residential building are further defined below. A building owned by state or local governments, public school districts or tribal agencies does not qualify as a sustainable building for purposes of the NSBTC.[205]

To qualify for the NSBTC for tax years ending on or before December 31, 2026, a building must achieve a silver or higher certification level in the LEED green building rating system or the Build Green New Mexico ("BGNM") rating system (with regard to residential buildings). The building's LEED rating or its BGNM rating determines the amount of credit per qualified occupied square foot. LEED is an acronym standing for Leadership in Energy and Environmental Design, and the LEED rating system establishes ratings for the design, construction and operation of green buildings.[206] BGNM is a rating system adopted by the Homebuilders Association of Central New Mexico and is based on the ANSI National Green Building Standard ("NGBS"), and provides four levels that can be attained; Bronze, Silver, Gold and the highest, Emerald. For purpose of the NSBTC, the BGNM rating system means the certification standards adopted by BGNM in November 2014, which includes water conservation.

The "qualified occupied square footage" of a building is the occupied space of the building as determined by: (a) the United States green building council for those buildings obtaining LEED

---

[204] §7-2-18.29A NMSA 1978.
[205] §7-2-18.29Q(13) NMSA 1978.
[206] The LEED system is a product of the U.S Green Building Council, which is a non-government affiliated non-profit 501(c)(3) organization that promotes sustainability in how buildings are designed, built, and operated.

certification; (b) the administrators of the BGNM rating system for those homes obtaining BGNM certification; and (c) the United States environmental protection agency for ENERGY STAR-certified manufactured homes.[207]

The NSBTC with respect to a residential building is calculated in accordance with Table 1.[208]

System Rating/Level	Qualified Occupied Square Footage	Tax Credit per Square Foot
LEED-H Silver or BGNM Silver	Up to 2,000	$3.00
LEED-H Gold or BGNM Gold	Up to 2,000	$4.50
LEED-H Platinum or BGNM Emerald	Up to 2,000	$6.50
Manufactured Housing	Up to 2,000	$3.00

Table 1 – NSBTC for Residential Buildings

The amount of the NSBTC with respect to a sustainable commercial building is calculated in accordance with Table 2.[209]

---

[207] §7-2-18.29Q(12) NMSA 1978.
[208] §7-2-18.29E NMSA 1978.
[209] §7-2-18.29D NMSA 1978.

Business-related Credits

LEED Rating Level	Qualified Square Footage	Tax Credit per Square Foot
LEED-NC Silver	First 10,000 Next 40,000 Over 50,000 up to 500,000	$3.50 $1.75 $.70
LEED-NC Gold	First 10,000 Next 40,000 Over 50,000 up to 500,000	$4.75 $2.00 $1.00
LEED-NC Platinum	First 10,000 Next 40,000 Over 50,000 up to 500,000	$6.25 $3.25 $2.00
LEED-EB or CS Silver	First 10,000 Next 40,000 Over 50,000 up to 500,000	$2.50 $1.25 $.50
LEED-EB or CS Gold	First 10,000 Next 40,000 Over 50,000 up to 500,000	$3.35 $1.40 $.70
LEED-EB or CS Platinum	First 10,000 Next 40,000 Over 50,000 up to 500,000	$4.40 $2.30 $1.40
LEED-CI Silver	First 10,000 Next 40,000 Over 50,000 up to 500,000	$1.40 $.70 $.30
LEED-CI Gold	First 10,000 Next 40,000 Over 50,000 up to 500,000	$1.90 $.80 $.40
LEED-CI Platinum	First 10,000 Next 40,000 Over 50,000 up to 500,000	$2.50 $1.30 $.80

Table 2 – NSBTC for commercial buildings

The terminology of the rating system is defined as follows:

- LEED-H is the LEED rating system for homes;
- LEED-NC is the LEED rating system for new buildings and major renovations;
- LEED-EB means the LEED rating system for existing

buildings;
- LEED-CI means the LEED rating system for commercial interiors;
- LEED-CS means the LEED rating system for the core and shell of buildings;
- LEED platinum means the rating in compliance with, or exceeding, the highest rating awarded by the LEED certification process;
- LEED gold means the rating in compliance with, or exceeding, the second-highest rating awarded by the LEED certification process; and
- LEED silver means the rating in compliance with, or exceeding, the third-highest rating awarded by the LEED certification process.[211]

The installation of a solar thermal system or a photovoltaic system eligible for the solar market development tax credit[212] may not be used as a component of qualification for the rating system certification level used in determining eligibility for the NSBTC, unless such credit has not been claimed with respect to that system and the building owner and the taxpayer claiming the sustainable building tax credit certify that a tax credit will not be claimed.[213]

Applying for the NSBTC

A person that is a building owner may apply to the EMNRD for a certificate of eligibility after the construction, installation, or renovation of the sustainable building is complete. Applications are considered in the order received. If the EMNRD determines that the building meets the requirements of a sustainable residential or commercial building, it issues a certificate of eligibility to the owner. The certificate will include the rating system certification level awarded to the building, the amount of qualified occupied square footage, and a calculation of the maximum amount of NSBTC for which the building owner would be eligible.

If the certification level for the sustainable residential building is

---

[211] §7-2-18.29Q[2]-[10] NMSA 1978.
[212] See §7-2-18.14 NMSA 1978.
[213] §7-2-18.29I NMSA 1978.

Business-related Credits

awarded on or after January 1, 2017, the EMNRD may issue a certificate of eligibility to a building owner who is the owner of the residential building at the time the certification level of the building is awarded or to the subsequent purchaser of the building with respect to which no credit has been previously claimed.[215]

Dollar Limitation on NSBTC's

There are limits on the amount of NSBTC that can be granted. The EMNRD may issue a certificate of eligibility only if the total amount of NSBTC certificates of eligibility under the ITA, the CIT, and FTA, the taxes against which the credit may be claimed, do not exceed in any calendar year an aggregate amount of:

1. $1,250,000 with respect to sustainable commercial buildings;
2. $3,375,000 with respect to sustainable residential buildings that are not manufactured housing; and
3. $375,000 with respect to sustainable residential buildings that are manufactured housing.[216]

However, in any tax year where applications for credits under categories 1, 2 or 3 are less than the limit for that type of sustainable building, the difference between the aggregate limit and the applications will be added to the aggregate limit of another type of sustainable building for which applications exceed the aggregate limit. Any excess not used in a tax year may not be carried forward to subsequent tax years.[217]

Claiming or transferring the NSBTC

To claim the NSBTC, the building owner must file Form RPD-41382, New Sustainable Building Tax Credit Approval, and enclose the certificate of eligibility issued by EMNRD and any other information the form may require. Once the TRD approves Form RPD-41382, the taxpayer can claim the NSBTC new by submitting Form RPD-41383, New Sustainable Building Tax Credit Claim Form, with the taxpayer's Form PIT-1,

Alternatively, once a holder or owner receives TRD approval of the credit, the credit may be sold, exchanged, or otherwise transferred. Form RPD-41384, *Notice of Transfer of New Sustainable Building Tax*

---

[215] §7-2-18.29F NMSA 1978.
[216] §7-2-18.29G NMSA 1978.
[217] §7-2-18.29H NMSA 1978.

Credit, is used to report a transfer of approved NSBTC.[218] Notice must be provided to the TRD within 10 days of a sale, exchange, or other transfer. The TRD will issue the new holder an approval for the credit transfer, a new credit number, and instructions for applying the credit to personal or corporate income tax due. An original building owner that is a partnership or other business association may pass TRD-approved credit to its owners by completing Sections I and II of Form RPD-41382 and following other instructions of that form.

If the approved amount of NSBTC for a tax year is less than $100,000, a maximum of $25,000 can be applied against the taxpayer's income tax liability for the tax year for which the credit is approved and the three subsequent tax years. If the approved amount is $100,000 or more, then increments of 25% of the total credit is applied in each of four tax years, including the tax year for which the credit is approved and the three subsequent tax years.[221]

If the sum of all NSBTCs that can be applied to a tax year exceeds the taxpayer's income tax liability for that tax year, the excess may be carried forward for a period of up to seven years.[222]

Married individuals who file separate returns for a tax year in which they could have filed a joint return may each claim only one-half of the new sustainable building tax credit that would have been allowed on a joint return.[223]

A taxpayer who claims a NSBTC with respect to a sustainable building owned by a partnership or other business association of which the taxpayer is a member may claim a credit only in proportion to the taxpayer's interest in the partnership or association. The total credit claimed in the aggregate by all members of the partnership or association cannot exceed the amount of the credit that could have been claimed by a sole owner of the property.[224]

---

[218] §7-2-18.29K NMSA 1978.
[221] §7-2-18.29L NMSA 1978.
[222] §7-2-18.29M NMSA 1978.
[223] §7-2-18.29O NMSA 1978.
[224] §7-2-18.29N NMSA 1978.

Business-related Credits

Important terms

A "sustainable residential building" is

1. a building used as a single-family residence as registered and certified under the BGNM or LEED-H rating system that:
   a. is certified by the United States green building council as LEED-H silver or higher or by BGNM as silver or higher;
   b. has achieved a home energy rating system index of 60 or lower as developed by the residential energy services network;
   c. has indoor plumbing fixtures and water-using appliances that, on average, have flow rates equal to or lower than the flow rates required for certification by WaterSense;
   d. if landscape area is available at the front of the property, has at least one water line outside the building below the frost line that may be connected to a drip irrigation system; and
   e. if landscape area is available at the rear of the property, has at least one water line outside the building below the frost line that may be connected to a drip irrigation system; or
2. manufactured housing that is ENERGY STAR-qualified by the United States environmental protection agency.[225]

"WaterSense" is a program created by the federal environmental protection agency that certifies water-using products that meet the environmental protection agency's criteria for efficiency and performance.[226]

A "sustainable commercial building" is

1. a multifamily dwelling unit, as registered and certified under the LEED-H or BGNM rating system, that is certified by the United States green building council as LEED-H silver or higher or by BGNM as silver or higher and has achieved a home energy rating system index of sixty or lower as developed by the residential energy services network, or

---

[225] §7-2-18.29Q[16] NMSA 1978.
[226] §7-2-18.29Q[18] NMSA 1978.

2. a building that has been registered and certified under the LEED-NC, LEED-EB, LEED-CS or LEED-CI rating system and that:
   a. is certified by the United States green building council at LEED silver or higher;
   b. achieves any prerequisite for and at least one point related to commissioning under LEED "energy and atmosphere", if included in the applicable rating system; and
   c. has reduced energy consumption beginning January 1, 2012 by 60% based on the national average for that building type as published by the United States Department of Energy as substantiated by the United States Environmental Protection Agency target finder energy performance results form, dated no sooner than the schematic design phase of development.[227]

"Manufactured housing" means a multi-sectioned home that is:
1. a manufactured home or modular home;
2. a single-family dwelling with a heated area of at least 36 feet by 24 feet and a total area of at least 864 square feet;
3. constructed in a factory to the standards of the United States Department of Housing and Urban Development, the National Manufactured Housing Construction and Safety Standards Act of 1974 and the Housing and Urban Development Zone Code 2 or New Mexico construction codes up to the date of the unit's construction; and
4. installed consistent with the Manufactured Housing Act and rules adopted pursuant to that act relating to permanent foundations.[228]

¶ 11.18.2 Sustainable Building Tax Credit (for tax years ending on or before December 31, 2016)

Prior to adopting the NSBTC, New Mexico had put in place a sustainable building tax credit ('SBTC')[229] very much like the NSBTC, except for some modifications the legislature had made in enacting the

---

[227] §7-2-18.29Q[16] NMSA 1978.
[228] §7-2-18.29Q[11] NMSA 1978.
[229] §7-2-18.14 NMSA 1978.

Business-related Credits

NSBTC. The SBTC applies to tax years ending on or before December 31, 2016. The following chart replicated from the EMNRD website outlines the differences between the NSBTC and the SBTC.[230]

		Old SBTC	**New SBTC**
Commercial (multi-family) Housing	Annual cap	$1,000,000	$1,250,000
	Credits	$.30 to $6.25/ sq. ft. depending on the LEED certification level and amount of square footage	Unchanged
	Maximum Size	500,000 sq. ft.	Unchanged
	Standard to Meet	LEED Silver or higher; 60% energy reduction from national average for same building type	Unchanged
Residential	Annual cap	$4,000,000	$3,375,000
	Credits	$2.50-$9.00/sq. ft. depending on LEED or Build Green NM certification level and amount of square footage	$3.00-$6.50/sq. ft. depending on LEED or Build Green NM certification level (same rate for all square footage)
	Maximize Size	3,000 sq. ft.	2,000 sq. ft.
	Standard to Meet	LEED Silver or higher or Build Green NM Silver or higher; HERS score of 60 or lower	LEED Silver or higher or Build Green NM October 2014 Silver or Higher, which includes water conservation standards; HERS score of 60 or lower

---

[230] http://www.emnrd.state.nm.us/ECMD/CleanEnergyTaxIncentives/SBTC.html. Last viewed October 14, 2016.

New Mexico Personal Income Tax Guide

		Old SBTC	New SBTC
	Water-saving Requirements	None	Must have indoor plumbing fixtures and water-using appliances that have average flow rates equal to or lower than the Environmental Protection Agency's "WaterSense" certification
			Requires a water line that can be connected to a drip irrigation system in the front and back of a residence in any potential landscaping areas
Manufactured Housing	Annual Cap	Included in residential building cap, with max for manufactured housing of $1,250,000	$375,000
	Credits	$3.00/sq. ft.	Unchanged
	Maximize Size	3,000 sq. ft.	3,000 sq. ft.
	Standard to Meet	EPA Energy Star Manufactured Housing	Unchanged
Additional Provisions	Credit start date	January 1, 2007	January 1, 2017
	Expiration of credit	December 31, 2016	December 31, 2026
	Cap reallocation	Can use remainder of commercial building annual cap for residential buildings	Remaining annual cap balance in any one category can be reallocated into another category, if needed
	Payout schedule	If <$100,000, max of $25,000/yr. until paid out; If >$100,000, 25% over four taxable years	Unchanged

Business-related Credits

	Old SBTC	New SBTC
Carryforward	Up to 7 years	Unchanged
Reporting	TRD compile annual report and in 2015 and every 5 years thereafter produce reports that analyze the effectiveness of this credit	TRD compile annual report and in 2019 and every 3 years thereafter produce reports that analyze the effectiveness of this credit

Qualifying for and Claiming the SBTC

An owner must apply for a certificate of eligibility from the EMNRD. After the EMNRD issues a certificate of eligibility, the building owner must complete Form RPD-41327, *Sustainable Building Tax Credit Approval*, and submit it to TRD with a copy of the certificate of eligibility and any other information that TRD requires. If the TRD approves the credit, the approved form is returned to the owner or holder. The SBTC allowed may be claimed against the owner's personal or corporate income tax liability or may be sold, exchanged, or otherwise transferred to another taxpayer.

If the holder is a partnership or other business association that passes the credit to its owners, each owner may claim a credit only in proportion to that owner's interest in the partnership or other business association. The total credit claimed may not exceed the amount of the credit that could have been claimed by a sole owner. The owner may pass the credit to its members by submitting Form RPD-41327 for each member, partner, shareholder, or beneficiary, who may claim a credit.

Once a taxpayer has received an approved RPD-41327, *Sustainable Building Tax Credit Approval*, he or she can apply the SBTC to his or her personal income tax due by submitting Form RPD-41329, *Sustainable Building Tax Credit Claim Form*, with Form PIT-1. Any excess SBTC may be carried forward for seven tax years from the tax year for which the credit was approved.

A TRD-approved holder may sell, exchange or transfer SBTCs to another taxpayer. Both the holder and the new holder, or their authorized representatives must notify the TRD within ten days of a sale, exchange, or other transfer by filing Form RPD-41342, *Notice of*

Transfer of Sustainable Building Tax Credit. This form also be used by a holder, other than the original building owner, who is a partnership or other business association passing the credit to its members, partners, shareholders, or beneficiaries.

Business-related Credits

¶ 11.19 Technology jobs (additional) tax credit

¶ 11.19.1 Overview

Research and development is the lifeblood of high technology industries and for states like New Mexico that wish to develop such industries, it is important to encourage the growth of R&D in their state. Over time, New Mexico has experimented with finding the right incentives to improve its economy,[231] and in 2015 it tried to optimize its two most significant R&D tax incentives by eliminating one and enhancing the other.

The credit that has been removed from the mix is the research and development small business tax credit (RDSBTC), which was repealed as of January 1, 2016.[232] This credit was, in any event, only effective for reporting periods through July 1, 2015. The RDSBTC is not an income tax credit; rather, it allows a qualified R&D small business to claim a RDSBTC equal to the sum of all gross receipt taxes or 50% of withholding taxes owed to New Mexico for the reporting period in which the business qualified for the credit.[233] For purposes of this old credit, a "qualified R&D small business" is a corporation, partnership, sole proprietorship or similar entity with 25 or fewer full-time employees (calculated on a full-time equivalent basis), with total revenues of no more than $5 million annually, and whose qualified R&D expenditures for the prior 12 months equaled at least 20% of its total expenditures for those calendar months. In any prior month, the business could not have more than 50% of its voting securities or other equity interest having the right to designate or elect the board of directors or other governing body owned directly or indirectly by another business.[234]

Through enactment of the new Technology Jobs and Research and Development Tax Credit Act[235] the state has enhanced its technology jobs tax credit (TJTC) and rechristened it as the technology jobs and research and development tax credit (TJRDTC). As of January 1, 2015, the rules of the new credit go into effect under the name of the TJTC,

---

[231] §7-9F-2 NMSA 1978, Effective January 1, 2016.
[232] HB2, 52nd Legislature, First Special Session, 2015, §24.
[233] §§7-9H-1 to 6 NMSA 1978.
[234] §§7-9H-2C NMSA 1978.
[235] HB2, 52nd Legislature, First Special Session, 2015, §10 to 18.

253

and then on January 1, 2016, the name of the credit is officially changed to the TJRDTC.[236] This credit, which is, in part, an income tax credit, has been enhanced by increasing the credit rate and by providing refunds to small businesses. For reporting periods between January 1, 2015, and June 30, 2015, a taxpayer who was eligible for the RDSBTC could claim either the RDSBTC or the TJTC, but not both.[237] The RDSBTC transitional rules are discussed below.

¶ 11.19.2 TJTC and TJRDTC

The following discussion will describe the TJRDTC and highlight the important modifications from the TJTC. As noted above, and it bears repeating, the TJTC becomes the TJRDTC on January 1, 2016, but the new TJRDTC provisions are applicable to qualified expenditures incurred on or after January 1, 2015, but under the name of TJTC. The TJTC rules apply for periods prior to that.

The TJRDTC is divided into two parts: the basic credit and the additional credit. In both cases the amount of the credit is doubled if the research takes place in a rural area. The basic credit equals 5% (4% prior to January 1, 2015) of the amount of qualified expenditures made by a taxpayer in conducting qualified research at a qualified facility.[238] The basic credit may be applied against the compensating tax, withholding tax, or gross receipts tax, excluding local option gross receipts tax.

The additional credit, which may be claimed against the taxpayer's income tax liability, requires incremental increases in R&D spending over a base amount of payroll expense. The additional credit equals 5% (4% prior to January 1, 2015) of the amount of qualified expenditures made by a taxpayer in conducting qualified research at a qualified facility, when the following requirements are met:[239]

1. the annual payroll expense of the taxpayer at the qualified facility is increased by at least $75,000 over the taxpayer's base payroll expense, and this increase has not been previously used to meet this requirement; and

---

[236] §7-9F-1 NMSA 1978, Effective January 1, 2016. HB2, 52nd Legislature, First Special Session, 2015, §23.
[237] HB2, 52nd Legislature, First Special Session, 2015, §22.
[238] §7-9F-5A NMSA 1978.
[239] §7-9F-5B NMSA 1978.

Business-related Credits

    2. there is at least a $75,000 increase in the taxpayer's annual payroll expense for every $1,000,000 in qualified expenditures claimed by the taxpayer in a tax year in the same claim.[240]

The taxpayer's "annual payroll expense" is the wages paid or payable to employees in the state[241] by the taxpayer in the tax year for which the taxpayer applies for the additional credit.[243] (The TJTC uses a one-year measuring period ending on the day the taxpayer filed for the additional credit.) The taxpayer's "base payroll expense" is the wages paid or payable by the taxpayer in the tax year prior to the tax year for which the taxpayer applies for an additional credit, adjusted for inflation.[244] (The TJTC uses a one-year measuring period ending on the day one year prior to the day the taxpayer applied for the additional credit.)

In calculating the annual payroll expense and base payroll expense, a taxpayer includes total wages paid to all employees at a qualified New Mexico facility.[245] "Wages" is defined as remuneration for services performed by an employee in New Mexico for an employer,[246] and has the same meaning as the definition of wages as that used for federal income tax withholding purposes.[247] Thus, wages used to meet the eligibility requirements of the TJRDTC are the same as those included in box 1 of Form W-2.[248] Any expenses not included as wages in Form W-2, such as expenses for employee health insurance, retirement plan contributions, or the value of employee stock options, are not included when calculating annual payroll expense and base payroll expense.[249]

During a tax year in which a taxpayer has been part of a business merger or acquisition or other change in business organization, the taxpayer's base payroll expense includes the payroll expense of all

---

[240] §7-9F-6B NMSA 1978.
[241] The language "in the state" was added by the TJRDTC Act.
[243] §7-9F-3B NMSA 1978.
[244] §7-9F-3C NMSA 1978. The adjustment is for any increase from the preceding tax year in the consumer price index for the United States for all items as published by the United States department of labor in the tax year for which the additional credit is claimed.
[245] §3.13.5.8A NMAC.
[246] §7-9F-3M NMSA 1978. Under the TJTC, wages included remuneration in cash or other form. It is not the clear whether the omission of the words "in cash or other form" from the revised statute has any significance.
[247] IRC §3401(a).
[248] §3.13.5.8A NMAC.
[249] §3.13.5.8B NMAC.

entities included in the reorganization for all positions that are included in the business entity resulting from the reorganization.[250] This rule concerning mergers or acquisition is new in the TJRDTC and does not appear in the TJTC.

Both the basic and additional credit are based upon "qualified expenditures," which is defined as expenditures, or an allocated portion of expenditures, made by a taxpayer in connection with qualified research at a qualified facility. The term includes expenditures for the following:

- depletable land and rent paid or incurred for land,
- improvements,
- the allowable amount paid or incurred to operate or maintain a facility,
- buildings,
- equipment,
- computer software,
- computer software upgrades,
- consultants and contractors performing work in New Mexico,
- payroll,
- technical books and manuals, and
- test materials.[251]

The amount of a qualified expenditure is the purchase price for the relevant property or service.[252] For allocated expenditures, the cost accounting methodology used for the allocation of the expenditure must be the same as the cost accounting methodology used by the taxpayer in its other business activities.

But qualified expenditures do not include any of the following: R&D expenditures reimbursed by a person who is not an affiliate of the taxpayer; any expenditure on property that is owned by a municipality or county in connection with an industrial revenue bond project; any expenditure on property for which the taxpayer has received any credit pursuant to the Investment Credit Act; or any

---

[250] §7-9F-3C NMSA 1978.
[251] §7-9F-3G NMSA 1978.
[252] §7-9F-7 NMSA 1978.

Business-related Credits

expenditure on property owned by the taxpayer or an affiliate before July 3, 2000.[253] An "affiliate" is a person who directly or indirectly owns or controls, is owned or controlled by, or is under common ownership or control with another person through ownership of voting securities or other ownership interests representing a majority of the total voting power of the entity.[254]

A qualified expenditure must be made for "qualified research," which has a definition similar to that used in the federal tax code with regard to the federal research tax credit. Qualified research is research that is —

1. undertaken for the purpose of discovering information:
   a. that is technological in nature; and
   b. the application of which is intended to be useful in the development of a new or improved business component of the taxpayer; and where
2. substantially all of the activities of which constitute elements of a process of experimentation related to a new or improved function, performance, reliability or quality, but not related to style, taste or cosmetic or seasonal design factors.[255]

For a research expenditure to qualify as a qualified expenditure, the research must take place at a "qualified facility," which is a facility in New Mexico at which qualified research is conducted, other than a facility operated by a taxpayer for the United States or any agency, department or instrumentality thereof.[256] A "facility" is a factory, mill, plant, refinery, warehouse, dairy, feedlot, building or complex of buildings located within the state, including the land on which it is located and all machinery, equipment and other real and tangible personal property located at or within it and used in connection with its operation.[257]

As noted above, the amount of the basic and additional credit for which a taxpayer is otherwise eligible is doubled if the qualified expenditures are incurred with respect to a qualified facility in a rural

---

[253] §7-9F-3G NMSA 1978. The TJTC also excludes expenditures for which the taxpayer received a credit under the Capital Equipment Tax Credit Act.
[254] §7-9F-3A NMSA 1978.
[255] §7-9F-3I NMSA 1978.
[256] §7-9F-3H NMSA 1978.
[257] §7-9F-3E NMSA 1978.

area.[258] A "rural area" is any area of the state other than the state fairgrounds, an incorporated municipality with a population of 30,000 or more according to the most recent federal decennial census, and any area within three miles of the external boundaries of an incorporated municipality with a population of 30,000 or more, according to the most recent federal decennial census.[259]

¶ 11.19.3 Applying for and Claiming the Basic Credit

A taxpayer may apply for approval of the basic credit by filing Form RPD-41385, *Application for Technology Jobs and Research and Development Tax Credit,* within one year following the end of the reporting period in which the qualified expenditure was made.[260] A taxpayer that has been granted approval for a basic credit by the TRD may claim the amount of the approved credit against the taxpayer's compensating tax, withholding tax or gross receipts tax, but excluding any local option gross receipts tax. Form RPD-41386, *Technology Jobs and Research And Development Tax Credit Claim Form,* is used for this purpose, and must accompany any return on which the taxpayer wishes to apply the credit. However, a taxpayer may not claim an amount of basic credit for a reporting period to the extent that it exceeds the sum of the taxpayer's compensating tax, withholding tax and gross receipts tax, excluding any local option gross receipts tax, due for that reporting period.[261] Any

---

[258] §7-9F-8 NMSA 1978.
[259] §7-9F-3K NMSA 1978. Under the TJTC a rural area is any area of the state other than a class A county, a class B county that has a net taxable value for rate-setting purposes for any property tax year of more than $3,000,000,000, the municipality of Rio Rancho and the area within three miles of the exterior boundaries of a class A county. By statute, county classifications are set every two years. A class B county has property valuation greater than 75,000,000 and population greater than 100,000; a B-Over class county has valuation of greater than 300,000,000 and population less than100,000, and a B-Under class county has property valuation greater than 75,000,0000 but less than 300,000,000 and population less than 100,000. §4-44-2 NMSA 1978. For a listing of county classifications, see: http://www.nmcounties.org/wp-content/uploads/2016/05/County_Classifications_2016.pdf. (Last viewed October 14, 2016).
[260] §7-9F-9A NMSA 1978. With respect to the TJTC, claims had to filed within one year after the end of the calendar year in which the qualified expenditure was made. See §3.13.5.9 NMAC.
[261] §7-9F-9 NMSA 1978. A *local option gross receipts tax* is a tax authorized to be imposed by a county or municipality upon the taxpayer's gross receipts, as that term is defined in the Gross Receipts and Compensating Tax Act and required to be collected by the TRD at the same time and in the same manner as the gross receipts tax. The term includes the taxes imposed pursuant to the Municipal Local Option Gross Receipts Taxes Act, Supplemental Municipal Gross Receipts Tax Act, County Local Option Gross Receipts Taxes Act, Local

Business-related Credits

amount of approved basic credit not claimed may be claimed in subsequent reporting periods for a period of up to three years from the date of the original claim.[262]

¶ 11.19.4 Claiming the additional credit

A taxpayer may apply for approval of an additional credit by filing Form RPD-41385 within one year following the end of the tax year in which the qualified expenditure was made.[263] A taxpayer that has been granted approval for an additional credit by the TRD may claim the amount of the approved additional credit against the taxpayer's income tax liability. Form RPD-41386 is used for this purpose, and that form must accompany the return.[264] However, except for the circumstances described below, a taxpayer may not claim an amount of additional credit for a tax year in which the additional credit being claimed exceeds the amount of the taxpayer's income tax due for that year.[265]

If a taxpayer is a qualified research and development small business and the amount of approved additional credit for the tax year in which the additional credit is being claimed exceeds the taxpayer's income tax liability, the excess will be refunded to the taxpayer as follows. If the taxpayer's total qualified expenditures for the tax year for which the claim is made is:

1. less than $3,000,000, the excess additional credit will be refunded to the taxpayer;
2. greater than or equal to $3,000,00 and less than $4,000,000, two-thirds of the excess additional credit will be refunded to the taxpayer; and
3. greater than or equal to $4,000,000 and less than or equal to $5,000,000, one-third of the excess additional credit will be refunded to the taxpayer.[266]

A "qualified research and development small business" is a taxpayer

---

Hospital Gross Receipts Tax Act, County Correctional Facility Gross Receipts Tax Act and such other acts as may be enacted authorizing counties or municipalities to impose taxes on gross receipts, which taxes are to be collected by the TRD in the same time and in the same manner as it collects the gross receipts tax. §7-9F-3F NMSA 1978.

[262] §7-9F-9C NMSA 1978.
[263] §7-9F-9.1A NMSA 1978. See §3.13.5.9 NMAC.
[265] §7-9F-9.1B NMSA 1978.
[265] §7-9F-9.1B NMSA 1978.
[266] §7-9F-9.1C NMSA 1978.

that:

1. employed no more than 50 employees as determined by the number of employees for which the taxpayer was liable for unemployment insurance coverage in the tax year for which an additional credit is claimed;
2. had total qualified expenditures of no more than $5,000,000 in the tax year for which an additional credit is claimed; and
3. did not have more than 50% of its voting securities or other equity interest with the right to designate or elect the board of directors or other governing body of the business owned directly or indirectly by another business.[267]

Married individuals filing separate returns for a tax year for which they could have filed a joint return may each claim only one-half of the additional credit that would have been claimed on a joint return.[268]

Any amount of approved additional credit not claimed against the taxpayer's income tax due for a tax year or refunded to the taxpayer may be claimed in subsequent reporting periods for a period of up to three years from the date of the original claim.[269]

¶ 11.19.5 Taxpayers who can claim the credit

Only a taxpayer can claim either the basic or additional credit. A taxpayer includes any of the following persons:

- a person liable for payment of any tax;
- a person responsible for withholding and payment or collection and payment of any tax;
- a person to whom an assessment has been made if the assessment remains unabated or the assessed amount has not been paid; or
- for purposes of the additional credit against the taxpayer's income tax pursuant to the TJRDTC and to the extent of their respective interest in that entity, the shareholders, members, partners or other owners of:
    o a small business corporation that has elected to be treated

---

[267] §7-9F-3J NMSA 1978. Note that the definition of a qualified research and development small business is different than the definition used for the RDSBTC.
[268] §7-9F-9.1E NMSA 1978.
[269] §7-9F-9.1D NMSA 1978.

Business-related Credits

> - as an S corporation for federal income tax purposes; or
>   - an entity treated as a partnership or disregarded entity for federal income tax purposes.[270]

A federal or state governmental unit or subdivision or an agency, department, institution or instrumentality thereof is not a taxpayer.

¶11.19.6 Credit recapture and reporting

If a taxpayer or a business successor ceases operations for at least 180 consecutive days within a 2-year period after claiming the basic or additional credit at a facility, the TRD will grant no further credit with respect to that facility. In addition, any approved, but unclaimed basic or additional credit will be extinguished, and within 30 days after the 180th day of the cessation of operations, the taxpayer must return the amount of tax for which an approved basic or additional credit was taken. A taxpayer is not considered to have ceased operations during reasonable periods of maintenance or retooling or for the repair or replacement of facilities damaged or destroyed or during the continuance of labor disputes.[271]

A taxpayer claiming a basic or additional credit must file reports with the TRD before June 30 of the year following a calendar year in which the taxpayer claims a credit and by June 30 of each of the two succeeding years. The reports must contain information describing the taxpayer's business operations in New Mexico that is sufficient for the TRD to enforce the recapture provisions. If a taxpayer fails to submit a required report, the amount of any basic or additional credit claimed for that year is subject to the recapture provision.[272]

¶11.19.7 Transition rules for the RDSBTC

A taxpayer that becomes eligible for a RDSBTC prior to January 1, 2016 but has not claimed the credit prior to January 1, 2016, may claim the credit under the provisions of the RDSBTC Act in effect prior to January 1, 2016.[273] The TRD will approve claims submitted but not approved prior to January 1, 2016 if the claim meets the requirements of the RDSBTC Act in effect immediately prior to January 1, 2016.

---

[270] §7-9F-3L NMSA 1978.
[271] §7-9F-11 NMSA 1978.
[272] §7-9F-13 NMSA 1978. HB 2, 52nd Legislature, First Special Session, 2015, §18.
[273] Recall that the RDSBTC is effective for reporting periods only through July 1, 2015.

Claiming the RDSBTC under this rule makes the taxpayer ineligible to claim a TJRDTC for the same reporting period. Therefore the rules of the RDSBTC Act in effect prior to January 1, 2016 remain relevant in this case.[274]

¶11.20 Veteran employment tax credit

Military veterans often have a hard time transitioning to civilian life. To encourage the full-time employment of newly discharged military veterans from the armed forces (within two years of their discharge), New Mexico offers employers a veteran employment tax credit for tax years beginning on or after January 1, 2012, but not after December 31, 2016. The amount of the credit equals the amount of wages paid each qualified military veteran during the tax year in an amount up to $1,000. A taxpayer who employs a qualified military veteran for less than the full tax year is eligible for a credit amount equal to $1,000 multiplied by the fraction of a full year for which the veteran was employed. To qualify for the credit, a taxpayer must not be a dependent of another.[276]

A "qualified military veteran" is an individual who meets these requirements:

- is hired within two years of receipt of an honorable discharge from a branch of the United States military;
- works at least 40 hours per week during the tax year for which the credit is claimed; and
- was not previously employed by the taxpayer prior to the individual's deployment.[277]

A taxpayer may claim the veteran employment tax credit for each tax year in which the taxpayer employs one or more qualified military veterans, but the taxpayer may not claim the credit for any veteran for more than one calendar year from the date of hire.[278] Only one employer may receive the credit for a specific veteran during a tax year. The credits allowed per qualified military veteran are limited to a

---

[274] HB2, 52ⁿᵈ Legislature, First Special Session, 2015, §22. See §§7-9H-1 to 7-9H-6 NMSA 1978.
[276] §7-2-18.28A NMSA 1978.
[277] §7-2-18.28I NMSA 1978.
[278] §7-2-18.28C NMSA 1978.

Business-related Credits

maximum of one year's employment and multiple employers may not receive a credit for more than one year combined for the same qualified military veteran.[279].

A husband and wife filing separate returns for a tax year for which they could have filed a joint return may each claim only one-half of the veteran employment tax credit that would have been claimed on a joint return.[280]

If the veteran employment tax credit approved by the TRD for a year exceeds a taxpayer's income tax liability for that year, the excess is not refunded to the taxpayer, but may be carried forward for up to three years. The veteran employment tax credit is not transferrable to another taxpayer.[281]

If the taxpayer owns an interest in a business that is taxed as a partnership under federal income tax rules and that business has met all of the eligibility requirements for the credit, the right to claim the credit may be allocated in proportion to the taxpayer's ownership interest. But the total credit claimed by all members may not exceed the total allowable credit.[282]

Applying for the credit

The taxpayer must certify and provide information establishing that the claimed employee is a qualified military veteran. Form RPD-41370, *Certification of Eligibility for the Veteran Employment Tax Credit*, is used for this purpose and it is attached to Form RPD-41371, *Application for Veteran Employment Tax Credit*, when applying for the credit. The taxpayer must provide a copy of the qualified military veteran's DD Form 214, *Certificate of Release or Discharge from Active Duty*, or other evidence acceptable to the TRD. The document must show the date the veteran was honorably discharged from a branch of the United States military. Evidence other than DD Form 214 should be approved through the TRD before submitting the application.

Once a qualified military veteran is approved on an application for a tax year, any credit requested by another employer for the same

---

[279] §7-2-18.28H NMSA 1978.
[280] §7-2-18.28E NMSA 1978.
[281] §7-2-18.28D NMSA 1978.
[282] §7-2-18.28F NMSA 1978.

military veteran on subsequent applications for the same tax year will be denied. Applications will be processed in the order in which they are received.[283]

Claiming the credit

Once the credit is approved, Form RPD-41372, *Veteran Employment Tax Credit Claim Form,* must be completed and submitted with the taxpayer's PIT return. Each owner of a pass-through entity that claims the credit must supply a schedule of the names, addresses, and the pro rata credit amounts of all other entity owners.

> **Comment**
>
> This is credit is virtually unused according to the state's *2015 New Mexico Tax Expenditure Report*. One reason may be that the amount of the credit, at only $1,000 per veteran employee, is too low to justify the compliance required. The benefit of the credit can be eaten up by amounts paid to CPAs and the cost of the time necessary to provide the information required by the TRD.

¶11.21 Film Production Credit

This credit is discussed fully in Chapter 12.

¶11.22 Renewable energy production tax credit

New Mexico has abundant resources for the production of renewable energy. It has over 320 days of sunshine a year that enables the production of electricity from solar energy. In addition, there is great wind potential on the high plains and rugged ridges in the eastern half of the state. In 2014, wind energy contributed 7% of New Mexico's electricity generation from a dozen operating wind farms. Recognizing its role as a fertile source for these renewable energy opportunities, New Mexico established a renewable portfolio standard that requires investor-owned electric utilities to acquire 20% of electricity sold in-

---

[283] Form RPD-41371 (Rev. 2015), Application for Veteran Employment Tax Credit Instructions.

state from renewable energy sources by 2020. Of that 20%, at least half must come from solar and wind energy.

To help increase the amount of renewable energy production in New Mexico, the state has introduced the renewable energy production tax credit ("REPTC") as an incentive to further the production of electricity from renewable sources for sale to unrelated customers. The credit may be claimed by a taxpayer who:

- owns a qualified energy generator that first produces electricity on or before January 1, 2018; or
- leases such facility from a county or municipality under authority of an industrial revenue bond if the qualified energy generator first produces electricity on or before January 1, 2018.[284]

The tax credit is available to the claimant for ten consecutive years beginning on the date the qualified energy generator begins producing electricity. The credit may not be claimed with respect to the same electricity production for which a REPTC has been claimed under the CIT.[285]

The claimant must file an individual New Mexico income tax return and not be a dependent of another taxpayer. A husband and wife who file separate returns for a tax year in which they could have filed a joint return may each claim only one-half of the credit that would have been allowed on a joint return.[286]

Qualified energy generator

A "qualified energy generator" is a facility with at least one-megawatt generating capacity located in New Mexico that produces electricity using a qualified energy resource and that sells that electricity to an unrelated person.[287] A "qualified energy resource" is a resource that generates electrical energy by means of a fluidized bed technology or similar low-emissions technology or a zero-emissions generation technology that has substantial long-term production potential and

---

[284] §7-2-18.18B NMSA 1978.
[285] §7-2-18.18B and §7-2A-19 NMSA 1978. See RPD-41227, Renewable Energy Production Tax Credit Claim Form Instructions (Rev. 9/2016), p. 2.
[286] §7-2-18.18J NMSA 1978
[287] §7-2-18.18F(2) NMSA 1978.

that uses only the following energy sources:

- solar light;
- solar heat;
- wind; or
- biomass (see inset).[288]

> ***Biomass*** for the purpose of this credit is organic material that is available on a renewable or recurring basis, and includes:
>
> - forest-related materials, including mill residues, logging residues, forest thinnings, slash, brush, low-commercial-value materials or undesirable species, salt cedar and other phreatophyte or woody vegetation removed from river basins or watersheds and woody material harvested for the purpose of forest fire fuel reduction or forest health and watershed improvement;
> - agricultural-related materials, including orchard trees, vineyard, grain or crop residues, including straws and stover, aquatic plants and agricultural processed co-products and waste products, including fats, oils, greases, whey and lactose;
> - animal waste, including manure and slaughterhouse and other processing waste;
> - solid woody waste materials, including landscape or right-of-way tree trimmings, rangeland maintenance residues, waste pallets, crates and manufacturing, construction and demolition wood wastes, excluding pressure-treated, chemically treated or painted wood wastes and wood contaminated with plastic;
> - crops and trees planted for the purpose of producing energy;
> - landfill gas, wastewater treatment gas and biosolids, including organic waste byproducts generated during the wastewater treatment process; and
> - segregated municipal solid waste, excluding tires and medical and hazardous waste.[289]

Computing the credit

The tax credit is computed on the basis of the amount of energy produced and which is available over a ten-year period. For energy produced using a wind- or biomass-derived qualified energy resource, the credit equals $.01 per kilowatt-hour of the first 400,000 megawatt-hours of electricity produced by the qualified energy generator in the tax year. The total amount of tax credits claimed by all taxpayers for a

---

[288] §7-2-18.18F(3) NMSA 1978.
[289] §7-2-18.18F(1) NMSA 1978.

Business-related Credits

single qualified energy generator in a tax year using such facility, however, may not exceed $.01 per kilowatt-hour of the first 400,000 megawatt-hours of electricity produced by the qualified energy generator.[290]

For a qualified energy generator using a solar light derived or solar heat derived qualified energy resource, the amount of tax credit varies based on the year of production following the date the generator first produces electricity using the qualified energy resource. Table 1 shows the amount of tax credit for the first 200,000 megawatt-hours of electricity produced by the qualified energy generator in the applicable tax year following the day the qualified energy generator first produces electricity. The total amount of tax credits claimed for a tax year by all taxpayers for a single qualified energy generator using a solar-light-derived or solar-heat-derived qualified energy resource is limited to the first 200,000 megawatt-hours of electricity produced by the qualified energy generator in the tax year.[291]

Production Tax Credits from Solar Energy[292]	
Tax Credit per kilowatt hour	Tax year
$.015	1st
$.02	2nd
$.025	3rd
$.03	4th
$.035	5t
$.04	6th
$.035	7th
$.03	8th
$.025	9th
$.02	10th

---

[290] §7-2-18.18C NMSA 1978.
[291] §7-2-18.18D NMSA 1978.
[292] See RPD-41227, Renewable Energy Production Tax Credit Claim Form Instructions, p. 2.

Applying for the Credit

The first step in earning the credit is to obtain certification of eligibility from the Energy, Minerals and Natural Resources Department ("EMNRD").[293] An application form may be found on the EMNRD website.[294] The total amount of electricity that may be produced annually by all qualified energy generators, including applications made by corporations (pursuant to §7-2A-19), may not exceed a total of 2,000,000 megawatt-hours plus an additional 500,000 megawatt-hours produced by qualified energy generators using a solar-light-derived or solar-heat-derived qualified energy resource. The EMNRD may estimate the annual power-generating potential of a generating facility for this purpose. Applications are considered in the order received. On approval, the EMNRD will issue a certificate to the applicant stating whether the facility is an eligible qualified energy generator and the estimated annual production potential of the generating facility, which shall be the limit of that facility's energy production eligible for the tax credit for the tax year.[295]

Allocation of the credit for partnerships

A taxpayer owning an interest in a business entity that is taxed as a partnership under federal law may be allocated all or a portion of the right to claim a REPTC without regard to proportional ownership under the following circumstances:

- the business entity qualifies for the REPTC and owns an interest in a business entity that is also taxed as a partnership for federal tax purposes and that qualifies for the REPTC; or owns, through one or more intermediate business entities that are each taxed as a partnership for federal tax purposes, an interest in a business entity that is also taxed as a partnership for federal tax purposes and qualifies for the REPTC;
- the taxpayer and all other taxpayers allocated a right to claim the REPTC own collectively at least a 5% interest in a qualified energy generator;
- the business entity provides notice of the allocation and the taxpayer's interest to EMNRD on prescribed forms; and

---

[293] §7-2-18.18G NMSA 1978.
[294] www.emnrd.state.nm.us/ECMD/CleanEnergyTaxIncentives/ProdTaxCredit.html. Last viewed October 14, 2016.
[295] §7-2-18.18G NMSA 1978.

Business-related Credits

- EMNRD certifies the allocation in writing to the taxpayer.[296]

Upon receipt of notice of an allocation of the right to claim all or a portion of the REPTC, the EMNRD must promptly certify the allocation in writing to the recipient of the allocation.[297]

Claiming the credit

The credit may be claimed by submitting the following to the TRD:

1. a completed Form RPD-41227, *New Mexico Renewable Energy Production Tax Credit Claim Form*, with a personal tax return;
2. the certificate of eligibility issued by EMNRD;
3. the Allocation Notice approved by EMNRD, if applicable; and
4. documentation of the amount of electricity produced by the facility in the tax year.[298]

If these requirements have been complied with, TRD will approve the REPTC and apply the credit as indicated on the claim form.[299]

The credit may be deducted from a taxpayer's New Mexico income tax liability for the tax year for which the credit is claimed. If a tax credit was issued with respect to a qualified energy generator that first produced electricity using a qualified energy resource on or after October 1, 2007, any credit excess of the taxpayer's income tax liability is refunded to the taxpayer. For credits with respect to electricity produced before October 1, 2007, if the amount of credit exceeds the taxpayer's income tax liability for the tax year, the excess may be carried forward for 5 tax years. The credit claimed for the current tax year must be applied first. If the amount claimed for a tax year is less than the income tax liability for that year, the unused credit from prior years is available for carry forward. When applying unused credits available for carry forward, the oldest credit is applied first.[300]

Once a taxpayer has been granted a REPTC for a given facility, the taxpayer is allowed to retain the facility's original date of application for tax credits for that facility until either the facility goes out of production for more than 6 consecutive months in a year or until the

---

[296] §7-2-18.18H NMSA 1978.
[297] §7-2-18.18I NMSA 1978.
[298] §7-2-18.18K NMSA 1978.
[299] §7-2-18.18L NMSA 1978.
[300] §7-2-18.18L(1) and (2) NMSA 1978.

facility's 10-year eligibility has expired.[301]

¶ 11.23 Venture Capital Investment Credit – The forgotten tax credit

It appears that no one has ever taken advantage of this credit.[302] Although it remains on the books, there is no tax form allowing a taxpayer to claim the credit. Instead the instructions to Form PIT-1 direct taxpayers that if they are in full compliance with the provisions of the New Mexico Venture Capital Act, they should contact (505) 827-1746 for more details. Perhaps the person waiting at that number is the tax law equivalent of the Maytag repairman.[303] Because of the credit's complexity and the difficulty in meeting the eligibility requirements, it becomes more unlikely as time goes on that anyone will ever take advantage of the credit. Nevertheless, we provide the following description of the credit for the sake of completeness.

A taxpayer who pays federal income tax on the gain from certain corporate stock (qualified diversifying business net capital gain) may claim the venture capital investment credit (VCIC) against the taxpayer's New Mexico income tax liability in an amount equal to 50% of the federal income tax paid (the capital gain tax differential), if the taxpayer allocates the gain to New Mexico.[304] This tax credit may only be deducted from the taxpayer's New Mexico income tax liability. Any portion of the credit that remains unused at the end of the taxpayer's tax year may be carried forward and used in succeeding years.[305]

The purpose of the VCIC is to encourage investment by venture capitalists in manufacturing and high tech corporations. The credit can be taken only with respect to an "active manufacturing business," which is a corporation that throughout the testing period (the five-year period a stock is held by a taxpayer[306)] is either actively engaged in manufacturing (using substantially all of its assets in manufacturing),

---

[301] §7-2-18.18M NMSA 1978.
[302] 2015 New Mexico Tax Expenditure Report, p. 183.
[303] For readers of generations younger than mine, the Maytag repairman allusion pertains to an old TV commercial showing a Maytag repair man sitting by the phone waiting for someone to call, but no one ever does because the product never breaks down.
[304] §7-2D-8.1A NMSA 1978.
[305] §7-2D-8.1B NMSA 1978.
[306] §7-2D-2I NMSA 1978.

Business-related Credits

start-up activities, or R&D activities.[307] A corporation is not an active manufacturing business if at any time during the testing period more than 10% of the total value of its assets is real property that is not used in the active conduct of a manufacturing business, or more than 10% of its net assets consist of stock of other corporations that are not subsidiaries. Stock and debt in any subsidiary corporation is disregarded and the parent corporation is deemed to own its ratable share of the subsidiary's assets and to conduct its ratable share of the subsidiary's activities. A corporation is considered a subsidiary if the parent owns at least 50% of the combined voting power of all classes of stock entitled to vote or at least 50% in value of all outstanding stock.[308]

In view of the fact that the VCIC rules are very complex and difficult to meet, and that the VCIC is unlikely to be used by many or even any taxpayers, the following discussion highlights the important features of the VCIC and leaves the interested reader to look to the Venture Capital Investment Act for more details.[309]

The credit appears to be inapplicable to current issuances of stock, although the wording (discussed below) of an election to treat stock issued after June 30, 1993 as "qualified diversifying business stock" leaves some doubt. The statute provides that the credit is only applicable to sales of "qualified diversifying business stock," which is stock in a corporation that is originally issued after June 30, 1994, but before July 1, 2001, if the following conditions are met: 1) the corporation is a qualified diversifying business at issuance; 2) the stock is acquired at its original issue in exchange for money or other property (not including stock), or as compensation for services (other than services performed as an underwriter of such stock), and 3) the corporation is an active manufacturing business and a New Mexico business throughout the testing period, and is a successful business at the end of the testing period.[310] Special rules apply to stock issued through options, warrants and convertible investments,[311] and to certain tax-free transfers of stock.[312] A "successful business" is a

---

[307] §7-2D-6A NMSA 1978.
[308] §7-2D-6B NMSA 1978.
[309] §§7-2D-1 through 7-2D-14 NMSA 1978
[310] §7-2D-4 NMSA 1978.
[311] §7-2D-9 NMSA 1978.
[312] §7-2D-10 NMSA 1978.

corporation that at the end of the taxpayer's holding period has experienced a net increase in valuation of at least $15,000,000.[313]

Nevertheless, the statute provides an exception: on any date after June 30, 1993, a taxpayer who holds stock of a corporation that has a commercial domicile in New Mexico and meets the requirements of the VCIC, may elect to have the stock treated as "qualified diversifying business stock" for purposes of claiming the VCIC.[314] This language appears to allow even stock issued on or after July 1, 2001 to qualify for the VCIC if this election is made. If that were the case, this election would render meaningless the limitation for stock issuances after June 30, 1994 to June 30, 2001.

The statute also provides a second election for taxpayers holding the stock of a corporation with a commercial domicile in New Mexico and for which the taxpayer's basis is lower than the stock's value. On any date after June 30, 1994, if such stock would have been treated as qualified diversifying business stock when issued, except that it was issued on or before June 30, 1994 when the corporation was without a New Mexico commercial domicile, the taxpayer may elect to use that date as the election date and treat the stock as having been sold on that date for an amount equal to its value and as having been reacquired on that date for an amount equal to such value.[315]

If the taxpayer makes one of the above elections to qualify otherwise nonqualified stock, and the taxpayer had not previously paid federal income tax on the qualified diversifying business net capital gain that accrued prior to that election, then the capital gain differential is an amount equal to 50% of the federal income tax paid by the taxpayer on the gain on the sale of that qualified diversifying business stock times the percentage derived by dividing the gain on such stock accruing since the election by the total gain on the stock accruing since its original acquisition without regard to the election.[316]

The "capital gain tax differential," which is the basis of the tax, is defined as an amount equal to 50% of the federal income tax paid by the taxpayer on qualified diversifying business net capital gains. The

---

[313] §7-2D-8A NMSA 1978.
[314] §7-2D-13A NMSA 1978.
[315] §7-2D-13B NMSA 1978.
[316] §7-2D-2A[2] NMSA 1978.

Business-related Credits

"qualified diversifying business net capital gain" is the net capital gain for the tax year determined under the Internal Revenue Code by taking into account only gains or losses from sales or exchanges of qualified diversifying business stock with a holding period of more than five years at the time of the sale or exchange."[317]

A "New Mexico business" is a corporation that throughout the testing period has its commercial domicile in New Mexico and all of its corporate directors who are also employees of the corporation are full-time residents of New Mexico; has at least two-thirds of all employees, at least two-thirds of its R&D and design employees, and at least two-thirds of its manufacturing employees as full-time residents of New Mexico; maintains an employee stock purchase plan, incentive stock option plan or similar plan by which employees may acquire equity ownership; and employs on a full-time basis an average of at least 50 full-time New Mexico residents.[318]

A "qualified diversifying business" is a domestic corporation that has its commercial domicile in New Mexico and for which the aggregate amount of money, other property and services received for stock as a contribution to capital and as paid-in surplus, plus the accumulated earnings and profits, does not exceed $25,000,000 (adjusted for inflation if the stock is issued after 1993).[319]

In the case of pass-thru entities, any gain or loss of a pass-thru entity that is treated as a gain or loss of any person holding an interest in that entity shall retain its character as qualified diversifying business capital gain or loss in the hands of that person.[320]

---

[317] §7-2D-2F NMSA 1978.
[318] §7-2D-7 NMSA 1978.
[319] §7-2D-5 NMSA 1978.
[320] §7-2D-12 NMSA 1978.

CHAPTER 12
FILM PRODUCTION TAX INCENTIVES

¶ 12.1 Overview

With interesting and varied landscapes, a semiarid climate offering over 320 days of sunshine, and but a short plane trip to and from Hollywood, New Mexico offers a very favorable environment for film production. To create a favorable business environment and entice production companies to take advantage of these beneficial attributes, New Mexico enacted a film production tax credit ("FPTC") in 2002 as part of the Film Production Tax Credit Act ("FPTCA").[1] New Mexico was one of the first states to enact a film production incentive, but approximately 35 states now have such incentives, as film production provides both interesting and high wage jobs. A provision of the FPTCA states that the purpose of the credit is to establish the film industry as a permanent component of the economic base of the state, develop a pool of professionals and businesses to supply and support the film industry, increase employment, improve the economic success of existing businesses, and develop the infrastructure necessary for a thriving film industry.[2] The Film Division of the Economic Development Department (hereinafter referred to as the Film Office) administers the New Mexico film production tax incentives in cooperation with the TRD.

The FPTC has proven very successful in increasing film production in New Mexico, which also has resulted in the development of a thriving film industry cluster.[3] Many skilled production and performing personnel now live in New Mexico, and a wide variety of

---

[1] Chapter 7, Article 2F NMSA 1978 (Laws 2011, Chapter 177, Section 3; Laws 2011, Chapter 165, Section 2).
[2] §7-2F-3 NMSA 1978.
[3] The term "cluster" has been defined as follows: "Clusters are geographic concentrations of interconnected companies, specialized suppliers, service providers, firms in related industries, and associated institutions (e.g., universities, standards agencies, trade associations) in a particular field that compete but also cooperate." Porter, Michael E., *Economic Development Quarterly*, Vol. 14 Issue 1, p15, 20p, 4 (Feb. 2000).

vendors for production equipment and facilities are now available in-state. In FY 2013, 58 productions were registered in New Mexico, resulting in $213 million in direct production spending and 216,461 production worker days.[4] Since its original enactment, the legislature has modified the law to enhance it, fine tune it, and, in some respects, limit it. In 2015, the name of the incentive was changed to the Film and Television Tax Credit ("FTTC") to recognize the significant role of television production in New Mexico, as exemplified by the success of the *Breaking Bad* television series. The new name also calls attention to amendments to the incentive that now apply to television. The provisions of the FTTC apply to productions with principal photography commencing on or after January 1, 2016 and the FPTC applies to productions with principal photography commencing before that date.

The Film Office endeavors to make the New Mexico film incentives user friendly. Their web site points out: 1) that there is no minimum budget or spend requirement; 2) submission of a distribution plan is not necessary; and 3) there is no application fee and no pre-qualification. The process begins with submission of a registration form and tax agreement prior to principal photography. A tax application is submitted to the Film Office after production (or after each tax year in which production expenditures occur). The TRD conducts an internal review of the qualifying expenditures to determine the approved claim amount. This takes five to six months. The company receives a check or deposit after filing their state return.[5] See ¶ 12.6 for more details on qualifying for and claiming the credit

¶ 12.2 Film and Television Tax Credit -- Principal Photography Commencing On Or After January 1, 2016

An eligible film production company ("FPC") may apply for a FTTC equal to 25% of direct production expenditures ("DPEs") and postproduction expenditures ("PPEs") made in New Mexico. These expenditures must be subject to taxation in New Mexico and, of

---

[4] MNP, New Mexico Film Production Tax Incentive Study, Phase I Report, pp. 9-10 (July 21, 2014).
[5] http://www.nmfilm.com/Overview.aspx. Last viewed October 14, 2016. The information on this site has been very useful in the production of this chapter.

Film Production Incentives

course, cannot have been claimed by another taxpayer for the FTTC. A FPC, for purposes of the FTTC, is a person that produces one or more films or any part of a film that commences principal photography on or after January 1, 2016.[6] "Principal photography" involves the production of a film during which the main visual elements are created.[7] The following are some important points concerning the FTTC, which are discussed in more detail below:

- This is a refundable credit, meaning that if the amount of credit exceeds the taxpayer's tax liability, the excess is refunded to the taxpayer.
- The FTTC rate is increased by 5%, up to 30%, for DPEs related to qualified production facilities.
- The FTTC rate is also increased by an additional 5%, up to 30%, for DPEs with regard to a standalone pilot intended for series television in New Mexico or with regard to series television productions intended for commercial distribution with an order for at least six episodes in a single season if the New Mexico budget for each of those six episodes is $50,000 or more.[8] A FPC applying for this additional credit is not eligible for the additional credit regarding qualified production facilities.[9]
- A FPC may also earn a separate tax credit of 15% of the payment of wages, fringe benefits and per diem for nonresident industry crew if services are rendered in New Mexico and other requirements are met.[10]
- The FTTC rate of 25% is reduced to 20% for expenditures that are attributable to a production for which a FPC received a tax credit under the federal new markets tax credit program.[11]

---

[6] §7-2F-2.1B NMSA 1978.
[7] §7-2F-2N NMSA 1978.
[8] §7-2F-7A NMSA 1978.
[9] §7-2F-7B NMSA 1978.
[10] §7-2F-9. NMSA 1978.
[11] §7-2F-6C NMSA 1978. The "federal new markets tax credit program" is a tax credit program codified in IRC §45D, which provides a 39% federal tax credit, taken over seven years, on investments made in economically distressed communities. §7-2F-2E NMSA 1978.

277

¶ 12.2.1 Requirements for direct production and postproduction expenditures

To qualify for the FTTC, DPEs and PPEs must be made in New Mexico and meet the following requirements:

- they must be directly attributable to the production of a film or commercial audiovisual product in New Mexico;
- they must be subject to taxation by New Mexico, and, in the case of PPEs, are for postproduction services performed in New Mexico;
- they may not include expenditures for which another taxpayer claims the FTTC; and
- they may not exceed the usual and customary cost of the goods or services acquired when purchased by unrelated parties. The Secretary of the TRD may determine the value of the goods or services when the buyer and seller are affiliated or the sale or purchase is not at an arm's length.[12]

An "affiliated person" is one who directly or indirectly owns or controls, is owned or controlled by, or is under common ownership or control with another person through ownership of voting securities or other ownership interests representing a majority of the total voting power of the entity.[13]

¶ 12.2.2 Direct production expenditures - definition

The FPTCA provides a list of specified categories of production expenditures that qualify as DPEs for the FTTC:

1. the payment of wages, fringe benefits or fees for talent, management or labor to a person who is a *New Mexico resident*;
2. the payment for standard industry craft inventory when provided by a resident industry crew in addition to its industry crew services;

---

[12] §7-2F-6B[1] NMSA 1978.
[13] §7-2F-2A NMSA 1978.

Film Production Incentives

> **FPCTA Amendment**: Within the definition of DPE, resident box rentals are now addressed. The language clarifies that equipment box rentals, regardless of how they are paid by the company, qualify when that resident is providing crew services on the same production. It is not a vendor relationship.

3. the payment for wages and per diem for a performing artist who is *not a New Mexico resident* and who is directly employed by a FPC if the FPC deducts and remits income tax, or causes New Mexico income tax to be deducted and remitted, at the maximum rate from the first day of services;
4. the payment to *a personal services business* on the wages and per diem paid to a performing artist of the business if:
    a. the personal services business pays gross receipts tax in New Mexico on the portion of those payments qualifying for the tax credit; and
    b. the FPC deducts and remits New Mexico income tax, or causes income tax to be deducted and remitted, at the maximum income tax rate on the portion of those payments qualifying for the tax credit paid to a personal services business where the performing artist is a full or part owner of that business or subcontracts with a personal services business where the performing artist is a full or part owner of that business; and

> **FPTCA Amendment**: Qualifying payments to nonresident actors paid through a Super Loan Out (discussed below in ¶ 12.2.3) are now limited to wages and per diem and benefits no longer qualify. The withholding tax rate is at the maximum of 4.9% for nonresident artists employed directly by the FPC or through a loan out company.

5. any of the following provided by a *vendor*:
    - the story and scenario to be used for a film;
    - set construction and operations, wardrobe, accessories and related services;

- photography, sound synchronization, lighting and related services;
- editing and related services;
- rental of facilities and equipment;
- leasing of vehicles, including New Mexico-based chartered aircraft for in-state transportation directly attributable to the production (but not aircraft for out-of-state transportation), provided that only the first $100 of the daily expense of a leased vehicle for in-state passenger transportation may be claimed as a DPE;
- food or lodging, but only the first $150 of lodging per individual per day is eligible as a DPE;
- commercial airfare purchased through a New Mexico-based travel agency or travel company for travel to and from New Mexico or within New Mexico directly attributable to the production;
- insurance coverage and bonding if purchased through a New Mexico-based insurance agent, broker or bonding agent;
- services for an external audit upon submission of an application for a FTTC where an audit by an accountant is required, and
- other direct costs of producing a film in accordance with generally accepted entertainment industry practice.[14]

> **FPTCA Amendment:** For credit claims in excess of $5 million, a CPA licensed to practice in New Mexico must conduct the required external audit.[15]

DPEs do not include expenditures for:

1. a gift with a value greater than $25.00;
2. artwork or jewelry, except that a work of art or a piece of jewelry may be a DPE if used in film production and the expenditure is less than $2,500;
3. entertainment, amusement, or recreation; or
4. subcontracted goods or services provided by a vendor when

---

[14] §7-2F-2.1A(1) NMSA 1978.
[15] See §7-2F-6I NMSA 1978.

Film Production Incentives

subcontractors are not subject to state taxation, such as equipment and locations provided by the military, government, and religious organizations.[16]

¶ 12.2.3 Nonresident performing artists

As noted above, there are two situations in which wages paid to a nonresident performing artist may qualify as DPEs: 1) payment of wages and per diem for a nonresident performing artist who is directly employed by a FPC, provided that the FPC from the first day of services rendered in New Mexico deducts and remits, or causes to be deducted and remitted, income tax at the maximum withholding rate (4.9%); and 2) payment to a personal services business (or loan out company) on the wages and per diem paid to a nonresident performing artist of the artist loan out company, if the loan-out company pays New Mexico gross receipts tax on the portion of those payments qualifying for the tax credit, and the FPC deducts and remits, or causes to be deducted and remitted, income tax at the maximum rate on the portion of those payments qualifying for the tax credit paid to a loan out company, where the performing artist is a full or part owner of that business, or subcontracts with a personal services business where the performing artist is a full or part owner of that business.

A "personal services business" is a business organization, with or without physical presence that receives payments for the services of a performing artist.[17] Such a business is often referred to as a loan out company or a super loan out company. The term "loan-out company" or "artist loan-out company" refers to a company that is established by performers as a way to shield them from potential liability and also provide some tax advantages. The performer would be employed by the loan-out company, which would then contract for the performer's services with the FPC. In this case, the loan-out company, and not the production company, is responsible for employment tax withholding. A "super loan out company" (SLO) is a loan-out company that is set up so that the payment for the services of nonresident talent and on-camera stunt performers with management companies will qualify for the refundable tax credit. The SLO must register its business in New Mexico; but, a physical presence is not required.

---

[16] §7-2F-2.1A(2) NMSA 1978.
[17] §7-2F-2K NMSA 1978.

The following are condensed versions of examples in the tax regulations that help explain these concepts.[18]

Example 1. A SLO receives payments for the services of a performing artist from a FPC. The SLO pays gross receipts tax on the payments and deducts and remits withheld income tax on the payments to the performing artist. The payment from the FPC to the SLO qualifies as a DPE.[19]

Example 2. The facts are the same as Example 1 except the SLO contracts with a payroll service company to deduct and remit withheld income tax on the payments to the performing artist. The payment from the FPC to the SLO qualifies as a DPE.[20]

Example 3. A SLO receives payments for the direct hires (performing artists who do not own their own company) from a FPC and pays gross receipts tax on the payments received. No tax is deducted and remitted on the payments for the direct hires because the direct hires are employees of the SLO company and wages are excluded from this requirement to withhold. The payment from the FPC to the SLO for the services of the direct hires qualifies as a DPE.[21]

Example 4. An actor loan-out company receives payments for the services of a performing artist from a SLO company. The SLO company executes a nontaxable transaction certificate to the actor loan-out company and pays gross receipts tax on the payments they receive from the FPC for the services of the performing artist. The SLO company, or the payroll company, by agreement with the production company, deducts and remits withheld income tax on the payments to the performing artist. The payment from the FPC to the SLO company for the

---

[18] See also the TRD presentation on nonresident performing artist, which is linked to at http://www.nmfilm.com/Summary.aspx. Last viewed October 14, 2016.
[19] §3.13.9.10B NMAC.
[20] §3.13.9.10C NMAC.
[21] §3.13.9.10D NMAC. The exclusion for the requirement to withhold is found in §7-3A-3I NMSA 1978 which states that excluding wages, a personal services business shall deduct and withhold an amount equal to the owner's share of net income multiplied by the highest rate for single individuals.

services of the performing artist qualifies as a DPE.[22]

Example 5. An actor loan-out company owned by the performing artist receives payments for the services of the performing artist who is a New Mexico resident. The company pays gross receipts tax on the payments received. No income tax is deducted or remitted on the payments due the performing artist from the company because the obligation to deduct and withhold does not apply to payments made to a New Mexico resident.[23] The payments from the FPC to the actor loan-out company qualify as DPEs.[24]

¶ 12.2.4 Limitation for performing artists

The FTTC is limited with regard to expenditures related to services of non-resident performing artists and featured resident principal performing artists. The amount of credit related to DPEs for the services of these performing artists may not exceed $5,000,000 for a production. This limitation does not apply to the services of background artists and resident performing artists who are not cast in industry standard featured principal performer roles.[25]

A "performing artist" is an actor, on-camera stuntperson, puppeteer, pilot who is a stuntperson or actor, specialty foreground performer or narrator; and who speaks a line of dialogue, is identified with the product or reacts to narration as assigned. A performing artist does not include a background artist.[26] A "background artist" is a person who is not a performing artist but is a person of atmospheric business whose work includes atmospheric noise, normal actions, gestures and facial expressions of that person's assignment; or a person of atmospheric business whose work includes special abilities that are not stunts; or a substitute for another actor, whether photographed as a double or acting as a stand-in.[27]

---

[22] §3.13.9.10E NMAC.
[23] See §7-3A-3C NMSA 1978.
[24] §3.13.9.10F NMAC.
[25] §7-2F-10 NMSA 1978.
[26] §7-2F-2J NMSA 1978.
[27] §7-2F-2B NMSA 1978.

> **FPTCA Amendment:** Resident non-lead actors are no longer subject to the $5 million tax credit limit.

¶ 12.2.5 Postproduction expenditures

To qualify for the FTTC, a PPE must be directly attributable to the production of a commercial film or audiovisual product and must be performed in New Mexico.[28] A "postproduction expenditure" is an expenditure for editing, Foley recording, automatic dialogue replacement, sound editing, special effects, including computer-generated imagery or other effects, scoring and music editing, beginning and end credits, negative cutting, soundtrack production, dubbing, subtitling or addition of sound or visual effects. The term does not include expenditures for advertising, marketing, distribution or expense payments.[29]

> **FPTCA Amendment:** "Postproduction services," not just "services," must now be performed in New Mexico to qualify.

¶ 12.2.6 Film and audiovisual product requirements

Both PPEs and DPEs must be made with regard to a film or a commercial audiovisual product. A "film" is a single medium or multimedia program intended for exhibition, excluding advertising messages other than national or regional advertising messages, that is: a) fixed on film, a digital medium, videotape, computer disc, laser disc or other similar delivery medium that can be viewed or reproduced; b) not intended to and does not violate the provisions of the criminal code regarding sexually oriented material harmful to minors;[30] and c) intended for reasonable commercial exploitation for the delivery medium used.[31] A "commercial audiovisual product" is a film or a videogame intended for commercial exploitation.[32]

When the FTTC is claimed with regard to a production, an acknowledgment to New Mexico must appear in the end screen credits that the production was filmed in New Mexico, and a state logo

---

[28] §7-2F-6B[2] NMSA 1978.
[29] §7-2F-2M NMSA 1978.
[30] See Chapter 30, Article 37 NMSA 1978
[31] §7-2F-2F NMSA 1978.
[32] §7-2F-2C NMSA 1978.

Film Production Incentives

provided by the Film Office must be included and embedded in the end screen credits of long-form narrative film productions and television episodes, unless otherwise agreed to in writing by the Film Office.[33]

> **FPTCA Amendment:** The state's logo must appear in the screen credits at a standard size as compared to other logos in the same end crawl for both features and television episodes.

¶ 12.2.7 Residency requirement for purposes of the FTTC

A "New Mexico resident" for purposes of the FPTCA is an individual who is domiciled in New Mexico any time during the tax year or who is physically present 185 days or more during the tax year. However, an individual, other than someone who meets the physical presence test, who changed his or her place of abode on or before the last day of the tax year to a place outside the state, intending to permanently live outside the state, is not a resident for periods after the change.[34]

¶ 12.2.8 Requirement for DPEs and PPEs to be a taxable transaction

The FTTC may not be claimed for DPEs or PPEs for which a FPC has delivered a nontaxable transaction certificate with regard to the Gross Receipts and Compensating Tax Act. Under that Act, the receipts from selling or leasing property and from performing services may be deducted from gross receipts or from governmental gross receipts if the sale, lease or performance is made to a qualified production company that delivers a nontaxable transaction certificate to the seller, lessor or performer.[35]

¶ 12.2.9 Requirements to Contract With Certain Vendors

A vendor is a person who sells or leases goods or services that are related to standard industry craft inventory, who has a physical presence in New Mexico and is subject to gross receipts tax and personal or corporate income tax but excludes a personal services

---

[33] §7-2F-6E NMSA 1978.
[34] §7-2F-2I NMSA 1978.
[35] §7-2F-6D NMSA 1978; §7-9-86 NMSA 1978.

business.[36] A FPC must make reasonable efforts to contract with a specialized vendor whose ordinary course of business directly relates to a standard industry craft inventory and that:
1. provides services;
2. provides inventory, for sale or lease that is *maintained in New Mexico* and represented by the specialized vendor; or
3. subcontracts similar standard industry craft inventory from other businesses with or without physical presence.[37]

If a FPC does not contract with a specialized vendor, but contracts with a vendor that provides services, does not sell or lease standard industry craft inventory and outsources inventory from out-of-state businesses for a FPC, the FPC must provide documentation of reasonable efforts made to find a specialized vendor.[39]

A "physical presence" in New Mexico means a physical address in New Mexico from which a vendor conducts business, stores inventory or otherwise creates, assembles or offers for sale the product purchased or leased by a FPC and the business owner or an employee of the business is a resident.[40] Any vendor (provider) providing goods or performing services and who occupies and maintains one or more physical places of business in New Mexico (not a virtual or online business), has established physical presence if the following conditions are present:
1. a provider of goods or services, or its employees, or representatives, is available at that provider's place of business during established times;
2. a provider of goods maintains an inventory of the goods sold at the provider's New Mexico place of business and those goods are held for sale in the vendor's ordinary course of business at that place of business; and
3. critical elements of any service performed by a service provider occur, are managed at, or coordinated from the service provider's place of business.[41]

---

[36] §7-2F-2.1C NMSA 1978.
[37] §7-2F-11A NMSA 1978.
[39] §7-2F-11B NMSA 1978.
[40] §7-2F-2L NMSA 1978.
[41] §3.13.9.9A NMAC.

Film Production Incentives

The following indicia are considered in determining if the above conditions are present:

1. the provider of the goods or services is a resident or has at least one laborer who is a New Mexico resident, as defined in the ITA;
2. a telephone is assigned for the exclusive use by the provider of goods or services at the provider's place of business;
3. the place of business has been designated for the use of the goods or services provided;
4. the place of business contains office furniture or equipment for the use by the provider;
5. the goods or services provider is identified by business name on a sign located in or adjacent to the place of business; and
6. a client or other persons can expect to communicate, either in person or by telephone, with the goods or services provider, or employees or representatives of the provider, at the place of business.[42]

> **FPCTA Amendment:** The definition of "physical presence" clarifies that either the owner or an employee of the vendor must be a resident.
>
> **FPCTA Amendment:** The term "Specialized Vendor" is now used to deter "pass-throughs." If a vendor sells, leases, or subcontracts a specific category of industry equipment or expendables, then they are considered specialized.[43]

¶ 12.2.10 Additional conditions for earning the FTTC

A FPC must submit information to the Film Office that demonstrates its conformity with the requirements of the FPTCA, including detailed information on each DPE and each PPE. The FPC must provide a projection of the credit claims it plans to submit in the fiscal year.

In addition, the FPC must agree in writing:

---

[42] §3.13.9.9B NMAC.
[43] Pass-through entities are not recognized because these vendors only invoice for goods or services without directly providing them and without taking on any liability. Pass-through entities do not meet the physical presence requirements of the statute. See http://www.nmfilm.com/nm-vendors.aspx.

1. to pay all obligations the FPC has incurred in New Mexico;
2. to post a notice at completion of principal photography on the web site of the Film Office that:
   a. contains FPC information, including the name of the production, the address of the FPC and contact information that includes a working phone number, fax number and email address for both the local production office and the permanent production office to notify the public of the need to file creditor claims against the FPC; and
   b. remains posted on the web site until all financial obligations incurred in the state by the FPC have been paid;
3. that outstanding obligations are not waived should a creditor fail to file;
4. to delay filing of a claim for the FTTC until the Film Office delivers written notification to the TRD that the FPC has fulfilled all requirements for the credit; and
5. to submit a completed application for the FTTC and supporting documentation to the Film Office within one year of the close of the FPC's tax year in which the expenditures in New Mexico were incurred for the registered project and that are included in the credit claim.[44]

¶ 12.3 Additional credit for use of qualified production facilities

The FTTC is increased by 5%, up to 30%, for certain expenditures where the principal photography is shot at a qualified production facility (QPF). The additional credit applies to DPEs that are directly attributable and paid to a resident who is hired as industry crew, or who is hired as a producer, writer or director working directly with the physical production and has filed a New Mexico income tax return as a resident in the two previous tax years. To qualify for the credit, production must be shot at a QPF for a minimum number of days that varies with the size of the budget of the production.

If the budget is not more than $30,000,000, at least 10 principal

---

[44] §7-2F-6F NMSA 1978.

Film Production Incentives

photography days must be shot in New Mexico at a QPF, and at least 7 of those days must be shot at a sound stage that is a QPF, with the remainder, if any, at a standing set that is a QPF. For each of the 10 days, industry crew is included only if working on the premises of those facilities for a minimum of 8 hours within a 24-hour period.

If the budget is $30,000,000 or more, at least 15 principal photography days must be shot in New Mexico at a QPF and at least 10 of those days must be shot at a sound stage that is a QPF, with the remainder, if any, at a standing set that is a QPF. For each of the 15 days, industry crew is included only if working on the premises of those facilities for a minimum of 8 hours within a 24-hour period.[45]

A "qualified production facility" is a building, complex of buildings, or building improvements and associated back-lot facilities in which films are or are intended to be regularly produced and that contain at least one of the following:

- sound stage with contiguous, clear-span floor space of at least 7,000 square feet and a ceiling height of no less than 21 feet; or
- standing set that includes at least one interior, and at least five exteriors, built or repurposed for film production use on a continual basis and which is located on at least 50 acres of contiguous space designated for film production use.[46]

> **FPTCA Amendment**: A QPF now includes a standing set when used as a filming location. Up to 3 days of principal photography at the qualified standing set counts towards the 10-day requirement at the soundstages, and up to 5 days towards the 15-day requirement. Crew members must work at least 8 hours within a given day at the QPF to constitute "principal days." The additional 5% applies to a resident producer, writer, and/or director when they have filed their NM income tax return as a full-time, in-state resident in the two previous tax years.

The term "industry crew" refers to a person in a position that is off-camera and who provides technical services during the physical

---

[45] §7-2F-8 NMSA 1978.
[46] §7-2F-2O NMSA 1978.

production of a film, but does not include a writer, director, producer, background artist or performing artist.[47]

A FPC that receives an additional credit for television pilots and series is not eligible for the additional credit for the use of qualified production facilities.[48]

¶ 12.4 Additional Credit--Television Pilots and Series

The FTTC is increased by an additional 5% with regard to DPEs for:

- a standalone pilot intended for series television in New Mexico, and
- series television productions intended for commercial distribution with an order for at least six episodes in a single season if the New Mexico budget for each of those six episodes is $50,000 or more.[49]

> **FPTCA Amendment**: In determining eligibility, the term "budget" now means the New Mexico budget.

A FPC applying for this additional credit is not eligible for the additional credit regarding qualified production facilities.[50]

DPEs that are payments to a nonresident performing artist in a standalone pilot are generally not eligible for the additional credit.[51] As an exception, payments to a nonresident performing artist for a television series may be eligible for the additional credit where:

1. a television series completes at least one season of the scheduled episodes for that series in New Mexico;
2. the FPC certifies the intention to produce a subsequent season to that series in New Mexico; and
3. the FPC, or its parent company, produces or begins production of an additional eligible television series in New Mexico during the same FPC's tax year as the television series.

---

[47] §7-2F-2H NMSA 1978.
[48] §7-2F-7B NMSA 1978.
[49] §7-2F-7A NMSA 1978.
[50] §7-2F-7B NMSA 1978.
[51] §7-2F-7C NMSA 1978.

Film Production Incentives

> **FPTCA Amendment**: In case of series television, the additional 5% payments to nonresident on-camera actors and stunt persons only applies when the FPC or parent company begins another television series in NM within the same tax year.

If these requirements are met, payments to a nonresident performing artist for the additional television series may also be eligible for this additional credit.[52]

> **FPTCA Amendment**: Standalone TV pilots are eligible for a 30% credit, excluding payments to nonresident performing artists, when documentation shows the intention for the series to be produced in New Mexico.

¶ 12.5 Additional Credit for Nonresident Industry Crew

A FPC employing nonresident industry crew may earn a separate tax credit equal to 15% of the payment of wages, fringe benefits and per diem for nonresident industry crew if the following requirements are met:

1. the service is rendered in New Mexico;
2. production designers, directors of photography, line producers, costume designers, still unit photographers and drivers whose sole responsibility is driving are excluded;
3. the nonresident industry crew must be employed by the FPC in New Mexico; and
4. the number of non-resident industry crew employees allowed for the credit is in accordance with following table:

Final NM Budget	Number of Positions Permitted
Up to $2,000,000	4
For each additional $1,000,000 over $2,000,000 up to $10,0000	1 additional
For each additional $5,000,000 in budget over $10,000,000 up to $50,000,000	1 additional
For each $10,000,000 in budget over $50,000,000	1 additional

---

[52] §7-2F-7D NMSA 1978.

Eight additional positions above the number allowed in the above table are allowed for a television pilot episode that has not been ordered to series at the time of New Mexico production, but only if the FPC certifies to the Film Office that the series is intended to be produced in New Mexico if the pilot is ordered to series.

No more than 30 positions are allowed, except that up to 10 additional positions may be permitted at the discretion of the Film Office if 5 other films are being produced in New Mexico at the time of the FPC's production.[53]

> **FPTCA Amendment**: The need to contract a services company to employ nonresident individuals is eliminated, as is the need for the Film Office to approve positions. Qualifying payments include wages, fringe benefits and per diem .

In addition to the above described four requirements, the FPC must make financial or promotional contributions toward educational or work force development efforts in New Mexico as determined by the Film Office, including:

- A payment to a New Mexico educational institution that administers at least one industry-recognized film or multimedia program, as determined by the Film Office, equal to at least 2.5% of the DPEs for the payment of wages, fringe benefits and per diem for nonresident industry crew made by the FPC to nonresident industry crew;[54] or
- Promotion of the New Mexico film industry by directors, actors or producers affiliated with the FPC's project through: social media managed by the state; radio interviews facilitated by the Film Office; enhanced screen credit acknowledgments; or related events that are facilitated, conducted or sponsored by the Film Office.[55]

¶ 12.6 Qualifying for and Claiming the FTTC

The first step that the FPC must take to obtain the FTTC is to register

---

[53] §7-2F-9A,B, & C. NMSA 1978.
[54] §7-2F-2L NMSA 1978.
[55] §7-2F-9D NMSA 1978.

Film Production Incentives

a project with the Film Office and file a tax agreement at least two weeks prior to the beginning of principal photography or services in New Mexico. After production, the FPC may apply for the credit by submitting Form RPD-41381, *Application for Film and Television Tax Credit*, to the Film Office. The application must be submitted within one year of the close of the FPC's tax year in which the DPEs were incurred. When the New Mexico Film Office receives the Tax Application, a memo is sent to the Film Unit at the TRD outlining the eligibility of the registered project and the credit percentage allowed and confirming that obligations have been met. If an external CPA audit is required (if requested credit exceeds $5 million), the audit results will be included with this memo. An auditor is then assigned to the project in order to determine the amount of expenditures eligible for the credit. An engagement letter is sent to the FPC requesting it to submit ledgers by secured electronic transfer. After receipt of information, the project is placed in queue for audit sampling, based on "first- in, first-out" from date of submission. On completion of the audit, the TRD approves the credit and issues a document granting it.

Once the FPC is determined to be eligible by the Film Office and has been approved by the TRD, credits are claimed by attaching a completed Form RPD-41228, *Film-Related Tax Credit Claim Form*, including Schedule A, to the FPC's New Mexico income tax return filed after the close of its tax year for authorization for payment. The return must be timely filed. For qualifying expenditures made after April 15, 2013, the credit may be claimed by filing New Mexico Form PTE, *New Mexico Information Return* for *Pass-Through Entities*. The amount of approved film credit is entered on line 18 of that form.

All DPEs and PPEs incurred during the tax year by a FPC must be submitted as part of the same income tax return. A credit claim may not be divided and submitted with multiple returns or in multiple years.[63]

The Film Office posts on its web site on a quarterly basis the projected amount of credit claims for the fiscal year and all information provided by the FPC that does not reveal revenue, income or other information that may jeopardize the confidentiality of income tax

---

[63] §7-2F-12E NMSA 1978.

returns.[64]

The TRD posts on its web site on monthly basis the aggregate amount of credits claimed and processed for the fiscal year so as to provide guidance to FPCs regarding the amount of credit capacity remaining in a fiscal year.[65] In this case, the term "fiscal year" means the state fiscal year beginning on July 1.[66]

> **FPTCA Amendment**: Submission deadline for each tax application is now one year from last qualifying production expenditure, incurred for the registered project, within the FPC's tax year.

As the above procedures may change, FPCs should discuss any changes with the FO before proceeding.

¶ 12.7 Payment of claim and aggregate amount of claims allowed

The FPC may apply all or a portion of the FTTC granted against personal income tax liability or corporate income tax liability. If the amount of the claimed credit exceeds the FPC's tax liability for the tax year in which the credit is being claimed, the excess will be refunded as described below.[69]

The date a credit claim is received by the TRD determines the order that it is authorized for payment.

The aggregate amount of FTTC and FPTC claims that may be paid out in in any fiscal year is $50,000,000. If FTTC or FPTC claims are not paid because the claims for the fiscal year exceed the above limitation, these claims are placed at the front of a queue for the next fiscal year.[70]

Credit claims authorized for payment are paid out as follows:

1. A credit claim of less than $2,000,000 per tax year is applied or

---

[64] §7-2F-6G NMSA 1978.
[65] §7-2F-56 NMSA 1978.
[66] §7-2F-2G NMSA 1978.
[69] §7-2F-6J NMSA 1978.
[70] §7-2F-12A NMSA 1978; Form RPD-41228, Film-Related Tax Credit Claim Form Instructions (Rev. 9/2016).

Film Production Incentives

paid immediately upon processing of the income tax return;
2. A credit claim amount of $2,000,000 or more but less than $5,000,000 in a tax year is divided into two equal halves, with one half applied or paid immediately upon processing of the income tax return and the remainder paid 12 months after the date of the first payment; and
3. A credit claim of $5,000,000 or more in a tax year is divided into three equal payments, with one-third applied or paid or immediately upon processing of the income tax return, one third paid 12 months following the date of the first payment and the last one third paid 24 months following the date of the first payment.[71]

Any of the above payments that are deferred into a future year are also subject to the total aggregate limit of $50,000,000 in payments in a fiscal year. However, any deferred amount is placed in the front of the queue in the next fiscal year. If a partial payment is made because the aggregate tax credit limit has been met in a fiscal year then the difference owed retains its original position in the queue.[72]

For purposes of determining the payment of credit claims, the Secretary of the TRD may require that credit claims of affiliated persons be combined into one claim if necessary to accurately reflect closely integrated activities of affiliated persons.[73]

> **FPTCA Amendment**: The $10,000,000 rollover option available in past years has expired.

¶ 12.7.1 Assignment of FTTC

A FPC that is eligible to receive a FTTC may make a one-time assignment of an authorized payment to a third-party financial institution or to an authorized third party either in a full or partial amount. If TRD procedures for the assignment are followed, the TRD will remit to the assignee that amount of tax credit approved by the TRD that would otherwise be remitted to the company.[74]

An "authorized third party" is an entity that holds the rights to a

---

[71] §7-2F-12B NMSA 1978.
[72] §7-2F-12C, D NMSA 1978.
[73] §7-2F-12F NMSA 1978.
[74] §7-2F-5A NMSA 1978.

film for which a FTTC may be claimed and initiates that film's production. A "financial institution" is a fund purposely created to produce a film, or a bank, savings institution or credit union that is organized or chartered under the laws of New Mexico or the United States and that files a New Mexico income tax return.

¶12.8 Reporting--accountability

In order to allow government leaders to assess the effectiveness of New Mexico film incentives, the Economic Development Department ('EDD") is required to collect and analyze data and report periodically to government committees. The FPTCA requires the EDD to:

- collect data to be used in an econometric tool that objectively assesses the effectiveness of credits;
- track the direct expenditures for the credits;
- with the support and assistance of the legislative finance committee staff and the TRD, review and assess the above analysis and create a report for presentation to the revenue stabilization and tax policy committee and the legislative finance committee that provides an objective assessment of the effectiveness of the credits; and
- report annually to the revenue stabilization and tax policy committee and the legislative finance committee on aggregate approved tax credits.[75]

The Film Office is required to develop a form on which the taxpayer claiming a credit would submit a report to accompany the application for the credit.[76]

With respect to the film on which the application for a credit is based, the FPC must report to the Film Office at a minimum the following information:

- the total aggregate wages of the members of the New Mexico resident crew;
- the number of New Mexico residents employed;
- the total amount of gross receipts taxes paid;

---

[75] §7-2F-5A NMSA 1978.
[76] §7-2F-5B NMSA 1978.

Film Production Incentives

- the total number of hours worked by New Mexico residents;
- the total expenditures made in New Mexico that do not qualify for the credit;
- the aggregate wages paid to the members of the nonresident crew while working in New Mexico; and
- other information deemed necessary by the Film Office and EDD to determine the effectiveness of the credit.[77]

For purposes of assessing the effectiveness of a credit, the inability of the EDD to aggregate data due to sample size does not relieve the department of its requirement to report all relevant data to the legislature. The Film Office must notify a FPC applying for a credit that information provided to the Film Office may be revealed in reports to the legislature.[78]

¶ 12.9 Film Production Tax Credit-- Principal Photography Commencing Prior to January 1, 2016

¶12.9.1 Overview

An eligible film production company ("FPC") may apply for a FPTC equal to 25% of DPEs and PPEs that are made in New Mexico. These expenditures must be subject to taxation in New Mexico and not be claimed by another taxpayer for the FPTC. For purposes of the FPTC, a FPC is a person that produces one or more films or any part of a film and that commences principal photography *prior to January 1, 2016.*[79] Principal photography means the production of a film during which the main visual elements are created.[80] The following are some important points concerning the FPTC, which are discussed in more detail below:

- This is a refundable credit, meaning that if the amount of credit exceeds the taxpayer's tax liability, the excess is refunded to the taxpayer.
- The FPTC rate is increased by 5%, up to 30%, for DPEs related to qualified production facilities.

---

[77] §7-2F-5C NMSA 1978.
[78] §7-2F-5D NMSA 1978.
[79] §7-2F-1U NMSA 1978.
[80] §7-2F-2N NMSA 1978.

297

- The FPTC rate is also increased by an additional 5%, up to 30%, for DPEs with regard to a standalone pilot intended for series television in New Mexico or series television productions intended for commercial distribution with an order for at least six episodes in a single season if the New Mexico budget for each of those six episodes is $50,000 or more.[81] A FPC applying for this additional credit is not eligible for the additional credit regarding qualified production facilities.[82]
- The FPTC rate of 25% is reduced to 20% for expenditures that are attributable to a production that for which a FPC received a tax credit under the federal new markets tax credit program.[83]

¶ 12.9.2 Requirements for direct production and postproduction expenditures

To qualify for the FPTC, DPEs and PPEs must be made in New Mexico and meet the following requirements:

- they must be directly attributable to the production in New Mexico of a film or commercial audiovisual product;
- they must be subject to taxation by the state of New Mexico and in the case of PPEs are for services performed in New Mexico;
- they may not include expenditures for which another taxpayer claims the FPTC; and
- they do not exceed the usual and customary cost of the goods or services acquired when purchased by unrelated parties. The secretary of the TRD may determine the value of the goods or services when the buyer and seller are affiliated persons or the sale or purchase is not an arm's length transaction.[84]

An "affiliated person" is one who directly or indirectly owns or controls, is owned or controlled by, or is under common ownership or control with another person through ownership of voting securities or other ownership interests representing a majority of the total voting

---

[81]. This statute applies post Jan. 1, 2016. §7-2F-1C[1] NMSA 1978 applies before Jan1, 2016.
[82] §7-2F-1C NMSA 1978.
[83] §7-2F-1D NMSA 1978.
[84] §7-2F-5B NMSA 1978.

Film Production Incentives

power of the entity.[85]

¶ 12.9.3 Direct production expenditures

The FPTCA provides a list of specified categories of production expenditures that qualify as DPEs for the FPTC:

1. Payment of wages, fringe benefits or fees for talent, management or labor to a person who is a New Mexico resident;
2. Payment for wages and per diem for a performing artist who is not a New Mexico resident and who is directly employed by the FPC, but only if the FPC deducts and remits, or causes to be deducted and remitted, income tax from the first day of services rendered in New Mexico at the maximum rate under law;

> **FPCTA Amendment**: Income tax withholding is now required for nonresident on-camera actors and stunt persons on production payroll at 4.9%, in addition to those actors paid through an actor loan out company. This rule applies for payments made on and after June 19, 2015, regardless of exemptions claimed or the number of days worked by these employed, nonresident actors in New Mexico.

3. Payment to a personal services business for the services of a performing artist (including stunt coordinators under a standard stunt performer's contract with the FPC),[86] if:

    - the personal services business pays gross receipts tax in New Mexico on the portion of those payments qualifying for the tax credit; and
    - FPC deducts and remits, or causes to be deducted and remitted, income tax at the maximum withholding tax rate on the portion of those payments qualifying for the tax credit paid to a personal services business where the performing artist is a full or part owner of that business or subcontracts with a personal services

---

[85] §7-2F-2A NMSA 1978.
[86] §3.13.9.7B NMAC.

business where the performing artist is a full or part owner of that business; and

> **FPCTA Amendment**: A personal service business includes an entity that may not have physical presence.

4. Any of the following provided by a vendor:
   a. the story and scenario to be used for a film;
   b. set construction and operations, wardrobe, accessories and related services;
   c. photography, sound synchronization, lighting and related services;
   d. editing and related services;
   e. rental of facilities and equipment;
   f. leasing of vehicles, not including the chartering of aircraft for out-of-state transportation, but
      i. New Mexico-based chartered aircraft for in-state transportation directly attributable to the production is considered a direct production expenditure, and
      ii. only the first $100 of the daily expense of leasing a vehicle for passenger transportation on state roadways may be claimed as a DPE;
   g. food or lodging; provided that only the first $150 of lodging per individual per day is eligible to be claimed as a direct production expenditure;
   h. commercial airfare if purchased through a New Mexico-based travel agency or travel company for travel to and from New Mexico or within New Mexico that is directly attributable to the production;
   i. insurance coverage and bonding if purchased through a New Mexico-based insurance agent, broker or bonding agent;
   j. services for an external audit upon submission of an application for a FPTC by an accounting firm that submits the application for the credit; and

Film Production Incentives

> **FPCTA Amendment**: The expenditure for a required external audit by a CPA licensed to practice in New Mexico requires the CPA to have a physical presence in New Mexico and to render the services in-state. The application would have to be submitted, and the expenditure paid, on or after June 19, 2015, for that cost to be eligible.

    k. other direct costs of producing a film in accordance with generally accepted entertainment industry practice.

DPEs include only those expenditures directly incurred and paid by the FPC to the vendor of the services or property and does not include expenditures incurred and paid by a third party even if incurred on behalf of the qualified production company.[87]

DPEs do not include expenditure for:

1. A gift with a value greater than $25.00.
2. Artwork or jewelry, except that a work of art or a piece of jewelry may be a direct production expenditure if it is used in the film production and the expenditure is less than $2,500;
3. Entertainment, amusement or recreation;
4. Subcontracted goods or services provided by a vendor when subcontractors are not subject to state taxation, such as equipment and locations provided by the military, government and religious organizations; or
5. A service provided by a nonresident employed in an industry crew position, other than a performing artist, where it is the standard entertainment industry practice for the FPC to employ a person for that position, except when the nonresident is hired or subcontracted by a vendor; and when the FPC, as determined by the Film Office and when applicable in consultation with industry, provides:
        a. reasonable efforts to hire resident crew; and
        b. financial or promotional contributions toward education or work force development efforts in New Mexico, including at least one of the following:
               i. a payment to a New Mexico public education

---

[87] §3.13.9.7A NMAC.

           institution that administers at least one industry-recognized film or multimedia program, as determined by the Film Office, in an amount equal to 2.5% of payments made to nonresidents in approved positions employed by the vendor;
      ii. promotion of the New Mexico film industry by directors, actors or executive producers affiliated with the production company's project through social media that is managed by the state;
      iii. radio interviews facilitated by the Office;
      iv. enhanced screen credit acknowledgments; or
      v.   related events that are facilitated, conducted or sponsored by the Film Office.[88]

Expenditures may not exceed the usual and customary cost of the goods or services when purchased by unrelated parties. The Secretary of the TRD may determine the value of the goods or services when the buyer and seller are affiliated or the transaction is not at arm's length transaction. An "affiliated person" is one who directly or indirectly owns or controls, is owned or controlled by, or is under common ownership or control with another person through ownership of voting securities or other ownership interests representing a majority of the total voting power of the entity.[89]

¶ 12.9.4 Nonresident performing artists

The FPTCA provide two cases where wages paid to a nonresident performing artist qualify as DPEs: 1) payment for wages and per diem for a nonresident performing artist who is directly employed by a FPC, provided that the FPC from the first day of services rendered in New Mexico deducts and remits, or causes to be deducted and remitted, income tax at the maximum withholding rate (4.9%); and 2) payment to a personal services business (or loan out company) on the wages and per diem paid to a nonresident performing artist of the artist loan out company, if the loan out company pays New Mexico gross receipts tax on the portion of those payments qualifying for the tax credit, and

---

[88] §7-2F-1T NMSA 1978.
[89] §7-2F-1B NMSA 1978;§7-2F-2A NMSA 1978.

Film Production Incentives

the FPC deducts and remits, or causes to be deducted and remitted, income tax at the maximum rate on the portion of those payments qualifying for the tax credit paid to a loan out company, where the performing artist is a full or part owner of that business, or subcontracts with a personal services business where the performing artist is a full or part owner of that business.[90]

See ¶ 12.2.3 for a discussion of personal service businesses and loan out companies and how they are used to qualify payments to nonresidents as DPEs.

¶ 12.9.5 Limitation on credit for performing artists

That amount of FPTCs related to the services of performing artists is limited to $5,000,000 with regard to nonresident performing artists and featured resident principal performing artists in a production. This limitation does not apply to the services of background artists and resident performing artists who are not cast in industry standard featured principal performer roles.[91]

A "performing artist" is an actor, on-camera stuntperson, puppeteer, pilot who is a stuntperson or actor, specialty foreground performer or narrator; and who speaks a line of dialogue, is identified with the product or reacts to narration as assigned, but does not include a background artist.[92]

> **FPTCA Amendment:** Resident non-lead actors are no longer subject to $5 million tax credit limit.

¶ 12.9.6 Postproduction Expenditures

To qualify for the FPTC, a PPE must be directly attributable to the production of a commercial film or audiovisual product.[93] A "postproduction expenditure" is an expenditure for editing, Foley recording, automatic dialogue replacement, sound editing, special effects, including computer-generated imagery or other effects, scoring and music editing, beginning and end credits, negative cutting, soundtrack production, dubbing, subtitling or addition of

---

[90] §7-2F-1T[1][c] NMSA 1978.
[91] §7-2F-1S NMSA 1978.
[92] §7-F-2J NMSA 1978.
[93] §7-2F-1B NMSA 1978.

sound or visual effects. The term does not include expenditures for advertising, marketing, distribution or expense payments.[94]

¶ 12.9.7 Film and audiovisual product requirements

Both PPEs and DPEs must be with regard to a film or commercial audiovisual product. The term "film" refers to a single medium or multimedia program, excluding advertising messages other than national or regional advertising messages intended for exhibition, that is a) fixed on film, a digital medium, videotape, computer disc, laser disc or other similar delivery medium that can be viewed or reproduced; b) is not intended to and does not violate the provision of the criminal code regarding sexually oriented material harmful to minors;[95] and c) is intended for reasonable commercial exploitation for the delivery medium used.[96] A "commercial audiovisual product" is a film or a videogame intended for commercial exploitation.[97]

When the FPTC is claimed on a production, an acknowledgment to New Mexico must appear in the end screen credits that the production was filmed in New Mexico, and a state logo provided by the Film Office must be included and embedded in the end screen credits of long-form narrative film productions and television episodes, unless otherwise agreed to in writing by the Film Office.[98]

> **FPTCA Amendment:** The State's logo must appear in the screen credits at a standard size as compared to other logos in the same end crawl for both features and television episodes.

¶ 12.9.8 Residency requirement for purposes of the FPTC

A "New Mexico resident" for purposes of the FPTCA is an individual who is domiciled in New Mexico any time during the tax year or who is physically present 185 days or more during the tax year. However, an individual, other than someone who meets the physical presence test, who changed his or her place of abode on or before the last day of the tax year to a place outside the state, intending to

---

[94] §7-2F-2M NMSA 1978.
[95] See Chapter 30, Article 37 NMSA 1978
[96] §7-2F-2F NMSA 1978.
[97] §7-2F-2C NMSA 1978.
[98] §7-2F-1M NMSA 1978.

Film Production Incentives

permanently live outside the state, is not a resident for periods after the change.[99]

¶ 12.9.9 Requirement for DPEs and PPEs to be a taxable transaction

The FPTC may not be claimed for DPEs or PPEs for which a FPC has delivered a nontaxable transaction certificate with regard to the Gross Receipts and Compensating Tax Act. Under that Act, the receipts from selling or leasing property and from performing services may be deducted from gross receipts or from governmental gross receipts if the sale, lease or performance is made to a qualified production company that delivers a nontaxable transaction certificate to the seller, lessor or performer.[100]

¶ 12.9.10 Vendor requirements

A "vendor" is a person who sells or leases goods or services that are related to standard industry craft inventory, who has a physical presence in New Mexico, and is subject to the gross receipts tax, the income tax, or the corporate income tax, but excludes a personal services business and services provided by nonresidents hired or subcontracted if the tasks and responsibilities are associated with:

- the standard industry job position of a director, a writer, a producer, an associate producer, a co-producer, an executive producer, a production supervisor, a director of photography, a motion picture driver whose sole responsibility is driving, a production or personal assistant, a designer, a still photographer, or a carpenter and utility technician at an entry level; and
- nonstandard industry job positions and personal support services.[101]

A FPC must make reasonable efforts, as determined by the Film Office, to contract with a specialized vendor that provides goods and services, inventory or services directly related to that vendor's ordinary course of business.

---

[99] §7-2F-2I NMSA 1978.
[100] §7-2F-1L NMSA 1978; see §7-9-86 NMSA 1978.
[101] §7-2F-1V NMSA 1978.

"Physical presence" means a physical address in New Mexico from which a vendor conducts business, stores inventory or otherwise creates, assembles or offers for sale the product purchased or leased by a FPC and the business owner or an employee of the business is a resident. Any vendor (provider) providing goods or performing services and who occupies and maintains one or more physical places of business in New Mexico (not a virtual or online business), has established physical presence for purposes of the FPTC if the following conditions are present:

1. a provider of goods or services, or its employees, or representatives, is available at that provider's place of business during established times;
2. a provider of goods maintains an inventory of the goods sold at the provider's New Mexico place of business and those goods are held for sale in the vendor's ordinary course of business at that place of business; and
3. critical elements of any service performed by a service provider occur, are managed at, or coordinated from the service provider's place of business.[102]

The following indicia are considered in determining if the above conditions are present:

- the provider of the goods or services is a resident or has at least one laborer who is a New Mexico resident, as defined in the Income Tax Act;
- a telephone is assigned for the exclusive use by the provider of goods or services at the provider's place of business;
- the place of business has been designated for the use of the goods or services provided;
- the place of business contains office furniture or equipment for the use by the provider;
- the goods or services provider is identified by business name on a sign located in or adjacent to the place of business; and
- a client or other persons can expect to communicate, either in person or by telephone, with the goods or services provider, or employees or representatives of the provider, at the place of

---

[102] §3.13.9.9A NMAC.

Film Production Incentives

business.[103]

> **FPCTA Amendment:** The definition of "physical presence" clarifies that either the owner or an employee of the vendor must be a resident.
>
> **FPCTA Amendment:** The term "specialized vendor" is now used to deter "pass-throughs." If a vendor sells, leases, or subcontracts a specific category of industry equipment or expendables, then they are considered specialized.

¶ 12.9.11 Additional conditions for earning the FPTC

A FPC must submit information to the Film Office that demonstrates its conformity with the requirements of the FPTCA, including detailed information on each DPE and PPE. The FPC must provide a projection of the credit claims it plans to submit in the fiscal year.

In addition, the FPC must agree in writing:

1. to pay all obligations the FPC has incurred in New Mexico;
2. to post a notice at completion of principal photography on the web site of the Film Office that:
   a. contains FPC information, including the name of the production, the address of the FPC and contact information that includes a working phone number, fax number and email address for both the local production office and the permanent production office to notify the public of the need to file creditor claims against the FPC; and
   b. remains posted on the web site until all financial obligations incurred in the state by the FPC have been paid;
3. that outstanding obligations are not waived should a creditor fail to file;
4. to delay filing of a claim for the FPTC until the Film Office delivers written notification to the TRD that the FPC has fulfilled all requirements for the credit; and
5. to submit a completed application for the FPTC and supporting documentation to the Film Office within one year

---

[103] §3.13.9.9B NMAC.

of the close of the FPC's tax year in which the expenditures in New Mexico were incurred for the registered project and that are included in the credit claim.[104]

> **FPCTA Amendment**: All qualifying projects must include the acknowledgement to the State of New Mexico. The State's logo must now appear in the screen credits at a standard size as compared to other logos in the same end crawl for both features and television episodes.

12.10 Additional credit for use of qualified production facilities

The FPTC is increased by an additional 5%, up to 30%, for certain expenditures on a production where the principal photography is shot a qualified production facility (QPF). The additional credit applies to DPEs that are directly attributable and paid to a resident who is hired as industry crew, or who is hired as a producer, writer or director working directly with the physical production and has filed a New Mexico income tax return as a resident in the two previous tax years. To qualify for the credit, production must shoot for a minimum number of days at a QPF based upon the budget of the production.

If the budget of a FPC in principal photography on or after April 10, 2015 is not more than $30,000,000, at least 10 principal photography days must be shot in New Mexico at a QPF, and at least 7 of those days must be shot at a sound stage that is a QPF, with the remainder, if any, at a standing set that is a QPF. For each of the 10 principal photography days, industry crew is included only if working on the premises of those facilities for a minimum of 8 hours within a 24-hour period.

If the budget of a FPC in principal photography on or after April 10, 2015 is $30,000,000 or more, at least 15 principal photography days must be shot in New Mexico at a QPF and at least 10 of those days must be shot at a sound stage that is a QPF, with the remainder, if any, at a standing set that is a QPF. For each of the 15 principal photography days, industry crew is included only if working on the premises of those facilities for a minimum of 8 hours within a 24-hour

---

[104] §7-2F-1N NMSA 1978.

Film Production Incentives

period.[105]

> **FPCTA Amendment**: QPFs now include a standing set when used as a filming location on or after April 10, 2015. Up to 3 days of principal photography at the qualified standing set count towards the 10 day requirement at the soundstages, and up to 5 days count towards the 15 day requirement. "Principal days" means that the crew members work at least 8 hours within a given day at the QPF.
>
> The additional 5%, when meeting the requirements for using a QPF, includes resident producer, writer, and/or director when they have filed their New Mexico personal income tax return as a full-time, in-state resident in the prior two tax years.

A "qualified production facility" is a building, or complex of buildings, building improvements and associated back-lot facilities in which films are or are intended to be regularly produced and that contain at least one of the following:

- sound stage with contiguous, clear-span floor space of at least 7,000 square feet and a ceiling height of no less than 21 feet; or
- standing set that includes at least one interior, and at least five exteriors, built or re-purposed for film production use on a continual basis and is located on at least 50 acres of contiguous space designated for film production use.[106]

The term "industry crew" refers to a person in a position that is off-camera and who provides technical services during the physical production of a film, but does not include a writer, director, producer, background artist or performing artist.[107]

A FPC that receives an additional credit for television pilots and series is not eligible for the additional credit for the use of qualified

---

[105] §7-2F-1C NMSA 1978.
[106] §7-2F-2O NMSA 1978.
[107] §7-2F-2H NMSA 1978.

production facilities.[108]

¶12.11 Additional Credit--Television Pilots and Series

The FPTC is increased by 5%, up to 30%, for DPEs for a standalone pilot intended for series television in New Mexico or on series television productions intended for commercial distribution with an order for at least 6 episodes in a single season, but only if the New Mexico budget for each of those 6 episodes is $50,000 or more

> **FPTCA Amendment**: Standalone TV pilots are eligible for a 30% credit DPEs when documentation is included showing the intention for the series to be produced in New Mexico upon "pick-up" and when applying for the credit after June 19, 2015. With regard to eligibility, "budget" means the New Mexico budget.

The FPTC may not be claimed for DPEs or PPEs for which a FPC has delivered a nontaxable transaction certificate with regard to the Gross Receipts and Compensating Tax Act. Under that Act the receipts from selling or leasing property and from performing services may be deducted from gross receipts or from governmental gross receipts if the sale, lease or performance is made to a qualified production company that delivers a nontaxable transaction certificate to the seller, lessor or performer.[109]

¶12.12 Qualifying for and Claiming the FPTC

Section 12.6 discusses the procedures for qualifying for a FTTC claim under FPTCA. Those procedures are similar to ones for making a FPTC claim. One important difference is that the tax application is made on Form RPD-41229, *Application for Film Production Tax Credit*, which reflects the laws applicable for projects that began principal photography before January 1, 2016

---

[108] §7-2F-7B NMSA 1978
[109] §7-2F-1L NMSA 1978; §7-9-86L NMSA 1978.

Film Production Incentives

¶ 12.13 Payment of claims and aggregate amount of claims allowed

¶ 12.13.1 Overview

The process for the payment of a FPTC claim is similar to that for FTTC claims. See ¶ 12.7. A FPTC credit claim is considered received by TRD only if the claim is made on a complete income tax return filed after the close of the tax year. All DPEs and PPEs incurred during the tax year by a FPC must be submitted as part of the return and paid pursuant to the rules of the statute. A credit claim may not be divided and submitted with multiple returns or in multiple years.[110] If a FPC files a complete and timely tax return before the credit is approved by the TRD, the FPC may claim the credit on amended return after the FPTC has been approved.[111]

The date a credit claim is received by the TRD determines the order that it is authorized for payment. The aggregate amount of claims for a credit that may be authorized for payment in any fiscal year is $50,000,000. A FPC that submits a claim for a FPTC that is does not receive the credit because the claims for the fiscal year exceed this limitation is placed at the front of a queue for the subsequent fiscal year.[112]

An important change in the law affects the rollover of any unused portion of the maximum $50,000,000 in credits to future years. Previously, if FPTC claims authorized for payment in a fiscal year, for fiscal years 2013 to 2015, was less than $50,000,000, then the difference, or $10,000,000, whichever is less, was added to the amount of claims that may be authorized for payment in the following fiscal year.[113] This rollover mechanism no longer exists.

> **FPTCA Amendment**: The $10M rollover option is no longer available.

Credit claims that are authorized for payment are paid according to the following rules:

---

[110] §7-2F-1J NMSA 1978.
[111] §3.13.9.8E NMAC.
[112] §7-2F-1E NMSA 1978.
[113] §7-2F-1F NMSA 1978.

1. a credit claim of less than $2,000,000 per tax year is paid immediately upon authorization for payment;
2. a credit claim of $2,000,000 or more but less than $5,000,000 per tax year is divided into 2 equal payments, with the first payment made immediately upon authorization of the payment and the second payment to be made 12 months following the date of the first payment; and
3. a credit claim $5,000,000 or more per tax year are divided into 3 equal payments, with the first payment made immediately upon authorization of payment, the second payment 12 months following the date of the first payment and the third payment made 24 months following the date of the first payment.[114]

See ¶ 12.7 for a further discussion of credit payout rules.

¶ 12.13.2 Assignment of FPTC

As in the case of the FTTC, a FPC that is eligible to receive a FPTC may make a one-time assignment of an authorized payment to a third-party financial institution or to an authorized third party either in a full or partial amount. These assignment rules are applicable to tax years beginning on or after January 1, 2015.[119] See ¶ 12.7.1 for a discussion of the assignment of the FTTC.

---

[114] §7-2F-1G NMSA 1978.
[119] §7-2F-5B NMSA 1978.

CHAPTER 13
REFUNDABLE CREDITS AND REBATES

¶ 13.1 Overview

New Mexico has ten refundable credits. Three are reported on Schedule PIT-CR, one is reported directly on the Form PIT-1, and the following six refundable credits are reported on Schedule PIT-RC:

- Tax rebate of a portion of property tax due from low-income taxpayers
- Tax rebate of property tax for elderly
- Low-income comprehensive tax rebate
- Credit for expenses for dependent child day care necessary to enable gainful employment to prevent indigency
- Refundable medical care credit for persons 65 or older
- Special needs adopted child tax credit

The first four of the above credits are targeted to help low-income residents, whose income must be below a certain level to qualify. The medical care credit is for the elderly who incur large unreimbursed medical expenses and the special needs adoption credit is to provide a subsidy to caring people who adopt a special needs child and are subject to significant care expenses as a result.

The working families credit, which also requires income qualification, is reported on Form PIT-1, line 25, and is discussed below at ¶ 13.9. Three business-related credits: the film production credit, the renewable energy production credit, and the technology jobs (additional) tax credit (for certain taxpayers) are also refundable and are discussed in Chapters 11 and 12.

The credits of Schedule PIT-RC are totaled on line 25 of that schedule and reported on Form PIT-1, line 24. Since four of the credits of the Schedule PIT-RC credits depend on taxpayers having a qualifying income based on a separate measuring standard, known as modified gross income, this concept is explained next.

¶ 13.2 Modified gross income ("MGI")

A taxpayer's eligibility for four of the credits and rebates of Schedule PIT-RC depends upon the taxpayer's level of MGI. The following table shows the levels of MGI required to qualify for each of the four credits that are dependent on MGI.

Qualifications for rebates and credits	
Persons with MGI of:	**May qualify for:**
$22,000 or less	Low income comprehensive tax rebate
$16,000 or less	Property tax rebate
$30,160 or less	NM child day care credit
$24,000 or less	Additional low income property tax rebate – for Los Alamos or Santa Fe countries only

MGI is different from AGI, federal taxable income, or New Mexico taxable income. MGI is a unique New Mexico income standard. At its essence, MGI is a comprehensive total of all income and compensation (subject to exclusions) of the taxpayer, the taxpayer's spouse (even if filing separate returns), and the taxpayer's dependents, received from all sources (regardless of whether the income is taxable by the federal government or New Mexico). No deductions or losses are allowed in computing MGI.[1] The two insets immediately below list MGI income and exclusions, and these in turn are followed by an inset adapted from Schedule PIT-RC which shows how the MGI calculation is made.

---

[1] §7-2-2L NMSA 1978. 2016 PIT-RC New Mexico Rebate and Credit Schedule Instructions, p. 4RC.

Refundable Rebates and Credits

MGI INCLUSIONS
MGI represents all income of the taxpayer, the taxpayer's spouse, and dependents, from whatever source, undiminished by losses, regardless if that income is taxable by the U.S. or NM, including: <ul><li>Compensation</li><li>Distributions from employee stock ownership plans or other employee benefit plans, except for medical benefits</li><li>The value of room and board received as compensation</li><li>Amounts received from endowment contracts</li><li>Unemployment compensation benefits (not including medical benefits)</li><li>Net profit from business (including self-employment)</li><li>Gains from dealings in property (unreduced by capital losses, and including capital gains and gain on the sale of a personal residence that is deferred or not subject to federal income tax)</li><li>Net rents (without offsetting the loss of one business, farm, or rental against the profit of another or against any other source of income)</li><li>Interest (including interest untaxed by the federal government or NM)</li><li>Dividends and royalties</li><li>Alimony and separate maintenance payments</li><li>Social security benefits (the full pension or annuity amount before deduction for Medicare or other deductions), pensions, annuities</li><li>Receipt of contribution withdrawals from deferred compensation plans</li><li>Income from life insurance and endowment contracts;</li><li>Gross gambling, gaming, and lottery winnings without reducing winnings by any losses</li><li>Discharge of indebtedness</li><li>Distributive share of income of partnership, S corporation, or similar pass-through entities</li><li>Income in respect of a decedent</li><li>Income from an interest in an estate or a trust</li><li>Workers' compensation benefits</li><li>Public assistance and welfare benefits (e.g., TANF or a similar program, welfare and general assistance benefits, and SSI)</li><li>Cost-of-living, moving, or other allowances received as compensation</li><li>Value of a legacy, devise, bequest, or inheritance received</li><li>Gifts received</li><li>Insurance or court settlements</li><li>Scholarships, fellowships, prizes, awards, or grants</li><li>Other cash prizes and awards</li><li>VA benefits[2]</li></ul>

---

[2] §7-2-2L NMSA 1978; §3.3.1.10 NMAC; 2016 PIT-RC New Mexico Rebate and Credit Schedule Instructions, p. 4RC.

MGI EXCLUSIONS
<ul><li>Medical care payments made by Medicaid, the State Human Services Department, the County Indigent Hospital Claims Fund, Champus, Veterans Administration (VA), or Workers' Compensation</li><li>Payments by any party or by Medicare or any similar plan for hospital, dental, medical, or drug expenses whether or not the payment is made directly to the insured/recipient or to a third-party provider, and whether or not a premium is paid</li><li>The value of room and board provided by federal, state or local governments or by private individuals or agencies based upon financial need and not as a form of compensation</li><li>The face value of food stamps or Women, Infants, and Children (WIC) vouchers</li><li>Payments pursuant to a federal, state or local government program directly or indirectly to a third party on behalf of the taxpayer when identified to a particular use or invoice by the payer</li><li>Payments for credits and rebates pursuant to the ITA and made for a credit against state income tax for the year (such as low income or property tax rebates or as child day care credit</li><li>Money lent to an individual with a legal obligation to repay</li><li>Rent subsidies, weatherization, energy, and housing; rehabilitation benefits, such as Section 8 housing assistance</li><li>Debts that have been discharged by a United States bankruptcy court</li><li>Stipends paid to foster grandparents[3]</li></ul>

---

[3] §7-2-2M NMSA 1978; §3.3.1.10 NMAC; 2016 PIT-RC New Mexico Rebate and Credit Schedule Instructions, p. 4RC.

Refundable Rebates and Credits

CALCULATING MGI
MGI generally, is all income of the taxpayer and household members, both taxable and nontaxable, and undiminished by losses. **NOTE:** If married filing separately, spouse's income is included.
➢ Wages, salaries, tips, etc. ➢ Social security benefits, pensions, annuities, and Railroad Retirement ➢ Unemployment and workers' compensation benefits ➢ Public assistance, TANF and Supplemental Security Income (SSI**)** ➢ Net pro t from business, farm, or rentals. **If a loss, enter zero. DO NOT enter a negative number.** ➢ Capital gains undiminished by capital losses. ➢ Gifts of cash or marketable tangible items received. (You must give the items a reasonable value.). ➢ All other income such as interest, dividends, gambling winnings, insurance settlements, scholarships, grants, VA benefits, trust income and inheritance, alimony, and child support
MGI equals the total of the above which is entered on line 12 and on line 13 of page 2 of Schedule PIT-RC.

¶ 13.3 Low-income comprehensive tax rebate ("LICTR")

A resident with MGI of $22,000 or less may claim a LICTR if the following conditions are met:

1. the resident is not a dependent of another,
2. the resident was not an inmate of a public institution for more than 6 months during the tax year, and
3. the resident was physically present in New Mexico for at least 6 months during the tax year.

The statute provides that the rebate is given in compensation for a portion of state and local taxes to which the resident has been subject during the tax year, but there is no requirement that the taxpayer show that any state and local taxes have been paid.[4]

The amount of the rebate depends upon the number of the taxpayer's exemptions and the amount of the taxpayer's MGI, as set out in the rebate table below. A rebate may be claimed even though a resident has no taxable income. A husband and wife who file separate returns for a tax year in which they could have filed a joint return may each claim only one-half of the tax rebate that would have been allowed on a joint return.[5]

The determination of total number of exemptions used in calculating the rebate starts with the number of exemptions allowable on the federal return (Form PIT-1, line 5). From this number is subtracted any exemptions and extra exemptions for those who do not qualify. This would include any spouse who does not meet the requirements for the credit stated above, plus dependents who are non-residents of New Mexico. Then two additional exemptions are added for each individual domiciled in New Mexico included in the return who is 65 years of age or older, plus one additional exemption for each individual domiciled in New Mexico included in the return who, for federal income tax purposes, is blind. One exemption is added for each minor child or stepchild of the resident who would be a dependent for federal income tax purposes if the public assistance contributing to the support of the child or stepchild was considered to have been contributed by the resident. These calculations are made in Schedule PIT- RC, as reproduced below.[6]

CALCULATE ALLOWABLE HOUSEHOLD MEMBERS AND EXTRA EXEMPTIONS

1. Number of exemptions from Form PIT-1, line 5. 1
2. a. Enter number of household members who **DO NOT** qualify. If all exemptions qualify, leave blank.................... 2a −
   See PIT-RC instructions.
   b. **Subtract** 2a from 1. Number of allowable household members. .... 2b =
   c. Extra Exemption: Enter **1** if you **or** your spouse (if married filing jointly) are blind for federal income tax purposes. Enter **2** if you **and** your spouse (if married filing jointly) are blind. .... 2c +
   d. **Add** lines 2b and 2c .... 2d =
   e. If you are 65 or older, enter **2** .... 2e +
   f. If married filing jointly and your spouse is 65 or older, enter **2** .... 2f +
   g. **Add** lines 2d, 2e, and 2f .... 2g =
   h. If you checked filing status (3) married filing separately on your Form PIT-1, enter the number of exemptions, if any, your spouse claimed on line 2g of your spouse's PIT-RC. .... 2h +
3. **Total. Add** lines 2g and 2h. Enter here and on line 13a on page 2 of this form .... 3 =

After determining the number of exemptions, the amount of rebate can be found using the following table reproduced from the

---

[4] §7-2-14A and B NMSA 1978.
[5] §7-2-14A NMSA 1978.
[6] §7-2-14C NMSA 1978.

Refundable Rebates and Credits

instructions to Schedule PIT-RC.

TABLE 1. 2015 Low Income Comprehensive Tax Rebate Table							
Modified Gross Income from PIT-RC, Line 13		Number of Exemptions from PIT-RC, Line 13a					
	But Not Over	1	2	3	4	5	6 or more
$ 0	$ 500	$ 120	$ 160	$ 200	$ 240	$ 280	$ 320
501	1,000	135	195	250	310	350	415
1,001	1,500	135	195	250	310	350	435
1,501	3,500	135	195	250	310	350	450
3,501	4,500	135	195	250	310	355	450
4,501	5,000	125	190	240	305	355	450
5,001	5,500	115	175	230	295	355	430
5,501	6,000	105	155	210	260	315	410
6,001	7,000	90	130	170	220	275	370
7,001	8,000	80	115	145	180	225	295
8,001	9,000	70	105	135	170	195	240
9,001	10,000	65	95	115	145	175	205
10,001	11,000	60	80	100	130	155	185
11,001	12,000	55	70	90	110	135	160
12,001	14,000	50	65	85	100	115	140
14,001	15,000	45	60	75	90	105	120
15,001	16,000	40	55	70	85	95	110
16,001	17,000	35	50	65	80	85	105
17,001	18,000	30	45	60	70	80	95
18,001	19,000	25	35	50	60	70	80
19,001	20,000	20	30	40	50	60	65
20,001	21,000	15	25	30	40	50	55
21,001	22,000	10	20	25	35	40	45

Source: Table 1 from Form 2016 PIT-RC Instructions

Example. Taxpayer is single with one dependent child, providing her with two exemptions. She has wages of $8,500 and child support of $5,000 for the 2015 tax year. Her MGI is $13,500 and her LICTR would be $65 provided that she meets the requirements of the statute. If a taxpayer's MGI is zero, the taxpayer may claim a rebate in the amount shown in the first row of the table appropriate for the taxpayer's number of exemptions.[7]

The rebate may be deducted from the taxpayer's New Mexico income tax liability for the tax year, and if the tax rebate exceeds the taxpayer's income tax liability, the excess is refunded to the taxpayer.[8]

¶ 13.4 Property tax rebate for persons 65 or older

A resident filing a New Mexico tax return may claim a tax rebate for a portion of the property tax due on his or her principal residence if he

---

[7] §7-2-14E NMSA 1978.
[8] §7-2-14F NMSA 1978.

or she is 65 or older, meets the rebate's MGI requirements, and is not a dependent of another. The amount of the rebate is the amount of property tax due on the taxpayer's principal place of residence for the tax year that exceeds the taxpayer's Maximum Property Tax Liability (MPTL). The MPTL varies with the taxpayer's MGI and is determined in the table below.[9] The rebate is limited to $250 ($125 for taxpayers who are married filing separately).

A resident who rents a principal place of residence from another person is also entitled to the rebate. In this case, the amount of property tax due is calculated by multiplying the gross rent for the tax year by 6%.[10] A resident residing in a long-term residential care facility (nursing home) which is subject to property taxation and which does not itemize rent in its billings may treat 32% of the amount billed to or for the benefit of the resident as the amount of gross rent. A "long-term residential care facility" is any facility which provides room, board and health care services to persons residing in the facility for more than a temporary period of time, but does not include any general or other hospital unless the hospital maintains a separate area for purposes of providing long-term room, board and health care services for persons not requiring admission to the hospital.[11]

The statute contains two sets of tax rebate tables. One rebate table is for taxpayers who live in counties that have adopted a resolution authorizing qualified taxpayers to claim a more generous amount of rebate.[12] No county has such resolution in effect at the time of this writing. The other table, shown below, is for taxpayers whose principal place of residence is in a county that does not have such resolution in effect for the tax year. The tax rebate that may be claimed is the

---

[9] §7-2-18 NMSA 1978.
[10] §7-2-18B NMSA 1978.
[11] §3.3.13.8A NMAC.
[12] §7-2-18J NMSA 1978. The resolution must provide that the county will reimburse the state for the additional amount of tax rebates paid to such taxpayers over the amount that would have otherwise been paid. The resolution may apply to one or more tax years and specify the period of time for which the rebate may be claimed by qualified taxpayers. The county must adopt the resolution and notify the TRD of the adoption by no later than September 1 of the tax year to which the resolution first applies. The TRD will determine the additional amounts paid to taxpayers of the county for each tax year and shall bill the county for the amount at the time and in the manner determined by the department. If the county fails to pay any bill within thirty days, the TRD may deduct the amount due from any amount to be transferred or distributed to the county by the state.

Refundable Rebates and Credits

property tax due each tax year that exceeds the amount shown as MPTL in the table below.

The tax rebate is not allowed to a resident who was an inmate of a public institution for more than six months during the tax year or who was not physically present in New Mexico for at least six months during the tax year for which the rebate could be claimed.[13]

A husband and wife who file separate returns for a tax year in which they could have filed a joint return may each claim only one-half of the tax rebate that would have been allowed on a joint return.[14]

ELDERLY HOMEOWNERS' MAXIMUM PROPERTY TAX LIABILITY TABLE		
Taxpayer's MGI (from PIT-RC, line 13)		MPTL
	But not over	
$0	$1,000	$20
1,001	2,000	25
2,001	3,000	30
3,001	4,000	35
4,001	5,000	40
5,001	6,000	45
6,001	7,000	50
7,001	8,000	55
8,001	9,000	60
9,001	10,000	75
10,001	11,000	90
11,001	12,000	105
12,001	13,000	120
13,001	14,000	135
14,001	15,000	150
15,001	16,000	180

---

[13] §7-2-18D NMSA 1978.
[14] §7-2-18E NMSA 1978.

> *Example.* Taxpayer is 68 years of age and owns a home on which he pays a property tax of $525. His MGI is $14,000. Thus, his MPTL is $150. The amount of his rebate is ($525 less $150) $275, but limited to $250.

If MGI is zero, a taxpayer may claim a tax rebate based upon the amount shown in the first row of the table. No tax rebate is allowed any taxpayer whose MGI exceeds $16,000.[15]

A "principal place of residence" is the resident's dwelling, whether owned or rented, and so much of the land surrounding it (not to exceed five acres) as is reasonably necessary for use of the dwelling as a home, and may consist of a part of a multi-dwelling or a multipurpose building and a part of the land upon which it is built. If a taxpayer has more acreage than is reasonably necessary to maintain a dwelling, the amount of the property tax billed must be adjusted to reflect the principal place of residence only. The instructions to Schedule PIT-RC[16] provide this example.

> *Example.* A taxpayer's principal place of residence is located on 25 acres. If only one acre is reasonably necessary to maintain the residence, the tax due on the land must be divided by the total number of acres for which property tax was billed. The property tax billed on the home is added this amount. The total is the amount used to calculate the rebate.

Fiscal year filers

Residents who file income tax on a fiscal year basis must determine their tax rebate by:

1. Determining the weight of each calendar year by dividing the number of days in each calendar year included in the taxpayer's income tax fiscal year by the number of days in the taxpayer's income tax fiscal year;
2. Multiplying the property tax paid in each calendar year by the weight determined for that year; and
3. Combining the results for the 2 calendar years.[17]

---

[15] §7-2-18H NMSA 1978.
[16] 2016 PIT-RC, New Mexico Rebate and Credit Schedule Instructions, p. 6RC.
[17] 3.3.13.8B NMAC.

Refundable Rebates and Credits

Refund of tax rebate

The tax rebate may be deducted from the taxpayer's New Mexico income tax liability for the tax year. If the tax rebate exceeds the taxpayer's income tax liability, the excess is refunded to the taxpayer.[18]

¶ 13.5 Additional Low-income property tax rebate

Los Alamos and Santa Fe counties are two counties that have adopted ordinances that provide a property tax rebate for low-income taxpayers.[19] An individual having a principal place of residence in a county that has adopted such an ordinance may claim a property tax rebate on the individual's personal income tax return, with respect to the property tax on such property, but the individual must satisfy the following conditions:

1. Is a low-income property taxpayer;
2. Is not a dependent of another individual;
3. Was not an inmate of a public institution for more than six months during the tax year; and
4. Was physically present in New Mexico for at least six months

---

[18] §7-2-18I NMSA 1978.
[19] In January of every odd-numbered year in which a county does not have in an ordinance effect, its board of county commissioners must conduct a public hearing on whether the property tax rebate should be made available. §7-2-14.3G NMSA 1978. At the hearing, if a majority of the elected members vote to adopt an ordinance, it must be adopted no later than thirty days after the public hearing. The ordinance must specify the tax years to which it is applicable. §7-2-14H NMSA 1978. If a county has adopted the property tax rebate, §7-2-14.4 NMSA 1978 authorizes the county's board of county commissioners to adopt a resolution to submit to electors the question of whether a property tax at a rate not exceeding $1.00 per $1,000 of taxable value should be imposed to fund the rebate. If a majority of electors approve, the rate should be certified by the department of finance and administration for any year the tax is imposed. Section 7-2-14.5A NMSA 1978 provides that the revenue produced by the tax must be placed in a separate fund in the county treasury and be pledged solely for the payment of the income tax revenue reduction resulting from the property tax rebate.

The above tax may be imposed for one, two, three, four or five years commencing with the property tax year in which the tax rate is first imposed. The board of county commissioners may direct that the rate be decreased for any year if imposition of the total rate is not necessary for such year. The board of county commissioners must direct that the imposition not be made for any property tax year for which the property tax rebate for low-income taxpayers is not provided or for any year in which the county has imposed a property transfer tax pursuant to the Transfer Tax Act. §7-2-14.5B NMSA 1978.

during the tax year for which the rebate is claimed.[20]

The amount of rebate is based on the MGI of the taxpayer and is determined in accordance with the following table:

LOW-INCOME TAXPAYER'S PROPERTY TAX REBATE TABLE		
Taxpayer's MGI (from PIT-RC, Line 13)		Property Tax Rebate
Over	But not over	
$0	$8,000	75% of property tax liability
8,000	10,000	70% of property tax liability
10,000	12,000	65% of property tax liability
12,000	14,000	60% of property tax liability
14,000	16,000	55% of property tax liability
16,000	18,000	50% of property tax liability
18,000	20,000	45% of property tax liability
20,000	22,000	40% of property tax liability
22,000	24,000	35% of property tax liability

Source: §7-2-14.3D NMSA 1978.

If a taxpayer's MGI is zero, the taxpayer may claim a tax rebate based upon the first row of the table. The tax rebate may not exceed $350 per return. No tax rebate is allowed any taxpayer whose MGI exceeds $24,000.[21]

A husband and wife who file separate returns for a tax year in which they could have filed a joint return may each claim only one-half of the tax rebate that would have been allowed on the joint return. The tax rebate in such case cannot exceed $175.[22]

The taxpayer's principal "place of residence" is the dwelling owned and occupied by the taxpayer and so much of the land surrounding it, not to exceed five acres, as is reasonably necessary for use of the dwelling as a home. A principal place of residence may consist of part of a multidwelling or a multipurpose building and a part of the land upon which it is built. If the acreage on which the residence sits is more than reasonably necessary to maintain a dwelling, the instructions to Schedule PIT-RC require the taxpayer to adjust the amount of property tax billed to reflect the principal place of residence only.[23]

---

[20] §7-2-14.3A and B NMSA 1978.
[21] §7-2-14.3E NMSA 1978.
[22] §7-2-14.3C NMSA 1978.
[23] §7-2-14.3J NMSA 1978, 2016 PIT-RC New Mexico Rebate and Credit Schedule Instructions, p. 7RC.

Refundable Rebates and Credits

The "property tax liability" is the amount of property tax resulting from the imposition of the county and municipal property tax operating impositions on the net taxable value of the taxpayer's principal place of residence, calculated for the year for which the rebate is claimed.[24]

The tax rebate is deducted from the taxpayer's New Mexico income tax liability for the tax year. If the tax rebate exceeds the taxpayer's income tax liability, the excess is refunded.[25]

¶ 13.6 New Mexico Day Care Credit

New Mexico provides assistance to employed adults with young dependents, by providing a tax credit for child day care expenses paid to caregivers. To qualify, the taxpayer must be a resident and meet the following conditions:

- either alone or with a spouse furnish over half the cost of maintaining the household for one or more qualifying dependents for any period in the tax year;
- is gainfully employed for any period for which the credit is claimed or, if a joint return is filed, both spouses are gainfully employed or one is disabled for any period for which the credit is claimed;
- compensates a caregiver for day care for a qualifying dependent to allow the resident taxpayer and spouse, if not disabled, to be gainfully employed;
- is not a dependent of another and is not a recipient of public assistance under a program of aid to families with dependent children (such as TANF), a program under the New Mexico Works Act,[26] or any successor program during any period for which the credit is claimed; and
- has a MGI, including child support payments, of not more than the annual income that would be derived from earnings at double the federal minimum wage (which at the time of this writing equals $30,160).[27]

---

[24] §7-2-14.3D NMSA 1978.
[25] §7-2-14.3F NMSA 1978
[26] §27-2B-1 NMSA 1978.
[27] §7-2-18.1B NMSA 1978. See 2016 PIT-RC New Mexico Rebate and Credit Schedule

The credit equals 40% of the compensation paid to a caregiver by the resident for a qualifying dependent (a child under age of 15), but may not exceed $480 for each qualifying dependent or a total of $1,200 for all qualifying dependents for a tax year. In computing the credit, compensation may not exceed $8.00 per day for each qualifying dependent.[28]

The credit for expenses for dependent child day care may only be claimed for expenses that occur during periods in which the taxpayer is gainfully employed.[29]

> *Example:* A single parent who provides over 50% of the support of a 10-year old dependent child incurred child care expenses for the entire year. She attended school and was not employed during January through May of the tax year, but on June 1 began a career and was employed for the remainder of the year. She can claim the credit for child care on only those expenses incurred during those months in which she was gainfully employed, June through December.[30]

An individual with federal tax liability may not claim an amount of credit from the state that is more than the difference between the amount of the state child care credit for which the taxpayer is eligible and the federal credit for child and dependent care expenses the taxpayer is able to deduct from federal tax liability for the same tax year. For first year residents, the amount of the federal credit for child and dependent care expenses may be reduced to an amount equal to the amount of federal credit for child and dependent care expenses the resident is able to deduct from federal tax liability multiplied by the ratio of the number of days of residence in New Mexico during the tax year to the total number of days in the tax year.[31]

Claiming the credit

Each caregiver must provide a Form PIT-CG, *New Mexico Caregiver's Statement*.[32] Using the information from these forms, the *Child Day Care*

---

[28] Instructions, p. 8RC.
[29] §7-2-18.1C NMSA 1978.
[30] §3.3.13.9C NMAC.
[31] Based upon the example in §3.3.13.9C(2) NMAC.
[32] §7-2-18.1E NMSA 1978.
2016PIT-RC New Mexico Rebate and Credit Schedule Instructions, p. 12RC.

Refundable Rebates and Credits

Worksheet, found in the instructions to Schedule PIT-RC, must be completed and attached to the Form PIT-1, together with any Form PIT-CG. The amount from Column G of the worksheet is entered on Schedule PIT-RC, line 19. From that is deducted any federal tax credit applied against federal income tax, resulting in the New Mexico daycare credit on line 22.

The credit is deducted from the taxpayer's New Mexico income tax liability for the tax year, and if the credit exceeds the taxpayer's income tax liability, the excess is refunded to the taxpayer.[33]

A husband and wife maintaining a household for one or more qualifying dependents and filing separate returns for a tax year for which they could have filed a joint return may each claim only one-half of the credit that would have been claimed on a joint return. They are eligible for the credit only if their joint MGI, including child support payments, if any, is not more than the annual income that would be derived from earnings at double the federal minimum wage.[34]

Important terms

A "caregiver" is a corporation or an individual 18 years of age or over who the resident pays for providing direct care, supervision and guidance to a qualifying dependent for less than 24 hours daily, and includes related individuals of the resident but not a dependent of the resident. The caregiver must furnish the resident with a signed statement of compensation paid by the resident to the caregiver for day care services, which must specify the dates and the total number of days for which payment has been made.[35]

The "cost of maintaining a household" consists of the expenses incurred for the mutual benefit of the occupants by reason of its operation as their principal place of abode, and includes property taxes, mortgage interest, rent, utility charges, upkeep and repairs, property insurance and food consumed on the premises; but the term does not include expenses otherwise incurred, including cost of clothing, education, medical treatment, vacations, life insurance, transportation

---

[33] §7-2-18.1F NMSA 1978.
[34] §7-2-18.1G NMSA 1978.
[35] §7-2-18.1A[1] NMSA 1978.

and mortgages.[36]

The term "dependent" is defined by §152 of the IRC, but also includes any minor child or stepchild of the resident who would be a dependent for federal income tax purposes if the public assistance contributing to the support of the child or stepchild was considered to have been contributed by the resident.[37] The term also includes a child of divorced or legally separated parents when the taxpayer meets all the special requirements of §§21(e)(5)[38] and 152(e) of the IRC.[39] Under IRC §21(e)(5), the federal credit for child-care expenses is allowed only to the custodial parent, meaning the parent having custody for the greater portion of the calendar year.[40] Although IRC §152(e) allows a child to qualify as a dependent of the noncustodial parent by agreement of the custodial parent if the conditions of IRC §152(e)(2) or (3) are met, IRC §21(e)(5) precludes the noncustodial parent from obtaining the benefit of the child care credit. This is likely with good reason, as the credit essentially operates as a subsidy to a parent who has to pay someone to watch his or her children so that the parent can work.

A "qualifying dependent" is a dependent under the age of 15 at the end of the tax year who receives the services of a caregiver.[41]

> **In Practice**: It is worth noting that the federal credit is available only for children under 13 years of age, while New Mexico's credit applies to a dependent under the age of 15. Because the credit is limited by the federal credit, it is possible that the taxpayer may not receive a New Mexico credit in the same year that he or she receives a federal child care credit. On the other hand, because the credit is available for dependents who are 13 and 14, unlike the federal credit, there is the possibility of receiving a New Mexico credit and not a federal credit.

A "disabled person" is a person who has a medically determinable physical or mental impairment, as certified by a licensed physician,

---

[36] §7-2-18.1A(2) NMSA 1978.
[37] §7-2-18.1A(3) NMSA 1978.
[38] Renumbered from IRC §44A(f)(5).
[39] §3.3.13.9A NMAC.
[40] IRC §152(e)(4)(A).
[41] §7-2-18.1A(6) NMSA 1978.

Refundable Rebates and Credits

which renders such person unable to engage in gainful employment.[42]

A "gainfully employed" person is one who is working for wages, salary, commissions or any other form of employee remuneration or any resident who engages in any business activity as a proprietor or partner and who is required to report and pay taxes under the provisions of the federal Self-Employment Contributions Act.[43]

¶ 13.7 Refundable medical care credit for persons 65 or older

A taxpayer 65 years of age or older and who is not a dependent of another taxpayer may claim a credit of $2,800 for medical care expenses paid by the taxpayer if those expenses equal $28,000 or more within a tax year and if those expenses are not reimbursed or compensated for by insurance or otherwise.[44] The expenses must be expended for the taxpayer or for the taxpayer's spouse or a dependent. A "dependent" is a dependent as defined under federal income tax rules.[46] Medical expenses which have been included in itemized deductions on federal Form 1040, Schedule A qualify for the credit.[47]

The taxpayer claims the credit by filing Form PIT-RC and entering the amount of the credit on line 23.[48] Taxpayers eligible to claim this credit are also eligible to claim the medical care expense exemption for persons 65 years or older (reported on line 17 of Schedule PIT-ADJ – see ¶ 8.3.12)[49] and the deduction for unreimbursed medical expenses (reported on Form PIT-1, line 16 – see ¶ 7.5). The tax credit is also allowed for out-of-state residents with income tax responsibility to New Mexico.[50]

A husband and wife who file separate returns for a tax year in which they could have filed a joint return may each claim only one-half of the credit, or $1,400, that would have been allowed on a joint return.[51]

---

[42] §7-2-18.1A(4) NMSA 1978.
[43] §7-2-18.1A(5) NMSA 1978; §3.3.13.9B NMAC.
[44] §7-2-18.13A NMSA 1978.
[46] IRC §152.
[47] 2016 PIT-RC New Mexico Rebate and Credit Schedule Instructions, p. 10RC.
[48] 2015 PIT-RC New Mexico Rebate and Credit Schedule Instructions, p. 10RC.
[49] §7-2-5.9 NMSA 1978.
[50] See 2015 PIT-RC New Mexico Rebate and Credit Schedule Instructions, p. 10RC.
[51] §7-2-18.13B NMSA 1978.

The credit may be deducted from the taxpayer's income tax liability, but if the credit exceeds the income tax liability for the tax year, the excess is refunded to the taxpayer.[52]

Important terms

"Medical care" is the diagnosis, cure, mitigation, treatment or prevention of disease or for the purpose of affecting any structure or function of the body. "Medical care expenses" are amounts paid for:

- the diagnosis, cure, mitigation, treatment or prevention of disease or for the purpose of affecting any structure or function of the body, if provided by a physician or in a health care facility;
- prescribed drugs or insulin (A "prescribed drug" is a drug or biological that requires a prescription of a physician.[53]);
- qualified long-term care services (as defined in IRC §7702B(c));
- insurance covering medical care, including amounts paid as premiums under Part B of Title 18 of the Social Security Act or for a qualified long-term care insurance contract (as defined in IRC §§7702B(b)), if the insurance or other amount is paid from income included in the taxpayer's adjusted gross income for the tax year;
- specialized treatment or the use of special therapeutic devices if the treatment or device is prescribed by a physician and the patient can show that the expense was incurred primarily for the prevention or alleviation of a physical or mental defect or illness; and
- care in an institution other than a hospital, such as a sanitarium or rest home, if the principal reason for the presence of the person in the institution is to receive the medical care available; provided that if the meals and lodging are furnished as a necessary part of such care, the cost of meals and lodging are medical care expenses.[54]

A "health care facility" is a hospital, outpatient facility, diagnostic and treatment center, rehabilitation center, freestanding hospice or

---

[52] §7-2-18.13C NMSA 1978.
[53] §7-2-18.13D(6) NMSA 1978.
[54] §7-2-18.13D(4) NMSA 1978.

Refundable Rebates and Credits

other similar facility at which medical care is provided.[55]

A "physician" is a medical doctor, osteopathic physician, dentist, podiatrist, chiropractic physician or psychologist licensed or certified to practice in New Mexico.[56]

---

[55] §7-2-18.13D(2) NMSA 1978.
[56] §7-2-18.13D(5) NMSA 1978.

¶ 13.8 Special needs adopted child tax credit

A taxpayer who adopts a special needs child (meeting the definition below) is entitled to a special needs adopted child tax credit.[57] The amount of credit is $1,000 and this amount is claimed against the taxpayer's tax liability for the tax year. If the amount of the credit exceeds the taxpayer's tax liability, the excess is refunded. There is no MGI test for this credit, but the taxpayer cannot be a dependent of another.[58]

A taxpayer may claim a special needs adopted child tax credit for each year that the child may be claimed as a dependent for federal taxation purposes by the taxpayer.[59]

A husband and wife who file separate returns for a tax year in which they could have filed a joint return may each claim only one-half of the special needs adopted child tax credit provided in this section that would have been allowed on a joint return.[60]

A "special needs adopted child" is an individual who may be over 18 and who is certified by the children, youth and families department or a licensed child placement agency as meeting the definition of a "difficult to place child" pursuant to the Adoption Act,[61] provided, however, if the classification as a "difficult to place child" is based on a physical or mental impairment or an emotional disturbance, the physical or mental impairment or emotional disturbance must be at least moderately disabling.[62]

Claiming the credit

To claim the credit taxpayers enter $1,000 for each special needs adopted child on line 24 of Schedule PIT-RC, unless the taxpayer is a married person filing separately, in which case $500 is entered for each child.

In the first year that the special needs adopted child tax credit is claimed, it is necessary to attach a copy of the certificate issued by the

---

[57] §7-2-18.16A NMSA 1978. This credit replaces the tax exemption for adopted special need children allowed by §7-2-5.4 NMSA 1978, which was repealed effected January 1, 2007.
[58] §7-2-18.16B and D NMSA 1978.
[59] §7-2-18.16C NMSA 1978.
[60] §7-2-18.16E NMSA 1978.
[61] 32A-5-1 NMSA 1978.
[62] §7-2-18.16F NMSA 1978.

Refundable Rebates and Credits

New Mexico Children, Youth and Families Department or the licensed child placement agency for each child adopted that year.[63]

¶ 13.9 Working families tax credit

An individual who is a resident of New Mexico for any part of a tax year[64] may claim a working families tax credit in an amount equal to 10% of the federal earned income tax credit (EIC) for which that individual is eligible for the same tax year under §32 of the IRC.[65] The EIC is a refundable federal income tax credit for low income working individuals and families.

The working families tax credit may be deducted from the income tax liability of an individual. If the credit exceeds the individual's income tax liability for the tax year, the excess is refunded.[66]

The amount of EIC that is reported on the 2015 federal Form 1040, line 66a; 1040A, line 42a; or 1040EZ, line 8a is entered on line 25a of Form PIT-1. The working families credit is entered on line 25 and is determined by multiplying the amount entered on line 25a by 0.10.

---

[63] 2016 PIT-RC New Mexico Rebate and Credit Schedule Instructions, p. 10RC.
[64] See 2016 PIT-1, Personal Income Tax Return, Instructions, p. 31.
[65] §7-2-18.15A NMSA 1978.
[66] §7-2-18.15B NMSA 1978.

CHAPTER 14
VOLUNTARY CONTRIBUTION OF REFUNDS

¶ 14.1 New Mexico System of Voluntary Contributions

As mentioned earlier, New Mexico utilizes its tax system to achieve social purposes. One mechanism it has adopted is the designation system of making contributions to worthy causes. Individuals may designate on their personal income tax return part or all of any refunds due to them to selected charities. Schedule PIT-D lists the various causes chosen by the legislature as worthy of such selection and taxpayers may allocate their refunds to these causes as they wish. These designated contributions are sometimes referred to as check-offs in the statutes authorizing them. The designated contributions are totaled on line 14 of the schedule and entered on line 40 of Form PIT-1.

If the amount of refund due on the return is determined by the TRD to be less than the sum of the amounts contributed, no contributions will be made or deducted. In this case, the TRD will disregard a direction to make an optional refund contribution.[1]

A taxpayer may not make a refund claim with respect to any optional refund contribution that was made by the TRD at the direction of the taxpayer.[2]

These voluntary contribution rules do not apply to income tax refunds subject to interception under the provisions of the Tax Refund Intercept Program Act and any voluntary contribution of such refunds is void.[3]

If the total amount contributed for any cause by all taxpayers is less

---

[1] §7-2-31.1C NMSA 1978
[2] §7-2-31.1D NMSA 1978.
[3] See §7-2C-1 to 7-2C-13 NMSA 1978. This Act covers the use of state income tax refunds as setoff against debts to public agencies including back child support, student loans, etc.

than $5,000 for three consecutive years, the statue providing the option to designate refunds to the cause is repealed effective the following January 1.[4]

The causes selected by the legislature as worthy of designation for voluntary contribution by taxpayers are discussed below.

¶ 14.1.1 Share with Wildlife

There are many benefits to protect and perpetuate the renewable wildlife resources of the state, and in 1981 the legislature enacted legislation providing a voluntary check-off designation of tax refunds to supplement any other state funding provided for that purpose. The check-off funds are intended to provide additional wildlife funds and not to take the place of the funding that would otherwise be appropriated.[5]

The funds are used to finance the Share with Wildlife program, which is a non-profit program of New Mexico Department of Game and Fish, supported exclusively by donations. Its mission is to assist all New Mexico wildlife in need. The program funds four general categories: research, public education, habitat protection, and wildlife rehabilitation.[6]

¶ 14.1.2 Veterans' State Cemetery Fund

This fund was established to increase the size of the Santa Fe National Cemetery to provide a lasting tribute to all veterans of New Mexico. When total contributions exceed $1,070,000, the cost of the additional land that will be purchased by the City of Santa Fe and deeded to the cemetery, the fund will send any proceeds over that amount to the Substance Abuse Education Fund.[7]

¶ 14.1.3 New Mexico Substance Abuse Education Fund

Substance abuse educational programs are provided in New Mexico schools, and to allow taxpayers to provide additional funding, individuals may designate all or a portion of their refunds to be

---

[4] §7-2-31.1B NMSA 1978
[5] §7-2-23 NMSA 1978.
[6] See http://www.wildlife.state.nm.us/conservation/share-with-wildlife/.
[7] §7-1-6.18 NMSA 1978and §7-2-28 NMSA 1978; City of Santa Fe Resolution No. 2013-2. The name of the fund has been changed from Veterans' National Cemetery Fund to Veterans' State Cemetery Fund. Chapter 7 [HB-185 (section 1)].

Voluntary Contribution of Refunds

contributed to New Mexico Substance Abuse Education Fund. This check-off is intended to be supplemental to any other funding, and is in not to take the place of the funding that would otherwise be appropriated. The program is administered by New Mexico Public Education Department, Coordinated School Health and Wellness Bureau.[8]

¶ 14.1.4 New Mexico Forest Re-Leaf Program

To support tree planting in New Mexico, voluntary contributions may be made to the Conservation Planting Revolving Fund. The Forestry Division of the EMNRD administers this fund and awards grants to plant trees on public lands in New Mexico communities through The New Mexico Forest Re-Leaf Program.[9]

¶ 14.1.5 National Guard Member and Family Assistance

Contributions are distributed to the Department of Military Affairs, which uses them to help members of the New Mexico National Guard activated for overseas service and their families.[10]

¶ 14.1.6 Kids 'N Parks Transportation Grant Program

The State Parks Kids 'n Parks Transportation Grant Program provides teachers with funds for buses to connect their students to the outdoors. Teachers must connect classroom learning to the outdoors and must evaluate their experiences. The State Parks Division of the EMNRD administers this grant program.[11]

¶ 14.1.7 Amyotrophic Lateral Sclerosis Research Fund

An individual may designate any portion of his or her income tax refund to the Amyotrophic Lateral Sclerosis Research fund.[12] This fund is created in the state treasury. Money in the fund is appropriated to the Board of Regents of the University of New Mexico for amyotrophic lateral sclerosis (Lou Gehrig's disease) research. Any money remaining in the fund at the end of a fiscal year reverts to the

---

[8] §7-2-30 NMSA 1978.
[9] §7-2-24.1 NMSA 1978. See http://www.emnrd.state.nm.us/SFD/ReLeaf/releaf.html. Last viewed October 14, 2016.
[10] §7-2-30.3 NMSA 1978.
[11] §7-2-30.2 NMSA 1978.
[12] §7-2-30.1 NMSA 1978.

State General Fund.[13]

¶ 14.1.8 Vietnam Veterans Memorial State Park

An individual may designate any portion of an income tax refund to the State Parks Division of the EMNRD for the operation, maintenance and improvement of the Vietnam Veterans Memorial State Park near Angel Fire, New Mexico.[14]

¶ 14.1.9 New Mexico Political Parties

An individual may make a voluntary contribution of $2 (no more, no less) to any state political party listed on Schedule PIT-D. With a joint return, each spouse may contribute $2 to a political party. To qualify as a "state political party," the organization must meet statutory requirements of §1-7-2A NMSA 1978 on January 1 of the tax year for which the return is filed.[15]

¶ 14.1.10 Veterans Enterprise Fund

Contributions to the Veterans' Enterprise Fund are used to carry out the programs, duties or services of the Department of Veterans Services.[16]

¶ 14.1.11 Lottery Tuition Fund

Contributions to the of the Lottery Tuition Fund will help support its objective of providing college tuition assistance for eligible New Mexico resident undergraduates.[17]

¶ 14.1.12 Horse Shelter Rescue Fund

Contributions to the Horse Shelter Rescue Fund help fund horse rescue and retirement facilities registered by the New Mexico Livestock Board to care for homeless horses in New Mexico. The New Mexico Livestock Board administers this fund.[18]

---

[13] §24-20-4 NMSA 1978.
[14] §7-2-30.4 NMSA 1978.
[15] §7-2-31 NMSA 1978.
[16] §7-2-30.5 NMSA 1978. See http://www.dvs.state.nm.us.
[17] §7-2-30.6 NMSA 1978.
See http://www.hed.state.nm.us/students/lotteryscholarship.aspx. Last viewed October 14, 2016,
[18] §7-2-30.7 NMSA 1978; §21.32.6.8 NMAC. See https://www.nmlbonline.com/index.php?id=23#. Last viewed October 14, 2016.

Voluntary Contribution of Refunds

¶ 14.1.13 Animal Care and Facility Fund

Individuals may voluntarily designate all or a portion of their refund to the Animal Care and Facility Fund to carry out the statewide dog and cat spay and neuter program.[19] In the case of a joint return, both individuals must make that designation.

¶ 14.1.14 Supplemental Senior Services

To help enhance or expand vital services to New Mexico's elderly population, individuals may designate that all or a portion of their income tax refund go to the Aging and Long-term Services Department.[20] Funds contributed are distributed statewide through the area agencies on aging for the provision of supplemental senior services throughout the state, including senior services provided through the north central New Mexico economic development district as the non-metro area agency on aging, the city of Albuquerque/Bernalillo county area agency on aging, the Indian area agency on aging and the Navajo area agency on aging. In a joint return, both individuals must make the designation.[21]

Any contribution is supplemental to any other funding and does not take the place of the funding that would otherwise be appropriated. The TRD is required to distribute to the aging and long-term services department 100% of all designated refund contributions which then distributes those funds statewide to area agencies on aging. The agencies on aging throughout the state are instructed in the authorizing statute to cooperatively establish a grant program based on need that is available to all senior service providers in the state that meet the requirements of the program.[22]

---

[19] §7-2-30.9 NMSA 1978. Applicable to tax years beginning on or after January 1, 2015.
[20] See http://www.nmaging.state.nm.us. Last viewed October 14, 2016.
[21] §7-2-30.8 NMSA 1978. Applicable to tax years beginning on or after January 1, 2015.
[22] §7-2-30.8E NMSA 1978.

CHAPTER 15

INTEREST AND PENALTIES

¶ 15.1 Interest on deficiencies

If tax is not paid on time, on or before the due date, interest accrues from the day after the due date until paid. Interest is computed on a daily basis, and New Mexico uses the same interest rate for deficiencies as does the federal government. The federal rate is set by a formula that provides that the interest rate on deficiencies is the sum of the Federal short-term rate plus 3 percentage points.[1] The rate is set quarterly. Interest cannot be waived by the TRD.

The formula for calculating daily interest is as follows:

> tax due × quarterly daily interest rate × no. of days late = interest due

The TRD website provides the following example.

> *Example.* Say that you owe $300 for the 4th quarter of 2010, due January 15, 2011. The daily rate for the 1st quarter of 2011 is 0.008219178%. If the tax-due date is January 15, 2011, and you are paying on January 30, 2011, the payment is 15 days late.
>
> Using the formula—Multiply $300 × 0.00008219178 × 15 = $0.37.

The applicable daily rates by quarter are published on the TRD website and are shown in the following table.[3]

---

[1] §7-1-67B NMSA 1978; IRC §6621(a). Prior to January 1, 2008, interest was calculated at the statutory rate of 15% per year.

[3] http://www.tax.newmexico.gov/Individuals/penalty-interest-rates.aspx. Last viewed October 14, 2016. See also TRD Bulletin B-400.4, revised 9/2016

New Mexico Personal Income Tax

Effective Interest Rates for Late Payment		
Period	Rate	Daily Rate
Prior to January 1, 2008	15%	0.041%
Apr. 1, 2008 - Jun. 30, 2008	6%	0.016393442%
Apr. 1, 2008 - Jun. 30, 2008	6%	0.016393442%
July 1, 2008 - Sep. 30, 2008	5%	0.013661202%
Oct. 1, 2008 - Dec. 31, 2008	6%	0.016393442 %
Jan. 1, 2009 - Mar. 31, 2009	5%	0.013661202%
Apr. 1, 2009 – Dec. 31, 2010	4%	0.010958904%
Jan. 1, 2011 - Mar. 31, 2011	3%	0.008219178%
April 1, 2011 – Sep. 30, 2011	4%	0.010958904%
Oct. 1, 2011 – Dec. 31, 2011	3%	0.008219178%
Jan. 1, 2012 – Dec. 31, 2012	4%	0.008196721%
Jan. 1, 2013 – Dec. 31, 2015	3%	0.008219178%
Jan. 1, 2016 – Mar. 31, 2016	3%	0.008196721%
Apr. 1, 2016 – Dec. 31, 2016	4%	0.010928962%

Interest is not ordinarily imposed on interest, nor on penalties.[4] As an exception, interest will continue to run on a civil penalty imposed on a person who willfully causes or attempts to cause the evasion of another's obligation to report and pay tax. In this case, the penalty equals the amount of tax evaded and interest and penalties thereon. The tax regulations construe the statute as specifically authorizing the assessment of interest on the penalty (the amount of tax evaded).[5]

If a jeopardy assessment has been made and the due date has not yet passed, interest begins to accrue on the sixth day following the jeopardy assessment.[6]

Interest does not stop accruing unless there is a specific statutory or regulatory exception. Thus, interest does not stop running where a taxpayer receives an extension of time or enters into a closing agreement or an installment agreement. Interest continues to accrue when a taxpayer appeals an adverse decision rendered at an administrative hearing or protests an assessment, unless payment has been made,[7] in which case interest accrues only until payment is tendered. Interest continues to accrue on the granting of a partial abatement of tax, the seizing of property under levy, the imposition of

---

[4] §7-1-67C NMSA 1978.
[5] §7-1-72.1 NMSA 1978; §3.1.11.18C NMAC.
[6] §3.1.10.18A(5) NMAC. See §7-1-59 NMSA 1978.
[7] See §3.1.7.9 NMAC.

Interest and Penalties

an injunction or a TRO, the furnishing of security, or the attempt to pay tax by a bad check. Ignorance of a successor with regard to a tax liability incurred by a predecessor in business, or the proper dissolution of a corporation does not stop interest from running.[8]

The statute and regulations provide the following exceptions where interest will stop accruing:[9]

- De minimis amount. If the amount of interest due at the time payment is made is less than $1.00, no interest is due.
- Combat duty. If a member of the armed services is serving in a combat zone under orders of the President of the United States, interest accrues beginning the day after any applicable extended due date. See ¶ 6.3.
- Prompt payment after demand. If demand is made for payment, including accrued interest, and if that amount is paid within 10 days from the date of demand, no interest is imposed on the amount paid for the period after the date of the demand.
- Managed audits. If a taxpayer completes a managed audit on or before the date required in the managed audit agreement, and payment of tax due is made in full within 180 days of the date the Secretary has mailed or delivered an assessment for the tax, no interest is due on the assessed tax.
- Credit for overpayment. When, as the result of an audit or a managed audit, an overpayment of a tax is credited against an underpayment,[10] interest accrues from the date the tax was due until deemed paid.
- Notice of outstanding records. If the TRD has issued a notice of outstanding records (see ¶ 16.1.6) and has not issued an assessment within 180 days of the notice or within 90 days after an approved extension of time, interest is paid from the first day following the day on which the tax is due until the tax is paid, excluding the period between either: the 180th day after giving a notice of outstanding records or books of account and the date of the assessment of the tax; or the 90th day after the expiration of the additional time granted the taxpayer to

---

[8] §3.1.10.18A(4) NMAC.
[9] §7-1-67A[1]-[7] NMSA 1978.
[10] See §7-1-29 NMSA 1978.

comply and the date of the assessment.
- No proper notice of outstanding records. If the taxpayer was not provided a proper notice of outstanding records or books of account, interest is paid from the first day following the day on which the tax becomes due until the tax is paid, excluding the period between 180 days prior to the date of assessment and the date of assessment.[11]

When a taxpayer receives an excess credit, rebate or refund, it is treated as a tax owed to the state. The due date of such "tax" is 30 days after the taxpayer receives it, unless a due date is provided by statute. Interest on this tax applies each month or fraction from the due date until paid. The person to whom the TRD mails an excess credit, rebate or refund is presumed to have received it seven days after the mailing, unless a preponderance of evidence indicates another date.[13]

¶ 15.2 Interest on overpayments

Interest is paid by the state to the taxpayer on the amount of tax that has been overpaid and that is subsequently refunded or credited.[14] The interest on overpayments is computed on a daily basis and accrues at the underpayment rate used by the federal government, which is the same rate applicable to deficiencies, described above.[15] Interest is never paid upon interest that has been previously been accrued.[16]

When a taxpayer is entitled to a refund of tax that was paid after its due date and on which the taxpayer had paid interest, the taxpayer is entitled to a refund of the interest that has been paid whether or not a refund of interest is specifically requested.[17]

Interest on an overpayment arising from an assessment by the TRD is paid from the date of overpayment until a date preceding the date of the credit or refund by not more than 30 days. Interest on an overpayment that does not arise from an assessment by the TRD, such

---

[11] §§7-1-67A(7); 7-1-11.2E NMSA 1978.
[13] §3.1.10.18C NMAC.
[14] §7-1-68A NMSA 1978.
[15] §7-1-68B NMSA 1978; IRC §6621(a).
[16] §7-1-68E NMSA 1978.
[17] §3.1.9.16A NMAC.

Interest and Penalties

as with the filing of a tax return, is paid from the date of the claim for refund until a date preceding the credit or refund by not more than thirty days.[18]

Since an overpayment resulting from a TRD assessment is computed from the date of overpayment rather than the date of a refund claim, it is important to determine how the overpayment arises. The determinative factor is whether the action establishing the tax liability was initiated by the taxpayer or by the TRD. Actions initiated by the TRD include, but are not limited to, an audit of the taxpayer's books and records or the issuance of a provisional assessment as a result of a taxpayer's failure to file any return or returns.[19] Actions initiated by the taxpayer include, but are not limited to, the filing of a tax return reporting a tax liability, whether or not payment accompanies the return. If a subsequent notice of assessment is issued by the TRD due to the failure of the taxpayer to accompany the return with full payment, the date from which interest is computed does not change.[20]

The tax law provides several cases where interest is not paid on overpayments, and these are as follows:

- De minimis amount. Interest is not paid if the amount of interest due is less than $1.00.[21]
- Grace period for TRD payment. Interest is not paid when the credit or refund is made within:
  - 55 days of the date of the claim for a refund for the tax year preceding the tax year in which the claim is made; or
  - 120 days of the date of the claim for a refund for any tax year more than one year prior to the year in which the claim is made.[22]
- Federal income tax prohibitions of interest on overpayment. The Internal Revenue Code does not provide for interest on federal refunds if the refund is caused by a net operating loss or capital loss carryback and certain credit carrybacks. In

---

[18] §7-1-68C NMSA 1978.
[19] §3.1.9.14B NMAC.
[20] §3.1.9.14A NMAC.
[21] §7-1-68D(1) NMSA 1978
[22] §7-1-68D(2) NMSA 1978.

addition, no interest is payable on a refund until a federal return is filed in a processible form.[23] When the federal rules would prohibit interest payment, then New Mexico would likewise prohibit interest payments.[24]

- Offset of audit adjustment. No interest is paid in the case of a credit resulting from overpayments found in a multiple-year audit and applied to underpayments found in that audit or refunded as a net overpayment.[25]
- Intercepted refunds. No interest is applicable if the TRD applies the credit or refund to an intercept program.[26]
- Early application of refund to estimated tax. No interest is applicable if the TRD applies the taxpayer's credit or refund to the taxpayer's estimated payment prior to the due date for the estimated tax payment.[27]
- Offset of prior liabilities. No interest is applicable if the TRD applies the taxpayer's credit or refund to offset prior liabilities of the taxpayer[28]
- TRD increases amount of refund. No interest is payable for the amount of credit or refund resulting from overpayments the TRD finds that exceed the refund claimed by the taxpayer on the return.[29]
- Film production credit. No interest is payable on a refund resulting from a film production tax credit.[30]

¶15.3 Civil penalties

¶ 15.3.1 Failure to pay tax or file a return.

If a taxpayer fails to file a return (regardless whether tax is owed) or pay tax when due, a civil penalty is imposed when the failure to comply is due to negligence or disregard of TRD rules and regulations, but without intent to evade or defeat a tax.

---

[23] IRC §6611(f) and (g).
[24] §7-1-68D(3) NMSA 1978.
[25] §7-1-68D(4) NMSA 1978; §7-1-29D NMSA 1978.
[26] §7-1-68D(5) NMSA 1978.
[27] §7-1-68D(5) NMSA 1978.
[28] §7-1-68D(5) NMSA 1978; §7-1-26E NMSA 1978.
[29] §7-1-68D(6) NMSA 1978; §7-1-26F NMSA 1978.
[30] §7-1-68D(7) NMSA 1978; §7-2F-1 NMSA 1978.

Interest and Penalties

The amount of the penalty equals the greater of:

- 2% per month or any fraction of a month from the date the tax was due multiplied by the amount of tax due but not paid, not to exceed 20% of the tax due but not paid; or
- 2% percent per month or any fraction of a month from the date the return was required to be filed multiplied by the tax liability established in the late return, not to exceed 20% of the tax liability established in the late return.[31]

If an extension to file or pay has been granted to an extended due date, the penalty is computed beginning with the first day following the extended due date.[32]

When a demand is made for payment of a tax, including penalties, and the tax is paid within ten days after the date of such demand, no penalty is imposed for the period after the date of the demand with respect to the amount paid.[33]

A penalty is not assessed against a taxpayer if the failure to pay results from a mistake of law made in good faith and on reasonable grounds.[34] If the there is a good faith doubt as to the taxpayer's liability, the Secretary may compromise the assessment of a civil penalty by entering into a closing agreement. The Secretary may not compromise the civil penalty because of the inability to pay or solely because of the threat of litigation. The Secretary may not compromise the civil penalty solely as an expedient means of disposing of a controversy.[35]

As previously noted, this civil penalty is imposed when the taxpayer negligently fails to file return or pay a tax when due. The term "negligence" means: 1) the failure to exercise that degree of ordinary business care and prudence which reasonable taxpayers would exercise under like circumstances; 2) inaction where action is required; and 3) inadvertence, indifference, thoughtlessness, carelessness, erroneous belief or inattention.[36]

---

[31] §7-1-69(A) NMSA 1978.
[32] §3.1.11.15 NMAC.
[33] §7-1-69(E) NMSA 1978.
[34] §7-1-69(B) NMSA 1978.
[35] §3.1.11.9 NMAC.
[36] §3.1.11.10 NMAC.

The regulations provide the following situations as indications that a taxpayer has not been negligent or in disregard of rules and regulations:

- the taxpayer proves the taxpayer was affirmatively misled by a TRD employee;
- the taxpayer, disabled because of injury or prolonged illness, demonstrates the inability to prepare a return and make payment and the inability to procure the services of another person to prepare a return because of the injury or illness;
- the taxpayer shows that physical damage to the taxpayer's records or place of business caused a delay in filing a return or making payment of tax;
- the taxpayer proves that the failure to pay tax or to file a return was caused by reasonable reliance on the advice of competent tax counsel or accountant as to the taxpayer's liability after full disclosure of all relevant facts, but failure to make a timely filing of a tax return, is not excused by the taxpayer's reliance on an agent;
- a taxpayer, within 12 months of the filing of a return by the original due date or by the extended due date and without action of the TRD, files an amended return reflecting tax due or additional tax due and full payment of any tax due accompanies the amended return;
- the IRS abates a federal penalty originally assessed for the same or similar reason as the New Mexico penalty; however, if a taxpayer, without requesting and receiving an extension of time for good cause, has failed to timely file an amended return per the IRS adjustments and to pay any additional income tax due within 180 days of the final determination of a federal adjustment, a penalty will be assessed; or
- a good faith doubt exists with regard to whether an out-of-state business has nexus with New Mexico and whether the state has jurisdiction over the taxpayer and its transactions into New Mexico, and the business volunteers to enter into an agreement with the TRD to register, report and pay gross receipts tax, corporate income tax or franchise tax or to collect and remit

Interest and Penalties

compensating tax as an agent.[37]

If a different penalty is called for in a compact or other interstate agreement to which New Mexico is a party, that penalty is applied to amounts due.[38]

If the failure to pay involves the willful intent to evade or defeat a tax, a penalty of 50% of the amount unpaid, or a minimum of $25.00, whichever is greater, is added to the unpaid amount.[39]

No penalty is imposed on tax due as the result of a managed audit or tax that is deemed paid by crediting overpayments found in an audit or managed audit of multiple periods.[40]

A taxpayer who has been assessed a civil penalty and who believes that there has been neither negligence nor disregard of rules or regulations may use all the legal remedies that are available for any assessed taxpayer, whether for tax, taxes, interest or penalty.[41]

Similar to the federal rules, any assessment of a civil penalty or demand for payment made by the TRD is presumed to be correct. As a result, the taxpayer has the burden of coming forward with evidence showing that the assessment is not correct.[42]

The civil penalty provisions do not apply when a taxpayer files a return with intent to defraud the state by making a claim for a tax credit or rebate, and no amount of tax is required to be paid on the return. However, in this case criminal prosecution of such person for tax fraud is available.[43]

The terms "willful attempt to evade" or "willful attempt to evade or defeat" means a conscious awareness of the obligation to pay taxes coupled with either reckless disregard for, or gross negligence with respect to whether the tax obligation is paid. A willful attempt to evade or defeat may occur either with respect to the obligation to report or the obligation to pay.

---

[37] §3.1.11.11 NMAC
[38] §7-1-69(C) NMSA 1978.
[39] §7-1-69(D) NMSA 1978.
[40] §7-1-69(G) NMSA 1978; §7-1-29 NMSA 1978.
[41] §3.1.11.8C NMAC
[42] §3.1.11.8D NMAC
[43] §3.1.11.13 NMAC. See §7-1-73 NMSA 1978;

A willful attempt to evade or defeat may include:

- engaging in business while not filing tax returns coupled with the knowledge that the business is subject to tax;
- filing tax returns without payment for an extended period of time while staying in business and paying other creditors;
- knowingly completing false tax returns or claiming exemptions, deductions, credits or other reductions of taxable amounts or taxes to which the taxpayer knows he or she is not entitled;
- hiding or transferring assets to hinder collection activity of the TRD; or
- advising or counseling any of the foregoing in the course of one's business as an attorney, accountant, bookkeeper, business consulting firm or tax preparer.[44]

The TRD has the burden of proving tax evasion or the causing or attempting to cause another to evade tax. In a protest before a TRD hearing officer, the officer must find by a preponderance of the evidence that either the taxpayer or other person who has been assessed for causing or attempting to cause the evasion of another's tax knew of the obligation to pay tax. Whether the taxpayer or the other person actually knew of the obligation to pay tax can be proved by reasonable inference from circumstantial evidence, and notwithstanding testimony to the contrary which the hearing officer finds not credible. Whether the taxpayer or other person exercised gross negligence or willful disregard for whether taxes were paid is an objective standard to be determined by the facts and circumstances.[45]

¶ 15.3.2 Innocent Spouse Relief

When a married couple files a joint federal return which results in an understatement of federal tax, a spouse can be relieved of the resulting liability in cases where the spouse did not know of the facts and circumstances of the cause of an understatement of tax and it would be inequitable to hold the spouse liable for the understatement. The provision of the Internal Revenue Code granting this relief is IRC§ 6015, which is generally referred to as the innocent spouse provision.

---

[44] §3.1.11.18A NMAC.
[45] §3.1.11.18B NMAC.

Interest and Penalties

The ITA more broadly provides that if the Secretary determines that taking into account all the facts and circumstances it is inequitable to hold the spouse or former spouse of a taxpayer liable for payment of all or part of any unpaid tax, the Secretary may decline to bring an action or proceeding to collect such taxes against the spouse or former spouse of the taxpayer. Of course, the abatement of taxes or enforcement against the spouse does not result in any abatement against the taxpayer.[46]

In addition, the regulations to the ITA provides spousal relief which mirrors that of IRC §6015, providing that the TRD may decline to bring an action or proceeding to collect taxes against a spouse or former spouse who is granted relief by the IRS pursuant to IRC§ 6015. Where the IRS grants relief in writing, the spouse who received such relief may provide a copy of the IRS's determination and request that the TRD cease any collection activity to the extent such relief was allowed by the IRS. The TRD may decline to pursue collection activity while an application for such relief is pending before the IRS, but the failure to seek or obtain such relief does not preclude the TRD from declining to bring an action or proceeding against a spouse or former spouse for collection of a community debt when bringing an action or proceeding would be inequitable.

The regulations are not to be construed to apply to offsets of refunds or credits to collect on community debts.[47]

The TRD will consider the following facts and circumstances when determining whether to bring an action or proceeding to collect community debt:

1. Did the spouse or former spouse have knowledge of the tax liability at the time that liability arose?
2. Did the spouse or former spouse have a meaningful opportunity to contest the assessment of tax at the time the assessment was made?
3. Has the spouse or former spouse cooperated with the TRD in collection and compliance efforts?
4. Can the state protect its interests without pursuing active

---

[46] §7-1-17.1 NMSA 1978; §3.1.12.13 NMAC.
[47] §3.1.12.13D NMAC.

collection efforts against the spouse or former spouse, including collection efforts against the other spouse or former spouse?
5. Has the spouse or former spouse benefited from the transfer of significant amounts of property from the other spouse or former spouse?
6. Was the spouse or former spouse given an opportunity to participate in the business decisions of the household during the periods when the debt arose?[48]

In addition to these facts and circumstances, in the case of a community debt arising from the conduct of a business within the state, the TRD will also consider the following factors:

- Did the spouse or former spouse participate in the conduct of the business, including responsibility for payment of taxes and other debts?
- Has the spouse or former spouse benefited from the conduct of the business?
- Did the spouse or former spouse know that the other spouse or former spouse had a business?[49]

The regulations require the TRD to weigh all applicable factors with no one factor being determinative. Each of these factors may be given different relative weight, depending on the facts and circumstances of the case.

A spouse or former spouse who believes he or she is entitled to relief may petition to the Secretary in writing, but has the burden of proof in establishing entitlement to the relief. The spouse or former spouse may protest a denial of relief.[50]

¶ 15.3.3 Civil penalty for bad checks

If any required payment is made by a bad check, a penalty in the amount of $20.00 will be imposed for each instance. This penalty is in addition to any other penalty that may be imposed.[51]

---

[48] §3.1.12.13A NMAC.
[49] §3.1.12.13B NMAC.
[50] §3.1.12.13E NMAC; §7-1-24 NMSA 1978.
[51] §7-1-70 NMSA 1978; §3.1.11.17 NMAC.

Interest and Penalties

A bad check is a check or draft to the order of the TRD, which the bank, as drawee, dishonors upon presentment by the TRD. "Dishonor" means the bank refuses to pay the amount of the check to the order of the TRD. The burden is on the taxpayer to prove that the taxpayer was not responsible for the bank's dishonoring of the check. The term "bank" includes any financial institution upon which a check or draft is drawn.[52]

¶15.3.4 Civil penalty--willful attempt to cause evasion of another's tax

Any person who willfully causes or attempts to cause the evasion of a taxpayer's obligation to report and pay tax may be assessed a civil penalty in an amount equal to the amount of the tax, penalty and interest attempted to be evaded.[53]

¶ 15.4 Criminal offenses

¶ 15.4.1 Tax fraud

Tax fraud is a criminal offense and can be either a misdemeanor or a felony, depending on the amount of tax involved. Persons convicted of tax fraud can be fined or sent to prison, or both.

A person is guilty of tax fraud in the following circumstances:

- a person willfully makes and signs a return, statement or other document that contains or is verified by a written declaration that it is true and correct as to every material matter, but the person does not believe it to be true and correct as to every material matter;
- a person willfully assists in, willfully procures, willfully advises or willfully provides counsel regarding the preparation or presentation of a return, affidavit, claim or other document regarding any matter arising under the tax law, knowing that it is fraudulent or knowing that it is false as to a material matter;
- a person files any return electronically, knowing the information in the return is not true and correct as to every material matter; or

---

[52] §3.1.11.16 NMAC.
[53] §7-1-72.1 NMSA 1978.

- a person with intent to evade or defeat the payment or collection of tax, or, knowing that the probable consequences of the person's act will be to evade or defeat the payment or collection of tax, removes, conceals or releases any property on which levy is authorized or that is liable for payment of tax, or aids in accomplishing or causes the accomplishment of the these acts.[54]

The term "willfully," as used above, means intentionally, deliberately or purposely, but not necessarily maliciously.[55] The burden of proof is upon the TRD in any proceeding involving the issue of whether a person has been guilty of fraud or corruption.[56]

If a person commits tax fraud when the amount of tax owed is $250 or less, the person is guilty of a petty misdemeanor.[57]

If a person commits tax fraud when the amount of tax owed is over $250 but less than $500, the person is guilty of a misdemeanor.[58]

If a person commits tax fraud when the amount of tax owed is over $500 but less than $2,500, the person is guilty of a fourth degree felony.[59]

If a person commits tax fraud when the amount of tax owed is over $2,500 but less than $20,000, the person is guilty of a third degree felony.[60]

If a person commits tax fraud when the amount of tax owed is over $20,000, the person is guilty of a second degree felony.[61]

For the above determinations, "tax" does not include civil penalties or interest.[62]

The penalty imposed for a petty misdemeanor is imprisonment for a definite term not to exceed six months or the payment of a fine of

---

[54] §7-1-73A NMSA 1978.
[55] §7-1-73H(2) NMSA 1978.
[56] §7-1-78 NMSA 1978.
[57] §7-1-73B NMSA 1978.
[58] §7-1-73C NMSA 1978.
[59] §7-1-73D NMSA 1978.
[60] §7-1-73E NMSA 1978.
[61] §7-1-73F NMSA 1978.
[62] §7-1-73H(1) NMSA 1978.

not more than $500, or both in the discretion of the judge.[63] The penalty for a misdemeanor is imprisonment for a definite term less than one year or the payment of a fine of not more than $1,000 or both, in the discretion of the judge.[64]

The penalty imposed for a fourth degree felony is a basic sentence of 18 months' imprisonment and the court may also impose a fine not exceeding $5,000.[65] The penalty imposed for a third degree felony is a basic sentence of three years imprisonment and the court may also impose a fine not exceeding $5,000.[66] The penalty imposed for a second degree felony is a basic sentence of nine years imprisonment and the court may impose a fine not exceeding $10,000.[67]

¶ 15.4.2 Other criminal violations

¶ 15.4.2.1 Penalty for attempts to evade or defeat tax

Any person who willfully attempts to evade or defeat any tax or the payment of any tax is guilty of a felony, and in addition to other penalties, will be fined upon conviction not less than $1,000 nor more than $10,000, or imprisoned for not less than one year nor more than five years, or both, together with the costs of prosecution.[68]

¶ 15.4.2.2 Interference with administration of revenue laws

Whoever by force, bribe, threat or other corrupt practice obstructs or impedes or attempts to obstruct or impede the administration of the tax law will be fined not less than $250 nor more than $10,000, or imprisoned for not less than three months nor more than one year, or both, together with costs of prosecution.[69]

¶ 15.4.2.3 Assault and battery of a TRD employee

Whoever assaults and batters or attempts to assault and batter a TRD employee acting within the scope of employment will be fined not less than $100 nor more than $500, or be imprisoned for not less than three days nor more than six months, or both, together with costs of

---

[63] §31-19-1B NMSA.
[64] §31-19-1A NMSA.
[65] §31-18-15A(10) and E(9) NMSA 1978.
[66] §31-18-15A(9) and E(9) NMSA.
[67] §31-18-15A(6) and E(6) NMSA.
[68] §7-1-72 NMSA 1978.
[69] §7-1-74 NMSA 1978.

prosecution. The magistrate courts have jurisdiction over these actions.[70]

¶ 15.4.2.4 Revealing information concerning taxpayers

A person who reveals any return or return information that is prohibited from being revealed[71] to another person or who uses a return or return information for any unauthorized purpose[72] is guilty of a misdemeanor and may be fined up to $1,000 or imprisoned up to one year, or both, together with the costs of prosecution. A person convicted of this offense may not be employed by the state for five years after the date of the conviction.[73]

---

[70] §7-1-75 MNSA 1978.
[71] See §7-1-8 NMSA 1978.
[72] See §§7-1-8 to 7-1-8.10 NMSA 1978 for circumstances under which return information may be released for authorized purposes.
[73] §7-1-76 NMSA 1978.

CHAPTER 16
AUDITS AND DISPUTES

¶ 16.1 Audit and Inspection of Books of Taxpayers

¶ 16.1.1 Notice of audit

In conducting an office or field audit, the TRD must provide a written dated notice of the commencement of the audit prior to or coincident with requesting a taxpayer's records and books of account. This notice requirement is inapplicable to fraud investigations.[1] At a minimum, the notice must state the tax programs and reporting periods to be covered and the date of commencement of the audit.[2]

¶ 16.1.2 Identification of auditors

Auditors and officials of the TRD must display identifying credentials to a taxpayer whose books are to be examined.[3]

¶ 16.1.3 Production of records and books of account

Auditors and other officials of the TRD designated by the Secretary are authorized to request and require the production of the taxpayer's records and books of account for examination, and these records must be made available when requested.[4] The TRD may inspect or audit the records and books of account of taxpayers at such times as the TRD deems necessary for the effective execution of its responsibilities.[5]

¶ 16.1.4 Reasonable hours

Upon request, taxpayers must make their records and books of account available for inspection at reasonable hours to TRD employees who present proper identification. Reasonable hours means any time during taxpayer's business hours but not less than between

---

[1] §7-1-11.2G NMSA 1978.
[2] §7-1-11.2A NMSA 1978.
[3] §7-1-11B NMSA 1978.
[4] §7-1-11B NMSA 1978; §3.1.5.15B(1) NMAC.
[5] §7-1-11A NMSA 1978.

the hours of 8:00 a.m. and 5:00 p.m. of any day except Saturday, Sunday, and state and federal holidays.[6]

¶ 16.1.5 Records include governmental returns, documents, reports and other attachments

The term "records" includes all copies of returns or reports that the taxpayer has filed with agencies of the federal government, agencies of New Mexico, and agencies of any sovereign state or Indian nation, tribe or pueblo located nationally or worldwide. The term also includes all returns, documents and reports, as well as any attachments, to any political subdivision of any state.[7]

¶ 16.1.6 Notice of outstanding records

In cases where the TRD has not received all the records it needs to complete and audit, the TRD may provide a dated, written notice of outstanding records or books of account no sooner than 60 days but no later than 180 days after the commencement of an audit. The notice can be provided earlier if the taxpayer provides a written request for early completion of the audit. The notice must indicate the outstanding records or books of account that have been requested but not received. If the taxpayer has provided all records and books of account requested, the notice must so indicate. The notice must provide reasonable descriptions of any records or books of account needed or the information expected to be contained in them and give the taxpayer 90 days to comply. The notice must state that if the taxpayer does not properly comply within 90 days, the TRD will proceed to issue an assessment of tax due on the basis of information available.[8] A taxpayer may make written request for additional time to comply, which should state the amount of time needed.[9]

¶ 16.1.7 Taxpayer records in possession of another

The TRD may inspect taxpayer records that are in the possession of another person. Except for banks, savings and loan associations, credit unions or similar financial institutions, the possessor is required to allow the inspection or audit by the TRD upon written request just as

---

[6] §3.1.5.14 NMAC.
[7] §3.1.5.12 NMAC.
[8] §7-1-11.2B NMSA 1978.
[9] §7-1-11.2C NMSA 1978.

Audits and Disputes

if the records were in the possession of the taxpayer. The failure of the possessor to allow inspection or audit by the TRD upon a reasonable request of the TRD is considered a violation of the provisions of the TAA and is subject to fine and imprisonment.[10] Requests to inspect or audit records of a taxpayer in the possession of a bank, savings and loan association, credit union or similar financial institution must be made in accordance with statutory rules concerning a state agency obtaining information from a financial institution.[11]

¶ 16.1.8 Enforcement by subpoena

The Secretary may serve or cause to be served a *subpoena duces tecum* upon a taxpayer or other person having custody of the taxpayer's records and books of account.[12]

¶ 16.1.9 Managed audits

The managed audit program is an effort to make tax administration more user- friendly by allowing qualified taxpayers to conduct managed audits or self-audits.[13] A "managed audit" is a review and analysis, or self-audit, conducted by a taxpayer to determine the taxpayer's compliance with a tax administered under the TAA and the presentation of the results to the TRD for assessment of tax due.[14]

No penalty is imposed on the tax due as the result of a managed audit.[15] In addition, if a taxpayer completes a managed audit by or before the date required, as provided in the audit agreement, and the payment of tax due is made in full within 180 days of the date the Secretary has mailed or delivered an assessment to the taxpayer, no interest is due on the assessed tax.[16]

To qualify for a managed audit, a taxpayer must first apply and then enter into a written agreement with the TRD. The decision to enter into a managed audit agreement is solely that of Secretary or the Secretary's delegate.[17] After entering into the agreement, the parties

---

[10] §3.1.5.16 NMAC.
[11] §§14-7-1 and 14-7-2 NMSA 1978.
[12] §3.1.5.13 NMAC.
[13] TRD, FYI 404, *Managed Audits for Taxpayers*, p. 1 (rev. 6/2016).
[14] §7-1-3J NMSA 1978.
[15] §7-1-69G[2] NMSA 1978.
[16] §7-1-67A(4) NMSA 1978.
[17] §7-1-11.1E NMSA 1978.

may subsequently modify it,[18] but the written agreement and any modifications must:

- be signed by the taxpayer or the taxpayer's authorized representative and by the TRD;
- contain a declaration by the taxpayer or the taxpayer's authorized representative that all statements of fact made by the taxpayer or taxpayer's representative in the application and the agreement are true and correct as to every material matter;
- specify the reporting period or periods, the type of receipts or transactions and tax to be audited, the procedures to be followed in performing the managed audit, the records to be used, the date of commencement of the audit and the date for the taxpayer's presentation of the results of the managed audit to the TRD; and
- include a waiver by the taxpayer of the limitations on assessments for the reporting period or periods to be audited.[19]

A managed audit may be limited in scope to certain periods, activities, lines of business, geographic areas or transactions, including the tax on:

- the receipts from certain sales;
- the value of certain assets;
- the value of certain expense items or services used; and
- any other category specified in the agreement.[20]

In determining whether to enter into an agreement for a managed audit the statute provides that the TRD may consider, in addition to other relevant factors:

- the taxpayer's history of tax compliance;
- the amount of time and resources the taxpayer has available to dedicate to the audit;
- the extent and availability of the taxpayer's records; and
- the taxpayer's ability to pay any expected liability.[21]

---

[18] §7-1-11.1C NMSA 1978.
[19] §7-1-11.1B NMSA 1978.
[20] §7-1-11.1A NMSA 1978.
[21] §7-1-11.1D NMSA 1978.

Audits and Disputes

In addition, TRD publication FYI-404, *Managed Audits for Taxpayers*, provides the following criteria that are to be used by the TRD:

- the TRD has not already selected the taxpayer for audit;
- the TRD is not currently pursuing collections on the taxpayer;
- the taxpayer demonstrates a willingness and ability to comply with New Mexico's tax laws;
- the taxpayer demonstrates an acceptable system of internal controls and business records;
- the taxpayer has not been the subject of a criminal investigation;
- the taxpayer has the resources available to conduct the audit;
- the taxpayer is not already in a legal dispute with the TRD over the taxability of the transactions that are the subject of the managed audit;
- the managed audit does not apply to existing liabilities;
- the taxpayer's outstanding liability was paid in full prior to requesting a managed audit agreement;
- the managed audit does not include transactions that are subject to a tribal gross receipts tax that the TRD administers on behalf of any tribe pursuant to a Gross Receipts Tax Tribal Cooperative Agreement;
- the taxpayer has not entered into and completed a managed audit for the same tax issue previously.[22]

The taxpayer must choose one of the following options under which the managed audit will be conducted:

> Option A – The taxpayer prepares the audit work papers with minimum guidance from the TRD. The taxpayer is issued a written statement stating that the taxpayer remains subject to audit by the TRD for the audit period.
>
> Option B – The taxpayer works with an assigned auditor to develop an audit plan, have work papers reviewed by the assigned auditor through the audit process, and, after completion and acceptance of the audit, is issued a written statement stating that the specific issue(s) in the audit period

---

[22] TRD, FYI 404, *Managed Audits for Taxpayers*, p.2 (rev. 6/2016)

covered by the agreement are closed to further audit.[23]

The taxpayer should present the results of the managed audit to the TRD on or before the date set for presentation in the managed audit agreement, and the TRD will assess the tax liability found to be due in accordance with the agreement. The TRD may review records, documents, schedules or other information to determine if the managed audit substantially conforms to the managed audit agreement.[24]

¶ 16.1.10 Federal audit adjustments

A taxpayer must file an amended return with the TRD if the taxpayer's federal income tax is adjusted as a result of: 1) an IRS audit; 2) the filing of an amended federal return that changed a prior election; or 3) any other change requiring federal approval. The amended return must be filed within 180 days of the final determination of the adjustment, together with the payment of any additional tax due.[25]

A "final determination" occurs on the happening of any of the following events:

- the taxpayer has made payment on any additional income tax liability resulting from the audit and has not filed a petition for redetermination or claim for refund for the portions of the audit on which payment was made;
- the taxpayer has received a refund resulting from the audit;
- the taxpayer has signed Form 870 or other IRS form consenting to the deficiency or accepting any overassessment;
- the taxpayer's time period for filing a petition for redetermination to the U.S. Tax Court has expired;
- the taxpayer enters into a closing agreement with the IRS; or
- a decision from the U.S. Tax Court, U.S. District Court, U.S. Court of Appeals, Court of Federal Claims (formerly the Court of Claims), or U.S. Supreme Court becomes final.[26]

---

[23] TRD, FYI 404, *Managed Audits for Taxpayers*, p.1 (rev. 6/2016).
[24] §7-1-11.1F NMSA 1978.
[25] §7-1-13C NMSA 1978.
[26] §7-1-13F NMSA 1978.

Audits and Disputes

¶ 16.1.11 Closing agreements

If the Secretary has a good faith doubt of a liability, then with the written approval of the Attorney General, the Secretary may compromise a liability for taxes by entering into a written closing agreement with the taxpayer that adequately protects the state. If a closing agreement is entered into after a court acquires jurisdiction, the agreement becomes part of a stipulated order or judgment disposing of the case.[27] The TRD may require the taxpayer to furnish security for payment of any taxes due under the agreement.[28]

A closing agreement is conclusive as to liability or non-liability for taxes relating to the periods covered in the agreement, and except for fraud, malfeasance, or misrepresentation or concealment of a material fact:

1. the agreement may not be modified by the state; and
2. in any suit, action or proceeding, the agreement or any determination, assessment, collection, payment, abatement, refund or credit made in accordance with the agreement may not be annulled, modified, set aside or disregarded.[29]

A liability may not be compromised because of a taxpayer's inability to pay, because of the threat of litigation, or as an expedient means of disposing of a controversy unless the Secretary has a good faith doubt as to the liability.[30] A closing agreement must address the facts giving rise to such good faith doubt. The specific periods of assessed liabilities must be detailed in the agreement.[31] The burden is upon the taxpayer to convince the Secretary that a good faith doubt exists by presenting evidence sufficient to overcome the presumption of correctness.[32]

¶16.2 Disputes

¶16.2.1 Exhaustion of administrative remedies

State courts do not have jurisdiction over any proceeding in which a

---

[27] §7-1-20A and B NMSA 1978.
[28] §7-1-20C NMSA 1978.
[29] §7-1-20D NMSA 1978.
[30] §3.1.6.14A NMAC.
[31] §3.1.6.14B NMAC.
[32] §3.1.6.14C NMAC.

taxpayer questions a tax liability or the application of any provision of the TAA, except as a result of an appeal by the taxpayer to the court of appeals from an order of a hearing officer, or as a result of a claim for refund.[33]

¶16.2.2 Election of remedies in disputing liabilities

A taxpayer who disputes a tax liability must either protest the assessment without making payment[34] or claim a refund after making payment.[35] Once one of these two remedies is pursued, the right to pursue the other is waived.[36] This choice is made when a taxpayer files a timely protest to an assessment or makes a timely claim for refund.[37] The taxpayer may not withdraw a protest, pay the assessment, and then claim a refund without permission from the TRD. Taxpayers may not "Pay Under Protest".[38]

> ***Example 1.*** A taxpayer files a timely protest to a notice of assessment. Prior to the administrative hearing, the taxpayer realizes that by paying the tax and claiming a refund, he would be able to commence a civil action in district court after the denial of the refund. The taxpayer then commences a civil action and asks that the administrative proceedings be discontinued. The Secretary will move to dismiss in district court on the grounds that the taxpayer made an election to pursue the administrative remedy by filing the protest and is precluded from pursuing a district court action.[39]

> ***Example 2.*** A taxpayer writes a letter to the TRD objecting to paying an assessment, but does not state the nature of the complaint or relief requested, nor is the complaint received within 30 days of the date of the assessment. The taxpayer has not filed a valid protest and still has the right to pay the assessment and claim a refund. Any one of the three defects noted above in the taxpayer's written objection would disqualify

---

[33] §7-1-22 NMSA 1978. See §7-1-26 NMSA 1978 for claims for refunds.
[34] As provided in §7-1- 24 NMSA 1978.
[35] As provided in §7-1-26 NMSA 1978.
[36] §7-1-23 NMSA 1978.
[37] §3.1.7.8A NMAC.
[38] §3.1.7.8B NMAC.
[39] Based upon §3.1.7.8C NMAC.

Audits and Disputes

it from being a valid protest.[40]

Nevertheless, the tender by a taxpayer and acceptance by the TRD of payment of a protested assessment prior to resolution of the protest constitutes an agreement whereby:

- the Secretary waives the taxpayer's election of remedies upon a resolution of the protest in favor of the taxpayer, which will permit the taxpayer to file a refund claim for the portion of the protested assessment resolved in the taxpayer's favor; and
- the taxpayer waives the accrual of interest on any refund arising from the portion of the protested assessment resolved in favor of the taxpayer.[41]

¶ 16.2.3 Disputing liabilities – administrative protest

A taxpayer may administratively dispute many of the significant TRD actions and present his or her case at a formal hearing. A taxpayer may administratively dispute:

- the assessment of any amount of tax;
- the application of any provision of the TAA, except the issuance of a subpoena or summons;[42] or
- the denial of or failure either to allow or to deny a credit or rebate or a claim for refund.[43]

The above matters are disputed by the filing of a written protest. The protest must identify the tax credit, rebate, property or provision of the TAA involved and state the grounds for the protest and the affirmative relief requested. The statement of grounds must specify the individual grounds upon which the protest is based and provide a summary statement of the evidence expected to be produced supporting each ground.[45] A protest may be made by filing form ACD-31094, *Formal Protest*. The taxpayer may supplement the statement any time prior to ten days before the hearing, or in accordance with the scheduling order if a scheduling order has been issued. To speed the

---

[40] Based upon §3.1.7.8D NMAC.
[41] §3.1.7.9 NMAC.8
[42] §7-1-24E NMSA 1978.
[43] §7-1-24A NMSA 1978.
[45] §7-1-24B NMSA 1978. See §3.1.7.12 A NMAC for the requirements of the statement of grounds.

review of the protest, copies of the evidence may be included with the statement of the grounds, although such evidence must still be introduced and admitted at the formal hearing to be considered by the hearing officer.[46]

TRD publication FYI 400, *Tax Audits and Protest Procedures*, explains that taxpayers must file a written protest within 90 days of the mailing date on the notice of assessment of tax, or within 90 days of the date the TRD receives the taxpayer's return showing a liability for tax.[47] Failure by a taxpayer to file a protest within a maximum of 90 days is jurisdictional, and the Secretary is without authority to consider any protest filed after that period.[48]

If a protest is not filed within the time required, the Secretary may enforce collection of any tax if the taxpayer is delinquent. The fact that the TRD did not mail the assessment or other peremptory notice or demand by certified or registered mail or otherwise demand and receive acknowledgment of receipt by the taxpayer will not be deemed to demonstrate the taxpayer's inability to protest within the required time.[49]

¶ 16.2.4 Informal conferences

The Secretary may schedule an informal conference in appropriate cases.[50] The regulations provide that upon the taxpayer's written request or the TRD's own initiative, the TRD will provide for an informal conference before setting a hearing on the protest at a time and place agreed to by the parties. Both parties may bring representatives and any pertinent documents.[51]

The purpose of an informal conference is to discuss the facts and legal issues and to hopefully resolve the issues, thereby avoiding the need for a formal hearing.[52] There is no restriction on the number of informal conferences that may be scheduled, but after the initial informal conference, additional informal conferences will be scheduled

---

[46] §3.1.7.12 B NMAC.
[47] See §7-1-24C NMSA 1978.
[48] §3.1.7.11 NMAC.
[49] §7-1-24C NMSA 1978.
[50] §7-1-24B NMSA 1978.
[51] §3.1.7.13A NMAC.
[52] §3.1.7.13B NMAC.

Audits and Disputes

only if the Secretary believes that they will help resolve the issues. If taxpayer fails to appear at the informal conference without reasonable notice, the protest may be scheduled for a formal hearing without further opportunity for an informal conference.[53]

¶ 16.2.5 Rules for formal hearings

Formal hearings are held in Santa Fe and are not open to the public except upon the taxpayer's request. Taxpayers may appear themselves or be represented by an employee, an attorney, a certified public accountant, or registered public accountant. Each party has the right of due notice, cross-examination, presentation of evidence, objection, motion, argument and all other rights of a fair hearing, including the right to discovery. Any witness who is hostile, unwilling or evasive, may be interrogated by leading questions and may also be contradicted and impeached by the party calling that person.

The parties may agree to the joint submission of stipulated facts if accepted by the hearing officer. The hearing officer may order the parties to stipulate to uncontested facts and to exhibits and may also order the parties to stipulate to basic documents regarding the controversy, such as audit reports, assessments, taxpayer returns and payments, correspondence, and to basic facts concerning the identity and business of a taxpayer.[54]

¶ 16.2.6 Hearing officer

A "hearing officer" is a person who has been designated by the chief hearing officer to serve as a hearing officer and who may be the chief hearing officer or an employee or contractor of the administrative hearings office.[55] It is the duty of the hearing officer to conduct fair and impartial hearings, avoid delay in the proceedings, and maintain order. The hearing officer has the powers necessary to carry out these duties, including the following:

- to administer or have administered oaths and affirmations;
- to cause depositions to be taken;
- to require the production and/or inspection of documents and

---

[53] §3.1.7.13C NMAC.
[54] §3.1.8.8 NMAC.
[55] §7-1-3F NMSA 1978; §3.1.8.9A NMAC.

other items;
- to require the answering of interrogatories and requests for admissions;
- to rule upon offers of proof and receive evidence;
- to regulate the course of the hearings and the conduct of the parties and their representatives therein;
- to issue a scheduling order, schedule a prehearing conference for simplification of the issues, or any other proper purpose;
- to schedule, continue and reschedule formal hearings;
- to consider and rule upon all procedural and other motions appropriate in proceeding;
- to require the filing of briefs on specific legal issues prior to or after the formal hearing;
- to cause a complete record of proceedings in formal hearings to be made; and
- to make and issue decisions and orders.[56]

The hearing officer acts *independently* in performing these functions and is not responsible to or subject to the direction of any officer, employee, or agent of the TRD.[57] To maintain impartiality, the hearing officer is prohibited from ex parte discussions with either party on any protested matter.[58]

When a hearing officer has substantial doubt as to whether he or she has a conflicting interest, the hearing officer must withdraw from the hearing. Whenever a party believes the hearing officer should be disqualified, the party may file a motion with the Secretary to seek disqualification and removal of the hearing officer. The motion should be supported by affidavits setting forth the alleged grounds for disqualification. The hearing officer has 25 days to accede or to reply to the allegations. If the hearing officer does not remove him or herself, the Secretary promptly reviews the alleged grounds and determines whether the hearing officer should be disqualified, in which case the Secretary's decision is final.[59] If the hearing officer is

---

[56] §3.1.8.9B NMAC.
[57] §3.1.8.9B[C] NMAC.
[58] §3.1.8.9D NMAC.
[59] §3.1.8.9D NMAC.

Audits and Disputes

disqualified, the Secretary will designate another person to act as hearing officer.

¶ 16.2.7 Evidence

The taxpayer has the burden of proof, except as otherwise provided by law. Relevant and material evidence will be admitted, and irrelevant, immaterial, unreliable, or repetitious evidence may be excluded. The hearing officer will consider all evidence admitted and take administrative notice of facts as provided in the New Mexico Rules of Civil Procedure for District Courts. Parties objecting to evidence must timely state their grounds and rulings on objections will appear in the record. Formal exception to an adverse ruling is not required. When an objection to a witness is sustained, the examining representative may make an offer of what the representative expects to prove by the answer, or the hearing officer may, with discretion, receive and have reported the evidence in full. Excluded exhibits, adequately marked for identification, must be retained in the record to be available for consideration by a reviewing authority.[60]

¶ 16.2.8 Hearing record

Hearings are electronically recorded unless the hearing officer allows recording by an alternative means approved by the New Mexico Supreme Court. A party may request that a hearing be recorded by alternative means, but unless that hearing officer rules otherwise, that party will be responsible for the cost, including the provision of the original transcript to the hearing officer and copies to opposing parties.[61]

¶ 16.2.9 Proposed findings, conclusions and briefs

After the close of the reception of evidence, the hearing officer may require, or any party may file, proposed orders, proposed findings of fact, and proposed conclusions of law, together with supporting reasons and briefs.[62]

---

[60] §3.1.8.10 NMAC.
[61] §3.1.8.11 NMAC.
[62] §3.1.8.12 NMAC.

¶ 16.2.10 Discovery

The parties are expected to accomplish discovery by the time of the hearing. Discovery is achieved by informal consultation, stipulation, deposition, requests for admissions, production of documents, and written interrogatories. If adequate discovery is not achieved, a party may request the hearing officer for an order to require depositions, production of records, or answers to interrogatories. Depositions may be taken orally or by written interrogatories and cross-interrogatories. Unless the hearing officer orders otherwise, responses to interrogatories, requests for production of documents, and requests for admission are due thirty days after service. A notice of deposition must be served on opposing parties at least five working days prior to the date of the deposition. The parties must cooperate in scheduling depositions and avoiding unnecessary expense and inconvenience to witnesses.[63]

¶ 16.2.11 Failure to comply with orders

If a party fails to comply with an order of the hearing officer for the taking of a deposition or otherwise relating to discovery, the hearing officer may take such action as is just, including the following:

1. infer that the evidence sought by discovery would have been adverse to the party failing to comply;
2. rule that the matter concerning which the order was issued be taken adversely to the party failing to comply;
3. rule that the noncomplying party may not introduce evidence or rely, in support of any claim or defense, upon testimony, documents, or other evidence of which discovery has been denied;
4. rule that a party may not object to introduction and use of secondary evidence to show what the withheld evidence would have shown; or
5. dismiss the protest or order that the protest be granted.[64]

These actions may be taken by written or oral order issued in the course of the proceeding or by inclusion in the decision of the hearing

---

[63] §3.1.8.13 NMAC.
[64] §3.1.8.14 A NMAC.

Audits and Disputes

officer.[65]

A party that had requested the Secretary to issue a subpoena may request the Secretary to seek the assistance of the court in the enforcement of the subpoena.[66]

¶ 16.2.12 Prehearing conference

The hearing officer may direct all parties to meet with the hearing officer for a prehearing conference to consider the following:

- simplification and clarification of the issues;
- stipulations and admissions of fact and of the contents and authenticity of documents;
- expedition in the discovery and presentation of evidence, including, restrictions on the number of expert witnesses;
- matters of which administrative notice will be taken; or
- such other matters that aid in the disposition of the proceeding, including disclosure of the identity of witnesses and documents or other exhibits to be introduced in evidence.[67]

The hearing officer may have the prehearing conference recorded,[68] and may enter an order in the record reciting the results of the conference. The order will include the hearing officer's rulings, together with directions to the parties, which will control the course of the proceeding.[69]

¶ 16.2.13 Motions

After the formal hearing is scheduled on a protest, all motions are addressed to the hearing officer with copies to the opposing parties. All written motions must state the order, ruling, or desired action and the grounds. Within ten calendar days after personal service or service by fax, or within thirteen calendar days after the motion is mailed or within a different time period set by the hearing officer, the opposing party must answer or be deemed to have consented to the requested relief. The moving party has no right to reply, except as permitted by

---

[65] §3.1.8.14 B NMAC.
[66] §3.1.8.14C NMAC.
[67] §3.1.8.15A NMAC
[68] §3.1.8.15B NMAC.
[69] §3.1.8.15C NMAC

the hearing officer.[70]

¶ 16.2.14 Appeals from hearing officer's decision

The party dissatisfied with the decision and order of the hearing officer may appeal to the Court of Appeals, but only on the same issues and upon the same theory asserted at the hearing. The appeal is based on the record at the hearing and not de novo. An appeal must be taken within thirty days of the date of mailing or delivery of the written decision and order to the protestant, or the decision and order are conclusive.[71] The procedure for perfecting an appeal is provided by the Supreme Court Rules of Appellate Procedure.[72]

Per the statute, the TRD may choose between hand delivering or mailing the written decision and order. The "date of mailing" is the time that the hearing officer's decision and order enclosed in a properly addressed envelope or wrapper is postmarked by the U.S. postal service. "Delivery" means time of hand delivery of the written decision and order to the taxpayer's business or residence.[73]

The court will set aside a decision and order of the hearing officer only if it is found to be:

- arbitrary, capricious, or an abuse of discretion;
- not supported by substantial evidence in the record; or
- otherwise not in accordance with the law.[74]

If the Secretary appeals a decision of the hearing officer that is upheld by the court, and either no further appeal is taken or may be taken, the court will award reasonable attorney fees to the protestant. If hearing officer's decision is upheld in part, the award is limited to attorney fees associated with the portion upheld.[75]

¶ 16.2.15 Conditions for refund or credit

A written claim for refund may be submitted to the TRD in the following cases: 1) a person paid tax or had tax withheld in excess of

---

[70] §3.1.8.16 NMAC.
[71] §7-1-25A NMSA 1978.
[72] §7-1-25B NMSA 1978; §3.1.8.18 NMAC; §3.1.8.19 NMAC.
[73] §3.1.8.17 NMAC.
[74] §7-1-25C NMSA 1978.
[75] §7-1-25D NMSA 1978.

Audits and Disputes

the person's liability; 2) a person has been denied a claimed credit or rebate; or 3) the TRD has taken possession of property pursuant to a levy from a person with a claim of prior right. The Secretary does not have statutory authority to initiate action in these cases and the affected person must initiate the claim.[76]

The TRD may grant a refund or credit only if all of these conditions are satisfied:

1. the tax has been erroneously paid and payment has been verified from the TRD or taxpayer's records;
2. the taxpayer has submitted a proper claim for refund; and
3. the Secretary has secured the prior approval of the Attorney General where required.[77]

The filing of a fully completed income tax return or a fully completed amended income tax return that shows an overpayment of tax, a credit or rebate claimed, constitutes the filing of a claim for refund, and no separate refund claim is required.[78] A return is "fully completed" when it complies with all the instructions for the return and contains all attachments required by the instructions.[79]

In response to a claim for refund for one type of tax, the TRD may credit the amount to be refunded against any other tax due from the taxpayer. The TRD must give a full accounting of the crediting transaction to the claimant.[80]

A taxpayer may not create a credit for a discovered overpayment by understating the amount due on current tax returns to offset amounts paid on prior returns.[81]

A credit or refund claim must be made within three years of the end of the calendar year in which:

1. the payment was originally due or the overpayment resulted from an assessment by the TRD, whichever is later;
2. property was levied upon; or

---

[76] §7-1-26 NMSA 1978A; §3.1.9.8A NMAC.
[77] §3.1.9.13A NMAC.
[78] §3.1.9.8A NMAC.
[79] §3.1.9.8B NMAC.
[80] §3.1.9.13B NMAC.
[81] §3.1.9.13C NMAC

3. an overpayment of New Mexico tax resulted from an IRS audit adjustment, a federal refund paid due to an IRS audit adjustment or an amended federal return, or making a change to a federal return for which federal approval is required.[82]

When a claim for credit is denied under Investment Credit Act, the Laboratory Partnership with Small Business Tax Credit Act, the Technology Jobs Tax Credit Act, or for the rural job tax credit or similar credit, a claim for the refund of the credit must be made no later than one year after the date of the denial.[83]

When a taxpayer under audit signs a waiver of the limitation on assessments,[84] the taxpayer may file a claim for refund of the same tax paid for the same period for which the waiver was given until a date one year after the later of the date of the mailing of an assessment issued pursuant to the audit, the date of the mailing of final audit findings to the taxpayer, or the date a proceeding is begun in court by the TRD with respect to the same tax and the same period.[85]

If the payment of an amount of tax was not made within three years of the end of the calendar year in which the original due date of the tax or date of the assessment occurred, a claim for refund of that amount of tax can be made within one year of the date on which the tax was paid.[86]

When a taxpayer has paid penalty for the failure to timely pay tax or file a return, but the taxpayer subsequently becomes entitled to a refund of part or all of the tax, the taxpayer is also entitled to a proportionate refund of the penalty paid whether or not the taxpayer specifically requests refund of the penalty.[87]

When a taxpayer has been assessed a tax in the cases of a fraudulent return, a failure to file, or because of an understatement of tax of more than 25% on a return, and that assessment applies to a period ending at least three years prior to the beginning of the year in which the assessment was made, the taxpayer may claim a refund for the same

---

[82] §7-1-26D(1) NMSA 1978.
[83] §7-1-26D(2) NMSA 1978.
[84] See §7-1-18F NMSA 1978.
[85] §7-1-26D(3) NMSA 1978; §3.1.9.12A NMAC.
[86] §7-1-26D(4) NMSA 1978.
[87] §3.1.9.16B NMAC.

Audits and Disputes

tax for the period of the assessment or for any period following that period within one year of the date of the assessment unless a longer period for claiming a refund is provided in the rules described above in this section.[88]

A claim for refund is valid if it states the nature of the complaint, the affirmative relief requested, and contains information sufficient to allow the processing of the claim. Information sufficient to allow processing of a claim includes:

1. taxpayer's name, address and identification number;
2. the type or types of tax for which the refund is being claimed;
3. the sum of money being claimed;
4. the period for which the overpayment was made;
5. the basis for the refund; and
6. a copy of the appropriate, fully completed amended return for each period for which a refund is claimed.[89]

A claim that does not include the required information is invalid and the TRD may return it to the taxpayer. Alternatively, the TRD may advise the taxpayer that the claim is invalid because of missing information. If the taxpayer resubmits the claim with the required information or, when the return is not returned, submits all required information, the claim becomes valid when the claim is re-submitted or the required information is supplied.[90]

If an overpayment of tax is found in any period as a result of an audit of multiple periods, that overpayment may be credited against an underpayment of the same tax found in another period under audit, provided that the taxpayer files a claim for refund for the overpayments identified in the audit.[91]

A refund of tax may be made at the discretion of the TRD in the form of a credit against future tax payments if future tax liabilities in an amount at least equal to the credit amount may reasonably be expected to become due.[92]

---

[88] §7-1-26D(5) NMSA 1978; §3.1.9.12B NMAC.
[89] §3.1.9.8D and E NMAC.
[90] §3.1.9.8F NMAC.
[91] §7-1-26F NMSA 1978.
[92] §7-1-26G NMSA 1978.

¶ 16.2.16 Claimant remedies

A person who has been denied a refund claim or who has submitted a valid refund claim upon which no action has taken within 120 days, may submit a written protest against the denial of, or failure to either allow or deny, the claim. The protest must be received by the TRD either:

- on or before 90 days after the date that the TRD has mailed to the claimant a written denial of the claim for refund; or
- within 90 days after the expiration of 120 days after the mailing of a claim to the TRD on which no action has been taken by the TRD.[93]

Alternatively, a person who has been denied a refund claim or who has submitted a valid claim for refund upon which no action has been taken within 120 days may commence a civil action. The civil action must be commenced within 90 days of the denial by the TRD or within 90 days after the expiration of 120 days after the mailing of the claim to the TRD upon which no action has been taken by the TRD.[94]

A claimant may not refile a claim that has been denied in whole or in part. If the claimant wishes to challenge the TRD's denial, the claimant must pursue one of the two remedies described above (protest or civil action). A claimant may, however, refile a claim within the statutory period if the TRD has not denied the claim in whole or in part and has taken no action on that claim within 120 days from the filing of the claim.[95]

A request for additional information by the TRD does not constitute "action".[96]

A written protest must set forth the following:

1. the circumstances of an alleged overpayment, a denied credit, a denied rebate, or a denial of a prior right to property levied upon by the TRD;
2. an allegation that, because of that overpayment or denial, the

---

[93] §3.1.9.9A NMAC.
[94] §3.1.9.9B NMAC.
[95] §3.1.9.9C NMAC.
[96] §3.1.9.9D NMAC.

Audits and Disputes

state is indebted to the taxpayer for a specified amount, including any allowed interest, or for the property;
3. a demand of the refund to the taxpayer of that amount or that property; and
4. the facts of the claim for refund.[97]

A civil action is commenced in the District Court for Santa Fe County by the filing of a complaint setting forth the circumstances of the overpayment, denied credit or rebate, or denial of a prior right to property levied upon by the TRD, and which alleges that the state owes the plaintiff the amount or property stated, together with interest, and which recites the facts of the refund claim. The plaintiff or the Secretary may appeal from any final decision or order of the district court to the court of appeals.[98]

¶ 16.2.17 Conclusiveness of court order on liability for payment of tax

Whenever the District Court of Santa Fe county or the court of appeals decides a case involving the decision of a hearing officer,[99] a denial of a refund claim,[100] a jeopardy assessment,[101] or whenever a federal court or a district court of New Mexico is involved in an action to collect a tax debt,[102] a final decision from that court or a higher court which reviewed the matter, and from which decision an appeal or review is not successfully taken, is conclusive as to the liability for the payment of tax.[103]

The TRD is given the authority to abate tax assessments in a number of appropriate circumstances:

- In response to a written protest against an assessment and before any court acquires jurisdiction of the matter, or when a notice of assessment is incorrect, the TRD may abate any part of an assessment determined to have been incorrectly, erroneously or illegally made. An abatement of $20,000 or

---

[97] §7-1-26C(1) NMSA- 9878.
[98] §7-1-26C(2) NMSA 1978.
[99] §7-1-25 NMSA 1978.
[100] §7-1-26 NMSA 1978.
[101] §7-1-59 NMSA 1978.
[102] §7-1-58 NMSA 1978.
[103] §7-1-27 NMSA 1978.

- In the case of a final court order that is not successfully appealed by the TRD which adjudges that a person is not required to pay any portion of a tax assessed, the TRD must cause the assessment to be abated.[105]
- When the Secretary enters into a closing agreement, the TRD must abate the appropriate amount of any assessment of tax.[106]
- The TRD will abate the amount of an assessment of tax that is equal to the amount of fee paid to or retained by an out-of-state attorney or collection agency from a judgment or the amount collected by the attorney or collection agency.[107]
- In response to a timely protest, the TRD may abate the portion of an assessment, including penalties and interest, representing the tax paid by another on behalf of the taxpayer on the same transaction, provided that the requirements of equitable recoupment are met. The protest may be made either by the taxpayer or by the person who claims to have paid the tax on the taxpayer's behalf.[108]

Records of abatements made in excess of $10,000 are available for inspection by the public. The TRD must keep such records for a minimum of three years from the date of the abatement.[109]

A notice of assessment is not effective until mailed or delivered to the taxpayer. Any time before this action occurs, an assessment can be cancelled by the TRD. The TRD considers a cancellation as an accounting process and not an abatement.[110]

¶ 16.2.18 Authority to make refunds or credits

In responding to a claim, but before a court obtains jurisdiction, the TRD may authorize payment of a claimed credit or rebate or refund an overpayment of tax erroneously made, together with interest. Amounts in excess of $20,000 or more require the prior approval of

---

[104] §7-1-28A NMSA 1978.
[105] §7-1-28B NMSA 1978.
[106] §7-1-28C NMSA 1978.-
[107] §7-1-28D NMSA 1978; §7-1-58 NMSA 1978.
[108] §7-1-28F NMSA 1978
[109] §7-1-28E NMSA 1978.
[110] §3.1.6.15 NMAC; §7-1-17 NMSA 1978.

Audits and Disputes

the Attorney General.[111]

If a final court order adjudges that a person has properly claimed a credit or rebate or made an overpayment of tax, the Secretary must authorize the payment.[112]

Any credit, or rebate to be paid, or any tax to be refunded a person may be offset against any amount of tax for which the person is liable. The TRD must give notice of this offset, and the taxpayer is entitled to interest until the tax liability is credited.[113]

In an audit of multiple periods in which both underpayments and overpayments have been made, the TRD will credit the tax overpayments against the underpayments, provided that the taxpayer files a refund claim for the overpayments. An overpayment is first applied to the earliest underpayment and then to succeeding underpayments. An underpayment to which an overpayment is credited is either deemed paid in the period in which the overpayment was made or in the period to which the overpayment was credited against an underpayment, whichever is later. If the overpayments exceed the underpayments, the net overpayment is refunded to the taxpayer.[114]

When a payment relating to a particular return or assessment exceeds the amount due, the TRD may apply the excess to the taxpayer's other tax liabilities, without requiring the taxpayer to file refund a claim. The liability is deemed paid either in the period in which the overpayment was made or applied, whichever is later.[115]

If upon review of an original or amended income tax return the TRD determines that there has been an overpayment of tax in excess of the amount due to be refunded as stated on the return, the TRD may refund the excess amount without requiring the taxpayer to file a refund claim.[116]

The records of refunds and credits made in excess of $10,000 are

---

[111] §7-1-29A NMSA 1978.
[112] §7-1-29B NMSA 1978.
[113] §7-1-29C NMSA 1978.
[114] §7-1-29D NMSA 1978.
[115] §7-1-29E NMSA 1978.
[116] §7-1-29F NMSA 1978.

available for inspection by the public. The TRD must keep such records for a minimum of three years from the date of the refund or credit.[117]

In response to a timely refund claim, the TRD may refund or credit a portion of an assessment paid, including applicable penalties and interest, representing the amount of tax previously paid by another on behalf of the taxpayer on the same transaction, provided that the requirements of equitable recoupment are met. The refund claim may be filed by the taxpayer or by the person who claims to have previously paid the tax on the taxpayer's behalf. Before granting the refund or credit, the Secretary may require a waiver of all rights to claim a refund or credit of the tax previously paid by another person.[118]

The term "overpayment" means an amount paid, pursuant to any law subject to administration and enforcement under the provisions of the TAA, by a person to the TRD or withheld from the person in excess of tax due from the person to the state at the time of the payment or at the time the amount withheld is credited against tax due.[119]

¶ 16.2.19 Awarding of costs and fees

In an administrative or court proceeding brought by or against the taxpayer in connection with the determination, collection or refund of tax, interest or penalty in which the taxpayer is the prevailing party, the taxpayer will be awarded reasonable administrative costs incurred in connection with an administrative proceeding with the TRD or the administrative hearings office, or reasonable litigation costs incurred in connection with a court proceeding.[120]

No agreement for or award of reasonable administrative costs or reasonable litigation costs in any administrative or court proceeding may exceed the lesser of 20% of the amount of the settlement or judgment or $50,000. A taxpayer awarded administrative litigation costs pursuant to the above rules is disqualified from receiving an award of attorney fees that is otherwise allowable to the protestant

---

[117] §7-1-29G NMSA 1978.
[118] §7-1-29H NMSA 1978.
[119] §7-1-3L NMSA 1978.
[120] §7-1-29.1A NMSA 1978.

Audits and Disputes

when the TRD appeals from a hearing officer decision.[121]

---

[121] §7-1-29.1E NMSA 1978; §7-1-25D NMSA 1978.

CHAPTER 17
TAX ADMINISTRATION

¶ 17.1 Overview

The New Mexico rules for the administration and enforcement of the PIT law under the ITA are contained in New Mexico Tax Administration Act (TAA)[1] and in the regulations thereunder. In addition to governing the administration and enforcement of the ITA, the TAA governs the administration of most other New Mexico taxes, as well.[2]

Enforcement officials

Individuals who enforce any of the provisions of the TAA must be furnished with identifying credentials. They may request the assistance of any sheriff or deputy sheriff or of the state police in order to perform their duties, which assistance is to be provided in appropriate circumstances.[3]

¶ 17.2 New Mexico Taxpayer Bill of Rights

The basic tone of the TAA is encapsulated in the New Mexico Taxpayer Bill of Rights, which was created to ensure that the rights of taxpayers are adequately safeguarded and protected during the assessment, collection, and enforcement of any tax. These rights have been created to ensure that the taxpayer is treated with dignity and respect, and to provide brief but comprehensive statements that explain in simple, nontechnical terms the rights of taxpayers.[4]

Taxpayers are afforded the following rights during assessment,

---

[1] §§7-1-1 to 7-1-83 NMSA 1978.
[2] §7-1-2 NMSA 1978.
[3] §7-1-79 NMSA 1978.
[4] **§7-1-4.1 NMSA 1978.** The TRD is given the responsibility to develop a publication that states the rights of taxpayers in simple, nontechnical terms and disseminate the publication to taxpayers, at a minimum, with the annual income and semiannual combined reporting system tax forms. §7-1-4.3 NMSA 1978.

collection and enforcement:

1. The right to available public information and prompt and courteous tax assistance.
2. The right to be represented or advised by counsel or other qualified representatives at any time in administrative interactions with the TRD as governed by the administrative protest procedures of the TAA[5] and the provisions of the Administrative Hearings Office Act.
3. The right to have audits, inspections of records and meetings conducted at a reasonable time and place.[6]
4. The right to have the TRD conduct its audits in a timely and expeditious manner and be entitled to the tolling of interest as provided in the TAA.
5. The right to obtain nontechnical information that explains the procedures, remedies and rights available during audit, protest, appeals and collection proceedings as provided in the TAA.
6. The right to be provided with an explanation of the results of and the basis for audits, assessments or denials of refunds that identify any amount of tax, interest or penalty due.
7. The right to seek review, through formal or informal proceedings, of any findings or adverse decisions relating to determinations during audit or protest procedures in accordance with administrative protest provisions[7] and the Administrative Hearings Office Act.
8. The right to have the taxpayer's tax information kept confidential unless otherwise specified by law, in accordance statutory confidentiality rules.[8]
9. The right to the abatement of an assessment of taxes determined to have been incorrectly, erroneously or illegally made (as provided in §7-1-28 NMSA 1978) and the right to seek a compromise of an asserted tax liability by obtaining a written determination of liability or nonliability when the TRD in good faith is in doubt of the liability (as provided in in §7-1-20 NMSA 1978).

---

[5] See §7-1-24 NMSA 1978 and attendant regulations.
[6] See §7-1-11 NMSA 1978;
[7] See §7-1-24 NMSA 1978.
[8] See §7-1-8 NMSA 1978.

Tax Administration

10. Upon receipt of a tax assessment, the right to be informed clearly that if the assessment is not paid, secured, protested or otherwise provided for (in accordance with the provisions of §7-1-16 NMSA 1978), the taxpayer will be a delinquent taxpayer and, upon notice of delinquency, the right to timely notice of any collection actions that will require sale or seizure of the taxpayer's property in accordance with the provisions of the TAA.
11. The right to procedures for payment of tax obligations by installment payment agreements (in accordance with §7-1-21 NMSA 1978).[9]

¶ 17.3 Authorized Representative

The Taxpayer Bill of Rights (paragraph 2 above) gives taxpayers the right to be represented or advised by counsel or other qualified representatives at any time in administrative interactions with the TRD as governed by the administrative protest procedures of the TAA[10] and the provisions of the Administrative Hearings Office Act. To represent a taxpayer, a person must provide the TRD written authorization signed by the taxpayer. Form ACD-31102, *Tax Information Authorization*, is provided for this purpose.[11] The TRD may reveal information that concerns the taxpayer if it is presented with proper authorization from the representative.[12]

Attorneys or accountants licensed to practice in New Mexico are exempted from the requirement to obtain written authorization. In addition, enrolled agents are exempted, but only with respect to income tax. Income tax includes personal income tax returns, pass-through entity tax returns, corporate income and franchise tax returns, s corporation income and franchise tax returns, and fiduciary income tax returns.

¶ 17.4 Delegation of Authority Rules

The Secretary of the TRD is responsible for administering the PIT and

---

[9] §7-1-4.2 NMSA 1978.
[10] See §7-1-24 NMSA 1978.
[11] See http://www.tax.newmexico.gov/Tax-Professionals/tax-authorization-procedure.aspx. Last viewed October 14, 2016.
[12] See §3.1.3.13 NMAC.

may act when authorized by the TAA. The Secretary's authority to act can be delegated to others, but only where specifically authorized by statute.[13] The term "Secretary" may also include the Deputy Secretary or a Division Director or Deputy Division Director if so delegated by the Secretary. However, the Secretary alone is invested with the power to issue subpoenas and summonses and may not delegate this authority.[14] Often a statute will refer to actions of the "Secretary or the Secretary's delegate" and this language includes the Secretary or any employee of the TRD exercising authority lawfully delegated to that employee by the Secretary.[15]

A delegation of authority by the Secretary to an employee of the division or an employee of the TRD is not required to be in writing.[16] The following persons are be considered to be employees of the TRD when acting as agents or authorized to represent or perform services for the TRD:

- The Secretary of the TRD or an employee of the TRD authorized by the Secretary.
- The New Mexico Attorney General, the Attorney General's deputies and assistants, district attorneys and the district attorneys' deputies and assistants.
- Persons employed by the Multistate Tax Commission and performing duties under the Multistate Tax Compact.[17]
- Persons acting under professional service contracts with the TRD.
- Any person acting as agent or authorized to represent or perform services for the TRD in any capacity with respect to any law made subject to administration and enforcement under the provisions of the TAA.[18]

When the ITA uses the word "department" this term includes the TRD, the Secretary or any employee of the TRD exercising authority

---

[13] §3.1.1.10A NMAC.
[14] §7-1-3U NMSA 1978.
[15] §7-1-3V NMSA 1978.
[16] §3.1.1.11 NMAC.
[17] See §§7-5-1 through 7-5-7 NMSA 1978.
[18] §7-1-3D NMSA 1978; §3.1.1.12 NMAC.

Tax Administration

lawfully delegated to that employee by the Secretary.[19]

¶ 17.5 Investigative Authority and Powers

The TRD has very broad investigative powers to establish or determine tax liability, collect tax, investigate criminal or fraudulent activities, and enforce any statute under the TAA. Thus, the Secretary or the Secretary's delegate may examine equipment, require the production of any pertinent records, books, information, or evidence, require the presence of any person, and require that person to testify under oath.[20] The TRD's broad investigative powers extend to persons other than the taxpayer who may be examined and include accountants, banks and financial corporations, lessors, vendors, buyers, corporate officers, corporate stockholders and general and limited partners.[21]

The term "person" is very broad and means any individual, estate, trust, receiver, cooperative association, club, corporation, company, firm, partnership, limited liability company, limited liability partnership, joint venture, syndicate, other association or gas, water or electric utility owned or operated by a county or municipality. The term also means, to the extent permitted by law, a federal, state or other governmental unit or subdivision, or an agency, department, or instrumentality thereof. With regard to tax fraud, attempts to defeat tax, causing another to evade tax, or interfering with the administration of revenue laws, a person also includes an officer or employee of a corporation, a member or employee of a partnership, or any individual who is under a duty to perform any act in respect of which a violation occurs.[22]

¶ 17.5.1 Subpoenas and summons

The Secretary is authorized to issue subpoenas and summonses as a means to enforcing the TRD's broad investigatory powers. These must bear the seal of the TRD and be attested by the Secretary. They must state with reasonable certainty the nature of the evidence required to be produced, the time and place of the hearing, the nature of the

---

[19] §7-1-3B NMSA 1978.
[20] §7-1-4A NMSA 1978.
[21] §3.1.1.14 NMAC.
[22] §7-1-3P NMSA 1978.

inquiry or investigation, and the consequences of a failure to obey. A subpoena or summons may not be made returnable less than ten days from the date of service.[23]

The TRD may seek the aid of the court if a person neglects or refuses to appear, to produce records or other evidence, to allow the inspection of equipment, or to give testimony as required. The court may issue an order requiring the person to appear and testify or to produce books or records, and, upon failure to comply, may punish the person for contempt.[24]

If a taxpayer, or an agent, nominee, or other person directed or controlled by the taxpayer, files an action to quash a subpoena or summons, the running of the period of limitations is suspended with respect to the tax liability under investigation while a proceeding and related appeals regarding the subpoena or summons is pending.[25]

¶ 17.6 Notice of Potential Eligibility Required

When the TRD mails out income tax refunds or other notices to taxpayers, it must include a notice to taxpayers whose income is within 130% of federal poverty guidelines (as defined by the United States census bureau) that they may be eligible for food stamps. The notice must include general information about food stamps, such as where to apply, based on information received from the Human Services Department by January 30 of each calendar year.[26]

¶17.7 Confidentiality of Returns And Other Information

New Mexico has very strict rules concerning the disclosure of confidential tax return information. Except when authorized by statute, it is unlawful for any person other than the taxpayer to reveal to any other person the taxpayer's PIT return or information from the taxpayer's PIT return.[27] Although a person can disclose the person's own information, a taxpayer cannot waive the applicability of the disclosure rules and allow TRD employees to disclose tax return

---

[23] §7-1-4B,C NMSA 1978.
[24] §7-1-4D NMSA 1978.
[25] §7-1-4E NMSA 1978.
[26] §7-1-4.4 NMSA 1978.
[27] §7-1-8 NMSA 1978. See §§7-1-8.1- 7.1.8.10 NMSA 1978.

Tax Administration

information.[28]

A "return" means any tax or information return, declaration of estimated tax or claim for refund, including any amendments or supplements to the return, required or permitted pursuant to a law subject to administration and enforcement pursuant to the TAA and filed with the Secretary or the Secretary's delegate by or on behalf of any person.[29]

"Return information" means a taxpayer's name, address, government-issued identification number and other identifying information. It also means any information contained in or derived from a taxpayer's return. Return information includes any information with respect to any actual or possible administrative or legal action by an employee of the TRD concerning a taxpayer's return, such as audits, managed audits, denial of credits or refunds, assessments of tax, penalty or interest, protests of assessments or denial of refunds or credits, levies or liens; or any other information with respect to a taxpayer's return or tax liability that was not obtained from public sources or that was created by an employee of the TRD. But "return information" does not include statistical data or other information that cannot be associated with or directly or indirectly identify a particular taxpayer.[30]

A number of statutory exceptions (as provided in §7-1-8.1 through §7.1.18.10) permit disclosure of taxpayer return information in prescribed situations. A discussion of these exceptions follows.

A. *Information provided to other TRD employees*

An employee of the TRD may reveal a return or return information to the taxpayer or to the taxpayer's authorized representative, or to another TRD employee whose official duties require the information. However, this exception does not require an employee to testify in a judicial proceeding, except as provided in paragraph D below.[31]

---

[28] There is no provision in the TAA allowing a taxpayer to "waive" the disclosure rules as applied to a TRD employee or former employee. Thus, the Secretary will not accept or approve a purported waiver of confidentiality from taxpayers who attempt to make lawful that which is unlawful for employees and former employees of the TRD. §3.1.3.11 NMAC.
[29] §7-1-3S NMSA 1978.
[30] §7-1-3T NMSA 1978.
[31] §7-1-8.1 NMSA 1978.

New Mexico Personal Income Tax

B. *Information required to be revealed*

The TRD is under obligation to reveal certain kinds income tax information,[32] as listed below:

- The TRD must furnish income tax returns and return information that is required under law to be made available to the public.
- The TRD must answer all inquiries concerning whether a person is a registered taxpayer for tax programs requiring registration (but may not answer inquiries concerning whether a person has filed a tax return); and
- With regard to tax abatements, the TRD must furnish upon request for inspection by a member of the public, the taxpayer name, abatement, refund or credit amount, tax program or business tax credit, and the date that the abatement, refund or credit was issued.[33]
- The TRD must furnish, upon request for inspection by a member of the public installment agreements in excess of $1,000.[34]

However, these rules may not be interpreted to require the release of information that would violate an agreement between the state and the IRS for sharing of information or any provision or rule of the IRC to which a state is subject.[35]

C. *Information that may be revealed to public*

Not all taxpayer information is confidential. Certain income tax information may be released to the public and may be revealed by an employee of the TRD:[36]

- information obtained through the administration of a law not subject to administration and enforcement under the TAA, but only to the extent that revealing that information is not otherwise prohibited by law;[37]

---

[32] §7-1-8.2 NMSA 1978.
[33] §§7-1-28E; 7-1-29G NMSA 1978.
[34] §7-1-21F NMSA 1978.
[35] §7-1-8.2B NMSA 1978.
[36] For rules concerning taxes other than income tax, see §7-1-8.3B NMSA 1978.
[37] §7-1.8.3A NMSA 1978.

Tax Administration

- a decision and order made by a hearing officer pursuant to the provisions of the Administrative Hearings Office Act with respect to a protest filed with the Secretary on or after July 1, 1993;[38]
- any written ruling on questions of evidence or procedure made by a hearing officer under the Administrative Hearings Office Act, but the name and identification number of the taxpayer requesting the ruling may not be revealed;[39]
- return information included in a notice of lien or release or extinguishment of lien;[40] and
- where payment warrants are issued in response to a claim for a refund that are required to be available for public inspection (that is, refunds and credits in excess of $10,000),[41] the warrants are not confidential information.[42]

A return or return information is not subject to the confidentiality rules once it is lawfully made public by a TRD employee or any other person, or is made public by the taxpayer.[43]

> **Example.** A loan company requests a TRD employee to provide the mailing address of a taxpayer and the amount of a state warrant which was processed as a refund or rebate from an income tax return. Since the requested information was derived from information contained in a taxpayer return, and the taxpayer had not made a claim for refund, it is unlawful for the employee to reveal this information.44

D. *Information that may be revealed to judicial bodies or with respect to proceedings or investigations and to administrative hearings office*

TRD employees may reveal the following income tax information to courts or the administrative hearing office.[45]

---

[38] §7-1.8.3D NMSA 1978.
[39] §7-1.8.3E NMSA 1978.
[40] §7-1-8.3F NMSA 1978.
[41] §7-1-29G NMSA 1978.
[42] §3.1.3.8 NMAC. (Issued under prior law.)
[43] §7-1-8D NMSA 1978.
[44] Based upon the example in §3.1.3.8 NMAC (Issued under prior law, but still appears relevant).
[45] §7-1-8.4 NMSA 1978; **§3.1.3.12 NMAC.**

Court, agency, or 3rd party	Information that may be disclosed
District court, appellate court, or a federal court	In responding to an order in an action relating to taxes or tax fraud or a crime involving taxes due to the state and in which the information is about a taxpayer who is party to the action and material to the inquiry, but with regard to information to be produced in court and admitted in evidence, only if subject to a court order protecting its confidentiality;
	In an action in which the TRD attempts to enforce an act with which the TRD is charged or to collect a tax; or in any matter in which the TRD is a party and the taxpayer has put the taxpayer's own tax liability at issue, in which case only information regarding the taxpayer may be produced, but TRD may reveal policy or interpretation of law arising regarding a taxpayer that is not a party.[46]
Bernalillo county metropolitan court or to a magistrate court	TRD employees may provide the last known address and date of that address for every person the court certifies owes fines, fees or costs to the court or who has failed to appear pursuant to a court order or a promise to appear.[47]
DA, a state district court or federal grand jury,	TRD employees may provide information for an investigation or proceeding related to alleged criminal tax law violations.[48]
Third party subject to a subpoena or levy issued pursuant to the TAA	TRD employees may provide the identity of the taxpayer involved, the taxes or tax acts involved, and the nature of the proceeding.[49]
Administrative Hearings Office	TRD employees may provide information relating to a protest or hearing, but only regarding the taxpayer who is a party, but this does not prevent revelation of TRD policy or interpretation of law arising from circumstances of a taxpayer that is not a party. The office must maintain confidentiality of this taxpayer information.[50]

---

[46] §7-1-8.4A NMSA 1978.
[47] §7-1-8.4B and C NMSA 1978.
[48] §7-1-8.4D NMSA 1978.

Tax Administration

Whenever an order for bankruptcy relief is entered under Title 11 of the United States Code with respect to a taxpayer, the taxpayer is deemed to have put his tax liability at issue, and the TRD is deemed to be a party to the bankruptcy proceeding. The bankruptcy court may enter an order allowing any other party in the bankruptcy case to obtain information from the TRD regarding the debtor-taxpayer upon showing relevance and need for the information. The TRD may release information pursuant to such an order.[51] The bankruptcy trustee, the United States trustee, and any court-appointed examiner or liquidating agent in a Chapter 11 case is deemed the taxpayer's authorized representative and the TRD may release information concerning the taxpayer and the taxpayer's tax liabilities to such representative.[52]

E. Information that may be revealed to national governments or their agencies

A TRD employee may reveal return information to a representative of the Secretary of the Treasury or a delegate under the terms of a reciprocal agreement with the federal government for the exchange of information; and to the national tax administration agencies of Mexico and Canada, but only if the receiving agency has entered into a written agreement with the TRD to use the information only for tax purposes and the information is subject to a confidentiality and penalty statute similar to those of New Mexico.[53]

> **Example.** A representative of the United States Treasury Department's Alcohol, Tobacco and Firearms Bureau (ATFB) requests a TRD employee to provide information contained in a taxpayer's return. Since the ATFB is not the authorized representative of the Secretary of the Treasury under a reciprocal agreement, it is unlawful for any TRD employee to

---

[49] §7-1-8.4E NMSA 1978.
[50] §7-1-8.4F NMSA 1978; For confidentiality provisions, see §7-1-8 NMSA 1978.
[51] §3.1.3.14A NMAC.
[52] §3.1.3.14B NMAC.
[53] §7-1-8.5 NMSA 1978. The Secretary must maintain a permanent record of the reciprocal agreements between the TRD and the representative of the Secretary of the Treasury for exchange of tax information. The proper representative of the Secretary of the Treasury must be identified in the agreement. Identification of proper representatives may be made by job title or job description. §3.1.3.10 NMAC.

New Mexico Personal Income Tax

fulfill the request.[54]

F. Information that may be revealed to certain tribal governments

A TRD employee may reveal return information to an authorized representative of an Indian nation, tribe or pueblo, located wholly or partially within New Mexico, but only if: 1) the information is provided pursuant to a written reciprocal agreement between the TRD and the Indian nation, tribe or pueblo for the exchange of that information for tax purposes only, and 2) the Indian nation, tribe or pueblo has enacted a confidentiality statute and penalty similar to those of New Mexico.[55]

G. Information that may be revealed to other states or multistate administrative bodies

New Mexico has entered into information sharing agreements with other states and the multistate tax commission. Under the terms of these agreements, a TRD employee may reveal return information in the following cases.

- Authorized representative of state or local governments. The TRD may disclose return information to an authorized representative of another state or an authorized representative of a local government of another state who is charged under the laws of that state with the responsibility for administration of that state's tax laws. This exception only applies if the receiving state or local government has entered into a written agreement with the TRD to use the return information for tax purposes only and that the receiving state has enacted a confidentiality statute and penalty similar those of New Mexico to which the representative is subject.[56]
- Multistate tax commission and federation of tax administrators. The TRD may disclose return information to the multistate tax commission, the federation of tax

---

[54] Based on the example in §3.1.3.10 NMAC.
[55] §7-1-8.6 NMSA 1978. The Secretary must retain all reciprocal exchange-of-information agreements between the TRD and Indian nations, tribes or pueblos which permit employees of the TRD to reveal to the information contained in the return of a taxpayer or other information about a taxpayer. §3.1.3.9 NMAC.
[56] The Secretary must retain all reciprocal exchange-of-information agreements between the TRD and other states that permit the TRD to reveal information contained in the return of a taxpayer or other information about a taxpayer. §3.1.3.9 NMAC.

Tax Administration

administrators or their authorized representatives, but only if the return information is used for tax purposes and is revealed by the multistate tax commission or the federation of tax administrators only to states that enacted a confidentiality statute and penalty similar those of New Mexico.[57]

A "state" is any state of the United States, the District of Columbia, the commonwealth of Puerto Rico and any territory or possession of the United States.[58]

H. Information that may be revealed to other state agencies

A TRD employee may reveal tax] information to other state agencies in the following cases (among others).

---

[57] §7-1-8.7 NMSA 1978.
[58] §7-1-3X NMSA 1978.

New Mexico Personal Income Tax

State Agency	Information that may be disclosed
Commissioner of Public Lands	Return information for use in auditing that pertains to rentals, royalties, fees and other payments due the state under land sale, land lease or other land use contracts
Secretary of Human Services or the Secretary's delegate	The last known address with date of all names certified to the TRD as being absent parents of children receiving public financial assistance, but only for the purpose of enforcing the support liability of the absent parents by the child support enforcement division or any successor organizational unit
Department of Information Technology	By electronic media, a database updated quarterly that contains the names, addresses, county of address and taxpayer identification numbers of New Mexico personal income tax filers, but only for the purpose of producing the random jury list for the selection of petit or grand jurors for the state courts;[59] and to the state courts, the random jury lists so produced
Public Regulation Commission	Information with respect to the Corporate Income and Franchise Tax Act required to enable the commission to carry out its duties
Director of the Workers' Compensation Administration or to the Director's authorized representatives	Return information to facilitate the identification of taxpayers that are delinquent or noncompliant in payment of fees[60]
Secretary of Workforce Solutions or the Secretary's delegate	Return information for use in enforcement of unemployment insurance collections pursuant to the terms of a written reciprocal agreement entered into by the department with the Secretary of Workforce Solutions for exchange of information[61]

I. Income tax information that may be revealed to private persons other than the taxpayer

A TRD employee may reveal to a corporation authorized under the Educational Assistance Act the last known address of every absent obligor of an educational debt owed the corporation or that the

---

[59] Pursuant to §38- 5-3 NMSA 1978.
[60] As required by §§52-1-9.1 or 52-5-19 NMSA 1978.
[61] §7-1-8.8L NMSA 1978.

Tax Administration

corporation has contracted to collect. This information may only be used by the corporation to enforce the educational debt obligations of the absent obligors.[62]

J. Disclosure to authorized representative

A TRD employee may reveal taxpayer information to a taxpayer's authorized representative.[63] The authorization of any person to be a representative of a taxpayer, other than in the case of an attorney or an accountant licensed to practice in New Mexico, or, with respect to income tax only, an enrolled agent, must be in writing, must contain sufficient information for the TRD to identify the taxpayer and the representative, and must be signed by the taxpayer.[64] Form ACD - 31102, *Tax Information Authorization*, is provided for this purpose.[65] See ¶ 17.3 for a discussion of authorized representatives.

K. Restrictions on process of revealing information

When revealing income tax return or return information described in paragraphs A through J above, the following rules must be observed:

- The information may only be revealed to a person specifically authorized to receive the information and the employees, directors, officers and agents of such person whose official duties or duties in the course of their employment require the information and to an employee of the TRD.
- The information may only be revealed for the authorized purpose and only to the extent necessary to perform that authorized purpose.
- The information must at all times be protected from being revealed to an unauthorized person by physical, electronic or

---

[62] §7-1-8.10 NMSA 1978. In 1981 the legislature established the New Mexico Educational Assistance Foundation (NMEAF), and the New Mexico Student Loan Guarantee Corporation (NMSLGC), which are §501(c)(3) corporations, to stimulate the availability of financial assistance for post-secondary education (New Mexico Code - Article 21A, Educational Assistance Act.). NMEAF operates New Mexico Student Loans (NMSL), a provider of student loans and a servicer of student loan programs for itself and others; and Community Outreach, a variety of programs assisting students and their families to save and pay for post-secondary education.
[63] §7-1-8.1B NMSA 1978; §3.1.3.13B NMAC.
[64] §3.1.3.13A NMAC.
[65] See http://www.tax.newmexico.gov/Tax-Professionals/tax-authorization-procedure.aspx. Last viewed October 14, 2016.

any other safeguards specified by directive by the Secretary.
- The information must be returned to the Secretary or the Secretary's delegate or destroyed as soon as it is no longer required for the authorized purpose.[66]

L. Requirement for a written agreement

Whenever a written agreement between a person and the TRD is required when revealing tax return or return information, the written agreement must meet the following requirements:

- list the name and position of any official or employee of the person to whom a return or return information is authorized to be revealed under the provision,
- describe the specific purpose for which the return or return information is to be used,
- describe the procedures and safeguards the person has in place to ensure that the requirements of Paragraph K, above, are met, and

provide for reimbursement to the TRD for all costs incurred by the TRD in supplying the returns or return information to and administering the agreement with the person.[67]

---

[66] §7-1-8B NMSA 1978.
[67] §7-1-8C NMSA 1978.

CHAPTER 18
RECORD RETENTION REQUIREMENTS

¶ 18.1 Required Taxpayer Records

Taxpayers must maintain books of account, documents and other records in a manner that permits the accurate computation of state taxes and provides the information required by statute.[1] The tax regulations go a bit further and require a taxpayer to maintain *all records* that are necessary to a determination of the correct tax liability.[2]

Upon request, taxpayers must provide the TRD with these records. There is no statutory time limit for the retention of books of account or other records, but the regulations state that all required records must be preserved unless the TRD has provided in writing that the records are no longer required.[3] However, this instruction should be taken in the context of the statute of limitations, which sets time limits for assessing tax.

¶ 18.1.1 Insufficient records and alternative methods used to determine taxes due

Records are considered insufficient if the taxpayer's state tax liability cannot be accurately or readily computed from taxpayer records. The inadequacy of records is a question of fact to be determined by the TRD. The failure of a taxpayer to keep adequate books of account or other records may cause the TRD to use alternative methods to determine or estimate taxes due.[4] The TRD may use any reasonable method of estimating a tax liability, including but not limited to using information about similar persons, businesses or industries, to estimate

---

[1] §7-1-10A NMSA 1978; §3.1.5.8A NMAC.
[2] §3.1.5.15B(1) NMAC
[3] §3.1.5.15I NMAC.
[4] §3.1.5.8B NMAC.

the taxpayer's liability.[5]

Several alternative methods may be used by the TRD, including, but not limited to the following:

- bank deposit method;
- documents and records of persons other than the taxpayer;
- federal returns and other government reports;
- cost of sales markup -- weighted percentage;
- net worth analysis;
- industry comparison; and
- provisional assessment of taxes based on best available information and allowing for any increase which may have occurred due to inflation, increased economic activity, or other reasons.

Any one or a combination of these methods or other methods may be used for reconstruction or verification of taxpayer records.[6]

¶ 18.1.2 Records reconstruction

The TRD may reconstruct the records of a person to establish or determine the extent of tax liability. The nonexistence or inadequacy of the records, for whatever reason, is the pertinent fact permitting reconstruction.[7]

> *Example.* A taxpayer's records for one audit year were destroyed accidentally. The TRD auditor is permitted to use the bank deposit method to reconstruct sales and income for that year.[8]

¶ 18.2 Alternative Storage Media

When storing or retaining records, taxpayers may convert hardcopy documents received or produced in the normal course of business to microfilm, microfiche, or other storage-only imaging systems, and may discard the original hardcopy. The term "hardcopy" refers to any

---

[5] §7-1-11D NMSA 1978.
[6] §3.1.5.8C- D NMAC.
[7] §3.1.5.9A NMAC.
[8] §3.1.5.9B NMAC.

Record Retention Requirements

documents, records, reports, or other data printed on paper.[9] A "storage-only imaging system" is a system of computer hardware and software that provides for the storage, retention and retrieval of documents originally created on paper. It does not include any system, or part of a system, that manipulates or processes any information or data contained on the document in any manner other than to reproduce the document in hardcopy or as an optical image.[10]

Documents which may be stored on these media include, but are not limited to, general books of account, journals, voucher registers, general and subsidiary ledgers and supporting records of details, such as sales invoices, purchase invoices, exemption certificates, and credit memoranda.

Microfilm, microfiche and other storage-only imaging systems must meet the following requirements insuring their integrity:

- Documentation establishing the procedures for converting the hardcopy documents to microfilm, microfiche or other storage only imaging system must be maintained and made available on request. Such documentation should, at a minimum, contain a sufficient description to allow an original document to be followed through the conversion system as well as internal procedures established for inspection and quality assurance.
- Procedures must be established for the effective identification, processing, storage and preservation of the stored documents, and for making them available for the period they are required to be retained.
- Upon request by the TRD, a taxpayer must provide facilities and equipment for reading, locating, and reproducing any documents maintained on microfilm, microfiche or other storage-only imaging system.
- When displayed on such equipment or reproduced on paper, the documents must exhibit a high degree of legibility and readability. Legibility is defined as the quality of a letter or numeral that enables the observer to identify it positively and quickly to the exclusion of all other letters or numerals.

---

[9] §3.1.5.15A(3) NMAC.
[10] §3.1.5.15A(5) NMAC.

Readability is defined as the quality of a group of letters or numerals being recognizable as words or complete numbers.
- All data stored on microfilm, microfiche or other storage-only imaging systems must be maintained and arranged in a manner that permits the location of any particular record.
- There is no substantial evidence that the microfilm, microfiche or other storage-only imaging system, lacks authenticity or integrity.[11]

¶ 18.3 Machine-Sensible Records

When machine-sensible records are used to establish tax compliance, these records must contain sufficient transaction-level detail so that the underlying details can be identified and made available to the TRD. A taxpayer may discard duplicated records and redundant information provided its recordkeeping and retention responsibilities are nevertheless being met.[12] A "machine-sensible record" is defined as a collection of related information in an electronic format and does not include hardcopy records that are created or recorded on paper or stored in or by an imaging system such as microfilm, microfiche or storage-only imaging systems.[13]

A taxpayer may demonstrate tax compliance with traditional hardcopy documents or reproductions, in whole or in part, whether or not the taxpayer also has retained or has the capability to retain records on electronic or other storage media.[14] However, if a taxpayer retains records in both machine-sensible and hardcopy formats, the taxpayer must make the records available to the TRD in machine-sensible format upon request of the TRD.[15] The TRD may request hardcopy printouts in lieu of retained machine-sensible records at the time of examination.[16] If hardcopy records are not produced or received in the ordinary course of transacting business (e.g., when the taxpayer uses electronic data interchange technology), such hardcopy records need

---

[11] §3.1.5.15G NMAC.
[12] §3.1.5.15C(1)(a) NMAC.
[13] §3.1.5.15A(4) NMAC.
[14] §3.1.5.15B(3) NMAC.
[15] §3.1.5.15B(2) NMAC.
[16] §3.1.5.15H(5) NMAC.

Record Retention Requirements

not be created.[17] Computer printouts that are created for validation, control, or other temporary purposes need not be retained.[18]

At the time of an examination, the retained records must be retrievable and convertible to a standard record format.[19] Taxpayers are not required to construct machine-sensible records other than those created in the ordinary course of business. A taxpayer who does not create the electronic equivalent of a traditional paper document or store the information in machine-sensible records in the ordinary course of business is not required to construct a machine-sensible record for tax purposes.[20]

¶18.3.1 Electronic data interchange requirements.

"Electronic data interchange" or EDI means the computer-to-computer exchange of business transactions in a standardized structured electronic format.[21] When a taxpayer uses EDI, the record detail, in combination with other records, must be equivalent to those contained in an acceptable paper record. For example, the retained records should contain the vendor name, invoice date, product description, quantity purchased, price, etc. Codes may be used to identify the data elements, provided that a method is provided allowing the TRD to interpret the coded information.[22]

A taxpayer may capture the information necessary to satisfy its record keeping responsibilities at any level within the accounting system and need not retain the original EDI transaction records provided the audit trail, authenticity and integrity of the retained records can be established.

> *Example.* A taxpayer using EDI technology receives electronic invoices from its suppliers. The taxpayer decides to retain the invoice data from completed and verified EDI transactions in its accounts payable system rather than to retain the EDI transactions themselves. Since neither the EDI transaction nor the accounts payable system capture information from the

---

[17] §3.1.5.15H(2) NMAC.
[18] §3.1.5.15G(4) NMAC.
[19] §3.1.5.15C(1)(b) NMAC.
[20] §3.1.5.15C(1)(c) NMAC.
[21] §3.1.5.15A(2) NMAC
[22] §3.1.5.15C(2)(a) NMAC.

invoice pertaining to product description and vendor name (i.e., they contain only codes for that information), the taxpayer also retains other records, such as its vendor master file and product code description lists and makes them available to the TRD. In this example, the taxpayer need not retain its EDI transaction for tax purposes.[23]

¶ 18.3.2 Electronic Data Processing Systems Requirements

The requirements for an electronic data processing accounting system are similar to that of a manual accounting system, in that an adequately designed accounting system should incorporate methods and records that will satisfy the statutory and regulatory recordkeeping requirements.[24]

¶ 18.3.3 Business Process Information

If requested by the TRD, the taxpayer must provide a description of the business process that created the retained records. The description must include the relationship between the records and the tax documents prepared by the taxpayer and the measures employed to ensure the integrity of the records.[25]

The taxpayer must be capable of demonstrating:
1. the functions being performed as they relate to the flow of data through the system;
2. the internal controls used to ensure accurate and reliable processing, and;
3. the internal controls used to prevent unauthorized addition, alteration or deletion of retained records.[26]

The following specific documentation is required for retained machine sensible records:
1. record formats or layouts;
2. field definitions (including the meaning of all codes used to represent information);
3. file descriptions (e.g., data set name); and

---

[23] §3.1.5.15C(2)(b) NMAC.
[24] §3.1.5.15C(3) NMAC.
[25] §3.1.5.15C(4)(a) NMAC.
[26] §3.1.5.15C[4][b] NMAC.

Record Retention Requirements

4. detailed charts of accounts and account descriptions.[27]

¶ 18.3.4 TRD access to machine-sensible records

The taxpayer may provide the TRD with access to machine-sensible records using a variety of means that take into account a taxpayer's facts and circumstances in consultation with the taxpayer. Such access will be provided in one or more of the following ways:

- the taxpayer may arrange to provide the TRD with the hardware, software and personnel resources to access the records;
- the taxpayer may arrange for a third-party to provide the hardware, software and personnel resources necessary to access the records;
- the taxpayer may convert the machine sensible records to a standard record format specified by the TRD, including copies of files, on a magnetic medium that is agreed to by the TRD;
- the taxpayer and the TRD may agree on other means of providing access to the machine sensible records.[28]

A taxpayer may create files solely for the use of the TRD. For example, if a database management system is used, the taxpayer may create and retain a file that contains the transaction-level detail from the database management system. The taxpayer should document the process that created the separate file to show the relationship between that file and the original records.[29] A "database management system" is a software system that controls, relates, retrieves and provides accessibility to data stored in a database.[30]

¶ 18.3.5 Records maintenance requirements

The taxpayer's computer hardware or software must accommodate the extraction and conversion of retained machine-sensible records.[31] The TRD recommends but does not require taxpayers to use the national archives and record administration's (NARA) standards for guidance

---

[27] §3.1.5.15C[4][c] NMAC.
[28] §3.1.5.15D(2) NMAC.
[29] §3.1.5.15F(1) NMAC.
[30] §3.1.5.15A(1) NMAC.
[31] §3.1.5.15D(2) NMAC.

on the maintenance and storage of electronic records.[32] A taxpayer may contract with a third party to provide custodial or management services of the records, but such a contract does not relieve the taxpayer of its responsibilities.[33]

---

[32] §3.1.5.15D(1) NMAC. The NARA standards may be found at 36 Code of Federal Regulations, Part 1234.
[33] §3.1.5.15F(2) NMAC.

CHAPTER 19

COLLECTION AND ENFORCEMENT

¶ 19.1 Assessments of tax

19.1.1 Methods of assessment

If the TRD determines that a taxpayer is liable for taxes in excess of $25.00 that are due and have not been assessed, the TRD is required to promptly assess the amount.[1] When taxes have been assessed and remain unpaid, the TRD may demand payment at any time, except if prevented by the statute of limitations.[2]

Assessments of tax are effective:

- when a tax return of a taxpayer is received by the TRD showing a liability for taxes;
- when a notice of assessment of taxes is mailed or delivered in person to the taxpayer stating the nature and amount of the taxes owed, demanding immediate payment, and briefly informing the taxpayer of the remedies available; or
- when an effective jeopardy assessment is made.[3]

Any assessment of taxes or demand for payment made by the TRD is presumed to be correct. The presumption of correctness also applies to any interest and penalty imposed.[4]

The effect of the presumption of correctness is that the taxpayer has the burden of coming forward with countervailing evidence tending to dispute the factual correctness of the assessment made by the TRD. Unsubstantiated statements that the assessment is incorrect cannot overcome the presumption of correctness. The presumption

---

[1] §7-1-17A NMSA 1978.
[2] §7-1-19 NMSA 1978.
[3] §7-1-17B NMSA 1978.
[4] §§3.1.6.12; 3.1.6.13 NMAC

exists even if the TRD has issued assessments using alternative methods of reconstruction of a tax or has estimated the tax.[5]

When a tax return is submitted by a taxpayer and received by the TRD, this self-assessment constitutes an effective assessment. Self-assessments by taxpayers are not, however, presumed to be correct.[6]

¶19.1.2 Delinquent taxpayers

Once taxes have been assessed or a demand for payment made,[7] the taxpayer becomes delinquent if within 90 days after the date of the assessment the taxpayer does not make payment, protest the assessment or demand for payment, or furnish security for payment. The taxpayer remains delinquent until:

- payment of the total amount is made;
- security is furnished for payment; or
- no part of the assessment remains unabated.[8]

Any taxpayer who protests only a portion of an assessment and neither pays the unprotested portion within 30 days after the date of assessment nor posts security covering the unprotested amount is delinquent until the unprotested amount is paid or security posted.[9]

A taxpayer does not become a delinquent if the assessment is a result of a managed audit and the taxpayer is still within the 180-day period allowed for payment in such cases.[10]

Any taxpayer who fails to provide security as required by the Secretary when protesting assessments or tax due in excess of $200,000 will be considered a delinquent taxpayer.[11]

A taxpayer that files a protest is nevertheless delinquent if he or she or an authorized representative fails to appear at the hearing as set or fails to perfect an appeal from any adverse decision to the next appellate level, unless the taxpayer pays the total taxes assessed and

---

[5] §3.1.6.12 NMAC.
[6] §3.1.6.10 NMAC
[7] As provided in §7-1- 63 NMSA 1978.
[8] §7-1-16A NMSA 1978.
[9] §3.1.6.8 NMAC.
[10] §7-1-16D NMSA 1978; §7-1-67A[4] NMSA 1978.
[11] §7-1-16B NMSA 1978; §7-1-54D NMSA 1978.

Collection and Enforcement

remaining unabated or furnishes security.[12]

¶ 19.1.3 Penalties and interest

Any civil penalty and interest may be collected concurrently and in the same manner as the tax to which it relates, without assessment or separate proceedings of any kind.[13]

¶ 19.1.4 Statutes of limitations on assessment or collection

The TRD may not make a tax assessment after three years from the end of the calendar year in which payment of the tax was due. Consequently, if there is no timely prior assessment, the TRD cannot begin a court proceeding for the collection of tax.[14] If the taxpayer's return understates his or her tax liability by more than 25%, the limitation period is extended to six years.[15] In case of a taxpayer's false or fraudulent return with intent to evade tax, the limitation on assessment and court proceedings is extended to ten years.[16]

If a taxpayer has failed to complete and file a return, the tax relating to the period for which the return was required may be assessed at any time within seven years from the end of the calendar year in which the tax was due. If there is no assessment within that period, the TRD may not initiate a court proceeding for the collection of such tax after the expiration of seven-year period.[17]

A taxpayer's federal tax may be adjusted as a result of an IRS audit or the filing of an amended return that changes an election or makes other changes requiring federal approval. If these adjustments result in an increased New Mexico income tax liability, that amount may not be assessed after three years from the end of the calendar year in which filing of a New Mexico amended return is required.[18]

If the taxpayer has signed a waiver of the limitations on assessment, an assessment of tax may be made or a proceeding in court begun

---

[12] §7-1-16C NMSA 1978.
[13] §7-1-30 NMSA 1978.
[14] §7-1-18A NMSA 1978.
[15] §7-1-18D NMSA 1978.
[16] §7-1-18B NMSA 1978.
[17] §7-1-18C NMSA 1978.
[18] §7-1-18E NMSA 1978; §7-1-13C NMSA 1978.

without regard to the time at which payment of the tax was due.[19]

Even if an assessment or notice of assessment is within the time limits of the statutes of limitations, no action or proceeding to collect taxes may be brought under an assessment or notice of the assessment after the later of either

- ten years from the date of the assessment or notice or,
- with respect to undischarged amounts in a bankruptcy proceeding, one year after the later of the issuance of the final order or the date of the last scheduled payment.[20]

An "action or proceeding" includes the filing of a lien, seizure of property through service of a warrant of levy, demand for security to cover the liability, sale of security which has previously been posted, demand for payment, civil action in district court, injunction to enjoin the taxpayer from engaging in business or foreclosure of a lien. The term does not include processing any payment made by a taxpayer when no other act has been initiated by the TRD after ten years from the date.[21]

¶ 19.1.5 Installment agreements

Under justifiable circumstances, the TRD may enter into a written agreement in which the taxpayer admits liability for the entire amount of taxes due and agrees to make monthly installment payments, but not for a period longer than 60 months. An installment agreement does not prevent the accrual of interest.[28] If an installment agreement is entered into after a court acquires jurisdiction over the matter, the agreement will be part of a stipulated order or judgment disposing of the case.[29]

The Secretary must require security for payment of the taxes admitted to be due, but if the taxpayer does not provide security, a notice of lien will be filed.[30]

---

[19] §7-1-18F NMSA 1978
[20] §7-1-19 NMSA 1978.
[21] §3.1.1.17 NMAC.
[28] §7-1-21A NMSA 1978.
[29] §7-1-21B NMSA 1978.
[30] §7-1-21C NMSA 1978. The lien is filed in accordance with the provisions of §7-1-38 NMSA 1978 and constitutes a lien upon all the property or rights to property of the taxpayer

Collection and Enforcement

Although an installment agreement is conclusive as to liability for the amount of taxes specified in the agreement, it does not preclude the assessment of any additional tax.[31]

Except in unusual circumstances that require the Secretary in his or her discretion to take action to protect the interests of the state, the Secretary may make no attempt to enforce payment by levy or injunction after entering into the agreement. But if installment payments are not made on time, if other conditions in the agreement are not met, or if the taxpayer does not make payment of all other taxes for which he or she is liable as they are due, the Secretary may enforce collection as if the agreement had not been made or may proceed against the security furnished.[32]

Records of installment agreements in excess of $1,000 are to be available for inspection by the public. The TRD must keep the records for a minimum of three years from the date of the installment agreement.[33]

¶ 19.1.6 Jeopardy assessments

If the Secretary has the reasonable belief that the collection of tax will be jeopardized by delay, the Secretary may immediately make a jeopardy assessment of the amount of tax believed to be in jeopardy.[34] A jeopardy assessment is effective upon the delivery of a document entitled *Notice of Jeopardy Assessment of Taxes* issued in the Secretary's name, stating the nature and amount of the taxes assertedly owed to the state, demanding immediate payment, and briefly informing the taxpayer of the steps that may be taken against him or her as well as of the available remedies. The jeopardy assessment document must be delivered either in person or by certified mail to the taxpayer against whom the tax liability is asserted.[35]

If a person does not pay the tax demanded or furnish satisfactory security within five days of the service of the notice of jeopardy assessment, the Secretary may immediately proceed to collect the tax

---

in that county in the same manner as provided for in §7-1-37 NMSA 1978.
[31] §7-1-21D NMSA 1978.
[32] §7-1-21E NMSA 1978.
[33] §7-1-21F NMSA 1978.
[34] §7-1-59A NMSA 1978.
[35] §7-1-59B NMSA 1978.

by levy on sufficient property of the taxpayer to satisfy the deficiency, or the Secretary may move to enjoin the taxpayer from doing business in New Mexico, or both.[36] The taxpayer may cause a levy or injunction to be stayed by filing with the TRD acceptable security in an amount equal to the amount of taxes assessed. A taxpayer to whom a jeopardy assessment has been made may dispute the jeopardy assessment by furnishing security and filing a protest, or he or she may pay the tax and claim a refund.[37]

¶ 19.2 Tax liens

¶ 19.2.1 Assessment as lien

If a person who is liable for tax neglects or refuses to pay after assessment and demand, the amount of the tax owed becomes a lien in favor of the state upon all property and property rights of the person, unless the person is entitled to protection under either §362 (automatic stay) or §1301 (stay of action against of co-debtor) of Title 11 of the United States Code (bankruptcy). The lien arises at the time both assessment and demand have been made and continues until the liability for payment is satisfied or extinguished. As against any mortgagee, pledgee, purchaser, judgment creditor, person claiming a lien, lienor for value or other encumbrancer for value, the tax lien is not be considered to have arisen or have any effect until notice of the lien has been filed.[38]

¶ 19.2.2 Notice of lien

A notice of the lien may be recorded in any county in the tax lien index and a copy must be sent to the affected taxpayer. Any county clerk presented with the notices must record them without charge. The notice of lien identifies the taxpayer, the date on which the tax became due, and the amount of tax asserted to be due, including applicable interest and penalties. The recording of the notice of lien is effective as to all property and property rights of the taxpayer.[39]

---

[36] §7-1-59C NMSA 1978.
[37] §7-1-59D NMSA 1978.
[38] §7-1-37 NMSA 1978. See Chapter 48, Liens and Mortgages NMSA 1978.
[39] §7-1-38 NMSA 1978.

Collection and Enforcement

¶ 19.2.3 Release or extinguishment of lien

When a taxpayer pays a substantial part of the tax due, the TRD will immediately file a document that completely or partially releases the lien in the county in which the notice of lien was filed.[40] The TRD may file a document releasing or partially releasing any lien when the filing of the lien was premature or did not follow requirements of law or when release or partial release would facilitate collection of taxes due. The county clerk must record these releases without charge.[41]

¶ 19.2.4 Statute of limitation on actions to enforce lien

When a notice of lien has been filed and a period of ten years has passed from the date the lien was filed, as shown on the notice of lien, the taxes, penalties and interest for which the lien is claimed are conclusively presumed to have been paid and the lien is extinguished. No action may be brought to enforce any lien so extinguished.[42]

¶ 19.2.5 Foreclosure of lien

Tax liens are foreclosed or satisfied by seizure and sale of property or property rights, except the lien in favor of a person who has redeemed the property and has a lien on the property for the amount paid in redemption.[43]

¶ 19.3. Levy of property

¶ 19.3.1 Seizure of property by levy for collection of taxes

A "levy" is the mechanism by which the TRD may take possession of or require the present or future surrender of any property or rights to property belonging to a delinquent taxpayer.[44] The TRD may collect tax from a taxpayer by levying upon the taxpayer's property or property rights and converting the property or property rights into money by

---

[40] §7-1-39A NMSA 1978.
[41] §7-1-39B NMSA 1978.
[42] §7-1-39C NMSA 1978.
[43] §7-1-40 NMSA 1978. Any person whose property has been levied upon shall have the right to pay the amount due, together with the expenses of the proceeding, or furnish acceptable security for the payment thereof according to the provisions of § 7-1-54 NMSA 1978 to the TRD at any time prior to the sale thereof. §7-1-47 NMSA 1978.
[44] §7-1-3H NMSA 1978.

New Mexico Personal Income Tax

appropriate means.[45] A levy is made in the following manner:
1. by taking possession of property pursuant a warrant of levy;
2. by the service of a warrant which orders the taxpayer or other person to reveal the extent of taxpayer's property in their possession and surrender it to the TRD, or to agree to surrender it or the proceeds in the future; or
3. by serving the warrant on:
    a. the taxpayer or other person possessing the taxpayer's property or property rights;
    b. upon the taxpayer's employer;
    c. upon any person or depositary owing or who will owe money to or holding funds of the taxpayer.[46]

Upon agreement between the TRD and a financial institution, the TRD may serve a warrant of levy on the financial institution in electronic format pursuant to the Electronic Authentication of Documents Act and the Uniform Electronic Transactions Act.[47]

¶ 19.3.2 Seizure of real property by levy

A levy on real property is made by personal service of a copy of the warrant of levy on the taxpayer-owner of the property, and by recording a copy of the levy in the county in which the property is located. The TRD must make every reasonable effort to send notice of the levy to each party with a recorded interest in the property.[48] Real property seized under warrant of levy is sold pursuant to the requirements of the TAA.[49]

¶ 19.3.3 Surrender of property upon service of levy on a financial institution

When a warrant of levy is served upon a financial institution in New Mexico, the financial institution must survey all checking accounts, savings accounts, escrows for collection, safety deposit boxes, trusts, certificates of deposit, and all other accounts or places in which it may possess or hold any property or property rights to belonging to the

---

[45] §7-1-31A NMSA 1978.
[46] §7-1-31B NMSA 1978.
[47] §7-1-31C NMSA 1978.
[48] §3.1.10.8 NMAC.
[49] See §§7-1-44 NMSA 1978 through 7-1-51 NMSA 1978.

Collection and Enforcement

taxpayer.[50]

A financial institution which is served with a warrant of levy must immediately surrender to the TRD any property or property rights of the taxpayer possessed or held by the institution as of the date of service. In failing to do so the financial institution becomes liable to the state in an amount equal to the value not surrendered. If the financial institution knows that another person possesses property or property rights of the taxpayer, it must immediately report this fact to an agent of the TRD. The financial institution is not required to reveal a mere expectation that the institution will come into the possession of the funds of the taxpayer, if there is no contractual or other legal obligation between the taxpayer, the financial institution or any third parties. A mere expectation does not constitute possession of funds.[51]

If a financial institution upon which a levy has been served complies with the above rules and the taxpayer subsequently deposits funds or property with the institution, the institution is not required to reveal this fact to the TRD until a new warrant of levy is served.[52]

The meaning of the term "financial institution" is very inclusive in this context and comprises any bank, savings and loan association, credit union, pawnshop, or any other similar entity that acts as a depository for another person's funds.[53]

¶ 19.3.4 Contents of warrant of levy

The contents of a warrant of levy must meet specific statutory requirements. In summary, the warrant of levy must -

1. bear on its face the authority for its service and compelling compliance with its terms;
2. identify the taxpayer, the amount of liability, and the date or approximate date on which the tax became due;
3. order the person on whom it is served to reveal the amount of taxpayer's property or property rights in the person's possession and the person's interest therein and to reveal the taxpayer's property or property rights that are, to the best of

---

[50] §3.1.10.9 A NMAC.
[51] §3.1.10.9 B NMAC.
[52] §3.1.10.9 C NMAC.
[53] §3.1.10.9D NMAC.

the person's knowledge, possessed by others;
4. order the immediate surrender of property, but allow a written agreement to surrender the property or the proceeds therefrom on a future date when the taxpayer's right would mature;
5. order the taxpayer's employer to surrender wages or salary in excess of the amount statutorily exempt from levy[54] owed to the taxpayer at the time of service and that may subsequently become owed until the full amount of the liability is satisfied or until notified by the TRD;
6. state the penalties for willful failure by any person to comply with its terms; and
7. state that the State of New Mexico claims a lien for the entire amount of tax asserted to be due, including applicable interest and penalties.[55]

¶ 19.3.5 Successive levies

If property or property rights upon which levy has been made is insufficient to satisfy a claim, the TRD may levy upon any other property or property rights of the person against whom the claim exists, until the amount due is fully paid. Successive levies are not necessary in the case of a levy served on the taxpayer's employer with respect to wages or salary of the taxpayer.[56]

¶ 19.3.6 Surrender of property subject to levy—penalty

Once a levy has been made on property or property rights, any person in possession of or obligated with respect to the property or rights, must surrender the property or rights, except for the part that at the time of demand is the subject of a bona fide attachment, execution, levy or other similar process. The surrender of the property can be avoided by the payment of the tax obligation. Anyone with a sufficient interest in the property can redeem the property by the payment of the obligation to the TRD.[57]

Any employer owing wages or salary to a taxpayer upon which a levy has been made must upon demand surrender to the TRD for each

---

[54] §7-1-36 NMSA 1978
[55] §7-1-32 NMSA 1978.
[56] §7-1-33 NMSA 1978.
[57] §7-1-34A NMSA 1978. See § 7-1-47 NMSA 1978 for redemption.

Collection and Enforcement

subsequent pay period that portion of the taxpayer's wages or salary not exempt from levy [58] and not subject to a prior bona fide attachment, execution, levy, garnishment or similar process, until the amount of the levy is satisfied in full or until notified by the TRD. The TRD must notify the employer promptly when the levy has been satisfied.[59]

A person that wrongfully fails or refuses to surrender or redeem any property or rights to property that is levied upon is liable for a civil penalty that is equal to the lesser of the value of the property or rights not so surrendered or the amount of the taxes for which the levy has been made.[60]

A surrender of property, property rights, or proceeds from the sale or disposition of property subject to levy discharges the obligation of the person in possession to the TRD. A surrender is a defense against the assertion of any obligation or liability to the delinquent taxpayer or any other person with respect to such property or rights to property arising from a surrender or payment.[61]

¶ 19.3.7 Stay of levy

A levy may not be made upon the property or property rights of any taxpayer who properly furnishes security.[62] A levy will be released upon the proper furnishing of security.[63]

¶ 19.3.8 Property exempt from levy

The money or property of a delinquent taxpayer not exceeding $1,000 is exempt from levy.[64] In addition, an employer of the taxpayer is exempt from levy on the greater of the following portions of the taxpayer's disposable earnings:

- 75% of the taxpayer's disposable earnings for any pay period; or
- an amount each week equal to 40 times the federal minimum

---

[58] See §7-1-36 NMSA 1978.
[59] §7-1-34B NMSA 1978.
[60] §7-1-34C NMSA 1978.
[61] §7-1-34D NMSA 1978.
[62] §7-1-35 NMSA 1978.
[63] See §7-1-54 NMSA 1978.
[64] §7-1-36A NMSA 1978.

hourly wage rate.[65]

"Disposable earnings" means that part of a taxpayer's wages or salary remaining after deducting amounts that are required to be withheld by law; and "federal minimum hourly wage" means the current highest federal minimum hourly wage rate for an 8-hour day and a 40-hour week, regardless of whether the employer is exempt under federal law from paying the federal minimum hourly wage rate.[66]

¶ 19.4 Sale of property

¶ 19.4.1 Notice of seizure and sale

As soon as practicable after levy, the TRD will notify the owner of the amount and kind of property seized and the total amount demanded in payment of tax.[67] In addition, TRD will as soon as practicable decide on a time and place for the sale of the property, make a diligent inquiry as to the identity and whereabouts of the owner and persons having an interest in the property and notify them of the time and place of sale. The validity of the sale is not affected if any person entitled to notice does not receive notice.[68]

¶ 19.4.2 Sale of indivisible property

If property subject to levy is not divisible so as to enable the TRD to raise the whole amount of the tax and expenses by selling part of the property, the taxpayer's whole interest in the property will be sold, but redemption before sale is always available.[69]

¶ 19.4.3 Requirements of sale

Perishable property may be sold immediately after seizure without publication or notice of sale. Imperishable property cannot be held for sale until after 30 days from the date of the levy, and not until after publication of a notice stating the time and place of the sale and describing the property to be sold in a general circulation newspaper in the county where the property was located when levied upon. The notice must run once each week for three successive weeks. The TRD

---

[65] §7-1-36B NMSA 1978.
[66] §7-1-36C NMSA 1978.
[67] §7-1-41 NMSA 1978.
[68] §7-1-42 NMSA 1978.
[69] §7-1-43 NMSA 1978.

must make special efforts to give notice of the sale to persons with a particular interest in special property and must, apart from the requirements stated above, advertise the sale in a manner appropriate to the kind of property to be sold.[70]

¶ 19.4.4 Sale at auction, minimum prices

Property that is levied upon, other than money, must be sold at public auction, which is required to take place at 1 pm on the steps of or in front of the courthouse of the county in which the property was located when levied upon. Alternatively, the property may be consigned to an auctioneer for sale. Payment must be in full and made immediately after the acceptance of a bid for the property. Stocks, bonds, securities and similar property may be negotiated or surrendered for money in accordance with regulations issued by the Secretary, notwithstanding the above.[71]

Before the sale, the TRD must determine a minimum price for which the property may be sold, and if no person offers the minimum price, the property may not be sold, but in this case the sale should be re-advertised and held at a later time. In determining the minimum price, the TRD must take into account the expense of making the levy and sale.[72]

¶ 19.4.5 Redemption before sale

A person whose property has been levied upon has the option prior to sale of either paying the amount due, together with the expenses of the proceeding, or furnishing security to the TRD. Upon payment or the furnishing of security, the TRD will restore the property to the person, and cease further proceedings as to the levy. A person with sufficient interest in the property or property rights to permit redemption and who redeems the property by paying the amount due has a lien against the property for the amount paid.[73]

¶ 19.4.6 Documents of title and legal effect of sale

Once property is sold and payment received, the TRD will deliver a certificate of sale to the purchaser of personal property and a deed to

---

[70] §7-1-44 NMSA 1978.
[71] §7-1-45 NMSA 1978
[72] §7-1-46 NMSA 1978
[73] §7-1-47 NMSA 1978.

the purchaser of realty. These documents of title must include a recitation of the TRD's authority for the transaction, the date of the sale, the interest in the property that is conveyed and the price paid by the purchaser.[74]

In case of personal property, the certificate of sale is:

1. prima facie evidence of the right of the TRD to make the sale and conclusive evidence of the regularity of the proceedings;
2. a transfer to the purchaser of all right, title and interest of the delinquent taxpayer in the property, subject to outstanding prior interests and encumbrances of record but free of any subsequent encumbrance;
3. in the case of stock certificates, notice to any corporation, company or association, when received, of the transfer and authority to record the transfer as if the record owner transferred or assigned the certificates;
4. if the subject of sale is securities or other evidences of debt, a good and valid receipt as against any person holding or claiming to hold possession of the securities or other evidences of debt; and
5. if such property consists of a motor vehicle as represented by its title, the certificate is notice of the transfer when received and authority to any official charged with registration of title to record the transfer on the official's books and records as if the record owner transferred or assigned the certificate of title.[75]

In the case of the sale of real property:

1. the deed of sale is prima facie evidence of the facts stated therein;
2. if the proceedings have been substantially in accordance with the provisions of law, the deed operates as a conveyance of all the right, title and interest of the delinquent taxpayer in and to the real property sold at the time the notice of lien was filed or immediately before the sale, whichever is earlier; and
3. neither the taxpayer nor anyone claiming through or under him

---

[74] §7-1-48 NMSA 1978.
[75] §7-1-49 NMSA 1978.

Collection and Enforcement

may bring an action after one year from the date of sale to challenge the conveyance.[76]

Money realized by levy or sale is first applied against the expenses of the proceedings. Any remaining amount is then applied to the tax liability for which the levy was made. Any balance remaining will be returned to a person legally entitled to it.[77]

¶ 19.4.7 Proceeds of levy and sale

The TRD may release a levy upon all or part of the property or property rights levied upon if it determines that such action will facilitate the collection of the liability and the interests of the state will continue to be protected. Such release will not prevent any subsequent levy.[78]

¶ 19.5 Injunctions and security

¶ 19.5.1 Enjoining delinquent taxpayer from continuing in business

The Secretary may seek an injunction from a state district court to have any delinquent taxpayer or other person who may be or may become liable for any tax enjoined from engaging in business in the state until the taxpayer ceases to be delinquent or until the taxpayer or person complies with other requirements, reasonably necessary to protect state revenues.[79]

The following are some examples where the Secretary may seek an injunction enjoining a taxpayer or other persons from doing business in the state:

- a taxpayer with a record of recurring tax delinquency;
- a taxpayer who does not respond to a jeopardy assessment by either paying the tax demanded or furnishing satisfactory security;
- a taxpayer who has a recurring record of attempting to pay taxes with bad checks;

---

[76] §7-1-50 NMSA 1978.
[77] §7-1-51 NMSA 1978.
[78] §7-1-52 NMSA 1978; §3.1.10.10 NMAC.
[79] §7-1-53A NMSA 1978.

- a successor in business who has wrongfully failed to withhold and pay over tax or has not made payment or surrendered property after demand of the TRD;[80]
- a tax protestor who, as a means of protesting taxation or other issues, refuses to comply with the tax law;
- a person who does not collect and pay over withholding tax from employees who perform personal services in New Mexico;
- a prime construction contractor with a principal place of business outside New Mexico, performing construction services in New Mexico, and who fails to comply with acceptable security requirements;[81]
- a person who has failed within 90 days to respond to the TRD's demand to file any tax return which was required to be filed on a date which occurred at least 45 days prior to the date of the demand to file.[82]

Upon application for an injunction against a delinquent taxpayer, the district court may issue an order temporarily restraining the taxpayer from doing business. The matter must be heard within 15 days, but a hearing may be held earlier upon written request of the taxpayer. Upon a showing of a preponderance of evidence that the taxpayer is delinquent, the court may enjoin the taxpayer from engaging in business in New Mexico until the taxpayer ceases to be delinquent. The court may also order the business premises of the taxpayer sealed by the sheriff and allow the taxpayer access only upon approval of the court.[83]

Upon application for an injunction against a person other than a delinquent taxpayer, the court may issue an order temporarily restraining the person from engaging in business. The matter should be heard within 15 days, except that a hearing may be held earlier if requested in writing by the person who is the subject of the TRO. The court may also without delay issue an injunction to the taxpayer in terms commanding the person who is the subject of the TRO to

---

[80] See §7-1-63 NMSA 1978.
[81] See §7-1-55 NMSA 1978.
[82] §3.1.10.11 NMAC.
[83] §7-1-53B NMSA 1978.

Collection and Enforcement

refrain from engaging in business until that person complies in full with the demand of the TRO to furnish security, if there is a showing that: (a) the person who is the subject of the TRO has been given proper notice of the hearing; (b) a demand by the TRD has been made upon the taxpayer to furnish security; (c) the taxpayer has not furnished security; and (d) the Secretary considers the collection from the person primarily responsible for the total amount of tax due or reasonably expected to become due to be in jeopardy.[84]

A TRO or injunction should not issue against any person who has properly furnished security. Upon a showing by any person against whom a TRO or writ of injunction has been issued that that person has properly furnished security, the court shall dissolve or set aside the TRO or injunction.[85]

A person who is subject to an impending injunction may take the following actions to avoid an injunction: pay the assessed tax, and, if applicable, submit a claim for refund, furnish acceptable security, make application for an extension of time,[86] or make application for and enter into an installment agreement.[87]

¶ 19.5.2 Security for payment of tax

When the TRD believes that it is necessary to ensure payment of a tax that is due or is reasonably expected to become due, it may require or allow a person to furnish acceptable security. The TRD will notify the person by mailing or by hand-delivering a written notice of the requirement to furnish security in the amount stated in the notice. If the person does not comply promptly, the TRD will make a written demand by certified mail or in person. Upon the failure to comply within 10 days of the date of the written demand, the Secretary may institute a proceeding to enjoin the person from engaging in business in the state.[88] The following examples illustrate some of the situations in which the TRD may require or allow the furnishing of security:

- the taxpayer is a delinquent taxpayer;

---

[84] §7-1-53C NMSA 1978.
[85] §7-1-53D NMSA 1978. See ¶19.5.2 for discussion of security for payment of tax.
[86] See §7-1-13 NMSA 1978
[87] See §7-1-21 NMSA 1978. §3.1.10.12 NMAC.
[88] §7-1-54A & B NMSA 1978; §7-1-53 NMSA 1978.

- the taxpayer is granted an extension of time to pay taxes;
- the taxpayer enters into an installment agreement;
- the taxpayer requests a stay of levy;
- the taxpayer requests permission to report and pay certain taxes on a quarterly or semiannual basis;
- the taxpayer wishes to avoid an impending restraining order or an injunction proceeding;
- the taxpayer wishes to stay the enforcement of a jeopardy assessment;
- a successor in business has failed to withhold the amount of the tax liability of the predecessor or to pay the tax or surrender the property;
- the taxpayer is conducting a business of a transient nature;
- the taxpayer has a recurring record of attempted payment of tax liabilities with bad checks;
- the taxpayer has failed to file any required tax returns within 45 days from the date the return was required to be filed;
- the taxpayer has engaged in business for more than three months during which period of time the taxpayer was not registered with the TRD or did not maintain an active identification number issued by the TRD.[89]

The term "security" means money, property or rights to property or a surety bond.[90] A surety bond must be conditioned upon payment no later than the date when the liability becomes conclusive. Other security than a surety bond may be acceptable and additional security can be requested as necessary.[91] Surety bonds accepted as security must be payable to the state of New Mexico upon demand by the Secretary or the Secretary's delegate and a showing to the surety that the principal debtor is a delinquent taxpayer. The Secretary will accept only those surety bonds underwritten by a company qualified to do business in New Mexico.[92]

When a serious and immediate risk exists that an amount of tax due

---

[89] §3.1.10.13A NMAC.
[90] §7-1-3W NMSA 1978.
[91] §7-1-54A NMSA 1978.
[92] §7-1-57 NMSA 1978; §3.1.10.14 NMAC.

Collection and Enforcement

or reasonably expected to become due will not be paid, the Secretary may require a person who is liable or prospectively liable for the tax to furnish security. Upon a refusal by the person to immediately comply, the Secretary may without notice apply to any state district court for an injunction enjoining the person from doing business.[93]

The Secretary may require taxpayers who protest an assessment or the payment of tax to furnish security whenever the total amount protested exceeds $200,000. If the taxpayer fails to provide security, the TRD may take all appropriate actions to collect the amount assessed, provided that any proceeds collected will be held as the security until the protest is resolved.[94]

The furnishing of security by a person liable for the payment of taxes will not prevent the imposition of interest due on deficiencies nor prevent the imposition of a civil penalty for failure to pay tax or file a return.[95]

¶ 19.5.3 Sale of or proceedings against security

If a liability for tax becomes conclusive, the TRD may move against the security by redeeming for cash or selling such security, or by compelling a surety directly to discharge the liability for payment of the principal debtor by serving demand upon him.[96]

¶ 19.6 Permanence of tax debt--civil actions to collect tax

Taxes due and assessed are personal debts of taxpayers to the state of New Mexico and may be collected by civil actions. Either the Secretary or Attorney General may bring these actions in state district court or in federal courts, but they may not bring an action or proceeding to collect taxes after ten years from the date of the assessment.[97] Final judgments may be enforced in courts of other states by the Secretary or Attorney General pursuant to agreement between the other state and New Mexico or by attorneys or other agents in that state retained by the TRD or the Attorney General. This remedy is in addition to any

---

[93] §7-1-54C NMSA 1978.
[94] §7-1-54D NMSA 1978.
[95] §3.1.10.13B NMAC.
[96] §7-1-56 NMSA 1978.
[97] §§7-1-58 and 7-1-19 NMSA 1978; §3.1.10.15A NMAC.

other remedy provided by law.[98]

When interest has been assessed on a tax liability, no action or proceeding to collect on the interest assessment may be brought by the TRD after ten years from the date of the underlying assessment, even though the interest assessment may have been made less than 10 years prior.[99]

¶ 19.7 Estoppel against state

In any tax proceeding, the TRD is estopped from obtaining or withholding requested relief if the adverse party shows that its action or inaction was in accordance with any regulation that was effective during the time the asserted liability arose or in accordance with any ruling addressed to the party personally and in writing by the Secretary, unless at the time that the asserted tax liability arose the ruling had been rendered invalid or superseded by regulation or by another ruling similarly addressed.[100]

¶ 19.8 Reciprocal enforcement of tax judgments

New Mexico courts enforce tax judgments of other jurisdictions, but only to the extent that the courts of other jurisdictions recognize and enforce similar tax judgments of New Mexico or its political subdivisions, agencies or instrumentalities. However, New Mexico property is exempt from execution for failure to pay another state's income tax on benefits of a pension or other retirement plan. The Attorney General, or the Secretary, with the Attorney General's permission, may employ on a contingency fee basis only bar members of other jurisdictions to recover taxes due New Mexico.[101]

---

[98] 7-1-58 NMSA 1978.
[99] §3.1.10.15B NMAC.
[100] §7-1-60 NMSA 1978.
[101] §7-1-65 NMSA 1978.

APPENDIX

A.1 Obsolete Provisions

A.1.1 Welfare-to-work tax credit (Obsolete)

Under the federal welfare-to-work program, which has since been repealed for persons employed after December 31, 2006, taxpayers who employed persons who had been long-term welfare recipients were entitled to a tax credit, known as the welfare-to-work credit. Under IRC Code section 51A, this credit equaled 35 percent of first-year wages and 50 percent of second-year wages, but only the first $10,000 of wages in a year are taken into account.[1]

New Mexico law provided a similar credit and a taxpayer who was entitled to claim the federal welfare-to-work credit with respect to a state-qualified employee in a state-qualified job could take a New Mexico welfare-to-work credit equal to 50% of the amount of the federal credit.[3] Since the federal credit has been repealed the state credit is now obsolete. However, the credit remains on the books and if the federal credit is ever revived the state credit will be revived as well.

Beginning January 1, 2008, a new federal work opportunity credit was established, but employers who qualify for the new federal work opportunity credit will no longer qualify for the New Mexico credit.

The state credit was available to any taxpayer who filed an individual Mexico income tax return and was not a dependent of another. The New Mexico credit could only be deducted from the taxpayer's income tax liability. Any portion of the tax credit that remained unused at the end of the taxpayer's tax year could be carried forward for 3 consecutive tax years. A husband and wife who filed separate returns for a tax year in which they could have filed a joint return could each claim only one-half of the tax credit that would have been allowed on a joint return.

---

[1] 26 U.S.C. Section 51A.
[3] §7-2-18.5 NMSA 1978.

New Mexico Personal Income Tax

The statute describes a "state-qualified employee" (SQE) as a "long-term family assistance recipient," defined under IRC §51A(c), as in effect before its repeal, who resides in a high-unemployment county during the period of employment for which the federal welfare-to-work credit applied with respect to that employee. A "high-unemployment county" is defined as a county in which the unemployment rate as reported by the labor department exceeded 10% in 6 or more months of the calendar year preceding the year for which the New Mexico credit was claimed. By January 31 of each year, the labor department was required to certify the high-unemployment counties for the preceding calendar year.

A "state-qualified job" is a job established by the taxpayer that:

- when first held by a SQE results in the total number of the taxpayer's employees exceeding the average number of the taxpayer's employees during the taxpayer's preceding tax year; or
- was a position previously filled by a SQE and was vacant prior to the hiring of the new state-qualified employee in that position.

To be eligible for the state credit, a taxpayer had to meet the following requirements:

- the hiring of an SQE could not displace any currently employed worker or position, including partial displacement such as a reduction in the hours of non-overtime work, wages or employment benefits, or infringement of promotional opportunities;
- the hiring of any SQE could not impair existing contracts for services or collective bargaining agreements, and employment could not be inconsistent with the terms of a collective bargaining agreement or involve the performance of duties covered under a collective bargaining agreement unless the employer and the labor organization concur in writing;
- a SQE could fill or perform the duties of an employment position only in a manner consistent with law, personnel procedures and collective bargaining contracts;
- no SQE could be employed or assigned:
    a. when an individual is on layoff from the same or any

Appendix

               substantially equivalent job;
       b. if the employer terminated the employment of a regular employee or otherwise caused an involuntary reduction of work force with the effect of filling the vacancy so created with a SQE; or
       c. to any position at a work site when there is an ongoing strike or lockout;

- SQEs had to be paid a wage substantially like the wage for similar jobs with the employer with appropriate adjustments for experience and training, but not less than the federal minimum hourly wage; and employers had to:
  - d. maintain health, safety and working conditions at not less than those of comparable jobs of the employer; and
  - e. maintain standard and customary entry-level wages and benefits and apply historical and normal increases in wages and benefits appropriate for experience and training of the SQE.

The labor department was required to determine whether the employee was a SQE and whether the job was a state-qualified job and to certify that fact to the employer. The taxpayer claiming the state credit had to provide a copy of the certification with respect to each employee for which the tax credit was claimed.

A taxpayer who otherwise qualified could claim his pro rata share of the credit with respect to SQEs employed by a partnership or other business association of which the taxpayer is a member. The total tax credit that could be claimed by all members of the partnership or association could not exceed the maximum amount of tax credit otherwise allowable with respect to each SQE.

A.1.2 2007 Individual Income Tax Credit

A taxpayer who filed a New Mexico income tax return for the 2007 tax year, and was a full-year or first-year resident and not a trust, estate or a dependent of another was allowed an income tax credit in the amount determined below. The credit was allowed even though the taxpayer had no taxable income for the 2007 tax year.[4] The credit was not

---

[4] §7-2-18.23 NMSA 1978.

allowed for a resident who was an inmate of a public institution for more than 6 months during the 2007 tax year.

The amount of tax credit is determined from the following tables:

Married taxpayers filing jointly:

Adjusted Gross Income		Credit Amount for Taxpayer and Spouse	Additional Credit Amount for Each Dependent[5]
Over	Not Over		
0	$30,000	$100	$50.00
$30,000	$50,000	$ 80.00	$40.00
$50,000	$70,000	$ 50.00	$25.00
$70,000		$ 0.00	$ 0.00

Taxpayers filing as single, head of household, married filing separately or as a surviving spouse:

Adjusted Gross Income		Credit Amount for Taxpayer	Additional Credit Amount for Each Dependent
Over	Not Over		
0	$30,000	$50.00	$50.00
$30,000	$50,000	$40.00	$40.00
$50,000	$70,000	$25.00	$25.00
$70,000		$ 0.00	$ 0.00.

If a taxpayer was liable for interest and penalties on the taxpayer's income tax liability for the 2007 tax year prior to the effective date of the credit, the interest and penalties was not recomputed due to the credit but could be applied to the penalty or interest due.

---

[5] The term Dependent is as defined by §152 of the Internal Revenue Code.

Appendix

If the tax credit exceeded the taxpayer's income tax liability, the excess was refunded to the taxpayer.

A.1.3 Tax rebate of property tax paid on property eligible for disabled veteran exemption

Any resident who files an individual New Mexico income tax return and paid property tax for the 1999 property tax year on property eligible for the property tax exemption authorized by Article 8, Section 15 of the constitution of New Mexico may claim a tax rebate for the amount of property tax paid.[6]

Section 15 directs the legislature to exempt from taxation property used as a veteran's principal place of residence, if the veteran has been determined under federal law to have a 100% permanent and total service-connected disability. Eligible property includes the community or joint property of husband and wife. The legislature is also directed to provide this exemption to the veteran's widow or widower if the widow or widower continues to occupy the property as a principal place of residence.

The tax rebate provided for in this section may be deducted from the taxpayer's New Mexico income tax liability for tax year 2000. If the tax rebate exceeds the taxpayer's income tax liability, the excess shall be refunded to the taxpayer.

The rebate provided for in this section may be claimed only on a return filed for tax year 2000. A husband and wife who file separate returns for tax year 2000 and could have filed a joint return for tax year 2000 may each claim only one-half of the tax rebate that would have been allowed on the joint return.

A.2 Information Returns

The Secretary may, by regulation, require any person doing business in the state to submit to the TRD information reports that are considered reasonable and necessary for the administration of any provision of law to which the Tax Administration Act applies.[7] In addition, The TRD may require any person doing business in New

---

[6] §7-2-18.7 NMSA 1978.
[7] §7-1-10F NMSA 1978.

Mexico to file information returns with regard to payments made in the course of business to another person.[8]

This requirement applies to payments made –

- by the State of New Mexico,
- by the governing bodies of any political subdivision,
- by any agency, department or instrumentality of the state or of any political subdivision, and,
- to the extent permitted by law or pursuant to an agreement entered into by the TRD, by any other governmental body or by an agency, department or instrumentality.

Automatic extension for 1099 information returns

The due date for Form 1099-MISC or *pro forma* 1099-MISC information returns that are required to be electronically filed is automatically extended to the first day of April of the year following the year for which the statement is made. This extended due date conforms to the federal due date for electronic filings of Form 1099-MISC.[9]

Rents and royalties from oil and gas properties

A payor of rents and royalties from oil and gas properties located in New Mexico who is required to file IRS Form 1099-MISC regarding such payments must file rent and royalty information with the TRD.[10]

Persons paying such rents and royalties on properties located in New Mexico are required to segregate the New Mexico rents and royalties paid from the rents and royalties paid everywhere and report only those rents and royalties from New Mexico properties to the TRD. The TRD will accept the information on magnetic media in lieu of paper returns, but the magnetic media must comply with the IRS reporting requirements. A person who has entered into an IRS agreement known as Consent For Internal Revenue Service To Release Tax Information will be deemed to have complied this requirement.[11]

---

[8] §7-2-20 NMSA 1978.
[9] §3.1.4.12H NMAC.
[10] §3.3.20.8A NMAC.
[11] §3.3.20.8A(2) NMAC.

Appendix

The due date for information returns required to be filed is June 15 of each year following the close of the previous calendar year.[12]

---

[12] §3.3.20.8B NMAC.

INDEX

A

Additional Low-income property tax rebate, 19, 323
Adjusted gross income (AGI), definition of, 14, 114
Adjustment to AGI
  additions
    contributions refunded when closing a §529 account, 137
    federal charitable deduction for which NM land conservation credit is claimed, 15, 138
    federal net operating loss carryover deduction, 15, 137
    interest and dividends from federal tax-exempt bonds, 15, 56, 135
  deductions
    armed forces active duty pay, 16, 150
      active duty pay defined, 16, 31, 40, 57, 63, 101, 120, 150, 153
      armed forces defined, 150
    deduction for contributions to a NM-approved §529 college savings plan, 120, 148
    deduction for organ donation-related expenses, 16, 57, 120, 151
    exemption for NM medical care savings account, 16, 120, 146
    exemption for persons age 65 or older, or blind, 15, 57, 120, 145
    income of persons age 100 years or older, 15, 40, 57, 120, 145
    interest received on U.S. Government obligations, 15, 56, 142
    medical care expense exemption for persons age 65 years or older, 16, 120, 151
    net capital gains deduction, 16, 149
    NM National Guard member life insurance reimbursements tax exemption, 120, 152
    NM net operating loss, 15, 137, 141
    NM tax-exempt interest and dividends, 15, 120, 140, 165
    non-resident U.S. Public Health Service members' active duty pay, 120, 153
    Railroad Retirement Act annuities and benefits, and Railroad Unemployment Insurance Act sick pay, 120, 144
    taxable refunds, credits, or offsets of state and local income taxes, 16, 41, 152
  Schedule PIT-ADJ, 15, 38, 41, 55, 101, 115, 120, 135, 136, 137, 138, 140, 142, 146, 153, 160, 329
Advanced energy income tax credit, 17, 189, 203
Affordable Housing Tax Credit, 17, 193, 194, 195
Agricultural biomass income tax credit, 17, 189, 209
Agricultural water conservation tax credit, 17, 47, 57, 189, 202
Allocation and apportionment of income
  allocation of income, 16, 163

community property, 17, 179
compensation earnings, 163
   disaster or emergency-related activities, 164
   fifteen-day rule, 163
   twenty-mile manufacturing rule, 163
   income or losses from pass-through entities, 170
   interest and dividends, 15, 39, 56, 135, 165
   other income not included elsewhere in Schedule PIT-B, 171
     gambling winnings, 171
     trading securities for one's own account, 172
     unemployment compensation, 172
   rent and royalties, 167
   retirement income, 166
     defined, 166, 167
apportionment of business and farm income, 16, 172
   headquarters operation, 177
   manufacturing business, 176
   payroll factor, 173, 176
   property factor, 173, 176
   sales factor, 173, 174, 176
   special industries, 16, 179
   three-factor formula, 173
income from sources both within and without NM, 157
Schedule PIT-B, 16, 44, 45, 61, 62, 75, 97, 106, 107, 131, 132, 153, 155, 157, 158, 159, 161, 162, 163, 164, 165, 166, 168, 169, 170, 171, 172, 173, 175, 180, 181
Schedule PIT-B Credit Bypass, 159
Amended returns, 13, 76, 84, 85, 231
   federal audit adjustment, 21, 362
   Form PIT-X, 84, 85
Amyotrophic Lateral Sclerosis Research Fund, 20, 337
Angel investment credit, 17, 46, 57, 189, 196
Animal Care and Facility Fund, 20, 339

Assessments of tax, 22, 389, 407
   jeopardy assessments, 22, 411
   methods of, 22, 407
Audit
   closing agreement, 342, 347, 362, 363, 378
   federal audit adjustment, 21, 362
   hours of inspection, 21, 357
   identification of auditors, 21, 357
   managed audit, 343, 349, 359, 360, 361, 362, 389, 408
   notice of, 20, 357
   production of records and books, 21, 357
   records
     enforcement by subpoena, 21, 359
     governmental returns, documents, reports, 21, 358
     in possession of another, 21, 358
     notice of outstanding records, 343, 344, 358
Authorized Representative, 22, 385

B

Blended biodiesel fuel credit, 17, 57, 213
   Form RPD-41322, 215
Blind or 65 or older, exemption, 15, 57, 120, 145
Business facility rehabilitation credit, 17, 47, 57, 189, 212

C

Cancer clinical trial tax credit, 17, 46, 58, 189, 216
Capital Gains Deduction, 16, 149
Civil action to collect debt, 425
Closing agreements, 342, 347, 362, 363, 378
Collection
   civil action to collect debt, 425
   penalty and interest, 409
COMMUNITY PROPERTY, 14, 17, 31, 113, 121, 129, 130, 131, 132, 133, 134, 135, 145, 179, 180
   IRS Form 8958, 132

Index

Confidentiality
  disclosure to authorized representative, 397
  information provided to other TRD employees, 389
  information required to be revealed, 390
  information that may be revealed to certain tribal governments, 394
  information that may be revealed to other state agencies, 395
  information that may be revealed to other states or multistate administrative bodies, 394
  information that may be revealed to public, 390
  requirement for a written agreement, 398
  returns and other information, 22, 388
Credits
  business-related credits, 9, 17, 189
    advanced energy income tax credit, 17, 189, 203
      coal-based electric generating facility, definition of, 204, 207
      Form RPD-41333, 204, 205, 206, 207
      Form RPD-41334, 206
      geothermal electric generating facility, definition of, 204, 208
      qualified generating facility, definition of, 47, 203
      solar photovoltaic electric generating facility, definition of, 204, 208
      solar thermal generating facility, definition of, 208
    affordable Housing Tax Credit, 17, 193, 194, 195
      Form RPD-41301, 195
    agricultural biomass income tax credit, 17, 189, 209
      agricultural biomass, definition of, 17, 47, 57, 189, 209, 211
      Form RPD-41361, 210
      Form RPD-41362, 210, 211
    angel investment credit, 17, 46, 57, 189, 196
      accredited investors, 197
    agricultural water conservation tax credit, 17, 47, 57, 189, 202
      Form RPD-41319, 203
      Form RPD-41320,, 197, 202
    attributes of, 191
    blended biodiesel fuel credit, 17, 57, 213
    business facility rehabilitation credit, 17, 47, 57, 189, 212
    cancer clinical trial tax credit, 17, 46, 58, 189, 216
      Form RPD-41358, 216, 218
    electronic card reading equipment tax credit, 17, 218
    geothermal ground-coupled heat pump tax credit, 17, 50, 58, 189, 219
    job mentorship tax credit, 17, 49, 58, 189, 222
      Form RPD-41279, 223
      Form RPD-41280, 223
      Form RPD-41281, 223
    land conservation incentives credit, 17, 47, 58, 189, 224
      Form RPD-41282, 227, 228
      Form RPD-41335, 227
      Form RPD-41336, 228
      qualified donations defined, 225, 226
    new sustainable building tax credits
      Form 41342, 251
      Form RPD-41327, 251
      Form RPD-41329, 251
      sustainable commercial building, defined, 247
    non-refundable credits, 189
    preservation of cultural property credit, 17, 58, 229
      Form PIT-4, 231
    refundable credits, 189, 190
    renewable energy production tax credit, 264
      biomass, defined, 266

Form RPD-41227, 269
qualified energy generator, defined, 51, 265, 267, 268, 269, 270
rural health care practitioner tax credit, 17, 236
   Form RPD-41326, 238
rural job credit, 17, 48, 58, 189, 232
   Form RPD-41238, 234
   Form RPD-41247, 234
solar market development tax credit, 17, 49, 58, 190, 239
sustainable and new sustainable building tax credits
   Build Green rating system, defined, 241
   LEED system, defined, 241
sustainable building and new sustainable building tax credits, 17, 50, 190, 240, 241, 244, 246, 248
   sustainable building, defined, 241
technology jobs (additional) tax credit, 17, 190, 192, 253
   additional credit, 18, 259
      annual payroll expense, defined, 255
      qualified expenditures, defined, 256
   basic credit, 17, 258
   Form RPD-41385, 258, 259
   Form RPD-41386, 258, 259
   qualified research, defined, 257
venture Capital Investment Credit, 18, 190, 270
veteran employment tax credit, 262
   Form RPD-41370, 263
   Form RPD-41371, 263, 264
veteran employment tax credit Form RPD-41370, 263
business-relatedcredits
   solar market development tax credit
      Form RPD-41317, 240
overview, 9, 17, 183

pre-approval of credits, 185
refundable credits
   day care credit, 19, 33, 52, 58, 314, 316, 325
      Form PIT-CG, 327
   medical care credit for persons 65 or older, 19, 53, 151, 313, 329
   Schedule PIT-RC, 30, 55, 184, 313, 314, 317, 319, 322, 324, 327, 332
   special needs adopted child tax credit, 332
   working families tax credit, 33, 53, 333
taxes paid to other states, 13, 17, 96, 185
three-year time limitation for claiming credits and tax rebates, 185

D

Delinquent taxpayers, 22, 408
Disputes
   administrative protest, 21, 365, 384, 385
   awarding of costs and fees, 21, 380
   conclusiveness of court order, 21, 377
   election of remedies, 21, 364
   exhaustion of administrative remedies, 21, 364
   formal hearing
      appeal to the Court of Appeals, 372
      discovery, 367, 370, 371
      evidence, 194, 263, 344, 349, 350, 363, 365, 367, 368, 369, 370, 371, 372, 387, 388, 391, 392, 402, 407, 420, 422
      failure to comply with orders, 21, 370
      hearing officer, 21, 102, 150, 350, 364, 366, 367, 368, 369, 370, 371, 372, 377, 381, 391
      hearing record, 21, 369

Index

    motions, 368, 371
    prehearing conference, 368, 371
    proposed findings, conclusions briefs, 21, 369
    rules for, 21, 367, 368
informal conference, 366

E

Electronic card reading equipment tax credit, 17, 218
    Form RPD-41246, 219
Electronic filing of returns, 12, 74, 76, 78, 432
Electronic payments, 12, 69, 76, 77
Enjoining delinquent taxpayer from continuing in business, 421
Estoppel against state, 23, 426
Extension of time to file and pay
    automatic extensions, 12, 80
    failure to file, pay or protest by extended due date, 13, 82
    good cause, 12, 78
    in general, 12, 78
    military personnel, 13, 82
    procedure for obtaining extensions, 12, 79

F

Federal audit adjustment, 21, 362
Filing requirements
    address of notices and payments, 12, 67
    date of payment, 12, 69
    due date of return and payments, 12, 68
    electronic filing of returns, 12, 74
    electronic payments, 12, 69, 76
    illegible postmarks, 12, 70
    individuals required to file, 12, 62
    name of spouse, 13, 82
    payments by mail, 12, 68
    private delivery services, 12, 70
    reproduction of income tax forms, 13, 83
    requirements of filed returns, 12, 73
    Saturday, Sunday or legal holiday, 12, 72
    tax preparer responsibilities with regard to electronic filing, 12, 78
    taxpayer identification number, 12, 64, 65
    tentative returns not allowed, 13, 83
    timely-mailed, timely-filed rule, 12, 69
Film and Television Tax Credit
    additional credit for nonresident 1ndustry crew, 18, 291
    additional credit for television pilots and series, 18, 19, 290, 310
    additional credit for use of qualified production facilities, 18, 19, 288, 308
    assignment of FTTC, 18, 295
    direct production expenditures
        audiovisual requirements, 18, 19, 284, 304
        basic requirements, 18, 19, 278, 298
    direct production expenditures, definition of, 18, 278
    direct production expenses
        limitation for performing artists, 18, 283
        nonresident performing artists, 18, 19, 281, 302
    vendor
        definition of and requirements, 286
    features, 277
    Film Office, 275, 276, 285, 287, 288, 292, 293, 296, 297, 301, 302, 304, 305, 307
    maximum amount of claims allowed, 18, 294
    payment of claims, 18, 294
    postproduction expenditures
        audiovisual requirements, 18, 19, 284, 304
        basic requirements, 18, 19, 278, 298
    postproduction expenses, definition of, 284, 303
    qualifying for and claiming the

FTTC, 18, 292
    additional requirements, 19, 287
    Form PTE, 293
    Form RPD-41228, 293, 294
    Form RPD-41381, 293
    reporting--accountability, 18, 296
    residency requirement, 18, 285
    start date, 276
    taxable transaction requirement, 285, 305
Film production incentives
    overview, 275
Film Production Tax Credit
    additional credit for qualified production facilities, 308
    additional credit for television pilots and series, 310
    assignment of FPTC, 19, 312
    direct production expenditures
        audiovisual product requirements, 304
        basic requirements, 18, 19, 278, 298
        definition of, 278, 299
    direct production expenses nonresident performing artists, 302
    features, 297
    limit on credit for performing artists, 303
    maximum amount of claims allowed, 311
    payment of claims, 311
    postproduction expenditures
        audiovisual product requirements, 304
        basic requirements, 18, 19, 278, 298
        definition of, 303
    qualifying and claiming the FPTC, 19, 310
        additional requirements, 18
    qualifying and claiming the FTTC
        additional requirements, 287
    residency requirements, 19, 304
    start date, 297
    taxable transaction requirement, 305, 310
    vendors, 19, 305

Film Production Tax Credit Act
    amendments made by, 279, 280, 284, 285, 289, 290, 291, 292, 294, 295, 303, 304, 310, 311
Form RPD-41334, 206
Form RPD-41372 credits
    veteran employment tax credit
        Form RPD-41372, 264
Forms
    Form PIT-4, 231
    Form PIT-CG, 327
    Form RPD-41227, 269
    Form RPD-41228, 293, 294
    Form RPD-41238, 234
    Form RPD-41246, 219
    Form RPD-41247, 234
    Form RPD-41279, 223
    Form RPD-41280, 223
    Form RPD-41281, 223
    Form RPD-41282, 227, 228
    Form RPD-41301, 195
    Form RPD-41317, 240
    Form RPD-41319, 203
    Form RPD-41320,, 197, 202
    Form RPD-41322, 215
    Form RPD-41326, 238
    Form RPD-41329, 251
    Form RPD-41333, 204, 205, 206, 207
    Form RPD-41335, 227
    Form RPD-41336, 228
    Form RPD-41342, 251
    Form RPD-41346, 221
    Form RPD-41348, 106
    Form RPD-41358, 216, 218
    Form RPD-41361, 210
    Form RPD-41362, 210, 211
    Form RPD-41370, 263
    Form RPD-41371, 263, 264
    Form RPD-41372, 264
    Form RPD-41381, 293
    Form RPD-41386, 258, 259
    FormRPD-41327, 251
    IRS Form 4972, 45, 75, 121, 166, 180
    IRS Form 8958, 132
    PIT-D, 59, 76, 335, 338
    PIT-X, 84, 85
    RPD-41385, 258, 259
    RRB-1099 and RRB- 1099-R, 145

Index

Schedule PIT-ADJ, 15, 38, 41, 55, 101, 115, 120, 135, 136, 137, 138, 140, 142, 146, 153, 160, 329
Schedule PIT-B, 16, 44, 45, 61, 62, 75, 97, 106, 107, 131, 132, 153, 155, 157, 158, 159, 161, 162, 163, 164, 165, 166, 168, 169, 170, 171, 172, 173, 175, 180, 181
Schedule PIT-CR, 45, 46, 53, 55, 184, 189, 222, 223, 313
Schedule PIT-RC, 30, 55, 184, 313, 314, 317, 319, 322, 324, 327, 332

G

Geothermal ground-coupled heat pump tax credit, 17, 50, 58, 189, 219
Form RPD-41346, 221

H

History of the personal income tax
    adoption of federal adjusted gross income, 11, 33
    benefits for low-income taxpayers, 11, 32
    economic, environmental, and social objectives, 11, 33
    in general, 11, 31
    tax rate changes, 11, 32
    today, 11, 34
    withholding and Estimated Tax, 11, 34
Horse Shelter Rescue Fund, 20, 338

I

Imposition of Tax on Individuals, 12, 61
Indian nation, tribe, or pueblo
    Income of a member, 15, 120, 145
Individual Income Tax Credit - 2007, 23, 429
Information Returns, 23, 431
Innocent Spouse Relief, 20, 350
Installment agreements, 22, 410

Interest
    collection of, 409
    on deficiencies, 20, 341
    on overpayments, 20, 344
Interest and dividends from federal tax-exempt bonds, 15, 56, 135
Interest received on U.S. Government obligations, 15, 56, 142

J

Jeopardy assessments, 22, 411
Job mentorship tax credit, 17, 49, 58, 189, 222

L

Land conservation incentives credit, 17, 47, 58, 189, 224
Levy of property
    contents of warrant of levy, 23, 415
    exempt property, 23, 417
    penalty for failure to surrender, 23, 416
    sale of property
        documents of title and legal effect of sale, 23, 420
        minimum prices, 23, 419
        notice of seizure and sale, 23, 418
        proceeds of levy and sale, 23, 421
        redemption before sale, 23, 419
        requirements of sale, 23, 418
        sale at auction,, 23, 419
        sale of indivisible property, 23, 418
    seizure of property by levy for collection of taxes, 22, 413
    seizure of real property by levy, 23, 414
    stay of levy, 23, 417
    successive levies, 23, 416
    surrender of property upon service of levy on a financial institution, 23, 414
Liens
    assessment as lien, 22, 412, 413

foreclosure of lien, 22, 413
notice of lien, 22, 412
release or extinguishment of lien, 22, 413
statute of limitation on actions to enforce lien, 22, 413
Lottery Tuition Fund, 20, 338
Low-income comprehensive tax rebate (LICTR), 19, 313, 317
Lump-sum
   10-year tax averaging option, 121
   defined, 120
   five-year averaging, 45, 181
   IRS Form 4972, 45, 75, 121, 166, 180

M

Managed audits, 343, 349, 359, 360, 361, 362, 389, 408
Medical care credit for persons 65 or older, 19, 53, 151, 313, 329
Medical expenses
   deduction of unreimbursed or uncompensated medical care expenses, 124
   medical care expense exemption for persons age 65 years or older, 16, 120, 151
   medical care expenses defined, 125
Military personnel
   income tax preferences, 13, 101
      armed forces active duty pay, 16, 150
   military pay of an enrolled member of an Indian nation, tribe, or pueblo, 14, 102
   residency and domicile, 103
   spousal issues
      Military Spouse Residency Relief Act, 14, 105
      nonresident spouse living in NM filing requirement, 107
      qualifying spouse living in another state, 106
      withholding exemption, 106
      withholding exemption Form RPD-41348, 106
   tax return filing extensions, 13, 82

Modified gross income (, 19, 34, 52, 314, 315, 316, 317, 318, 319, 320, 321, 322, 324, 325, 327, 332

N

National Guard Member and Family Assistance, 20, 337
National Guard member life insurance reimbursements tax exemption, 120, 152
Net income, 9, 14, 111, 112, 115, 117
Net operating losses
   federal net operating loss carryover deduction, 15, 137
   NM net operating loss, 15, 137, 141
New Mexico Day Care Credit, 19, 325
New Mexico Forest Re-Leaf Program, 20, 337
New Mexico medical care savings account, 120, 146
New Mexico Political Parties – designated contribution, 20, 338
NM tax-exempt interest and dividends, 15, 120, 140, 165

O

Organ donation-related expenses, 16, 57, 120, 151

P

Pass-through-entities
   definition of, 66
Penalties
   civil
      failure to pay tax or file a return, 20, 346
      innocent spouse relief, 20, 350
      mistake of law made in good faith and on reasonable grounds, 347
      negligent or in disregard of rules and regulations, 348
   for bad checks, 20, 352
   collection of, 409

Index

criminal offenses
  assault and battery of a TRD employee, 20, 356
  attempts to evade or defeat tax, 20, 355
  interference with administration of revenue laws, 20, 355
  revealing information concerning taxpayers, 20, 356
  tax fraud
    instances of, 353
    misdemeanors and felonies, 354
  tax fraud:, 354
Personal exemptions
  additional exemptions for low- and middle-income taxpayers, 14, 122
  amount of deduction, 122
  deduction of, 14, 122
  exemption for persons age 65 or older, or blin, 15, 57, 120, 145
  number of, 122
Persons age 100 years or older, income of, 15, 40, 57, 120, 145
Preservation of cultural property credit, 17, 58, 229
Private delivery services, 12, 70
Property tax rebate for persons 65 or older, 19, 58, 319

R

Railroad Retirement Act, 120, 144
Rebates
  additional Low-income property tax rebate, 19, 323
  low-income comprehensive tax rebate (LICTR), 19, 313, 317
  modified gross income, 19, 34, 52, 314, 315, 316, 317, 318, 319, 320, 321, 322, 324, 325, 327, 332
  property tax rebate for persons 65 or older, 19, 58, 319
Reciprocal enforcement of tax judgments, 23, 426
Record retention requirements
  alternative methods used to determine taxes due, 22, 399
  alternative storage media, 22, 400
  business process information, 22, 404
  electronic data interchange requirements, 22, 403
  electronic data processing systems requirements, 22, 404
  insufficient records, 22, 399
  machine-sensible records, 22, 402
  records maintenance requirements, 22, 405
  required taxpayer records, 22, 399
  TRD access to machine-sensible records, 405
Refunds
  authority to make refunds or credits, 21, 378
  claimant remedies, 21, 376
  conditions for refund or credit, 21, 372
  designation of contributions causes/charities
    Amyotrophic Lateral Sclerosis Research Fund, 20, 337
    Animal Care and Facility Fund, 20, 339
    Horse Shelter Rescue Fund, 20, 338
    Lottery Tuition Fund, 338
    National Guard Member and Family Assistance, 20, 337
    New Mexico Forest Re-Leaf Program, 20, 337
    New Mexico Political Parties, 20, 338
    Share with Wildlife, 20, 336
    Supplemental Senior Services, 20, 339
    Tax Refund Intercept Program, 335
    Veterans Enterprise Fund , 20, 338
    Vietnam Veterans Memorial State Park, 20, 338
  check-offs, 335

443

in general, 19, 335
Schedule PIT-D, 59, 76, 335, 338
payment of, 73
Refunds, credits, or offsets of state and local income taxes, 16, 41, 152
Renewable energy production tax credit, 18, 51, 190, 264
Residency and Domicile
domicile defined, 13, 94
EXAMPLE OF IMPACT OF RESIDENCY, 13, 99
First-year residents, 98
Leaving residents, 98
residency defined:, 13, 93
Residents who come and go, 99
Rural health care practitioner tax credit, 17, 236
Rural job tax credit, 17, 48, 58, 189, 232

S

Section 529 accounts, 16, 40, 120, 137, 148, 149
Security for payment of tax, 23, 423
sale of or proceeds against security, 23, 425
Solar market development tax credit, 17, 49, 58, 190, 239
Special needs adopted child tax credit, 19, 53, 313, 332
State and local tax add back, 14, 126
Statute of limitations, 22, 409
to enforce lien, 22, 413
Supplemental Senior Services, 20, 339
Sustainable building and new sustainable building tax credits, 17, 50, 190, 240, 241

T

Tax preparers
requirements for tax return preparers—penalties, 13, 83
Tax rates for individuals
tax rate schedules, 16, 113, 155, 156

tax tables, 16, 44, 156
Tax Refund Intercept Program Act, 335
Taxable income
computing, 14, 115
overview, 9, 10, 14, 16, 57, 111, 155
statutory method, 14, 115
tax return method, 14, 111, 113, 115, 121
Taxpayer Bill of Rights, 21, 383, 385
Taxpayer Identification Number, 12, 64, 65
Technology jobs (additional) tax credit, 17, 190, 192, 253
TRD
investigative authority and powers, 22, 387
issuance of subpoenas and summons, 22, 387
notice of potential eligibility for food stamps required, 22, 388
Secretary delegation of authority, 22, 385

U

U.S. Public Health Service, nonresident members' active duty pay, 120, 153
Uniform Division of Income for Tax Purposes Act (UDITPA), 16, 161

V

Venture Capital Investment Credit, 18, 190, 270
Veteran employment tax credit, 262
Veterans Enterprise Fund , 20, 338
Vietnam Veterans Memorial State Park, 20, 338

W

Welfare-to-work tax credit, 23, 427
Working families tax credit, 33, 53, 333

www.ingramcontent.com/pod-product-compliance
Lightning Source LLC
Chambersburg PA
CBHW071234300426
44116CB00008B/1038